HIDDEN AGENDA

U.S./NATO Takeover of Yugoslavia

Edited by John Catalinotto
and Sara Flounders

International Action Center
New York

Hidden Agenda
U.S./NATO Takeover of Yugoslavia

ISBN 0-9656916-7-5

International Action Center
39 West 14th Street, Suite 206
New York, NY 10011

Phone: (212)633-6646
Fax: (212)633-2889
Website: www.iacenter.org
E-mail: iacenter@iacenter.org

Cover Design: Lal Roohk

Library of Congress Cataloging-in-Publication Data

Hidden Agenda: U.S./NATO Takeover of Yugoslavia/ edited by John Catalinotto and Sara Flounders.
p.cm.
Includes index.
ISBN 0-9656916-7-5 (pb : alk.paper)
1. Yugoslavia—History—1992- 2. North Atlantic Treaty Organization—Armed Forces—Yugoslavia. 3. Kosovo (Serbia)—History—Civil War, 1998—Participation, American. 4. Operation Allied Force, 1999. 5. International Tribunal for the Prosecution of Persons Responsible for Serious Violations of International Humanitarian Law Committed in the Territory of the Former Yugoslavia since 1991. 6. United States—Foreign Relations—Yugoslavia. 7. Yugoslavia—Foreign Relations—United States.
I. Title: U.S./NATO takeover of Yugoslavia. II. Catalinotto, John. III. Flounders, Sara

DR1319 .H53 2002
949.703—dc21

2002017188

CONTENTS

Preface

We were days from sending the final pages of *Hidden Agenda* to the printer on September 11, 2001, when the devastating attack on the World Trade Center abruptly changed everyone's priorities. The stunned population in New York felt a horror and a fear they had never known before, along with sympathy for and solidarity with the immediate victims. A media blitz spread these feelings throughout the United States.

After an apparent initial confusion, the Bush administration exploited the new atmosphere to whip up a war frenzy, gathering support for aggression in Central Asia and repression at home in the name of a war against terror. No longer even bothering to consult with their NATO allies, the Pentagon soon sent its bombers to turn one of the poorest countries on earth into rubble. As it had wrecked the Yugoslav infrastructure in 1999 and the Iraqi in 1991, the U.S. military machine went after Afghanistan. They again inflicted cluster bombs and depleted uranium shells on a civilian population.

From the morning of September 11 all our routine work stopped here at the International Action Center. We turned our attention to the new crisis. We began an all-out mobilization against the coming war. We helped shape a new national coalition called A.N.S.W.E.R., or Act Now to Stop War and End Racism. By September 29, A.N.S.W.E.R.'s call had brought over 20,000 mostly young people to Washington and another 20,000 to San Francisco to protest.

According to the official U.S. story, Osama bin Laden's group Al Qaeda was responsible for the attacks inside the U.S. Al Qaeda is composed of the groups from all over the Middle East that the CIA had armed and used against the USSR. The CIA had backed and nurtured these forces to benefit U.S. strategic interests not only in Afghanistan but also in Bosnia and in Kosovo, and against progressive, secular and socialist forces throughout the Middle East and Central Asia. Now, according to Bush, they are no longer heroes of the fight against Communism, but they have become the new "evil" in the world.

We don't know what group carried out the attacks. But if it was from the Middle East, we think Bush and company know why. The U.S. war against Iraq, its murderous sanctions, its support for the Israeli occupiers of Palestinian lands, and the Pentagon's own military occupation of Saudi Arabia and other countries of that region had created sufficient reason for a deep and massive anger against the United States.

Saudi Arabia and other countries of that region had created sufficient reason for a deep and massive anger against the United States.

U.S. Middle East policies have enriched a handful of U.S. and other Western corporations and a small number of local collaborators. The masses are mired in poverty. More educated sectors are frustrated, seeing no opportunity for growth and watching exported U.S. films and media swamp and smother local customs and mores as the local oil reserves start running out.

With the assault on Afghanistan having now driven out the Taliban and apparently crushed Al Qaeda, Washington now threatens to bring wars to more areas of the world. Bush has threatened Somalia, Yemen and the Philippines with military intervention. A gang of old Cold Warriors from in and out of the administration is pushing for an invasion of Iraq. North Korea, Syria, even Cuba and the revolutionary forces in Colombia are on the hit list.

It has become even more important that we continue our work on the book exposing the U.S./NATO war against Yugoslavia. How could we explain the new wars without rooting out the motives of past wars? How could we examine the motives of these wars without seeing who profited from the adventures that risk millions of lives? By carefully examining the NATO war against Yugoslavia we can provide perspective on the present wars and the Pentagon's goals.

NATO leaders claimed they waged war on Yugoslavia to end massacres there. But the U.S. overthrew the only government in the region that resisted its rule, and NATO wound up with bases in Croatia, Bosnia, Hungary, Macedonia, Albania and Kosovo.

Likewise, the current "war on terror" is leading to a whole series of U.S. military bases in Uzbekistan, Tadjikistan, Kyrgistan, and Afghanistan, and increased U.S. military influence in Pakistan and India. U.S. oil companies will have a lock on the oil and natural gas of the Caspian Sea and on the oil pipelines from that sea both to Europe through the Balkans and to the Indian Ocean through Afghanistan.

U.S. bombing turned hundreds of thousands of Kosovo's residents into refugees. On an even grander scale, the U.S. bombing of Afghanistan has added millions to the already millions of Afghani refugees. Dislocation, hunger and cold will condemn hundreds of thousands of these people to death, many of them young children. This is an example of the U.S. using terror, and on a monstrous scale.

In Kosovo today the unemployment rate hovers above sixty percent. Can anyone believe that the U.S. conquest of Afghanistan, with or without its NATO allies, will lead to a life of prosperity for the population?

To justify the war against Yugoslavia the U.S. and its NATO allies set up the International Criminal Tribunal for the former Yugoslavia in The Hague. Now the Bush administration has invoked military tribunals, with the intention of trying its "enemies" before the Pentagon alone.

With these new threats before us, it is important that the world refuse to let the kangaroo court in The Hague get away with its attempt to rewrite history. NATO's leaders want to condemn President Slobodan Milosevic of Yugoslavia to cover up their own crimes. Stopping this frame-up is part of the struggle against war, a struggle that grows more vital each day.

Sara Flounders and John Catalinotto
December 15, 2001

Acknowledgments

Hidden Agenda: U.S./NATO Takeover of Yugoslavia is the result of the worldwide movement that arose in opposition to NATO's war against Yugoslavia. This, the second volume published by the International Action Center on NATO intervention in the Balkans, traces the machinations of Western policy since 1997.

At the time the IAC published its first book on the dismemberment of Yugoslavia, *NATO in the Balkans,* there was a small but dynamic group of organizers who opposed U.S./NATO expansion into the Balkans and Eastern Europe. This group grew. As activists in Belgium, the U.S., Germany, Canada, Italy, and Greece began to communicate with each other and with their counterparts in Yugoslavia, their outrage, their political analyses and their research developed. They examined the escalation of Western war efforts in the Balkans. In their work, they warned that NATO expansion threatened the peace and the well being of all of the people of Eastern Europe.

We are indebted to these activists and scholars who are the main contributors to this book. They provide the historical record that documents the war crimes, systematic ethnic demonization of the Serbian people, the media lies and the illegitimacy of The Hague Tribunal, the so-called International Criminal Tribunal for the Former Yugoslavia (ICTY). Prior to, during and after the seventy-eight day bombing campaign, as the entire Yugoslav nation resisted, every week many thousands of activists in the United States and Europe, and Asia were in the streets, protesting U.S./NATO aggression.

The authors of these articles were part of this world movement. When the bombing ended, the anti-war movement did not. The anti-NATO activists organized a series of tribunals that documented NATO crimes, citing explicit violations of international laws and conventions. Ramsey Clark's Nineteen Point Indictment of NATO for Crimes Against Peace, War Crimes and Crimes Against Humanity became the basis for these tribunals. Some of the papers from these meetings are found here, as well as excerpts from the two-volume *NATO Crimes in Yugoslavia: Documentary Evidence* (the "White Book"), compiled by the Yugoslav Ministry of Foreign Affairs; this book catalogues with photographs, documents and testimonials the devastation NATO wreaked on Yugoslavia.

The resistance to NATO continues. Former President Slobodan Milosevic's response to the NATO-created Tribunal at The Hague expresses this resistance.

The International Action Center depends to a great extent on voluntary labor, so the proofreading, editing, indexing, layout, and the myriad tasks that people undertook to get this book in print owe absolutely everything to the people who cooperated in this endeavor.

The truth is in the details, so we are indebted to Janet Mayes, Milos Raickovich, Michael Bar Am, and Bill Wayland for numerous proof readings.

No history book is useful without a good index, and for that Herculean effort we thank Carol Holland, Marie Jay, Janet Mayes and Sarah Sloan. Janet Mayes was also important in the technical work involved in production and for posting a great deal of this material on the IAC web site (www.iacenter.org). Lal Roohk was responsible for cover design; her use of photographs and maps, and thoughtful artistry enhanced the attractiveness and usefulness of the book. Polly Sylvia spent hours combing photo archives, books and cyber sources for the photo section. Sharon Ayling, Heather Cottin and Kathy Durkin worked on the publicity for this book and in the final drafting of many small pieces that turn a raw manuscript into a book. Nick Pavlica's excellent advice helped broaden the reach of *Hidden Agenda*. We also thank Milo Yelesiyevich for his helpfulness.

Hidden Agenda: U.S./NATO Takeover of Yugoslavia would not be in your hands were it not for the generous financial support of people who knew that this volume had to be published. Our call for funds to have the book printed was met with an outpouring of assistance we feared was not possible, with the Balkans relegated to history and the "Bush Doctrine" dominating the news.

ACKNOWLEDGMENTS FOR DONATIONS

This book wouldn't have been produced without the tremendous support and financial assistance of many people who we list here.

We recognize the support given by the People's Rights Fund throughout the duration of this book's production. We thank Jack Massen for encouraging our progress at every step. We give special thanks to Boris Vukovich for his generosity and confidence in this project. Kosa Martjak and John Martjak have been wonderful in their backing of this undertaking.

We also acknowledge and appreciate the financial contributions of the following individuals:

Benefactors: Stuart H. Anderson, Eric Brill, Phyllis Lucero, Tijana Nikov, Mihailo Petrovic, M.D.

Sponsors: Olga Zugec Emmel, Steven Prescop, David Winkler.

Supporters: Alvin Dorfman, Natalia Ganson-Myshkin, M.D., Irene H. Harhaj, Z. Logar, Zoran Marinkovic, Carrie Schuchardt, John Schuchardt, Nadja Tesich, Sharon Wallace.

Donors: Gordana Adzic, Radoslav Adzic, Dr. Bob Allen and Family, Bogdan Baishanski, Allan Billings, Archie Wayne Blumhorst, Wanita L. Blumhorst, Carl Boggs, Conrad Brenner, Stephen Burke, A.E. Carney, Lillian Carney, R. Cvijanovic, J.H. Diggle, Lorna Diggle, Dusan Dragic, Gregory S. Elich, George V. Fatsi, Judi Friedman, Lou Friedman, James Fujii, Harlan Girard, Patricia Hilliard, Richard Hugus, Miroslav Ivkovic, Nick Karas, Wayne Kelpien, Merle Krause, Norman Kristic, Irene Leiby, Dr. George Marchelos, George Markham, Damir Medakovic, Virginia J. Miller, Zagorka Milutinovic, Dave Morton, Milan O'Bradovich, Ann Prosten, Helena Prudkov, Beatrice Reiner, Jan Reiner, Frank Roemhild, Margaret Roemhild, Leonard D. Sanford, Jr., Ethel Sanjines, Mirjana Sasich, Olivera Savin, Michael Shaw, Forest Simmons, Susan Simmons, Vassie Sinopoulos, Radmilo Stanojevic, Bill Stivers, Bill Thompson, June Thompson, Aleksandar Topalovic, Mildred P. Vajagich, Wil Vannatta, Radmila Veselinovic, Andrea G. Vider-Myers, Maurina A. Ladich-Wallis, Richard R. Wallis, Joseph Yuskaitis, Gordana Zivanovic, Srbislav Zivanovic, Nick Zunich.

Friends: Alessandra Areni, Melvin E. Bell, Anne B. Blake, Anne Brenner, William Brenner, J. Deegan, Milijana P. Drakulich, Nikola Drakulich, Dave Duncan, Morris Einhorn, Darlene Gakovich, Radmilo M. Gregovic, Gloria K. Hannas, Parmenio A. Iglesias, Tika Jankovic, Albina Kozlowski, Chris Kozlowski, Vladislav Krasnov, Roberto O. Lozano, Saul Marcus, Jim Morgan, Dr. Austin Murphy, Harvey Parhad, M.D., Salwa E. Parhad, M.D., Michael E. Piston, Barbara Popovic, Radoje Popovic, John Przedpelski, Rade Savija, Dragoslav Siljak, Jerry Sommerseth, Sarah Standefer, Martha Vinick, Daniel Visnich, Myrna Vos, Paul Vos, Jim Yarker.

We appreciate all of the anonymous contributions that were donated so that this important book could be published.

Authors

MUMIA ABU-JAMAL, an award-winning journalist, is an African American on Death Row in Pennsylvania wrongfully convicted of killing a police officer—a crime another man confessed to. He has become an international symbol of the fight against the death penalty and the racist U.S. prison system with his weekly political column. He also authored three books: *Live From Death Row, All Things Censored* and *Death Blossoms.*

BRIAN BECKER, a co-director of the IAC, was a leading organizer of anti-war protests during the 1999 U.S./NATO aggression against Yugoslavia. He also coordinated sanctions-breaking trips to Iraq since the mid-1990s. After September 11, 2001, he helped found the national anti-war coalition A.N.S.W.E.R. (Act Now to Stop War and End Racism).

RICHARD BECKER is a West Coast coordinator of the IAC, who represented the IAC at popular tribunal hearings internationally. He has made solidarity trips to Iraq and Palestine, is a regular commentator on Pacifica radio forums on the Middle East and an organizer of anti-sanctions activities.

ELLEN CATALINOTTO is an anti-war activist and a certified nurse-midwife who has delivered over 1,200 babies, mostly in hospitals serving the poorer neighborhoods of New York City.

JOHN CATALINOTTO, anti-war activist since the 1960s, when he organized GIs against the Vietnam War, is co-editor of *Hidden Agenda* and of *Metal of Dishonor*—about U.S. use of depleted uranium weapons. He was a key organizer of the IAC's popular tribunals about Yugoslavia.

JUDI CHENG is a graduate student at the City University of New York and a youth organizer for the International Action Center. She helped organize for the June 10, 2000, tribunal in New York.

MICHEL CHOSSUDOVSKY is a professor of economics, University of Ottawa, author of *The Globalization of Poverty: Impacts of IMF and World Bank Reforms*, published by Third World Network, Pinang, and Zed Books. He has written articles exposing the role of these financial institutions in the Third World, including Eastern Europe.

RAMSEY CLARK, U.S. attorney general in the Lyndon Johnson administration, international lawyer and human rights advocate, went to Belgrade in March 1999 and again in May 1999 to show his solidarity during the bombing. He has opposed U.S. interventions in Vietnam, Grenada, Panama, Nicaragua, Libya, Somalia, Iraq, the Balkans, Sudan and many other countries. He has authored or contributed chapters to *Crime in America; The Fire this Time: U.S. War Crimes in the Gulf; Metal of Dishonor; NATO in the Balkans, The Children are Dying,* and many other books.

MICHEL COLLON is an anti-war and alternative-media activist and journalist for the weekly newspaper of the Belgian Workers Party, Solidaire. He is a leading anti-NATO spokesperson in Europe, who has written two books on the Balkans, *Liar's Poker*, which will be published in English by the IAC in February 2002, and *Monopoly*.

HEATHER COTTIN has taught in high school for 35 years, and has been active in the civil rights, anti-war and women's movements. The widow of Sean Gervasi, she has continued his work analyzing developments in the Balkans, has contributed to *NATO in the Balkans* and to building the Jewish-Serbian Friendship Society.

THOMAS DEICHMANN is editor of *Novo* magazine and a free-lance journalist based in Frankfurt. He is editor of *Noch einmal für Jugoslawien: Peter Handke* (Once Again for Yugoslavia). Deichmann's article "The picture that fooled the world" about a misleading TV image from Trnopolje camp exposed anti-Serb propaganda during the civil war in Bosnia.

DR. JANET EATON is a biologist, environmentalist and educator from Nova Scotia, Canada, and a researcher at the International Systems Institute. She co-founded the Institute for Global Perspectives.

GREGORY ELICH is a political activist and independent researcher who has published dozens of articles on the Balkans and Southeast Asia. He lectures on the series of interviews he did with Serbian refugees from the Krajina in Croatia, as well as on the deprivations caused by U.S. sanctions against Iraq.

LESLIE FEINBERG has authored *Transgender Warriors* and *Stone Butch Blues*. S/he is the winner of the ALA Gay and Lesbian Literature Award, and Lamba Literary Awards. On her many campus talks, Feinberg is known for linking together the many forms of oppression in class society and for speaking for unity and solidarity.

SARA FLOUNDERS, a co-director of the IAC, who accompanied Ramsey Clark to Yugoslavia during the bombing in 1999, led anti-war protests in the U.S. at that time and the tribunals that followed. A solidarity organizer, she has coordinated trips to Iraq and traveled to Palestinian during the Al Aqsa Intifada. Flounders co-edited *Hidden Agenda, NATO in the Balkans, Metal of Dishonor*, and *Challenge to Genocide: Let Iraq Live*.

LENORA FOERSTEL has been North American Coordinator of Women for Mutual Security since 1990 and is on the board of the Women's Strike for Peace. A cultural historian, she recently edited the book, *War, Lies and Videotape*, about corporate and governmental control of the media.

ROLAND KEITH, a Canadian official who was a monitor for the Kosovo Verification Mission assigned to maintain the peace in Kosovo in the winter of 1998-1999, has been an authoritative voice on what he sees as the failed role and misuse of that mission.

GREGOR KNEUSSEL, Sinologist and political activist in Vienna, Austria. He helped organize the Yugoslav-Austrian Solidarity Committee and the December 4, 1999, tribunal in Vienna, which found Austrian officials guilty of contributing to war crimes in the Balkans.

GLORIA LA RIVA is a trade union leader and a West Coast organizer for the IAC. She accompanied Ramsey Clark to Yugoslavia twice during the 1999 war, where she filmed footage for her video, *NATO's Targets*, and again in June 2001. La Riva also produced and edited the prize-winning documentary video on Iraq, *Genocide by Sanctions*. She is a leading spokesperson for the Peace for Cuba Committee of the IAC.

BARRY LITUCHY teaches modern European history at Kingsborough Community College, City University of New York. He has written extensively on the Yugoslav events and on the World War II concentration camp at Jasenovac. He organized a group that interviewed refugees in Yugoslavia in 2000, publishing the transcripts in "If They Find Me, They Will Kill Me."

EVANGELOS MAHAIRAS was president of the Association of Athens Lawyers (Bar Association) Athens from 1981-1984, honorary president since 1985, elected in 1986 president of the Greek Peace Movement and in 1990 president of the World Peace Council. He is a fighter for peace, human rights and the environment.

SLOBODAN MILOSEVIC was elected president of the Serbian Republic of Yugoslavia in 1989, serving until 1997, when he was elected president of the Federal Republic of Yugoslavia. He is a founder and president of the Socialist Party of Serbia. Since June 2001 he has been held prisoner at The Hague, Netherlands, charged with war crimes in a pro-NATO court.

MONICA MOOREHEAD is on the Board of the National Campaign to Free Mumia Abu-Jamal and coordinator of Millions for Mumia. She is a journalist who has written and spoken extensively on prisons and racism in the U.S. and on the relationship between military costs and social-service cuts.

MICHAEL PARENTI, educator, lecturer and frequent commentator on radio and television, traveled to Yugoslavia following the 1999 war. He is the author of *Democracy for the Few; Inventing Reality: the Politics of the Mass Media; The Sword and the Dollar: Imperialism, Revolution and the Arms Race*; and *To Kill a Nation: the Attack on Yugoslavia*.

MILOS PETROVIC helped organize for anti-NATO popular tribunals in the U.S., and was active with the IAC in California.

DR. CARLO PONA is a physicist and anti-depleted-uranium activist with the Nino Pasti Foundation in Rome, member of Scientists Against the War (Italy) and active organizer of the popular tribunal in Italy called the Clark Tribunal, exposing NATO war crimes in the Balkans.

DORIS PUMPHREY & GEORGE PUMPHREY are authors of the book, *Ghettos and Prisons in America—The anti-racist struggle in the USA: A question of Survival,* Published in 1981 by the American Commission of the Movement against Racism and for Friendship among Peoples (MRAP), Paris.

MILOS RAICKOVICH, Serbian-American composer and anti-war activist, is also a music teacher in New York City's schools and colleges.

MICHAEL RATNER, civil rights attorney on the National Board of the Center for Constitutional Rights, took the U.S. government to court for violating the War Powers Act in its undeclared war against Yugoslavia, as he had earlier for its undeclared war against Nicaragua.

SHANI RIFATI, originally from the Romani community in Kosovo, publishes an English-language newsletter about Romani affairs called the *Voice of Roma,* reporting on conditions facing the oppressed Roma people in Kosovo and in the world. He has organized relief for Roma refugees from Kosovo who fled to Italy.

REAR ADMIRAL ELMAR SCHMAEHLING resigned from the German Navy in January 1990 after criticizing the ongoing arms race and NATO's nuclear "flexible response" strategy with its "first use" option. He is a leading spokesperson for Germany's peace movement, and helped establish the European Peace Forum in 2001.

R.M. SHARPE is a journalist and photographer with special emphasis on political developments in the Caribbean, especially the U.S. intervention in Haiti, as well as in the Balkans.

SARAH SLOAN is on the IAC staff and organizer in the anti-globalization movement and of the anti-war coalition, A.N.S.W.E.R. (Act Now to Stop War and End Racism) formed after September 11, 2001.

NADJA TESICH, filmmaker, novelist and playwright, was born in Yugoslavia and frequently travels there. Her two novels, *Shadow Partisan* and *Native Land,* take place in Yugoslavia.

BILL WAYLAND is a journalist, anti-war activist and expert on developments in the former USSR and in the Balkans.

GARY WILSON is a journalist and researcher who has written extensively on the breakup of Yugoslavia, especially in the New York-based weekly *Workers World* newspaper. He maintains the popular web site, www.workers.org, and several Marxist lists. His articles have been reprinted worldwide.

A Brief Chronology of Yugoslavia*

1870s

Nationalist uprisings sweep the Balkans including the Bosnia-Hercegovinian Uprising of 1875; in Bulgaria, "The April Uprising" of 1876; and in Macedonia, the Razlovtsi Uprising in 1876.

1878

With the Balkans in full revolt and ungovernable, the Ottoman Empire is defeated in the Russo-Turkish War of 1877-78. The European Imperial powers (Germany, Austria-Hungary, France, Britain, Italy, Russia) meet at the Congress of Berlin and divide rule over countries of the Balkans among themselves. The nationalist movements are then crushed by the European powers. Austria-Hungary occupies Bosnia-Herzegovina.

1912-1913

The Balkan Wars: Popular nationalist uprisings sweep the Balkans.

1914

Serbian student's assassination of Austrian ruler in Sarajevo in Bosnia-Herzegovina, an Austrian colony, marks beginning of World War I.

1914-1918

World War I. Serbs hold off Austrians for more than a year. More than 800,000 Serbs are killed in the war.

1918

Creation of the Kingdom of Serbs, Croats and Slovenes.

1929

The Kingdom becomes Yugoslavia, which means Land of the Southern Slavs.

1941

Nazi Germany and fascist Italy impose the Axis Tripartite Pact on Prince Paul, regent of Yugoslavia, who signs pact rather than resist.

March 27

Anti-fascist coup overthrows Prince Paul.

April 6

Axis troops invade Yugoslavia and bomb Belgrade, the center of anti-fascist resistance. Yugoslavia is partitioned between Germany, Italy, Hungary and Bulgaria. A "Greater Croatia" is formed under the pro-Nazi Ustashe led by Ante Pavelic;

---

* The information outlined here for the period 1980-1996 can be found in detail in the book, *NATO in the Balkans,* published by the International Action Center in 1998.

"ethnic cleansing" of Serbs, Roma (Gypsies) and Jews begins. Greater Albania, including Kosovo, is formed by Italy and Germany.

Two movements emerge to fight German occupation. One is a Serbian nationalist movement, called the Chetniks, led by General Dragoljub Mihajlovic, who are royalist and tied to the Serbian Orthodox Church. The other is a Communist-led Partisan movement, led by Josip Broz Tito, which gives representation and involvement to all the many nationalities of Yugoslavia. This Partisan movement becomes the biggest resistance movement in Eastern Europe. Allied powers at first refuse to support Partisans. Later, in 1943, civil war breaks out between the two movements.

1941-1944

300,000 to 700,000 Serbs, Romas and Jews slaughtered in a death camp at Jasenovac in Nazi Croatia.

1943

In Jajce, Bosnia, the Anti-fascist Committee of National Liberation (AVNOJ) is founded. Yugoslav federation created in liberated territory. Allied powers recognize the Partisan movement as center for anti-fascist resistance.

1944

The Partisan army liberates Belgrade. Some 1,014,000 Yugoslavs die in World War II, half of them Serbs.

1945-1991

The Socialist Federation of Yugoslavia is founded as a multi-ethnic state. National rights are guaranteed for every nationality. A unique constitution includes affirmative action provisions (multi-ethnic, multi-lingual and multi-religious) and establishes wide autonomy for the six republics. It creates a rotating presidency between each member republic in the federation. Large landed estates are broken up and distributed to farmers. Private ownership of large industry is ended. Manufacturing, mining and the infrastructure are extensively developed. A decent standard of living is established for all for the first time in the Balkans, with free medical care, free education, a right to a job, one month paid vacation for all. Housing, transportation and utilities are made affordable. Literacy reaches over ninety percent.

1948

Break between Yugoslavia and the Soviet Union.

1949

First IMF loans to Yugoslavia are meant to exacerbate break with the other socialist countries, particularly with the Soviet Union.

1980s

Yugoslav foreign debt reaches $20 billion in 1980. By 1988 the foreign debt was $33 billion. In exchange for continued loans, the IMF demands economic reforms that bring an end to many socialist measures and severely weaken the socialist economy. The IMF program creates spiraling inflation, shuts many industries, cuts social programs and increases tensions among the nationalities and republics.

1989-1991

With the overturn of Soviet allies in Eastern Europe and the collapse of the USSR, nonaligned Yugoslavia is no longer needed as a buffer state between NATO and the Warsaw Pact. U.S. and European powers begin a march to reshape all of Eastern Europe.

1990

In November, the Bush administration and Congress pass the 1991 Foreign Operations Appropriations Law. It cuts off loans, credits and even trade for any part of Yugoslavia that does not declare independence within six months. It restricts funding to elements judged "democratic" by the U.S., including the fascist Ustashe movement and other right-wing organizations. The law specifically includes IMF and World Bank funding as well. This is widely recognized as a "death sentence" for Yugoslavia, which has become dependent on the IMF and World Bank loans.

1991

The Council of Europe follows the U.S. lead and demands that Yugoslavia break up or face economic blockade. Fascist organizations not seen in forty-five years suddenly revive in Yugoslavia, with covert support from the United States, Germany, and Austria.

January 25

Officers in the Yugoslav army publish a "Generals' Manifesto," assessing the threat from NATO powers to destroy Yugoslavia as a Socialist Federation now that there is no longer a Soviet Union. It calls for unity within Yugoslavia and preparations for self-defense.

May 5

Croatian fascists attack the Yugoslav government and call for expulsion of all Serbs living in Croatia. For hundreds of years, more than thirty percent of Croatia's population had been Serbs.

June 25

Slovenia and Croatia declare independence. Right-wing parties come to power. U.S. backs pro-fascist Croat leader Franjo Tudjman, who uses anti-Serb propaganda in his rise to power, reviving the Ustashe and using the fascist symbols and slogans from the Nazi era. Tudjman's regime imposes capitalism and strips all minorities (specifically including Serbs) of citizenship, jobs, pensions, passports, and land ownership. It will expel 500,000 Serbs by 1995. Germany immediately recognizes the new regimes and encourages the small, multi-ethnic republic of Bosnia-Hercegovina to secede. Tensions rise in Bosnia as secessionist forces receive aid and encouragement from Germany and the U.S.

1992

March 8

The *New York Times* publishes a Pentagon *White Paper* that asserts a U.S. dominant role in every corner of the earth. For Europe, a U.S.-dominated NATO is to be the only military pact.

March 19

Bosnian Muslims, Croats, and Serbs reach agreement in Lisbon for a unified state. The continuation of a peaceful multi-ethnic Bosnia seems assured. But the U.S. sabotages the agreement. The U.S. convinces Alija Izetbegovic (head of the right-wing Party for Democratic Action in Bosnia) that it will back him if he unilaterally declares a sovereign Bosnia under his presidency. Other political parties, including Muslim ones, are excluded from the government. Some Muslim leaders object and are smashed by PDA and U.S. military power.

May 27

An explosion in a food line in Sarajevo, Bosnia, kills fourteen people and wounds 100. The media charges that a mortar fired from Bosnian Serb positions is responsible. Weeks later a UN investigation proves the mortar could not have been fired from Bosnian Serb positions. But the international outrage against Serbs becomes the excuse for imposing sanctions on the Yugoslav government.

May 30

The UN Security Council votes to follow the Bush administration's lead and impose tough economic sanctions on the Yugoslav government. Exports, imports including oil and foreign investments are banned, and shipping on the Danube River is shut down. This all creates economic dislocation in Yugoslavia and its neighbors.

November 29

Air Force Chief of Staff Gen. Michael J. Dugan (ret.) and George Kenney publish an opinion piece in the *New York Times* entitled "Operation Balkan Storm: Here's a Plan." It says: "A win in the Balkans would establish U.S. leadership in the post-Cold War world in a way that Operation Desert Storm never could." They propose enlisting Britain, France, and Italy to use massive air power against Serbia, using aircraft and Tomahawk missiles to destroy Serbia's electricity grid, refineries, storage facilities, and communications. Six and a half years later, it happens.

1993

The economic strangulation of Yugoslavia imposed by U.S. law and European sanctions reduces the per capita income of Serbia from $3,000 (1990) to $700.

February 22

At U.S. Ambassador Madeleine Albright's insistence, the UN Security Council votes to create the International Criminal Tribunal for the Former Yugoslavia, in violation of the UN Charter. (Resolutions 808 and 827)

1994

February 5

Some sixty-eight people die in an open-air market in Sarajevo. The attack is blamed on the Serbs. This provides the excuse for NATO to bomb Bosnian Serb positions, NATO's first active military intervention abroad. Later, a report by the United Nations concludes that Izetbegovic's PDA forces had themselves carried out the attack it to justify war on the Bosnian Serbs.

June

Six U.S. generals help Izetbegovic's forces attack other Bosnian Muslim leaders in Bihac and Tuzla. The attacks violated the cease-fire and a UN-declared safe area. U.S. bombers under NATO command assist the attack.

1995

July 12

A "Council for Peace in the Balkans" calls for a "strategic and sustained" air campaign against Serbia. This "Council" consists of Zbigniew Brzezinski, Frank Carlucci, Hodding Carter, Max Kampelman, and Jeanne Kirkpatrick, all former top officials in the U.S. government.

July 17

The U.S. media reports an alleged massacre as Izetbegovic's troops pull out of Srebrenica in Bosnia. UN investigating teams report a year later that they could not find a single eyewitness to any atrocity, even though they interviewed hundreds of Muslims in Srebrenica and in Tuzla, where the majority of refugees were taken. Based on charges of a massacre, European countries stop efforts to maintain peacekeepers under UN flag. U.S./NATO military involvement is now accepted.

August 4

"Operation Storm," is launched. U.S./NATO aircraft destroy Yugoslav radar and air defenses, clearing the way for the Croatian military's offensive against the Krajina region of Croatia. U.S. EA6B electronic warfare aircraft jam Yugoslav communications and monitor Yugoslav military movements, delivering photos and intelligence reports to Croat military forces advancing into Krajina. Some 300,000 Serbs are expelled from Croatia and 14,000 are killed. The attack is led by Brig. Gen. Agim Ceku—the future head of the Kosovo Liberation Army—with massive U.S. support.

"Operation Storm" was planned by Military Professional Resources, Inc. (MPRI), a Pentagon contractor made up of retired U.S. generals and combat experts, working under contract to the Pentagon to "train" the Croatian military.

August 28

Another explosion hits a Sarajevo marketplace, killing thirty-seven civilians. Almost immediately, NATO launches over 4,000 bombing raids against the Bosnian Serbs. Later analysis of the crater and debris prove that the bomb was dropped off a roof by Izetbegovic's forces, which NATO knew at the time, according to *New York Times* Balkans bureau chief David Binder in a report in *The Nation* magazine on October 2, 1995.

November 21

Dayton (Ohio) Peace Accords are signed at Wright-Patterson Air Force Base. NATO bombing forces Bosnian Serb government and the Yugoslav government to accept U.S./NATO partition and occupation for Bosnia. The pact divides Bosnia into three area: Croatian, Bosnian Muslim, and Serbian. Sixty thousand NATO troops, including 20,000 U.S. troops, are sent to Bosnia, all under U.S. command. Troops are to remain six months; as of the end of 2001, they are still there. A new U.S./NATO base is established in Hungary and another in Tuxla, Bosnia. *Newsweek* of December 14, 1995, writes that "U.S.-led NATO forces will have nearly colonial powers in Bosnia."

1997

Sali Berisha becomes head of Albania with U.S. support and allows the U.S. to set up military bases in Albania. Berisha agrees to let the CIA take charge of the Albanian secret police. The attempt to dismember Yugoslavia centers now in Kosovo, a region of the Serbian Republic for over 600 years but with a majority population ethnically Albanian. The Kosovo Liberation Army sets up its headquarters on Berisha's estate in Albania. In November, the KLA kills Qamil Gashi, the Albanian chairperson of Serbian Socialist Party in Kosovo.

1997-1998

KLA goes through "rapid and startling growth," bolstered by mercenaries from the U.S. and Germany. According to *Jane's Defense Weekly*, the KLA includes U.S. Special Forces and British SAS units. It is not a liberation army. It is an arm of NATO.

1998

With the Albanian president of Kosovo, Ibrahim Rugova, on the verge of an agreement with Milosevic to restore Kosovo autonomy, the KLA steps up its terrorist attacks. Yugoslav police retaliation and attempts to curtail the KLA are put forward as a reason for NATO to intervene.

1999

January 15

The "Racak Massacre." KLA forces use a military setback in the town of Racak to set up a media coup, claiming dead KLA soldiers were civilians. William Walker, head of the Kosovo Verification Mission and former U.S. ambassador to El Salvador, arrives and declares his indignation at the atrocities committed by "the Serb police forces and the Yugoslav Army." [See chapter on Racak by Doris Pumphrey and George Pumphrey for details of how the so-called "massacre" was set up.--Editors]

Walker's declaration is widely reported in the U.S. media and used as a justification for further U.S. and NATO intervention.

March

Talks begin in Rambouillet, France. The U.S. draws up a document and presents it to the KLA and the Yugoslav government. There are no negotiations. Both sides are told to "take it or leave it." The document requires Yugoslav withdrawal from Kosovo, the introduction of a NATO occupying force with total powers, and a plebiscite to decide on independence for Kosovo. Not reported in the media at the time is that the document also gives NATO forces the right to occupy all of Yugoslavia, not just Kosovo. Members of the U.S. negotiating team brags that they intentionally set the bar too high for Milosevic to accept. "He needs a good dose of bombing, and that's what he's going to get," one is quoted as saying. [See Richard Becker's chapter on Rambouillet for details.]

March 24

NATO begins seventy-eight days of air strikes against Kosovo and Serbia.

April 4

NATO bombs the Monastery of Holy Mother and the Monastery of St. Nicholas in Kursumlija (both built in the twelfth century). At least fourteen other monasteries are bombed by the middle of April.

April 12

NATO bombs a train on a bridge over Grdelica gorge, killing ten civilians and wounding sixteen.

April 15

NATO bombs a refugee convoy on the road from Prizren to Djakovica, killing seventy-four civilians.

April 22

NATO bombs residence of President Milosevic, but assassination attempt fails.

April 23

NATO bombs the offices of Serbian Television, killing sixteen workers there.

April 24

NATO uses cluster bombs on Doganovici, killing five children and many adults.

April 27

NATO bombs residential district in Surdulica, killing twelve children and many adults.

May 1

NATO bombs bus on the Luzan Bridge, killing fifteen children, nineteen adults.

May 13

NATO cluster bombs kill seventy-nine refugees in Prizren. NATO bombs kill eighty-seven Albanians in Korisa, Kosovo the same day. At first NATO denies responsibility, then changes its story and says it did the bombing, but against a military target. It says the Serbs used the Albanians as human shields. Reporters from the London *Independent* report seeing scraps of flesh and scattered possessions, but no sign of a military presence. The *Los Angeles Times* also reports that the only targets were the tractors and wagons of refugees.

May 27

NATO bombs Chinese embassy in Belgrade, killing three and injuring twenty-seven.

June 3

The Yugoslavian government accepts terms proposed by the G-7 and Russia for ending the war. The terms are similar to those of Rambouillet except that Kosovo remains part of Serbia and the occupying forces, though made up largely of NATO countries, would officially be acting in the name of the United Nations. These are exactly the conditions Milosevic agreed to before the bombing started.

June 10, 1999 to Summer 2000

Kosovo remains occupied by NATO troops under United Nations aegis, divided into U.S., British, French, German and Italian zones. Under direct NATO occupation, more than 300,000 Serbs and people of other and mixed nationalities are driven out of Kosovo. In Summer of 2000, the U.S. and European Union organize parties that oppose Milosevic's Socialist Party of Serbia in Yugoslav election and give them $41 million.

2000

September 24

Milosevic is narrowly defeated in the popular vote for president of Yugoslavia by Vojislav Kostunica.

October 5

To avoid a runoff election, SPS opponents, called the Democratic Opposition of Serbia, stage a coup and overthrow the Socialist Party of Serbia.

2001

March 31

New authorities in Belgrade arrest Milosevic to comply with the U.S. deadline. They hold him in prison in Belgrade.

June 28

Belgrade officials break Yugoslav Constitution by turning Milosevic over to U.S. authorities to be brought before the International Criminal Tribunal for the former Yugoslavia in The Hague on war-crimes charges.

Abolish NATO and Its Court

SARA FLOUNDERS

What is the cause of a decade of wars that have ripped apart the Socialist Federal Republic of Yugoslavia?

Is this all due to the mad machinations of one evil individual—Slobodan Milosevic? This is the official charge of the International Criminal Tribunal for the Former Yugoslavia based at The Hague.

Is history ever so simple?

Are the continuing wars in the Balkans, as the media always presents them, a new cycle of "endless ethnic hatred" among the small nationalities of the region? Or are there powerful outside class forces involved in reshaping the region?

What is the hidden agenda of U.S. and West European corporate powers in this process? Is their acquisition of the major industries, infrastructure and resources of the Balkans and Eastern Europe a mere accident?

Are the resulting NATO bases in every country in the region unconnected to this transfer of ownership?

An investigator at the scene of a crime would look not only at what happened and how it unfolded but, most important, who stood to benefit. Not only the stated reasons for the war must be examined. The beneficiaries of this extreme action must be identified. Who will own the industries and natural resources? Who will get the contracts to rebuild the bombed infrastructure? Who will profit as the collectively owned industries and services are privatized?

An examination of the court, which today has the power to indict and order the arrest and prosecution of any political figure, is just the first step in understanding the forces controlling events in the region. Who established the court and what order it would impose in the region will explain a great deal about the role of outside powers in all the events of the past decade.

The proceedings of this court are of great importance to the political leaders and generals of the countries who carried out the war against Yugoslavia. When the smoke of media propaganda and war frenzy clears, how will the people of the world view this savage onslaught by the world's largest military power, in an alliance with other powerful states, on a country smaller than the state of Ohio in size and population?

Imagine a court that allows sealed indictments, closed hearings, secret trials and hearsay evidence. Imagine a court that can change the rules on procedure and evidence at any time, even during a trial.

Imagine a court where there is no jury and there is no independent appeals body. There is no bail.

Imagine a court where a defendant or their lawyers have no right to cross-examine a witness or even to know the identity of a witness. These secret prosecution witnesses do not even have to appear in court or answer any questions. The prosecutors release statements of the anonymous witnesses to the media in a continuing stream and they are reported in great detail. Visitors to the defendant are prevented from speaking to the media.

Imagine a court that asserts the right to bar an attorney from visiting or to disqualify a defendant's attorney for any reason, including the reason that the attorney is not friendly to the court.

Imagine a court that is paid for, staffed and assisted by private corporations and multi-billionaires, who have an enormous financial stake in the decisions.

This is the International Criminal Tribunal for the Former Yugoslavia (ICTY). A court where the countries ochestrating the proceedings are the very countries that bombed Yugoslavia for seventy-eight days, dropped thousands of cluster bombs and radioactive DU bombs, bombed 480 schools and thirty-three hospitals along with market places, bridges and refugee convoys.

This is the court where former President of Yugoslavia Slobodan Milosevic is on trial.

President Milosevic was kidnapped at Washington's demand and in violation of Yugoslavia's constitution, federal courts and parliament and taken to a prison cell in the Netherlands. He is to stand trial charged with responsibility for all the crimes and wars of the 1990s.

At his arraignment on July 3, 2001, President Milosevic stated his position strongly and clearly: "I consider this tribunal to be a false tribunal and the indictment a false indictment." Then he only had time to charge, "This trial's aim is to produce false justification for the war crimes NATO committed in Yugoslavia," before the judge ordered his microphone cut off.

His full response to the court has been included in this book. It is a vital historical record. Anyone reading it would understand immediately why it has been suppressed by the very powers that have placed him in the dock.

President Milosevic argues that the ICTY represents an effort by the most powerful countries to destroy even a semblance of sovereignty for small and developing countries. It is an apparatus created without any standing in existing international law, treaties or the United Nations Charter.

The kidnapping and imprisonment of President Milosevic raises in the starkest way the need for a critical examination of this court, its power and its purpose. Of fundamental importance is the issue of who is charged, who is not and why. Is there any power that can contest this court?

THE REAL ISSUES

Four years ago in a book the International Action Center published, *NATO in the Balkans: Voices of Opposition*, we described the coming war in Yugoslavia and its far-reaching consequences. The goals of the 1999 war, who would gain and who would lose, its tactics and justifications were already clear before the 1995 signing of the Dayton Accords.

NATO in the Balkans proved to be a valuable weapon in mobilizing resistance in the face of a propaganda barrage that reached new levels of hysteria. Thousands of people bought the book so quickly we had to reprint to keep up with the demand. The book was translated into Serbian and Greek, and substantial sections printed in French, German and Italian. It became a weapon in the fight against NATO's war.

Since that time, the two and half months of bombing, the forcible occupation of Kosovo, the overthrow of the elected government of Yugoslavia, and the kidnapping of its president and the new NATO invasion of Macedonia have changed the entire terrain. A new evaluation of a widening occupation was needed.

In this latest book published by the International Action Center, *Hidden Agenda: U.S./NATO Takeover of Yugoslavia,* we have gathered a series of thoughtful articles that challenge the media hysteria surrounding NATO's bombing and evaluate the deeper issues involved in the war. Their authors are analysts and anti-war organizers, mainly from NATO countries, who had the courage before, during and after the 1999 war to challenge the lies of NATO's rulers.

Former U.S. Attorney General Ramsey Clark makes a compelling case in his powerful chapters of "Indictment of U.S./NATO For Crimes Against Peace, War Crimes and Crimes Against Humanity." The crimes are summarized into nineteen charges. The international conventions, treaties and laws that the U.S. government and the NATO military command violated are cited at the end of each of the nineteen charges.

In his chapter, "The Greatest Purveyor of Violence," Clark puts the war in the Balkans in the perspective of 100 years of past U.S. wars, interventions and coups.

THE ICTY—AN ILLEGITIMATE VICTORS' COURT

The proceedings of any court give a cloak of legitimacy to the examination of any crime, whether it is a small robbery, a crime of passion or a financial fraud. In a trial all the evidence is supposed to be heard and weighed by impartial jurists and judges. A trial has standing as an official record. Over many centuries even those carrying out the most horrendous acts of slavery, piracy, and colonialism have sought to legitimize their conduct with laws and court proceedings. The conquered are placed in the dock. The victims are declared guilty of their own destruction. We challenge this scenario.

NATO pressured the UN Security Council to establish this court as a political weapon. It has all the credibility that a budget of tens of millions of dollars and endless press coverage can buy. It has the power of police forces in twenty countries to enforce its indictments.

As Jamie Shea, the official spokesperson for NATO bragged, "NATO countries are those that have provided the finances to set up the Tribunal, we are among the majority financiers." Madeleine Albright had this court set up in 1993 in violation of the United Nations Charter when she was the U.S. Ambassador to the UN. Since its creation it has served to justify step-by-step NATO's military occupation of the entire region. For eight years every act, every threat, every bombing by U.S. generals commanding NATO was preceded by a campaign of completely unsubstantiated charges from unidentified witnesses released by this court to the media with all the weight of law. The media dutifully reported these charges without ever researching or questioning them.

With the establishment of this court and the ability to arrest anyone in the region, NATO wields a big club over the head of any political leader who dares offer the least resistance. The court claims to be holding hundreds of secret indictments.

Any discussion of this ad hoc court must reach beyond the issue of its illegality, its financing by multi-national corporations and its unusual procedures. It is impossible to look at the court without first conducting a serious examination of the decade of outside interventions, grueling sanctions and financing of paramilitary organizations. All of this the court refuses to examine.

The political role of the ICTY has been to focus all blame on internal struggles among nationalities, which lived together in peace for fifty years. This is a little like trying to understand World War I, which started in Sarajevo, by looking at the motives of the Serbian student who assassinated Archduke Ferdinand of Austria. History has confirmed that World War I was a war between the great powers for a re-division of colonies worldwide.

Any investigative body that even pretended to be fair must scrutinize the military alliance that initiated seventy-eight days of bombing, review the targets and weapons used, and examine the explanations and justifications the generals and politicians gave for today's occupation. It must ask if this was a decision made quickly under extreme duress of rapidly unfolding events or was it the result of planning and premeditation.

The ICTY is obviously no impartial, fair court. We join with those around the world who are calling for this court to be abolished.

PEOPLE'S TRIBUNAL AGAINST NATO'S WAR

A large section of the *Hidden Agenda* recapitulates the information presented at the various popular tribunals held throughout 1999 and 2000 around the world that found the U.S. and NATO leaders guilty of crimes against peace, war crimes and crimes against humanity for the 1999 aggression against Yugoslavia. At the June 10, 2000, final hearing in New York, the prosecution presented evidence showing first how the media propaganda prepared the war with a web of lies. Then it showed how think tanks and Cold War ideologists laid out the motiviation and strategy for the war, as well as how U.S./NATO forces provoked hostilities, proving intent—a crime against peace. Witnesses described the damages purposely caused to Yugoslav civilians, or war crimes. This was followed by the crimes perpetrated against the population in occupied Kosovo; these are considered crimes against humanity.

Section II explains a most powerful weapon in the Pentagon's arsenal—a completely subservient media. This was a war promoted as a humanitarian intervention. It was supposed to stop crimes of unspeakable magnitude. During the war, the State Department stated that more than 100,000 people were in mass graves, some others claimed 500,000 missing and feared dead. An Internet search shows that more than 1,000 stories describing mass graves, massacres, mutilations and rapes were published or broadcast. After the war forensic teams from seventeen countries spent five months digging in Kosovo at every major site of an alleged massacre. Not one mass grave was found.

A picture is worth a thousand words. In preparing this book we reviewed thousands of pictures. The evidence is overwhelming and irrefutable. In the Photo Section III, we have tried to encapsulate into a few pages the images that tell the story of the calculated destruction of the civilian infrastructure.

CRIMES AGAINST PEACE

The aim of this latest book is to document that NATO is not only guilty of war crimes, but NATO's very existence is a crime. Section IV defines NATO as a criminal conspiracy with a global appetite. We document that the NATO powers were driven not by humanitarian concerns, but by the transnational corporations and banks' lust for profits.

The corporate powers needed this war; the U.S. strategists needed an enemy. U.S. strategy was aimed at redefining NATO into an aggressive military alliance of U.S. and Western Europe for domination with colonial control of Africa, Asia and the Arab world—and of Eastern Europe and the Balkans. This war was a criminal conspiracy to consolidate the hold on global markets by Washington in alliance and in competition with the European powers.

Today there are new NATO bases in Croatia, Bosnia, Macedonia, Albania, Kosovo and Hungary. Nearly every country in Eastern Europe is standing in line to join NATO. On March 29, 2001, Bulgaria signed an agreement allowing NATO troops to be permanently based on Bulgarian soil. None of this is accidental. This is the plan of the "New World Order."

At the intense negotiations at Rambouillet, France, before the war began, Washington issued an outrageous ultimatum. NATO must be given free access to all of Yugoslavia's airports, roads, ports and communication facilities or face devastating destruction. To the NATO leaders, Milosevic's great crime as the President of Yugoslavia was his resistance to these demands. Even after seventy-eight days of NATO bombing, Yugoslavia still refused to accept foreign troops on its soil beyond Kosovo. NATO Secretary General George Robinson told a meeting of the NATO alliance ministers on Oct 10, 2000, "We all know that in southeastern Europe and the former Yugoslavia there is an enormous opportunity for us."

This "opportunity" is an insatiable need, an addiction. The U.S. military is today larger than the armed forces of all the other members of the United Nations Security Council combined. Weapons are the largest and most profitable export item for the U.S. economy. The United States leads in the sale of weapons to other countries. Half the annual budget for the next decade for the countries of Eastern Europe will be spent on weapons procurements so that the equipment of these "emerging economies" is interchangeable with NATO equipment. This is a bonanza for U.S. military industries.

The oil-rich states of the Persian/Arabian Gulf region have become debtor nations because these U.S. puppet states spend most of their treasury on U.S. weapons. The U.S. economy today is dependent on militarism. The military industries enrich only a few corporate shareholders. Meanwhile, past, present and planning for future wars absorbs the tax dollars of half the U.S. federal budget.

WAR CRIMES — BOMBS DROP ON SERBIA

In June 2000 the chief prosecutor of this specially created court for war crimes in Yugoslavia, Carla Del Ponte, refused even to examine charges brought against the U.S. government and the NATO military alliance for the use of internationally prohibited weapons such as cluster bombs, the bombing of civilian targets such as schools, hospitals, heating plants, market places and refugee convoys.

In Section V of *Hidden Agenda* we present the research on environmental catastrophe, the use of radioactive weapons and the calculated targeting of the civilian infrastructure including schools, hospitals, heating plants and communications. This material is irrefutable and damning, as is a selection from the Yugoslav government's *White Book* listing each bombing attack that we publish in the appendix. Its impact will be felt far beyond the Balkans and by future generations.

NATO'S WAR CONTINUES

Section VI brings in the issues of U.S. and European intervention since the war. A budget of over $100 million dollars was spent to fix the Yugoslav elections of September 2000. Meanwhile the IMF and Western banks applied coordinated economic strangulation to force the privatization of nationally owned industries and drastic cuts in social services. This created further pressure for compliance. Politicians who Washington openly boasted it had placed in office kidnapped Milosevic.

Meeting all of Washington's demands has not guaranteed peace, stability or prosperity as the countries of Eastern Europe and the former Soviet Republics have learned. Even tiny U.S. protectorates like Macedonia, which bowed to Washington's demands, seceded from the Yugoslav Federation and allowed the stationing of foreign troops, now are being torn apart. A still larger NATO presence and a new round of concessions are the stated price to disarm an invasion by a guerrilla force which is armed and financed by NATO and which can still bring about dismembering of Macedonia.

The media hype during NATO's 4,000 bombing sorties in 1995 in Bosnia and Herzegovina and its 38,400 sorties in 1999 against Serbia and Montenegro was that this was emergency action—a humanitarian war to stop massacres on an unprecedented scale. Now it is clear this was not an emergency action. It is a long-term occupation of the entire region.

CRIMES AGAINST HUMANITY

The end of the NATO bombing was not the end of the war. NATO's occupation of Kosovo shows that peace and reconciliation are not on the agenda. Section VII explains the enormous impact of what in international law is labeled "Crimes Against Humanity." We show that NATO had a conscious policy to repress and expell from Kosovo of all nationalities who opposed occupation. Cultural monuments, churches were looted and industries seized. The Roma of Kosovo, the most oppressed people of the region, suffered the most systematic persecution, along with the Serbs.

Has this war resolved the crisis, as promised? Have the NATO occupation of the entire region and the stationing of more than 65,000 troops in Kosovo and Bosnia brought peace, reconciliation or stability? No. 150,000 Serbs, Roma, Gorani and Kosovo Albanians who opposed foreign occupation have been driven out of Kosovo after it was forcibly ripped away and occupied militarily. And war has begun in Macedonia.

In July 2001 the new government of Yugoslavia met with NATO generals. At the meeting, according to Beta News Agency, Serb Deputy Prime Minister Nebojsa Covic, Yugoslav Minister of Foreign Affairs Goran Svilanovic, Yugoslav General Ninoslav Krstic and Police General Goran Radosavljevic were informed about the plan on military cooperation by the commanders of American forces in Germany. The plan is the granting of a ninety-nine-year lease to NATO for Camp Bondsteel in Kosovo. Washington also wants to lease the radar base on Kopaonik Mountain, which the Yugoslav Army equipped with British technology and the Yugoslav military airport in Sjenica would be adapted for landing of American and NATO heavy transporters.

The Appendix reports some of the most important public responses to the fraudulent charges brought by NATO's court at The Hague. This is the material gathered internationally by People's Tribunals to Indict NATO for War Crimes. Powerful meetings were held in Berlin, Kiev, Rome, Vienna and New York, with hearings in dozens of other cities, and a mass protest in Athens. A Berlin lawyer has brought civil charges against the federal government there for damages to the people of Varvarin, a town in Serbia, during a bombing attack on it in 1999.

The hearings confirmed in a living way that in this epoch, not only the victors write the history. The efforts of many hundreds of thousands of people in a whole variety of forms to record the truth of the war and to challenge the war propaganda is important for the living struggle against NATO. It will continue to resonate.

NATO'S CONTRADICTIONS

NATO's biggest problem is that the capitalist market, which it imposed on the Balkans and the world by force, by stealth and by promises of greater prosperity, has been unable to provide a better life or a higher standard of living, than the planned economies it destroyed. Globally in the past decade, although the wealth of the top 200 billionaires has doubled, hundreds of millions have been impoverished. Two hundred billionaires own more than the combined incomes of two billion people.

In Kosovo, today divided into five zones of direct NATO control, the unemployment rate is sixty percent. In Bosnia, where more than $5 billion has been spent since NATO forced the signing of the Dayton Accords, the economy is in ruins. What can Serbian Prime Minister Zoran Djindjic and his band of collaborators expect to solve with the $1.3 billion in loans they received for selling Milosevic to The Hague Tribunal? If they even receive it?

The insatiable capitalist market has not only brought war to Yugoslavia. The entire region from the Adriatic to Siberia has suffered the most dramatic lowering of life expectancy in recorded history, according to the 1999 UN Development Report. Whole industries that provided jobs, benefits and pensions for millions of workers have been sold off for pennies and cut up for scrap metal. In capitalist terms they were redundant and not profitable even if they supplied needed products or services. Free day care, health care and education have collapsed. Drug addiction, alcoholism and prostitution have soared in the resulting chaos and demoralization.

During a decade of unparalleled corporate profits in the United States, conditions for millions of working people actually deteriorated. Now in the coming phase of stagnation and economic downturn, what conditions can be expected?

It is the heritage of the Partisan resistance against Nazi occupation that Washington fears today. During World War II the largest resistance army in Europe against Nazi occupation was built among the many diverse nationalities of the Balkans. Fifty years later, Washington used jet aircraft in 4,000 bombing sorties in Bosnia and over 38,000 sorties in Yugoslavia along with years of economic sanctions and political destabilization to overwhelm the same region. The Pentagon has erected at

Camp Bondsteel in Kosovo the largest base built since the Vietnam War because it fears that resistance will erupt again.

THE MOVEMENT AGAINST THE WAR

It is important to have an honest evaluation of our own movement against war and corporate globalization. The collapse of the socialist countries and the years of war propaganda were effective in creating great confusion.

In many NATO countries, such as Spain, Italy and Portugal, the overwhelming majority of the people were against the NATO war, but the movements were unable to derail the war. Only in Greece was the popular movement able to concretely resist NATO. Elsewhere, in the face of a crushing U.S. juggernaut, many who had opposed past wars instead became totally complicit. This disoriented the peace movement. These turncoats included the Social Democratic parties and many Green parties of Europe, the "Olive" coalition in Italy and others who were in office and actually directed their country's participation in the war. Nevertheless, by early June 1999, public attitudes in many of the European NATO countries had turned against the bombing.

By that time even in the U.S. the domestic support for the war was thin. Even when the barrage of propaganda was at its most intense, half the population of the U.S. was still not for sending U.S. troops. Ever since the Vietnam War distrust and skepticism of the assurances of political leaders regarding land wars runs too deep.

The Pentagon well understood that a protracted war and especially a ground war would awaken massive opposition in the U.S. and throughout Europe. The air war was intensified to force Yugoslavia to capitulate. The generals' recurring nightmare is that any casualties among the more than 65,000 troops, at least among U.S. troops stationed in the region, could quickly undermine the occupation.

The United States may have the world's largest military machine but ultimately this government cannot control the forces it has unleashed. There is a rising global movement against this ruthless competition and spiraling economic chaos. Six months after NATO's bombing of Yugoslavia a new movement against corporate globalization was born in Seattle. Hundreds of thousands of young activists have focused on the brutal policies imposed by the International Monetary Fund, the World

Bank and the trade agreements such as NAFTA and the FTAA, and the World Trade Organization. This is a movement outraged at sweatshop conditions, prisons, environmental devastation and capitalist chaos.

We are confident that the material published in this book will contribute toward the judgment of history. NATO means continuing war, crisis and colonial domination. Here at home NATO's existence means greater poverty and repression. This book is our effort to develop an understanding and to plant seeds of resistance. Resistance is needed, resistance is possible. The new movement against corporate globalization has shown that resistance will grow.

August 2001

I.

CHALLENGE
TO
THE HAGUE
TRIBUNAL

Patriots Will Soon Rule Serbia

PRESIDENT SLOBODAN MILOSEVIC

President Milosevic made this statement December 11, 2001, at an appearance before the International Criminal Tribunal for the Former Yugoslavia in The Hague, Netherlands, after being "indicted" for alleged crimes in Bosnia and Herzegovina

I want to tell you that what we have heard here, this miserable text, is the ultimate absurdity. I deserve credit for the peace in Bosnia, not the war. The responsibility for the war lies with the powers that have been breaking up Yugoslavia and with their agents in Yugoslavia, not with Serbia, not with the Serbian people and not with Serbian policy. This is an attempt...

> Here the court turned off President Milosevic's microphone. Later in the debate on unifying the "indictments," President Milosevic continued.

All that we have heard today from the so-called prosecution only confirms that the focus here entirely misses the point, but so as to not have the mike turned off again, I will stick to arguments that respond to your question.

It is entirely clear to me why this false prosecution insists on "unifying." It is because of September 11. They want to divert attention from the accusations against me concerning Kosovo since those accusations inevitably open the question of the Clinton administration's collaboration with terrorists in Kosovo, including [Osama] bin Laden's organization.

Second, regarding what we have heard today, they are conscious that, if they focus on Kosovo, they cannot, regardless of the illegality of this court, avoid having the main perpetrators of the crimes committed against my country and my people, starting from Clinton, [Madeleine] Albright and [Gen. Wesley] Clark and then also the others, appear before this body, nor could they avoid the appearance here of many peace brokers whose activities and cooperation in searching for peace refute the accusations—I would say, monstrous accusations—that have been made here.

So, their reasons for attempting to "unify" are totally pragmatic and aimed at the protection of those who have committed crimes against my country, and are not, as they claim, intended to ensure an efficient trial since they certainly do not care if I get tired out or not. I have told you before what I think about that.

As for their crowning argument, the accusation that we were motivated by the aim of creating a "Greater Serbia," that argument can be very easily disproved and I think that no reasonable person should dare to use that argument, which they have put forward as the mythical basis for all crimes. Nobody should try any longer to impute, to impose, or to abuse that argument in any way.

Here are irrefutable facts: On April 28, 1992, the Federal Republic of Yugoslavia was formed. On April 28, 1992, that is, before the conflicts began, before the civil war broke out, that Constitutional Assembly declared, in its official document, our position: that the Federal Republic of Yugoslavia has no territorial pretensions regarding any of the former Yugoslav republics. This is absolutely enough evidence to totally reject the nonsense that they are trying to impute.

I would remind you as well, that at the very beginning, in May 1993, with our maximum efforts, the Vance-Owen Plan was accepted and was then signed in Athens, including by Serbian representatives. The acceptance of that plan clearly shows that we regarded peace as the greatest goal and highest value for all Yugoslav peoples and refutes this mythical idea.

Finally, during those ten years in Yugoslavia, life itself has entirely disproved these accusations of national or religious discrimination, since the Federal Republic of Yugoslavia remained the only part of the old Yugoslavia to preserve its multinational character and in which there was no discrimination on national or religious grounds. Those ten years confirm that. The same goes for Kosovo. Maybe you do not know, but the government of the Autonomous Province of Kosovo and Metohija in 1998 and 1999—that is, during the war, until those who committed aggression installed their mercenaries in power—was formed of Serbs, Albanians, Muslims, Turks, Goranies, Roma and Egyptians. Serbs were a minority in that government. How can the notion that there was national discrimination be reconciled with that fact?!

Our delegation in Rambouillet [France, February-March 1999] was comprised of representatives of all these nationalities as well. How does that jibe with this monstrous imputing of national discrimination?! Do you know that in 1998, after ten years of total peace in Kosovo—ten years when no one got killed, ten years when no one got arrested, when dozens of daily papers printed in Albanian could be purchased on every corner, when education in primary and secondary schools was in Albanian—when, after ten years, terrorism broke out, organized by foreign secret services out of the outcasts of the Albanian mafia all over Europe, we formed local police forces in Albanian villages, where citizens chose their policemen. They carried weapons. All of them were ethnic Albanians. These Albanian policemen, and also Albanian mail carriers, Albanian supervisors, and other Albanians within the state apparatus, were all targets of threats, attempted murders, assassinations and outright butchery, all committed by Albanian terrorists.

In 1998 Albanian terrorists killed more Albanians than Serbs. It is truly remarkable that in all of our state structures, and in our Socialist Party as well, membership corresponded to the ethnic composition of our citizens—there were Serbs, Albanians, Turks, Hungarians, Ruthenians, Romanians, Bulgarians and all the others. Which one of these groups would ever go along with a program of national, religious, or racial discrimination, such as has here been imputed?

These two "indictments," for Croatia and Bosnia, were expressly launched for one purpose only: to drown the "indictment" concerning Kosovo because talking about Kosovo opens up the whole issue of terrorism—this apart from the fact that it is clear that in Croatia and Bosnia we worked for p eace, not war. We have assisted our people in order to help them survive rather than becoming, as they did in World War II, victims of genocide. Many times we have said publicly, and I have said this myself, that we want our people to be free and equal in the territories where they have lived for centuries. But at the same time, this should not be at the expense of any other people.

The example of the Federal Republic of Yugoslavia and its very good interethnic relations during the whole period of conflicts demonstrates this best. During the conflict in Bosnia no Muslim was expelled from Serbia. During the conflict in Croatia no Croat was expelled from Serbia. More than that, during the conflict in Bosnia—look at the records at UNHCR—over 70,000 Muslim refugees found shelter in Serbia. What nation, what tens of thousands of people, would seek shelter among those who had committed aggression against them?

Do you know that more Muslims live in Serbia than in Bosnia and Herzegovina? The Muslims in Bosnia and Herzegovina were pushed into that disaster, into that war, so that those outside forces, appearing as supporters of Muslims, could hide their responsibility for the deaths of many times more—millions of Muslims—in accordance with their interests of enslaving the world and a new colonialism.

Especially, I cannot understand that someone could dare to speak here about Kosovo implicitly as if it were something outside Serbia. Kosovo is Serbia and Kosovo will remain Serbia, but the terrible situation in Kosovo and Metohija will continue as long as it is subject to illegal occupation. Illegal because it was made possible based on an abuse of the United Nations and of Security Council Resolution 1244. This resolution does envisage the presence of UN security forces; however, the forces in Kosovo have violated their UN authorization by allowing further savageries by the Albanian terrorists, among other things.

Thousands of Serbs and other non-Albanian residents of Kosovo have been killed and kidnapped, tens of thousands of Serb homes have been burned down, more than a hundred churches have been destroyed and burned down, all under the auspices of the international forces that came there to guarantee safety for all.

And today, after these cartoon-like elections, those fine Serbian MPs come by plane from Belgrade to do their job as deputies and under military escort get into that so-called parliament. This situation will last as long as the occupation. A similar situation under Turkish occupation lasted for all of 500 years. This one won't last that long, and in the very moment it ends, Kosovo will again be completely under Serbian control, and here we are talking not only about Kosovo, but of Serbia as well, since Serbia too will be ruled again and soon by patriots. Patriots will rule in other countries as well, instead of this scheme of new colonialism and the establishing of various puppet governments.

I think that all we heard here today, which is in total contradiction to the truth, has shown how failed these "indictments" are. I can only understand them as a statement of anger and revenge for the fiasco that NATO has suffered in the attempt to militarily occupy Yugoslavia. I can tell you that I am proud that I commanded the armed forces of Yugoslavia that have stopped NATO, since this has shown that a country, even a small one, having a strong will to defend its freedom and defend the idea of freedom and equality of nations and peoples, can succeed. I am here as a punishment for our standing up against the danger of the biggest tyranny that has threatened humanity.

What of substance can be scraped from these accusations is nothing more than the mud and dregs of a decade-long media war aimed at demonizing both Serbia and the Serbian people, as well as the Serb leadership, and myself, and even my family. Because the media war preceded the real one and had as its goal convincing public opinion in the West that we are villains, regardless of the fact that we never provided any grounds for that.

You have read here today how on April 6, 1992, the European Union recognized Bosnia and Herzegovina. This was done under the influence of the then foreign affairs minister of Germany, Hans Dietrich Genscher, because April 6, 1941, was the day when Hitler started the attack on Yugoslavia and bombed Belgrade. There was a wish, in this way, to communicate that the outcome of World War II had been changed. I would never blame such a desire on the German people, but some politicians have held onto the evil, which we fought against together. In this way, these politicians realized a revenge in greater measure, for they have succeeded in killing us using the hands of our Allies, the Americans, English and French, with whom we fought together in two world wars, against that very same evil.

Here the court interrupts President Milosevic. He then resumes.

I have already told you about my relation to this court; no matter that Judge Robinson says my relation to it is of no consequence for you. Therefore, what you are going to do is your business, and I can only tell you that every argument used here to support "unifying" is not true, does not stand, is not correct, and cannot be justified in any way. So, the arguments are false, as the indictment is false; and you will do what you please, and that is your problem.

We have heard many arguments against the idea raised by the prosecution. Everything they bring up, and this will become more apparent as they go on, shows that their entire case stands on glass legs and is taken from the dregs of the media war, not from real facts, especially not from facts that could have some legal weight. The vocabulary and structure of all their arguments entirely matches what we have heard in political pamphlets or the media, which only shows that it was all cooked in the same kitchen, nothing else.

If I were you, I would, personally, regardless of your status, to which I object, a fact that is not unknown to you, reject such ideas. They want to put aside Kosovo only because it opens the matter of collaboration with the terrorists, which does not correspond with current policies. At this moment they are falsifying historical facts for the sake of daily policies, and that is something that even this illegal tribunal should not allow. ...

Blaming the Victim

RAMSEY CLARK

On June 10, 2000, the International Tribunal on U.S./NATO War Crimes in Yugoslavia held its final hearing in New York City. The evidence of U.S. and NATO aggression and war crimes against Yugoslavia was clear, compelling and massive. All who participated in the long process of gathering, presenting and evaluating it had a strong sense of accomplishment and a belief that if effectively communicated, the information gathered and work done by this tribunal would help deter the U.S. and NATO members from major violence against their chosen enemies. This tribunal was a people's tribunal, a forum for those who opposed aggression in the Balkans.

Another tribunal, the International Criminal Tribunal for the Former Yugoslavia (ICTY) in The Hague, Netherlands, had indicted Yugoslav President Slobodan Milosevic in May 1999 for war crimes in Kosovo. It was during the U.S. assault and well before the decision of the people's tribunal in New York that found the U.S and NATO leaders guilty. The ICTY indictment was so political and unsupportable, and Yugoslavia remained so strong that few took it seriously. Above all, the overwhelming evidence that the U.S. and NATO were the aggressors and committed war crimes throughout Yugoslavia was so clear that the risk of any real threat from the indictment seemed remote.

In the early 1960s when African Americans were beaten by the police in Alabama, Mississippi and other states, then charged with assaulting an officer, lawyers in the Department of Justice labeled the offense "resisting assault." That phrase applies perfectly to the conduct of President Milosevic. As the President of the Federal Republic of Yugoslavia he was sworn to protect and defend the sovereignty of his nation and the lives and property of its people from foreign aggression. Every citizen has the same duty.

The simple truth and the legal defense to the charges against President Milosevic is that he did all that he could to protect his country from military aggression by a superpower—and Western European countries it manipulated—that had the capacity to destroy all of Yugoslavia without ever setting foot on its soil. U.S. planes attacked civilians, civilian housing and facilities and utilities and properties essential to human life every day for seventy-eight days with aerial bombardments against which there was no defense.

The U.S. simultaneously motivated and financed domestic insurrection within Yugoslavia. For seeking to protect his country and its people, and to demonize Yugoslavia for history and make itself seem virtuous, the U.S. caused the indictment of President Milosevic to be obtained before an illegitimate court created at U.S. insistence in violation of the Charter of the United Nations, corrupting international law.

Can peace be found by punishing only the defeated weak after the fact, while the powerful victor engages in widespread military and economic warfare and spends ever more money on ever more dangerous arms? Because the Nuremberg Tribunal and the military trials following the Pacific war were created by victor nations who chose defeated enemy leaders for prosecution and defined their crimes, the criminality of the victors' conduct in bombing and burning civilian populations by the hundreds of thousands over whole cities, like Tokyo, Berlin, Hamburg, Dresden and scores of others and the use of atomic bombs against overwhelmingly civilian populations in Hiroshima and Nagasaki have never been established in international law.

U.S. bombing in North Korea from 1950 to 1953 was the principal contributing cause of the deaths of three million civilians. Cities in North Vietnam and civilian areas in and outside "free fire zones" in South Vietnam were the direct object of attack by United States aircraft, artillery and ground forces for years, contributing to the wartime death toll of several million Vietnamese. In 1983, the U.S. bombed civilian sites in Grenada, whose total population is 110,000, killing several hundred including sixteen patients in the public mental hospital.

In 1986, the U.S. bombed the sleeping Libyan cities of Tripoli and Benghazi in surprise early morning attacks killing hundreds of civilians and damaging four foreign embassies. Yet Libya is demonized and threatened with a criminal tribunal and two of its citizens have been tried and one convicted in an illegal proceeding before a one-time, one-case court on practically no evidence—and what little evidence there was was questionable—for allegedly sabotaging the plane that crashed in Lockerbie, Scotland.

In 1989, the U.S. bombed civilians in Panama from the Atlantic to the Pacific, killing two thousand people or more. U.S. forces had occupied Panamanian soil throughout the century. They surrounded and forced the surrender of President Manuel Noriega from Vatican offices where he sought sanctuary. Yet the U.S. had paid Noriega $200,000 a year to serve its interests. It then took the president of Panama to Florida by force, tried and convicted him of crimes against the U.S. and he remains imprisoned in Florida. His wife and family are refused permission to remain in the U.S. to visit him.

In Iraq in 1991 all major cities and utilities and infrastructure supporting civilian life, buildings, water, power, transportation, communication, food production, storage and distribution, health care, schools, churches, mosques, synagogues and and foreign embassies were the direct object of U.S. aerial and missile attacks. Many tens of thousands civilians were killed directly and many more indirectly. The U.S. claims it had 159 casualties, a third from friendly fire, none from combat. Economic sanctions since August 6, 1990, have caused the death of one and a half million people in Iraq, many of them infants and children.

And these are only a handful of the scores of illegal U.S. military interventions, attacks and economic assaults in the last century.

Where power has impunity even though it wreaks violence on the poor, the weak and the defenseless, then corrupts truth and justice, there can be no hope for peace and little hope for humanity.

August 2001

The Greatest Purveyor of Violence

RAMSEY CLARK

*Based on a talk June 10, 2000, in the auditorium of Rev. Martin Lu-
ther King, Jr. High School in New York summarizing the evidence presented at the International Tribunal for U.S./NATO War Crimes in
Yugoslavia.*

Let me remind everyone of some words from our spiritual host today, Dr. Martin Luther King, Jr., for whom this high school of hopes
and dreams is named. They are words that were very important to him,
spoken in 1967 at the height of American anguish over the war in Vietnam, before the fever broke, and exactly one day short of one year before he was murdered for saying what he believed.

They are words of enormous courage and patriotism–if that's not an
unpopular concept–or at least patriotism as I see it. And they are the
most important words for our time. They are not chest-beating words
like "Give me liberty or give me death," which means, "Do what I say
or I'll kill you." They are not pompous words like "Damn the torpedoes!
Full speed ahead." They are not even modest words like "Nuts!" the
words uttered by General Anthony McAuliffe during the Battle of the
Bulge when he was asked to surrender.

What Dr. King said was, "The greatest of purveyor of violence on
earth is my own country."

The incredible thing is that we don't all feel that constantly every
day, because it is perhaps the most abundant truth of our time. Brian
Becker mentioned the $300 billion that the Pentagon will spend on arms
next year. That's a small part of it actually, but that happens to exceed
the combined military budgets of the rest of the countries on the United
Nations Security Council. One of the new "great evils" that we are seeking to make enemies of—the incredible people of the People's Republic
of China—spend only a tenth of that, $34 billion, on their military.

But our arms include the vast majority of all weapons of mass destruction that exist on the planet. They include far and away the most
sophisticated and deadly delivery systems. They include the capacity for
ecocide. They could easily render Mother Earth a moonscape with literally only two launches from Trident II nuclear submarines. These can

cover a hemisphere–half the world–and strike in one launch 408 centers of human population with warheads ten times more powerful than the one that incinerated Nagasaki.

What utter madness.

This morning I talked about the long, hard, and often deadly roads that so many who came here traveled. Today has provided a glimpse of those roads, from the speakers and from the films and from the documents that you've been given. And the scenery wasn't pretty. It was hard to take.

How could we let this happen? What terrible failure of human will and courage could permit it to happen, could restrain us from tearing the place down? I'm not going to summarize the evidence. I don't think it's necessary. You have heard about as much of human violence and misery in one day as anyone ought to have to hear in a lifetime.

THE CASE SPEAKS FOR ITSELF

The case is what Roman law called *res ipsa loquitur*. It's obvious. It speaks for itself. Who needs to say anything about it? If each of us can't see it and understand that simple point by now, there's no hope. What we have seen and heard answers the question, "Isn't understanding the obvious more important than an investigation of the obscure?"

Let's just listen to what NATO says. They say it's true that they didn't intercede to save a single person being assaulted. They said that, but it's obvious. Look at their technique. Until there was a cease-fire they never set foot in Kosovo or in Yugoslavia, did they? They just bombed from a distance. They bombed defenseless people. They killed thousands directly by violence and tens of thousands more over who knows how long, indirectly, by the variety of violence that they used.

It should be clear beyond question that the war crimes committed are almost beyond counting. I mentioned earlier how pathetic it seems that there's such an uproar about Amnesty International's report of four acts of violence against civilians. I saw evidence of hundreds of such acts on my two trips to Yugoslavia, one at the beginning in late March and one toward the end in late May and early June, hundreds of different direct assaults on civilians. There was no other purpose.

These were not mistakes. Nearly all of the bombing was that way.

We must remember that the long struggle for freedom is between remembering and forgetting. We have to remember. When the war was going on NATO was telling us how many armored vehicles it hit. If you were reading the general media about three months ago you read that it was overestimated by about tenfold. They weren't hitting military targets. They were bombing to break the country down.

You can't break the spirit of the people of Yugoslavia, but you can sure make life miserable for them. Anyone who saw 50,000 defiant people out in Republic Square, asking to be bombed, knows that.

Remember Jaleh Square in Iran in the last days of the shah, where the people wore burial shrouds and were accommodated by the shah with Huey helicopters manufactured in the United States. The copters' .50-caliber machine guns killed 2,500 Iranians on "Black Friday," August of 1978. The U.S. supported the shah to the bitter end and seeks to overthrow the successor government to this day.

The people of Yugoslavia, they stood on the bridges and the bridges were bombed. You can't break their spirit but you can set them back so far. You can make their future difficult.

Read the nineteen counts in the indictment for what they are. They are nineteen ways of killing. How many ways of killing are there? Each one is deadly in its own design, some immediate and ghastly, some slow, torturous and wasting, from radiation, illness without medicine, malnutrition, chemical or other pollution in the environment—for your children and your grandchildren and generations in the future. NATO used high-tech killing methods for seventy-eight days, without the perpetrators of the crimes suffering casualties or any imminent accountability. If we can't stop publicized mass murder, what hope is there for peace or justice?

Some of NATO's targets are hardest to forget. The sorrows of the many families we saw who had lost loved ones are not forgetable. I remember on the first trip in the first days of the bombing coming into Novi Sad and seeing a huge apartment complex just half smashed down, and the rest unlivable with stunned survivors still seeking the missing. How many people were in there? How do you mistake an apartment complex just south of the Hungarian border for a military target?

NATO hit Hungary a few times, too, of course. High-tech weapons are not as accurate as they claim. U.S. bombs or rockets also hit Bulgaria and Macedonia. Kosovo was devastated. These bombing were deliberate.

You remember, day after day, pictures of the U.S. bombing Pristina, bombing the heart of Pristina, proudly announcing it and the flames coming up for the world to see on CNN. And then we must remember when the cease-fire came and NATO troops occupied Pristina they looked at horror at the heart of Pristina and said, "Look what the Serbs have done to Pristina!"

What fools they take us for and make of us. Have we no memory of their boasting about their bombing? I remember meeting the chancellor of the University of Pristina, about the fifth or sixth day of the bombing, and already three or four important buildings devoted to higher education in Kosovo had been destroyed there. Can that be anything but the basest of crimes? It was murder, mass murder by war machines that the American citizens pay for.

GREEK CONSULATE DESTROYED

Nis is in the far south. It's the last big city, down toward Bulgaria and Greece on the main highway, the international highway that comes from Athens to Western Europe. All the trucks go through Nis. The beautiful Greek Consulate-General is the first building you see as you enter the city from the south. It marks the gateway for Greek people entering Yugoslavia as they travel all the way into Germany and Scandinavia. Sixty percent of European Greek trade comes up that highway.

The Greek Consulate was virtually destroyed by bombing, like the Chinese Embassy in Belgrade, which overlooks the Saba River. The Yugoslav people brought piles of flowers to each to show their love and sorrow at what had been done.

I remember the hospital in Nis, a huge complex with a courtyard. It looked like a city in WWII where urban warfare had gone on. All the buildings were pockmarked, some badly damaged. We saw five unexploded cluster bombs still sticking in the ground or lying there, unexploded and dangerous. A hospital yard, hit with cluster bombs designed to rip apart anybody within hundreds of yards of the place.

It's a bad rap for mother, but they call the large container for bomblets the "mother bomb." That's the huge metal cylinder that breaks open and unleashes—depending on the model—400 or more hand grenade-type cluster bombs that explode, sending razor-sharp pieces of metal into the surroundings. This was in the middle of a major regional hospital complex.

Two of Amnesty International's complaints were about strafing of refugees. NATO forces strafed refugees and civilians many times, all of which added to the many war crimes they committed.

An important story appeared in the press in the United States this Thursday [June 8, 2000]. It came apparently from pressures generated by new revelations of the slaughter of Koreans fifty years ago in late June-early July of 1950 at a place called No Gun Ri. Already there was a big dispute about whether it really happened, with the U.S. denying and explaining what happened. But even the Encyclopedia Brittanica states that three million civilians died in northern Korea and 500,000 in the south from 1950-1953.

We speak of revelations, but a lot of people have known about this for a long time. Then there is an effort to make it appear that No Gun Ri was the only offense during the whole Korean war. The U.S. leveled Pyongyang, but they treat this like it was nothing. Everything became focused on this one bridge incident. And now they claim it didn't happen. The same day an Air Force colonel released a memo that reported that the Army had been asking the Air Force for military support to strafe columns of refugees before No Gun Ri.

If we don't reveal the truth, if we don't stand on the truth, if we don't spread the truth every place we possibly can, does anyone believe U.S. and NATO assaults will not happen again in fifty years, in five years, and in five months—on and on?

Look at the power and presence of U.S. arms everywhere. The largest naval armada since WWII is in the Persian/Arabian Gulf right now. This is U.S. power, and nobody who lives in the Gulf region wants it there. Certainly the Muslim populations don't want it there for good reason, religious and human, and yet there it is. Who dares defy that kind of power?

The truth of what happened in Kosovo and throughout Yugoslavia is clear. The important first step in our process in this tribunal is to have our judges declare the truth as they see it. The toil and sacrifice of thousands of people have gathered it over the last fifteen months and brought it here for presentation.

But justice is truth in action. Without action there can be nothing but sorrow and rage. And now we begin the new road. It's a steeper, harder road.

The hardest thing that I had to say in Yugoslavia was on an occasion when I spoke at the University of Belgrade. It was a cruel thing to say, but it had to be said. "You're enduring bombing now that seems unbearable, but it will be worse when the bombing ends."

How can you tell people something like that? But you have to tell the truth. Vietnam struggled against the French and the Americans for thirty years, from 1945 to 1975, and prevailed. They drove them out. Sanctions remained on Vietnam for twenty years from 1975 to 1995. We paid no attention to it. Yet there can be no question that those sanctions caused more human misery and caused more human deaths than thirty years of war.

People who had nothing but a pair of pants and maybe some shoes and a rifle and a sack of ammunition, a little bowl for rice, living underground for months and months and gone from home and loved ones for years, never gave up.

And yet soon after the war ended many Vietnamese were taking to the sea in open boats because with economic strangulation and human isolation the future seemed hopeless at home.

LOOK AT IRAQ

Look at Iraq—nine years of sanctions. Malnutrition. Twenty-five percent of the infants born there today at weights of less than two kilos, which means that you're lucky if you make it, or maybe you're unlucky if you make it, depending on how you define luck. Because if you do make it, that is if you live, the probability that vital organs won't develop, the probability of mental retardation and physical damage, of short lives full of pain and suffering, is very high. British doctors started declaring Iraq a "generation of dwarfed people" more than five years ago, yet the sanctions and more bombing continue.

The imperative need is for us to act, to organize and act. There will be no justice, however well known the truth is, unless we act on it. And we have to define carefully what must be done. NATO won't replace the United States as the greatest purveyor of violence on earth, but it will make U.S. capacity to purvey violence much greater.

One thing we notice is that U.S. political leaders prefer it when soldiers from other countries are the ones that have to stand on the ground out there and perhaps get caught between conflicts that these leaders created in Kosovo and elsewhere, in the rising violence.

Let's look at another human tragedy just for a moment to see what follows if we fail to act. We all know how profoundly distressed we were and are about violent deaths in Rwanda in 1994. Hundreds of thousands of people were killed. What was behind it? How does it happen that the prevailing governments of Uganda and Rwanda and Burundi are all governments that the U.S. supported? Yesterday we read in the papers that 1.7 million people have been killed in eastern Zaire or eastern Congo—as it's called now—in the last two years. That's three times the number of people killed in Rwanda, where the U.S. didn't intercede but promoted the overthrow of the prior government.

More Rwandan refugees may have died in Zaire/Congo since 1994 than in Rwanda that year. Now satisfied with the new government, Washington supports its repression of the people and prosecutes victims of this regime's violence in the International Criminal Tribunal for Rwanda. The U.S. and other NATO members created the Rwandan conflict very much as they created the conflicts in Yugoslavia, forcing the division of Yugoslavia by balkanizing it into small, contentious but dependent segregated peoples in Slovenia, Croatia, Bosnia, Macedonia and Kosovo.

The rate of violence in all those regions is higher than it has ever been and growing higher. And the impoverishment of the people is the deepest it's been since World War II and growing deeper. It's because the U.S. knows how to coordinate these nineteen techniques for killing, to dominate.

It's imperative first that we find the truth, that can set us free, but that we realize that the truth won't act without human energy and commitment. It will take our vision and courage and compassion and energy and perseverance for the rest of our lives and for those who come after. There is no more important business for humanity.

So we ask our tribunal to find the truth. And then we ask all of us to act to abolish NATO now, to provide reparations for all the peoples of Yugoslavia. Start with the poorest and most deprived and discriminated against always, that's where my heart is and it will never be elsewhere.

That means you start with the poorest, but you neglect no one. There is no other way to live together. We need new concepts of federation, not segregation.

Whoever decided to use the word "Balkanize" to describe political fragmentation that will create perpetual war never imagined in their wildest dreams how the Balkans would be Balkanized by NATO into the tiniest fragments not unlike cluster bombs. The masters of apartheid never had such dreams themselves, that you could break a country up and hold it in so many shards and set them against each other so you could dominate and exploit their labor and the resources of their land.

We ask the court to weigh the evidence and decide it truly, and we ask all of us to enlist for the duration in the struggle to overcome the powers that are impoverishing the great majority of the people of the planet, who are overwhelmingly the peoples with beautiful darker skin.

Indictment of U.S./NATO

For Crimes Against Peace, War Crimes and Crimes Against Humanity

RAMSEY CLARK

Written July 1999 and used as a basis for hearings leading up to the International Tribunal for U.S./NATO War Crimes in Yugoslavia held on June 10, 2000, in New York.

THE LIST OF CHARGES

THE COMPLAINT

This Complaint is presented to end the scourge of war, prevent future violations of fundamental human rights, protect international and national organizations, governments and institutions and to hold those convicted of the violations alleged accountable for their acts.

The Governments, Organizations and Individuals named herein are charged with:

Crimes against Peace, War Crimes, Crimes against Humanity and Other Offenses in Violation of the Principles of the Nuremberg Tribunal (Nuremberg), The Hague Regulations (Hague) and Geneva Conventions (Geneva) and Other International and National Laws;

Grave Violations of the Charter of the United Nations (UN Charter), the North Atlantic Treaty (NAT), other international treaties, International Law, the Federal Constitution and Domestic Laws of the United States, the Basic Laws of Other Nations Including the United Kingdom, the Federal Republic of Germany, Turkey, the Netherlands, Hungary, Italy, Spain and other Governments of NATO members and the Federal Republic of Yugoslavia.

Grave Violations of the Universal Declaration of Human Rights (UDHR), the International Covenant on Civil and Political Rights (ICCPR), the International Covenant on Economic, Social and Cultural Rights (ICESCR), the Genocide Convention, and Other International Covenants, Conventions, Treaties, Declarations and Domestic Laws named herein.

A. DEFENDANTS

1. President William J. Clinton, Secretary of State Madeleine Albright, Secretary of Defense William Cohen and Commanding Generals, Admirals, U.S. personnel directly involved in designating targets, flight crews and deck crews of the U.S. military bomber and assault aircraft, U.S. military personnel directly involved in targeting, preparing and launching missiles at Yugoslavia, the government of the United States personnel causing, condoning or failing to prevent violence in Yugoslavia before and during NATO occupation and Others to be named.

2. The United Kingdom, Prime Minister Tony Blair, the Foreign Minister, the Defense Minister and Commanding Generals, Admirals, U.K. personnel directly involved in designating targets, flight crews and deck crews of the U.K. military bomber and assault aircraft, U.K. military personnel directly involved in targeting, preparing and launching missiles at Yugoslavia, the government of the United Kingdom personnel causing, condoning or failing to prevent violence in Yugoslavia before and during NATO occupation and Others to be named.

3. The Federal Republic of Germany, Chancellor Gerhard Schroeder, the Foreign Minister, the Defense Minister and Commanding Generals, Admirals, German personnel directly involved in designating targets, flight crews and deck crews of the German military bomber and assault aircraft, German military personnel directly involved in targeting, preparing and launching missiles at Yugoslavia, the government of the Federal Republic of Germany personnel causing, condoning or failing to prevent violence in Yugoslavia before and during NATO occupation and Others to be named.

4. The Government of every NATO country that participated directly in the assaults on Yugoslavia with aircraft, missiles, or personnel and Commanding Generals, Admirals, NATO personnel directly involved in designating targets, flight crews and deck crews of the NATO military bomber and assault aircraft, NATO military personnel directly involved in targeting, preparing and launching missiles at Yugoslavia, the governments of the NATO countries' personnel causing, condoning or failing to prevent violence in Yugoslavia before and during NATO occupation and Others to be named.

5. The Governments of Turkey, Hungary, Italy and others who permitted the use of airbases on their territory to be used by U.S., or other military aircraft and missiles for direct assault on Yugoslavia.

6. The North American Treaty Organization (NATO), Secretary General Javier Solana, Supreme Commander General Wesley K. Clark.

7. For Condemnation: Each NATO member that voted to authorize military assaults on Yugoslavia.

B. THE CHARGES

1. Planning and Executing the Dismemberment, Segregation and Impoverishment of Yugoslavia.

The United States, Germany, NATO and other defendants engaged in a course of conduct beginning in, or before 1991 intended to break the Federal Republic of Yugoslavia into many parts, segregate different ethnic, religious and other groups among and within newly balkanized borders, weaken the Slav, Serb, Muslim and other populations by causing and prolonging internal violence and by direct assaults by the United States and certain NATO members. As a consequence Yugoslavia, which had 25 million people in an integrated society and economy, is now comprised of many small nations, the largest of which is Serbia. Defendants intend to divide Yugoslavia until all parts of Yugoslavia have fewer than 5 million people, each to be overwhelmingly of a single ethnic origin and religion, to have severely impaired economies largely dominated by foreign interests, in which two groups, Orthodox Christian Serbs and Muslims suffer severest casualties, most extensive property damage, a vast reduction of productivity now down by three-quarters or more, and a generation of impoverishment.

UN Charter; Declaration on the Inadmissibility of Intervention in the Domestic Affairs of States and the Protection of their Independence and Sovereignty (Non Intervention Decl.), 1965 USGA Res. 2131.

2. Inflicting, Inciting and Enhancing Violence between Muslims and Slavs.

The United States and other defendants engaged in a course of conduct beginning in or before 1991, to cause Muslims and Orthodox Christian Slavs to engage in protracted fratricidal violence, in wars of attrition, similar to conflicts in Afghanistan and Chechnya between Muslims and Russian Slavs, which caused death, destruction and division in Bosnia, Kosovo and elsewhere between the groups and dangerous frictions and enmity between two major peoples the U.S. government considers its enemies, Slavic peoples and Muslims, in other regions, weakening both. Tactics included both providing and depriving select Muslim groups of arms to attack others, or adequately defend themselves in Bosnia; motivating, training and supplying KLA with arms to attack Yugoslav police and military to seize control of Kosovo during NATO occupation and attack Serbs and others; preventing outside efforts to prevent and control the violence; committing, causing and condoning violence against persons displaced by U.S. and NATO bombing campaigns, and by KLA and Yugoslav police and military ground actions; causing and supporting clashes between Yugoslav military/police/civilian groups and KLA/paramilitary/civilian groups; condoning and failing to prevent assaults on displaced persons returning to and persons who remained in Kosovo, both before and after the NATO/U.S. occupation of Kosovo. In 1999, the U.S. caused the largest numbers of deaths, injuries and destruction by aerial and missile assaults against all elements in the population and its life support systems.

UN Charter, Art. 2; Non Intervention Declaration; Resolution on the Definition of Aggression (Res. on Aggression), 1997 UNGA Res. 3314.

3. Preventing and Disrupting Efforts to Maintain Unity, Peace and Stability in Yugoslavia.

From the beginning of its efforts to implement its plans for dismemberment and destruction of Yugoslavia, the U.S. acted to prevent any interference, negotiation, or other efforts within Yugoslavia, or by other nations, leaders, or individuals to prevent the accomplishment of its intended purposes. Its techniques included political, military and economic threats and control of highly publicized peace negotiations much like those at Dayton, Ohio, during the Bosnia struggle, at Rambouillet, France, in 1999, which created an appearance of earnest peace negotiations, but offered Yugoslavia only two choices, agree to foreign military occupation, or expect a devastating military assault.

UN Charter; Non Intervention Declaration; Resolution on Aggression; Pact of Paris 1928, Art. I and II.

4. Destroying the Peace-Making Role of the United Nations.

The United States acted and coerced other nations to act to block the United Nations from performing its duties under the UN Charter to prevent conflict, control violence and maintain peace in Yugoslavia in violation of the Charter of the UN and threatening its viability as an international institution capable of maintaining peace and ending the scourge of war.

UN Charter; Non Intervention Declaration; Resolution on Aggression, Pact of Paris 1928, Art. I and II.

5. Using NATO for Military Aggression against and Occupation of Non-Compliant Poor Countries.

The United States acted and coerced other nations to act to cause NATO to authorize direct military assaults on Yugoslavia in violation of the UN Charter and the North Atlantic Treaty relying overwhelmingly on U.S. weaponry and military technology and to cause NATO members to provide and finance the majority of the military forces to occupy Kosovo for the foreseeable future thereby employing the wealth and power of the rich former colonial powers of Europe against the poor and defenseless people of Yugoslavia.

United Nations Charter; North Atlantic Treaty 1949, Art. I.

6. Killing and Injuring a Defenseless Population throughout Yugoslavia.

Beginning on, or before March 24, 1999, the United States, without a declaration of war by the Congress, aided and abetted by certain NATO members, including the United Kingdom, Germany, Turkey, Spain and the Netherlands, as well as Hungary, Croatia, Italy and others, commenced a war of missile and aerial bombing assaults, often indiscriminate in its targeting, against the populations of Yugoslavia, intentionally killing and injuring many thousands of Serbs, Albanians, Romas, Muslims, Orthodox Christians, Roman Catholics, foreign nationals throughout Yugoslavia with malice aforethought.

Hague, Art. 22 and 23; Geneva 1949, Art. 19; Nuremberg, Principle VI a, b and c; U.S. Constitution, Art. I, Sec. 8, cl. II.

7. Planning, Announcing and Executing Attacks Intended to Assassinate the Head of Government, Other Government Leaders and Selected Civilians.

The United States planned, announced and carried out missile and aerial bombardment attacks intended to assassinate the Head of Government of Yugoslavia, members of his family, other government leaders and selected civilians to destroy existing government leadership and terrorize it and its closest personal support into submission.

UN Charter, Art. 2, Convention on the Prevention and Punishment of Crimes Against Internationally Protected Persons (Protected Persons Convention); U.S. Army Field Manual 27-10; U.S. Presidential Executive Order 12333 (Ex.Order 12333); Geneva Conventions 1977, Protocol I Additional (Geneva 1977), Art. 48, 51.

8. Destroying and Damaging Economic, Social, Cultural, Medical, Diplomatic and Religious Resources, Properties and Facilities throughout Yugoslavia.

Beginning on, or before March 24, 1999, the United States, aided and abetted by certain NATO members, including United Kingdom, Germany, Turkey, Spain and the Netherlands and others, including Croatia, Hungary and Italy, commenced a systematic missile and aerial bombing assault on resources, properties and economic, social, cultural, medical, diplomatic and religious facilities intentionally destroying and damaging them throughout Yugoslavia to crush the productive, economic, social, cultural, diplomatic and religious viability of the whole society.

Hague, Art. 22 and 23; Geneva 1949, Art. 19; Geneva 1977, Protocol I, Additional, Art. 48, 52, 53; UN Charter, Art. 2; Protected Persons Convention; U.S. Army Field Manual 27-10; Exec. Order 12333; Geneva 1977, Art. 48, 51; ICESCR.

9. Attacking Objects Indispensable to the Survival of the Population of Yugoslavia.

Beginning on or before March 24, 1999, the United States, aided and abetted by others, for the specific purpose of depriving the population of Yugoslavia of food, water, electric power, food production, medicines, medical care and other essentials to their survival, engaged in the systematic destruction and damage by missiles and aerial bombardment of food production and storage facilities, drinking water and irrigation works for agriculture, fertilizer, insecticide, pharmaceutical, hospitals and health care facilities, among other objects essential to human survival.

Hague 1907, Art. 22 and 23; Geneva 1949, Art. 19; Nuremberg 1970, Principles VIa, b and c; Geneva 1977, Art. 48, 54.

10. Attacking Facilities Containing Dangerous Substances and Forces.

The United States attacked chemical plants and storage facilities, petroleum and natural gas refining, processing and storage facilities, fertilizer plants and other facilities and locations for the specific purpose of releasing and scattering toxic, radioactive and other dangerous substances and forces into the atmosphere, soil, ground water and food chain to poison the environment and injure the population.

Nuremberg Principle VI; Hague, Art. 22 and 23; Protocol for the Prohibition of the Use in War of Asphyxiating, Poisonous or Other Gases, Geneva 1925 (Poisonous Substances Protocol); Geneva 1977, Protocol I Additional, Art. 48, 51, 56.

11. Using Depleted Uranium, Cluster Bombs and Other Prohibited Weapons.

The United States used prohibited weapons capable of mass destruction and inflicting indiscriminate death and suffering against the population of all Yugoslavia. Despite knowledge of its deadly long-term effect on life and warnings of the U.S. Nuclear Regulatory Commission, the U.S. attacked Yugoslavia with depleted uranium missiles, bombs and bullets. These depleted uranium weapons spread radioactive matter into the atmosphere, soil, ground water, food chain and solid objects, placing the Yugoslav population at risk of death, genetic damage, cancers, tumors, leukemia and other injuries for generations. Cluster bombs were used extensively, spraying deadly razor sharp metal shards over wide areas against hospitals, churches, mosques, schools, apartment developments and other heavily populated places inflicting death, injury and property damage. The use of other illegal weapons is under continuing investigation.

Hague, Art. 22 and 23, Geneva 1977, Art. 48, 51, 54, 55, POONA Indictment for the Subversion of Science and Technology 1978 (POONA Indictment).

12. Waging War on the Environment.

The United States aerial and missile assault intentionally created a widespread, long-term and severe environmental disaster in Yugoslavia. Air pollution from overflights alone multiplied normal impurities in the atmosphere. Thousands of tons of explosives unleashed enormous quantities of chemicals into the air, raised clouds of dust and debris from places hit and started fires that often raged for days. Chemical, petro-chemical, oil and gas refinery, storage and transmission facilities purposely targeted in the vicinity of Belgrade, Novi Sad, Nis and other major cities exposed huge populations to dangerous and noxious pollution. Depleted uranium scattered across Kosovo and the remainder of Serbia will threaten life for generations.

Hague, Art. 22 and 23; Geneva 1977, Art. 48, 51, 54, 55; Stockholm Declaration of the United Nations Conference on the Human Environment 1972; Principles I, II (UN Conf. on Human Environment), et al.

13. Imposing Sanctions through the UN that Are a Genocidal Crime against Humanity to Achieve Impoverishment and Debilitation of the People of Yugoslavia.

The United States began an economic attack on Yugoslavia designed to break it up politically and tear it down economically before 1989. It caused the International Monetary Fund (IMF) to use its strongest shock therapy to attack Yugoslav productivity, add to its foreign debt burden and expose national wealth to foreign capital by forcing removal of trade barriers and privatizing vital public industry, commerce, utilities and facilities. In May 1991 U.S. Secretary of State Baker stopped all U.S. aid programs to all six Yugoslav Republics and vetoed future IMF credits, creating an enormous economic incentive and powerful political argument for political opposition to Belgrade to separate other Republics from Serbia. The U.S. forced UN sanctions against Yugoslavia, but relieved Republics that seceded from Yugoslavia of sanctions. Such sanctions devastated the entire economy of Yugoslavia to the degree that a normal growth rate free of U.S. coercion would require thirty years to return Yugoslavia to its 1989 levels of productivity. Per capita production value for all six Republics of Yugoslavia in 1989 was $6,220. Today [July 1999] for Serbia and Montenegro, the remaining Republics of Yugoslavia, it is $1,510. Ninety percent of all trade was among the six republics before the break-up. All former republics have suffered economically, but Yugoslavia now, with barely forty percent of its 1990 population, including Kosovo, has had a far greater decline economically than the favored northern Republics of Slovenia and Croatia, which are today more overwhelmingly Roman Catholic than before their secession. The sanctions against Yugoslavia continue and Serbia, excluding Kosovo, is barred from receiving any planned reparations and aid to rebuild from bomb damage and economic attrition. The sanctions have had a far more damaging effect on life, health, the economy and the quality of life in Yugoslavia than the military assault, increasing death rates, lowering life expectation, reducing nutrition and health care and driving production down. As in Iraq, and elsewhere, the sanctions are an economic crime, a crime against humanity and genocide.

Nuremberg, Principle VI c, Crimes Against Humanity; Genocide Convention; Geneva 1977, Art. 48, 54, 55.

14. Creating an Illegal Ad-Hoc Criminal Tribunal to Destroy and Demonize Serb Leadership.

The United States acting through defendant Madeleine Albright coerced the UN Security Council to create ad hoc criminal tribunals for Yugoslavia and Rwanda in violation of the UN Charter to destroy and demonize enemy leaders in those two countries and threaten leaders elsewhere. The UN Charter does not authorize creation of criminal tribunals. The U.S. strongly opposes the International Criminal Tribunal treaty approved by 120 nations at Rome in July 1998 and in the process of ratification by nations now. It did so because it does not intend to subject its leaders or military forces to the jurisdiction of an independent international Court and the rule of international law. By targeting individual enemies in ad hoc courts and charging them with genocide, it achieves their isolation internationally, pressures their own countries to remove them from power, corrupts and politicizes justice and uses the appearance of neutral international law to adjudicate and punish enemies as war criminals and establish itself as an innocent champion of justice.

UN Charter, Statute of the International Court of Justice (Statute ICJ); UDHR; ICCPR.

15. Using Controlled International Media to Create Support for U.S. Assaults Anywhere and to Demonize Yugoslavia, Slavs, Serbs and Muslims as Genocidal Murderers.

The United States defendants have systematically controlled, directed, manipulated, misinformed and restricted press and media coverage concerning Yugoslavia and the U.S. assaults on it to gain public support for the massive bombardment of a defenseless Yugoslavia, including Kosovo, as had been done in Libya, Iraq, Afghanistan, Sudan and elsewhere. The international media has supported and celebrated U.S. political goals of further fragmentation of Yugoslavia and other areas, segregating each region; demonizing selected government officials, other leaders, generals, military officers and soldiers as genocidal murderers; controlling other nations by the threat of popularly supported missile and air assaults and crippling economic sanctions and stimulating acceptance and support from the U.S. public for future operations against other nations and to increase military budgets to support an expanding global role for U.S. military presence and control.

16. Establishing the Long-term Military Occupation of Strategic Parts of Yugoslavia by NATO Forces.

The United States has coerced defendant NATO members and others to provide and support military occupation forces for the occupation of Kosovo, as it did in Bosnia, in order to physically control key parts of Yugoslavia to enforce permanent separation and segregation of States and peoples, to further injure the populations, to create barriers to immigration from Asia Minor, Arab states in the Middle East, North Africa, and former southern republics of the USSR, and elsewhere; to provide a buffer between Europe and the regions described by controlling the territory of divided, segregated and impoverished Slavs, Serbs, Orthodox Christians, Albanians, and others; to exploit the resources of the region; and to prepare and condition NATO members for future participation against other nations.

UN Charter; NAT, Art. I; Non Intervention Decl.

17. Attempting to Destroy the Sovereignty, Right to Self Determination, Democracy and Culture of the Slavic, Muslim, Christian and Other Peoples of Yugoslavia.

The United States has attempted to destroy the Sovereignty of Yugoslavia, the rights of its people to self determination, the democratic institutions it has developed and its culture that defines the heritage, values and traditions of its people. The United States overthrew the democratically elected Mossadegh administration in Iran in 1953, which it replaced with the Shah of Iran, who ruled absolutely for twenty-five years; the democratically elected Arbenz government of Guatemala, which was followed by forty years of brutal governments; the democratically elected Lumumba government of the Congo in 1962, which was followed by the violent dictatorship of Mobutu Sese Seko for thirty-five years; the democratically elected Allende government of Chile, which promised health, education, social and economic justice, which was re-

placed by a reign of terror and military dictatorship under General Pinochet now sought by Spain and other nations for human rights violations.
Popularly elected leaders in Vietnam, Pakistan, the Philippines, Panama,
Haiti and elsewhere were replaced by U.S. surrogates. The U.S. has opposed, assaulted and blockaded Cuba and its people for forty years. The
UN General Assembly voted 155 to 2 to condemn the U.S. for its blockade of Cuba in December 1998. The U.S. has maintained repressive
governments on five continents in too many countries to name; all seeking to destroy the cultures that define the people, their history, character,
values, arts, literature, music, with commercially exploitative products
having no substantive worth and one overriding purpose—profits from
the poor. A goal of U.S. policy is to entrench the belief that only one
system works, capitalism, that only one culture has value, that of the
U.S. and western European, and that history will end with the globalization of U.S. culture.

UDHR; ICCPR; ICESCR.

**18. The Purpose of the U.S. Actions Being to Dominate, Control
and Exploit Yugoslavia, Its People and Its Resources.**

The long term purpose of all the acts complained of is to dominate,
control and exploit the poor nations of the world and the poor people of
the U.S. and other rich countries to further enrich and empower concen-
trations of wealth and neutralize the whole population of poor, overwhelmingly darker skinned people with fear, powerlessness, poverty,
bread and circus.

**19. The Means of the U.S. Being Military Power and Economic
Coercion.**

The United States with a near monopoly on nuclear weapons, military aircraft, missiles, advanced armored vehicles, firepower, equipment,
and highly sophisticated technology continuously expands its physical
power to destroy, expending more on its military power than the rest of
the UN Security Council members combined. This year, U.S. military
expenditures will be near 300 billion dollars. The demonized People's
Republic of China will spend 34 billion dollars, acquiring far less in destructive power for each dollar. The U.S. sells more destructive arms to
other governments and groups seeking to overthrow governments than
the rest of the arms-selling countries combined. Often the intention is
that they "kill each other," a preferred means of achieving domination.

The U.S. does not sell arms it cannot destroy without incurring significant casualties. The U.S. uses its enormous economic power to coerce foreign governments to comply with its wishes, without regard to the interests of the people of those foreign countries. The threat of economic sanctions alone coerces countries to meet U.S. demands contrary to their sovereignty and self-interest.

C. RELIEF SOUGHT

1. Freedom for all Balkan peoples to form a federation of their choice to provide political, civil, social, economic and cultural independence and viability for all the peoples of the region.

2. Comprehensive efforts to create mutual respect, common interests and bonds of friendship among and between Muslims, Slavs and all national, ethnic and religious groups in the Balkans.

3. Strict prohibition on all forms of foreign interference with or disruption of efforts to establish unity, peace and stability in the Balkans.

4. Restoration of peace-making functions of the UN and reform of the UN to make it effective.

5. The abolition of NATO.

6. Full accountability by individuals and governments for criminal and other wrongful military assaults and economic injustice, including sanctions inflicted on all the people of Yugoslavia, their lives, resources, properties and environment to include criminal prosecutions and reparations sufficient to place all the population in the condition it would be in had it not suffered the wrongs inflicted on it, together with resources with which to build a better future of the peoples' choice.

7. Abolition of the illegal ad hoc international criminal tribunal for Yugoslavia and reliance on a legal international tribunal of worldwide non-discriminatory jurisdiction capable of equal justice under the law.

8. Providing adequate media access to inform the world of the human destructiveness of the use of high technology weapons by the U.S. against poor and defenseless people and the practice of genocide by sanctions.

9. Removing all foreign troops from the Balkans at the earliest feasible moment and U.S. troops from NATO countries and elsewhere immediately.

A broader range of relief and reform may be found in Chapter 12 of *The Fire This Time* [Thunder's Mouth Press, 1992]. It is drawn from the experiences and recommendations of the Commission of Inquiry and the International War Crimes Tribunal, which heard evidence in 20 countries concerning the assault on Iraq in 1991, the continuing assaults on Iraq thereafter and the genocidal sanctions that continue to this day.

SCOPE OF THE INQUIRY

The Commission of Inquiry will focus on U.S. criminal conduct, aided and abetted by NATO, because of the dominant U.S. role in the military and other wrongful acts against Yugoslavia. The U.S. did not incur a single casualty to itself while causing thousands of deaths in Yugoslavia. The U.S. is also the focus because of the peril of continuing U.S. conduct to all the people of Yugoslavia and the risk of aerial and missile strikes against other nations in view of its recidivist record.

The Commission of Inquiry will seek and accept evidence of criminal acts by any person or government, related to the conflict, because it believes international law must be applied uniformly. It believes that "victors' justice" is not law, but the extension of war by force of the prevailing party. U.S. propaganda and international media coverage demonized Yugoslavia, its leadership, Serbs and Muslims to fit its purposes, but rarely noticed the criminal destruction of Yugoslavia by U.S. acts as set forth in this complaint.

Comprehensive efforts to gather and evaluate evidence, objectively judge all the conduct that constitutes crimes against peace, war crimes and crimes against humanity and to present these facts for judgment to the court of world opinion requires that any serious fair effort focus on the United States. The Commission of Inquiry believes its focus on U.S. criminal acts is important, proper, and the only way to bring the whole truth, a balanced perspective and impartiality in application of legal process to this great human tragedy.

The Breakup of Yugoslavia

EVANGELOS MAHAIRAS

Beginning in 1990 Germany and the United States sought and achieved the breakup of Yugoslavia in two stages—1992-1995 and 1998-1999. The German government aimed at this division because it wanted to include as territory of its "vital interest" Slovenia and Croatia, the most economically developed states of the Yugoslavian confederation. These states were old allies in the Second World War (the Ustashi fascist group in Croatia and the nationalists in Slovenia). Through them Germany would achieve access to the Adriatic Sea.

The United States was interested in the more recently established states (Bosnia, Serbia, the former Socialist Republic of Macedonia), which controlled the only route from east to west and from north to south though the Balkan mountains. The Balkan area, along with Romania, Bulgaria, Turkey and the Arab nations, forms a European-Middle East bloc, which the United States wants to control (including the former states of the Soviet Union—Kazakhstan, Azerbaijan, Turkmenistan, Tajikistan) for the complete exploitation of the great oil resources of the Caspian Sea.

Toward accomplishing this goal, one year before the dissolution of the Socialist Federation of Yugoslavia—specifically, on November 5, 1990—the Congress of the United States passed bill 101-513 concerning "appropriation of funds for operations abroad." A paragraph in this bill specifically devoted to Yugoslavia initiated that country's dissolution. In a single order, completely without forewarning, the United States cut off all forms of credit and loans to Yugoslavia in the event that within six months separate elections did not take place in each state of the federation.

As a consequence, Yugoslavia—no longer able to conduct foreign trade—was condemned to commercial bankruptcy, which reinforced the divisive tendency of its states, especially that of the stronger. Another crucial reason for the split was a provision in the bill that states holding separate elections would receive direct economic aid (not channeled through the federation). A third provision stated that even if separate elections did not take place, the United States could (openly now, and in addition to actions of the CIA and other secret services) economically support "democratic" factions or movements by way of "emergency humanitarian aid and promotion of human rights." Finally, a fourth provision obliged the American representatives in all international organizations such as the World Bank and International Monetary Fund, etc., to use their vote and influence to have their organizations apply the particulars of the bill.

The United States funded the states so as to dissolve the federation. The U.S. also supported parties and movements that would promote this process. Meanwhile, Germany shipped arms to Slovenia, Croatia, Bosnia and Herzegovina, and also trained "revolutionary corps" in special German camps to be sent into the states at the proper time to face federal forces.

In February 1991, on the initiative of Germany and with the support of countries decisively influenced by the U.S., like Great Britain, Italy and the Netherlands, the European Community backed the U.S. decision: If Yugoslavia did not announce multi-party elections, it would face economic isolation.

In the meantime, Croatian and Slovenian fascist associations in the U.S., Germany and Austria solicited money and arms, which they sent to the northern Yugoslavian states. In March of 1991, fascist organizations in Croatia demonstrated, calling for the overthrow of the socialist government and the expulsion of all Serbs from Croatia. On March 5, 1991, they attacked the federal army base at Gospic. Thus, civil war began.

On June 25, 1991, Slovenia and Croatia declared their independence. In Croatia the extreme right wing party, "Democratic Union," seized power. This party used the flag, emblems, and slogans of the pro-Nazi Ustashi party. Citizenship, property rights, employment, retirement benefits and passports were granted only to Croats and to no other ethnic group. Thus, 300,000 Serbs who were under threat armed themselves.

Federal forces intervened in Slovenia, where units of the autonomous militia had taken over posts on the Italian, Austrian and Hungarian borders. At once, on Germany's initiative, the European Community threatened the federal government with economic sanctions and obliged it to withdraw its forces, given that within three months Slovenia and Croatia would undertake independence and participate in negotiations for a "peaceful solution."

Of course the negotiations failed, and these two states, armed by Germany, officially declared their independence in October 1991. First Germany hastened to accord diplomatic recognition; then the other European countries and the USA, as well as the European Community in January 1992.

This recognition of independence reinforced the tendency to separation in Bosnia-Herzegovina. The Muslim party, headed by Aliya Izetbegovic, was in charge there. Its program was the establishment of theocratic Muslim rule and the expulsion of Serbs and Croats from Bosnia. Serbs were then thirty-one percent of the Bosnia population. Supported by Serbia and ethnic groups, they were prepared for conflict, ready to oppose whatever the European Community presented to Cyrus Vance from the USA and Lord Owen of the European Community as a "peace plan for Bosnia."

In the meantime, the UN Security Council, with the approval of Motion Number 757/1992, established sanctions against the Yugoslavian Federation as responsible for civil war within its territory. In May 1992, the UN General Assembly granted membership to Slovenia and Croatia, and on September 22, 1992, it expelled the Yugoslavian Federation. The result of these acts was the cessation of operations by the Yugoslavian Army against Slovenia and Bosnia. The civil war, however, continued till 1995.

In 1993, American officers undertook training of the Croatian army, which was now armed by the United States. In return the U.S. received bases on the Croatian islands of the Adriatic. American officers also took on training the Bosnian army as well as directing operations against the Bosnian Serbs who were besieging Sarajevo. Finally, NATO intervened supporting Bosnia with bombing from 1993 to 1995. NATO's pressure forced the Bosnian Serbs, who were also pressured by Milosevic, to accept the conducting of "peace negotiations" at Dayton, Ohio, where a neo-colonial agreement was drawn up involving two points—the establishment of a strong force of 60,000 NATO troops in Bosnia and the writing of the "Bosnian Constitution."

According to this Constitution, Bosnia was made up of three democratic states—Muslim, Croat and Serbo-Bosnian—under the supreme authority of the Swedish official appointed by the UN Security Council, who had full executive powers in all matters and even the right to reject the decisions of the three local governments as well as to overrule the prime ministers and the appointed ministers. This supreme official would work in close cooperation with the Supreme Military Council as well as with various sources of funding or gifts. The Security Council, in turn, appointed an "Associate Director of Police" who would be under the head Director and would have a force of 1,700 policemen at his disposal.

The economic policies of the country would be controlled by the officers of Bretton Woods and the European Bank of Reconstruction and Development. The first Director of the Central Bank of the country was appointed by the International Monetary Fund. And neither he nor those succeeding him would be citizens of Bosnia or Herzegovina, or of a neighboring state.

On August 3, 1995, Croat forces supported by the U.S. and headed by an American general launched a decisive attack in Krajina, expelling 300,000 Serbs, killing 14,000 people, and burning tens of thousands of Serbian homes as well as Orthodox churches and monasteries.

THE ROLE OF NATO

According to a statement of the Pentagon published in the New York Times on March 8, 1992, "The first aim [of the United States] is to block the appearance of a new adversary. ... First, the U.S. must show the leadership necessary to establish and protect a new order that holds the promise of convincing potential competitors that they need not aspire to a greater role or pursue a more aggressive posture to protect their legitimate interests. ... Finally, we must also maintain the necessary means to overthrow potential adversaries, ambitious to attain a broader local or global role." In Europe, specifically, this plan foresees that: "It is of fundamental importance to preserve NATO as the primary instrument of Western defense and security as well as a channel of exercising American influence and its participation in issues of European security. ... We must seek to prevent the emergence of European-only security arrangements which would undermine NATO."

Applying these views, the United States torpedoed the European Community's proposals for the peaceful solution of the Bosnian problem (the Vance-Owen plan of 1992 and the Vance-Stolemberg plan of 1993) in order to impose its own plan (the Dayton Agreement).

In the meantime, bases were established in Albania, the former Socialist Republic of Macedonia and Hungary, and NATO aimed to extend
its sphere to the socialist countries of Eastern Europe and the Baltic
states, for the full encirclement of Russia and the access of the United
States to the Caspian Sea. According to American journalists, the Danube is more important for Europe than the Mississippi is for commerce
in the United States. Thus, all the countries in the Danube valley must be
brought under the NATO umbrella and thereby under the influence (and
exploitation) of the USA.

This is the reason that, although the Yugoslavian Federation had essentially broken up in 1995 (Serbia and Montenegro alone remained in
the federation), any peaceful settlement in Bosnia was excluded and
NATO intervention took place, resulting in the total success of American plans for its dominance in the Balkans. The Serbian opposition per-
sisted, however. It had to be eliminated.

For this purpose the United States, Germany, Austria and other countries armed ethnic Albanian groups. In Kosovo and southern Serbia units
of the "Kosovo Liberation Army" (UCK are the initials in Albanian) had
been forming with uniforms and arms provided by the U.S. Army,
funded by the CIA as well as international aid. A continuous flow of
arms and military supplies came from Germany.

Because these units were not strong enough to defeat the Serbian
forces, the Western forces developed unprecedented propaganda concerning supposed genocide against the Albanians in the Kosovo area.
They finally decided on direct NATO intervention with horrendous aerial bombardment (31,000 bombs, ammunition with depleted uranium),
which forced Serbia to submit.

Western propaganda, as it had been throughout the Bosnian civil
war, was as effective as the depleted uranium weapons. There were daily
reports in all the mass media against Serbia, involving, for example, the
bomb that exploded in a Sarajevo market (which finally proved to be an
act of provocation to invite NATO intervention). Their accusations of
the rape of Muslim women, which from the fall of 1992 to the spring of
1993 scandalized western news broadcasts citing figures of 100,000, but
finally with research reduced significantly to 40,000, later to 4,000 and
finally to only seven women who testified to being victims.

These false or exaggerated reports provoked widespread outrage in western public opinion and among blindfolded "human welfare organizations," which saw criminal acts only on the part of Bosnian Serbs. The Muslims and Croat militaries were presented as angelic in behavior, even though they executed unarmed Serbs, raped women, and burned homes, churches and monasteries. It is significant that in the Special Tribunal formed to judge war crimes in Bosnia, sixty Serbs were indicted but only six Bosnians and Croats.

In turn, regarding Kosovo the Western media reported that the Serbs expelled 300,000 ethnic Albanians, committed mass killings of unarmed citizens and all sorts of atrocities. Finally it was shown that prior to the NATO bombings only some 20,000 to 25,000 people had taken refuge in Albania and the former Yugoslavian Republic of Macedonia. After the onset of the bombing more than 250,000 ethnic Albanians had fled to save themselves from the bombs. As for genocide, the "mass graves" about which there were daily references in the Western media were never found.

To be sure, there was the atrocity of Srebrenica, but on the opposing side there were the atrocities of Bihac and Krajina, about which not a word appeared in the Western press, just as there were no references either during the course of its militia action or after the bombing to the crimes of the UCK against Serbs and other ethnic groups in Kosovo, which the UCK called "police duties"! These actions put into effect the total removal of Serbs, Gypsies, Turks and Jews from Kosovo through killings, burning of villages, churches and monasteries, and unprecedented terrorism.

But for the UCK there, "purification of Kosovo" was not enough. Its action was extended to the area of Presovo (southern Serbia), though without success, since there the UCK faced the Serbian army, and to the former Yugoslavian Republic of Macedonia. There of course the UCK would disband with the complete cooperation of NATO, the USA and the European Community. The problem was whether the UCK would stop there or extend its action. That depended on the U.S. agenda for the region. The UCK could have been used as a means of exerting pressure on Greece to compromise on the issues of Cyprus and the Aegean Sea. Greece's allies had been habitually involved in such "friendly" actions from the time of the establishment of modern Greece up to today.

THE ROLE OF THE UN SECURITY COUNCIL

For the illegal (criminal) acts of NATO in Yugoslavia, enormous responsibilities are borne by the United Nations Security Council, which violated virtually all the regulations of Articles 44-50 of the UN Charter. According to Article 46 of the Charter, plans to use armed force will depend on the Security Council in consultation with the Committee of the Military Council of Article 47. This power is not relegated to NATO or "any other" military alliance. The Military Council of the UN would never permit the use of bombs with depleted uranium or bombing of unarmed civilians, schools, nurseries, hospitals and churches, as NATO did in Yugoslavia.

Moreover, the Security Council established the ad hoc International Tribunal to judge war crimes in Bosnia and Kosovo. But the UN Charter nowhere provides the right to establish such a court. Article 92 founded the International Court based in The Hague. Its members are elected by the General Assembly and the Security Council from a list of the permanent Administrative Court that was founded by The Hague agreement of 1907.

This Administrative Court can assemble a unit that can render judgments concerning a particular issue, in agreement, however, with regulations (Article 26, par. 3, of its charter). The expenses of this court would be covered by the UN in a manner determined by the General Assembly.

Thus, the Security Council does not have the right to establish an ad hoc court. That Court is illegal. It is a court of expediency and its mission was to serve the political purposes of the powers that supported its establishment. It is significant that its expenses are covered not by the United Nations but by "benefactors" from the U.S., from multi-national corporations and entrepreneurs like George Soros! The manner of establishment and funding also belies its manner of functioning.

Milosevic's abduction in violation of the Constitution and justice system of Yugoslavia was the first step. The justice system would be completely put to shame in what followed. However, the greatest crime of the U.S. and its followers (Great Britain, Germany, the Netherlands, Italy) was the debasing of the UN. The next step will be its dissolution. For the hopes of the peoples as expressed in the prologue of its charter are not in agreement with the imperialist "New World Order."

"We the Peoples of the United Nations, determined to save coming generations from the scourge of war, which twice during our time brought insufferable pain to mankind; once more proclaiming our belief in human rights, in human dignity and worth, in equal rights of men and women and large and small nations, we unite our efforts to achieve these goals."

The imperialists, however, desire global rule and not the equality of small and large nations. They wish to impose their will with war using bombardment and any other criminal means (Vietnam, the Gulf War, Bosnia, Yugoslavia and later). From their position in the UN they license NATO as the supreme arbiter of all international crises over the length and breadth of the earth, though it is not an international organization but a military alliance of Western forces.

Preface to Milosevic Statement

From the moment President Slobodan Milosevic announced his intention to defend himself at his arraignment on July 3, 2001, the Registry of the ICTY did all in its power to deny him access to legal advice. This was a clear violation of the fundamental right to assistance of counsel.

On July 4, 2001, Ramsey Clark informed the Registry that he had been requested by President Milosevic to consult on legal matters and that he would arrive for meetings on July 6 and 7.

The Registry responded on July 5 that consultation could not be approved until Mr. Clark was cleared by security officers and his legal qualifications were established.

There followed a Kafkaesque interchange for nearly four weeks during which Mr. Clark was offered a two hour monitored non-lawyer visit at which the Registry said it would be improper to discuss the facts or law of the case.

Despite submission of a ten-page memorandum demonstrating without question the right of a person in custody who has chosen to defend himself to assistance of counsel, the Registry finally flatly refused to permit any attorney consultation. Mr. Clark prepared and forwarded on July 20 an Emergency Motion with attachments totaling thirty-five pages for Trial Chamber III seeking a court order directing the Registry to respect the right to assistance of counsel and permit legal consultation. The Motion was received by the Registry on July 23. The registry confirmed receipt of the Motion and assured Mr. Clark's office it had been distributed to the Judges.

On July 26, 2001, Mr. Clark's office called the Chambers of Presiding Judge May and was told they were unaware of the Motion but that they would find it and they should be called the next morning.

Later that day Mr. Clark wrote the following note to Judge May:

> Federal Express confirmed that it delivered the documents at 2:10 p.m., Monday, July 23 to the Tribunal. On July 24, when my office called Mr. Christian Rhode at the Registry he assured us that the Motion had been distributed to the judges of Trial Chamber III on Monday afternoon, adding his comment that the Tribunal "does not have the last word on this issue."
>
> Today, concerned that we had received no response to the Motion my Office called Ms. Featherstone, Senior Legal Officer for Trial Chamber II and was told that she had not yet received the Emergency

Motion, and after further inquiring, Ms. Janice Kearns, your secretary, confirmed the Motion had not been received by your office.

I must add that I am deeply concerned about the actions of the Registry, its veracity, its disregard for the fundamental rights of persons in custody and the severe effects its violations of President Milosevic's rights may have on his defense. Absent an adequate explanation, I will seek an inquiry and full accountability for its conduct.

On the next morning, Friday, July 27, the Senior Legal Officer for the Trial Chamber called from The Hague an hour before the office opened in New York to say the Tribunal was granting the relief sought and a fax would be sent within the hour. The fax was from the Senior Legal Officer, not Judge May, but it confirmed the right of an accused "to have adequate time and facilities for the preparation of his defense and to communicate with counsel of his choosing," and that Mr. Clark would "be allowed to visit the accused for a reasonable time as requested, for legal consultation with the right of confidentiality."

Absurd as it seems, on August 13 Mr. Clark received a letter by mail from the Registrar dated July 26 which said in part:

I acknowledge receipt of your "Emergency Motion for and order Directing the Registry..." dated 20 July 2001, addressed to Trial Chamber III of the International Tribunal, presided by Judge May. I have considered whether to file your "motion" and thereby submit it to the Trial Chamber and to parties of the proceedings. ...I see no legal basis to file your "Emergency Motion" with the Trial Chamber. Your "Motion" will be added to the correspondence records of the Registry. Please do not hesitate to contact me should you have further questions or comments on this matter.

Are we to believe the Trial Chamber reads and answers the correspondence records of the Registry, or that the Registry plays games with the rights of prisoners?

Mr. Clark met with President Milosevic on Monday, July 30, Tuesday, July 31 and Wednesday, August 1, during which time they were able without interference to discuss issues concerning the legality of the ICTY and preparation of the defense.

These were the only confidential legal consultations President Milosevic was allowed from July 3 through the pre-trial conference on August 30. Several lawyers had short monitored meetings, some waiting for days and all arbitrarily controlled by the Registry.

Mr. Clark's meetings enabled him to prepare a Motion to Dismiss the indictment based on the illegality of the Tribunal and the illegality of the surrender of President Milosevic to the ICTY by the Republic of Serbia, which the Registry refused to file. President Milosevic succeeded in filing his copy of the motion with the prison commander late in the afternoon of August 9, the last day it could be filed.

The meetings also enabled Mr. Clark to prepare a draft memorandum for President Milosevic to use in defending himself without an attorney at the Pre-Trial Conference set for August 30, 2001. It was sent by Federal Express on August 17 for arrival on his birthday August 20 with instructions to the Registry that it could be opened only in President Milosevic's presence and was not to be read by the ICTY. It was planned that President Milosevic would make changes and return the memorandum to Mr. Clark's office for retyping. After sending the memo, Mr. Clark left for Rwanda and other African stops before arriving in Amsterdam on August 29.

On arrival in Amsterdam, Mr. Clark was not permitted to meet President Milosevic. Incredibly, the Registry claimed President Milosevic's right to assistance of counsel by Mr. Clark was only "temporary." Later in the afternoon Mr. Clark learned the draft memorandum was not delivered to President Milosevic until 3 p.m. that day. The two were able to discuss the memorandum but only by phone that evening. Thus, after holding the memorandum for over a week the Registry had given it to the accused, who was deprived of assistance of counsel, only on the eve of a hearing of great importance to his freedom and the rule of law.

As to its own access to the memorandum, which was sent as confidential attorney mail, and having decided that Mr. Clark's status had been "only of temporary nature," the Registry later wrote, "Consequently, the envelope addressed to the accused will be treated in accordance with the practice for non-privileged communications..." and opened by the ICTY. Not only do gentlemen not read other people's mail, to intercept internal documents of the prosecution or defense in a criminal proceeding is a criminal obstruction of justice. This is how the ICTY respects fundamental human rights.

The memorandum edited by President Milosevic with his pen became the "fat document," "a thirty-six-page written broadside against

The Hague Court" that Reuters reported President Milosevic "brandished" in its August 30 news release on the Pre-Trial Conference.

The memorandum, as hurriedly edited by President Milosevic, follows in the next chapter.

Illegitimacy of the 'Tribunal'

PRESIDENT SLOBODAN MILOSEVIC

There are three fatal legal flaws in the so-called International Criminal Tribunal for the Former Yugoslavia. Each has disastrous consequences for the human quest for peace, the rule of law, democracy, truth and justice.

1. The Charter of the United Nations Does Not Empower the Security Council to Create a Criminal Court

The UN Security Council has seized power it does not possess, corrupting the Charter of the United Nations, placing itself above the law and threatening "We Peoples of the United Nations" with a lawless future in which a superpower employs the scourge of war to have its way. Nothing in the history of the planning, drafting, discussion, approval or ratification of the UN Charter implies or is consistent with an intention to empower any body created by, or under, the Charter to establish any criminal tribunal. The words of the Charter and their textual inferences, the structure and allocation of power and duties, including those in the incorporated Statute for the International Court of Justice, all negate the existence of any capacity under the Charter to ordain criminal courts. The Criminal Tribunal for Former Yugoslavia is illegitimate and its creation a corruption of the United Nations.

There would never have been a United Nations if its Charter stated, or implied, that a criminal court could be created under its authority. No one who believes in historical truth, or that words have meaning can, after examining the history of its creation and its text, contend that the Charter of the United Nations empowers the Security Council to create a criminal court.

An International Criminal Court Can Be Created Only By A Multinational Treaty Or Amendment To The Charter Of The United Nations

The national representatives who have served on the Security Council and in the General Assembly and the scholars, lawyers and experts who have labored for more than thirty years to bring into being an international criminal court have recognized that the only lawful and binding way such a court can be created is by an agreement among nations through a treaty agreed upon for that purpose, or by amending the Charter of the United Nations under its strict provisions regulating amendments to authorize, or establish a court.

When an International Criminal Court was finally agreed upon in July 1998 by 120 nations meeting in Rome, it was by treaty which had been studied, drafted and debated for years. The United States, the most powerful participant in that long process, consistently sought to weaken the treaty to exempt U.S. leaders and military personnel from prosecution before it. Having failed, the U.S. was then the most prominent and powerful of the handful of nations that refused to sign. As of August 1, 2001, thirty-seven nations, the Netherlands the most recent, had ratified the treaty.

The United States is vigorously trying to persuade, coerce, or bribe nations not to ratify.

Creation Of The International Criminal Tribunal For The Former Yugoslavia Was A Lawless Act Of Political Expediency By The United States Designed To Demonize And Destroy An Enemy And Frustrate Creation Of A Legitimate International Criminal Tribunal

At the insistence of the U.S. the Security Council nearly fifty years after it came into being forged a new and powerful weapon capable of demonizing a nation and its people and depriving individuals of their liberty for the rest of their lives and placed it largely in the hands of the United States. The principal precedents for such pseudo judicial actions over several millennia preceding the creation of the UN are trials of leaders and soldiers of vanquished populations by the victors in war, and courts used by colonial powers to control and punish subjugated peoples. The precedents are many and the violence and cruelty and hatred they usually exposed and caused was extreme.

Unless It is Limited By The UN Charter And International Law, The Security Council Can Do Whatever It Chooses To Do

If it is not restrained by the United Nations Charter, the Security Council can commit any act it desires, disregarding all law. Early proponents of United States world power claimed such unbridled discretion for the Security Council publicly. Thus in 1950 John Foster Dulles wrote:

"The Security Council is not a body that merely enforces agreed law. It is a law unto itself... No principles of law are laid down to guide it, it can decide in accordance with what it thinks is expedient."

If unchallenged, this concept of Security Council power means that the most powerful international organ created by the Charter of the United Nations "to end the scourge of war" is above all law, domestic and international.

But absolute discretion is the very definition of lawlessness and has been called "more destructive of freedom than any other of man's inventions," by U.S. Supreme Court Justice William O. Douglas. All rights of all nations, races, religions, cultures, political parties and individuals are thereby subordinated to the will of the Security Council, and the single superpower that too often will dominate it. All but fifteen nations are excluded from Security Council counsels. Each of the five permanent members can veto its actions.

The Security Council is subject to domination by a single nation. The representative of each member votes as instructed by the national government that appoints him and to serve the interests of that government, not as an international statesman serving all peoples and the purposes for which the UN was created. The Security Council is inaccessible, anonymous and less responsive to democratic processes than any other international political institution.

2. A One-Time, One-Episode Court Targeting One Country, Created By International Political Power to Serve Its Geo-Political Interests Is Incapable of Equality and Conducive of Division and Violence

The illegitimate Criminal Tribunal for the Former Yugoslavia corrupts justice and law because it is incapable of acting equally among nations, or within the politically targeted nation. It will increase violence, division and the risk of war with neighboring nations and peoples and within Yugoslavia among the segments of the society the U.S. policy of balkanization of Former Yugoslavia has set against each other and against the new government the U.S. has installed for its own purposes. If the United Nations Charter had authorized the Security Council to create criminal courts, it could not create a court for one nation, or episode for political purposes, to persecute selected groups, or persons and such a court is incapable of equal justice under law. An ad hoc court violates the most basic principles of all law. Equality is the mother of justice. An international court established to prosecute acts in a single nation and primarily, if not entirely, one limited group, is pre-programmed to persecute and incapable of equality.

If the Security Council can create a criminal court to prosecute conduct in a single country like Yugoslavia, it can appoint a court for any country, selecting enemies or political and economic opportunities for targeting one at a time, while never exposing itself or those who comply with its wishes to such selective prosecution. If the U.S. or any ally or client state it chose to protect was the subject of a serious effort by the Security Council to be honored with a criminal tribunal in its own name, the U.S. would veto the threatened action.

A Court created only for crimes in one country is by definition discriminatory, incapable of equal justice, a weapon against chosen enemies, or antagonistic interests and war by other means. If there is to be any international criminal court, it must act equally as to all nations, with none above the law. The ad hoc tribunal for a single nation corrupts international law.

By its very nature, the ad hoc Tribunal can be created only after the conduct the Security Council decides justifies creation of the Court since there is no other excuse for its creation. It is in every case ex post facto. This violates an ancient principle of law. It also requires the Security Council, if there is to be a rational basis for its action, to make some preliminary claim to finding of facts, a task such a political body is not designed for, that inherently incriminates a country or faction by placing the imprimatur of the Security Council of the United Nations on a political decision of fact necessary to justify creation of the Tribunal. The very charge of the Security Council—genocide, crimes against peace, war crimes, or crimes against humanity—demonized any person thereafter accused.

The Selection Of A Nation For Prosecution On Political Findings Of Genocide, War Crimes And Crimes Against Humanity Creates A Compulsion To Convict

Investigators, prosecutors and administrative personnel who join a temporary Tribunal to pursue allegations of humanity's greatest crimes against a people and leaders already demonized will feel they have failed if there are not convictions. The very psychology of the enterprise is persecutorial. Few judges appointed to serve on a Tribunal created under such circumstances will feel free to acquit any but the most marginal, or clearly mistaken, accused, or to create an appearance of objectivity.

Powers That Create Ad Hoc International Criminal Tribunals Divert Attention From Their Own Offenses, Or Failures, Or Those Of Allies And Their Political Surrogates While Continuing To Inflict And Threaten Mass Destruction With Impunity

The ad hoc Tribunal which targets a country is incapable of prosecuting what may be greater crimes committed in the same conflict, by a power, coalition ally or political agents that was and remains a much greater source of violence and threat to peace. Most often the power that forced the creation of the target tribunal to further damage and demonize their enemy is shielded from criticism by the avalanche of propaganda against the accused, supported by the appearance of United Nations neutrality and peacemaking efforts.

What court will consider the criminality of aerial bombardment by U.S. aircraft of defenseless civilians, their housing, water systems, power plants, factories, office buildings, schools, hospitals, which takes thousands of lives directly and causes billions of dollars of property damages in Belgrade, Nis, Novi Sad and scores of other cities, towns and villages? What threat to peace continues from the U.S. bombing of the Chinese Embassy?

Who will be held accountable for the devastation of Pristina by NATO planes, or the attacks on refugee columns in Kosovo and Metohija? Is the U.S. use of cluster bombs exploding razor-sharp metal fragments over an area as large as a soccer field in the courtyard at the hospital in Nis no crime? Will the Security Council act to prevent and punish the use of depleted uranium by the U.S., which is as indiscriminate in its radiation as the air, the water, the soil and food chain it touches and contaminates for millions of years?

International law accepts bombing of defenseless civilian populations by a militarily advanced technology that can destroy a country without even setting foot on its soil because the superpower controls international prosecutions and determines violations. The dominant element in modern military power is mass destruction. Victors are nations with the greatest capacity for mass destruction. This places civilian populations at maximum peril. Infrastructure supporting civilian life, buildings, water, power, transportation, communication, food production, storage and distribution, health care, schools, churches, mosques, synagogues, foreign embassies were the direct object of U.S. aerial and missile attacks. Several thousands of civilians were killed directly and many more indirectly.

In 1998, the U.S. directed twenty-one Tomahawk Cruise missiles from international waters to destroy the El Shifa pharmaceutical plant in Khartoum, Sudan, which provided more than half the medicines available for a people who are very poor and have been unable to replace that supply. The U.S. continues to support insurrection in the South of Sudan and threaten Sudan with prosecution in an ad hoc international criminal tribunal.

NATO does not claim it prevented violence within Kosovo and Metohija among the Serbian, ethnic Albanian and other peoples. In fact, NATO accelerated that violence. It bombed Serbia for seventy-eight days, targeting civilians and citizens, destroying billions of dollars worth of civilian facilities, using illegal weapons including cluster bombs, destroying the civilian Serbian TV and radio buildings. It bombed Kosovo and Metohija heaviest of all, destroying most of Pristina, killing thousands of Albanians, Muslims, Serbs, Romany, Turks and others, and causing hundreds of thousands of people to flee from Kosovo and Metohija. Damage to the Yugoslavia military was negligible. In the summer of 2001 the U.S. continues to use cluster bombs in northern and southern Iraq, which it attacks on most days.

And in 1999, when the U.S. and NATO countries came into Kosovo and Metohija as a "security force," they refused to intervene on the ground to protect people who were endangered in the province.

There will be no remedy or relief for Serbian victims of atrocities, some 500,000 purged by Croatia with the approval if not on instructions of the U.S., forever from their homes in Krajina, the more than 330,000 permanently purged from Kosovo and Metohija since the ceasefire in 1999, or for the thousands of Serbs, Romany and others killed by the U.S. and NATO bombing assaults, or by the U.S.-supported terrorist organization, the so-called KLA, before, during and after the assaults. The Macedonians killed, injured and driven from their homes by U.S.-condoned if not instigated KLA aggressions that threaten civil war in Macedonia and general war in the Balkans will not lead the Security Council to create a Court to prosecute the perpetrators.

Major Powers Are Not Accountable For Their Actions Which Cause War, Insurrection And Violence Within Targeted Countries

There will be no accountability by the U.S., Germany and other nations whose acts and pressures forced the breakup of Yugoslavia, stripping Slovenia, Croatia, Bosnia, Macedonia and attempted stripping of parts of Serbia like Kosovo and Metohija.

The U.S. and several European nations have Balkanized the region in the most artificial and forced apartheid the Balkans or any other part of the world has ever known. Their acts have made peace, stability and prosperity impossible. Economic viability of small fragmented parts depends on foreign economic interests, which intend to dominate and exploit the region. The new apartheid leads to U.S.-planned conflicts between the Western Catholic Croatians and the Eastern Orthodox Serbs, creating conflict and a wall between Western and Eastern Europe. More dangerous, it sets the stage for violence, encouraging international conflicts between Slavic peoples and Muslims to decimate and debilitate the obstacles to the U.S. world order. Kosovo and Metohija, as a part of Serbia, and Macedonia are current examples in a long list of tragic and avoidable violence between Muslims and Slavs, which has occurred to different extents in Afghanistan, Dagestan, Chechnya, Kazakhstan, Kirgistan, Tajikistan, Turkmenistan, Uzbekistan and Bosnia.

A Federal Republic Of Balkan States Long Set Against Each Other By Foreign Powers Was Formed To Establish Peace, Cooperation And Prosperity

The idea of Yugoslavia, a Balkan federation to heal divisions and provide a better chance for living together in peace and prosperity, was seen as important in the years after World War I as a means to peace. While the idea floundered between the two worst wars in history, it worked with remarkable success after World War II, in which it was ravaged but unconquered. An independent and unified Federal Republic of Yugoslavia was a long-term successful solution for South Slavic peoples. It was a bulwark of the Non-Aligned Movement. With the collapse of the Soviet and Eastern bloc economy it was the remaining socialist government threatening capitalist control of Europe. With its mixed-market economy it offered an example to former Eastern bloc countries for revival of their economic and political independence. With a successful, functioning Federal Republic of Yugoslavia there was living proof history had not ended, that more than one economic system was possible.

After the collapse of the Eastern bloc economy a greater Balkan federation, a Southeastern European Union, was seen by many in the region as the means to prevent economic exploitation, avoid violence and develop a strong and independent political, social and economic region.

Foreign capital and the geopolitical interests of the U.S. considered this a dangerous obstacle to their plans for the new world order, globalization, new colonialism.

The United States Having Demonized Yugoslavia Attacks It With Impunity And Persecutes Its Leadership

The U.S. mercilessly bombed Yugoslavia for seventy-eight days. It tried to assassinate me by bombing my home, offices and other places, where it believed I might be. It attempted to kill Libya's head of state Muammar Qaddafi in its 1986 raid on Tripoli and Iraqi president Saddam Hussein on numerous occasions beginning in 1991, including its 1993 cruise missile attack on the Al Rashid Hotel in Baghdad at a time it believed he would be there meeting international Islamic leaders.

Through economic sanctions, the most extreme and overt form of forced impoverishment and economic assault, the U.S. has coerced the

Security Council into complicity in the longest deadliest and cruelest genocide of the last decade, the sanctions against its enemy Iraq, which have killed at least 1.5 million people, the majority children. The United States has forced economic sanctions against Yugoslavia, severely damaging its civilian economy and eroding its will to independence.

Can a criminal tribunal for Yugoslavia, which ignores pervasive violence by the U.S. and diverts public awareness from United States conduct and legitimizes by silent acceptance aerial and missile assaults on civilians and illegal weapons use against one country after another, making its repetition expected before it occurs, contribute to the hope for the rule of law, justice or peace?

The United States, itself immune from control or prosecution and above the law, uses its power to cause the persecution of enemies it selects to terrorize and further demonize. It manufactures and sells arms to chosen nations, to groups seeking to overthrow governments it opposes, uses illegal weapons against defenseless people with impunity, continues to consolidate and expand its near monopoly of nuclear weapons and sophisticated rocketry, spends trillions on unilateral protection from Star Wars, assuring a continued arms race while poverty overwhelms billions, hunger cripples millions, starvation takes hundreds of thousands of lives and AIDS spreads among poor nations.

It cripples international environmental protection, undermines control of nuclear weapons by threatening to withdraw from long-standing protections of the ABM and Non-Proliferation treaties. It refuses to ratify treaties to protect life from land mines, which it continues to manufacture, sell and deploy. It threatens to undermine a treaty controlling biological and chemical warfare. And the United States regularly engages in covert operations and violent military interventions in other nations in violation of their sovereignty and law.

The so-called ICTY is not just another arrow in the arsenal of the United States with which it persecutes and demonizes enemies and corrupts international law. The ICTY celebrates inequality in the rule of law, using criminal sanctions to destroy selected leaders and governments.

It is a poisonous arrow destructive of the foundations of peace among independent nations of equal rights and dignity.

3. The International Criminal Tribunal for the Former Yugoslavia is Incapable of Protecting Fundamental Rights, or Providing Due Process of Law

Such an ad hoc Tribunal has a temporary and limited purpose without helpful precedent, common tradition or relevant experience. It lacks power to enforce orders, or compel the disclosure of evidence and presence of witnesses, particularly for the defense.

It is not capable of finding facts fairly, or defining and applying legal principles equally. It cannot do justice.

The statutory mandate for the ICTY makes it hostile to concern for the rights of those accused before it, because it is told the crimes charged have occurred and the accused have been demonized.

The right to assistance of counsel, so firmly established in international law, has been denied and frustrated by the Tribunal even in its most prominent cases. The Registry denied to me the right to consult with lawyers of my choice on legal matters for several weeks after my arraignment.

The Registrar wrote that for the one attorney who visited me during that time and for only two hours, it would have been "inappropriate" to discuss the case because the conversation was monitored and confidences would be violated. Lawyers from Yugoslavia I asked to consult were still denied approval and visas to enter the Netherlands seven weeks after my arraignment. The only exception led to a monitored two hours visit.

Instead I was held in solitary confinement. I was able to visit my wife only after more than two weeks imprisonment and then only through soundproof glass using monitored telephones. She was prohibited from speaking with the press and kept isolated from all public contacts while in the Netherlands, a virtual prisoner in her hotel room, except as she traveled between the airport, the prison and the hotel.

The Ad Hoc Tribunal Is Intended To Demonize And Destroy, Not To Fairly Determine Facts, Protect Rights Of The Accused, And Apply Legal Principles Equally

Unfair phenomena are inherent in the purpose and the nature of a temporary ad hoc tribunal, struggling without personnel who are part of a legal tradition, far removed from the place the accused came from and the events occurred where the court is charged by its creator not to presume innocence, but that terrible crimes have occurred and the accused are from the group that committed them. They do this to protect the real criminals, the NATO leaders who killed thousands of innocent people in NATO's criminal aggression.

Truth Is Beyond The Reach And The Purpose Of The Ad Hoc Tribunal, Which Is Intended To Punish, Destroy And Divide

It has been impossible in all cases before powerless ad hoc Tribunals for the accused to obtain needed evidence and witnesses for their defense. The ICTY has been unable to obtain custody of many accused in the former Yugoslavia and has resorted to, or condoned, improper and illegal means to pressure their surrender.

Ad Hoc Tribunal Terrorizes And Punishes Those In Yugoslavia Who Dared To Oppose NATO Aggression And To React To Criminal Acts Of Terrorists Who Were Killing Serbs, Albanians, Muslims, Turks, etc.

In Yugoslavia, the U.S., in violation of international and domestic laws of both Yugoslavia and the U.S., has installed a government of its choice in the Republic of Serbia and ousted President Milosevic from the presidency of the Federal Republic of Yugoslavia by bombing, economic coercion including sanctions, physical threats, covert operations and corruption of the electoral process.

The U.S. Creates Client Governments By Forcing Elections, Using Millions Of Dollars To Purchase Unity For Its Candidate, Then Financing A Campaign That Buys Votes And Corrupts Democracy

The U.S. injected more than $100,000,000 to defeat the Government of Peoples Unity that was in power until October 2000.

The U.S. has intervened in many foreign elections and often installed governments subservient to its interests by that means.

The creation of an ad hoc international criminal tribunal with threats and indictments of the leadership of the government it seeks to remove is an additional devastating assault on the democratic process and the government targeted for destruction.

My Abduction and Surrender To The ICTY By A U.S.-Installed Serbian Government Was Done In Violation Of The Constitutions Of The Federal Republic Of Yugoslavia, The Republic Of Serbia, The Statute Creating The ICTY, While The Federal Constitutional Court Of Yugoslavia Reviewed The Request For Surrender, For A Bribe Of, Supposedly, 1.3 Billion Dollars.

The U.S.-installed government of Serbia abducted and surrendered me in violation of the Constitutions of the Federal Republic of Yugoslavia and the Republic of Serbia and its Laws while the request for surrender was under review by the Constitutional Court of Yugoslavia, which had forbidden any act related to surrender until the Court's final decision. That was also a violation of the UN Security Council Resolution creating the Tribunal, which provides that surrender shall be accomplished in accordance with the domestic laws of the nation requested to make the surrender. The United States threatened to block $1.3 billion in international loans and aid for Yugoslavia unless the surrender was accomplished by a date it set. Such conduct and the participation and acceptance of it reveals contempt for the rule of law by the Tribunal, the new government of Serbia and the United Nations.

The illegal seizure of an individual and his delivery to isolation in the prison of an illegal international criminal tribunal in a distant nation threatens the freedom of everyone. For the United Nations to engage in, or accept, international kidnapping of political leaders tells the world the old ways of violence, deceit and coercion are its ways. Those ways will be met in the only way they can be met, by the same means.

The New U.S. Installed Government Of Serbia Is Using Its Police Power To Crush Political Opposition In Serbia

The current government of Serbia is engaged in crushing and demonizing its domestic political opposition. The regime will surrender accused persons to the ICTY in violation of its own laws as it surrendered me in order to destroy political opposition at home and receive payments of money and support from abroad for the ruling politicians. It acts to frustrate any support or investigation for my defense, even attempting first to deny entry to and then to deport Ramsey Clark when he flew to Belgrade in June to discuss my political persecution. In the hope of eliminating rival domestic political power, it put hundreds of people in detention on purely political grounds.

That government may fabricate evidence, destroy evidence and control and coerce witnesses to assist in convictions by the ICTY, and it will seek to frustrate defense efforts to obtain documents, other evidence and witnesses in Yugoslavia needed for the defense in The Hague.

The People Of Serbia And Yugoslavia Risk A Tragic Future From The External Manipulation And Control Of Their Governments

The new government of Serbia is a puppet for the United States. If there is any expectation a U.S.-supported government might be better for the people of Serbia, or Yugoslavia, ask Iranians if they believe they fared better under the Shah of Iran, enthroned in 1953 by the U.S. for 25 years, than they would have under democratically elected President [Mohammed] Mossadegh and elected successors. Was a long line of military governments which brutally repressed the people of Guatemala for decades better for the people than democratically elected President [Jacobo] Arbenz who was removed by United States forces in 1954? Was Mobutu, who for four decades brutalized, bankrupted and corrupted the country, better for the people than democratically elected Patrice Lumumba assassinated with U.S. complicity in 1960? Did General [Augosto] Pinochet better serve democracy, human rights and the welfare of the people for decades than the democratically elected Salvador Allende murdered in a U.S. supported *golpe* in Chile in 1973? It would be difficult to find four greater national tragedies in the last fifty years, all brought about by the United States determination to control those regions.

Ask the people of the several score other countries who have lived under U.S. supported tyrannies, "our SOB's," as FDR [Franklin Delano Roosevelt] called Somoza in Nicaragua, how they benefited. An ad hoc criminal tribunal created to crush the leadership of the opposition to a U.S.-installed government cannot bring peace, reconciliation, protect human rights, or enable a people to live and prosper together. It will create fear, hatred, division and violence.

Consider the peoples of the poorest countries of the world during these last decades obediently struggling to repay loans for projects and purposes they did not choose and that never benefited them while their own citizens die from hunger and preventable illnesses. Consider the economies of Eastern Europe or of the former Yugoslav republics and ask why per capita income is often less than half, sometimes less than twenty-five percent what it was just twelve years ago. Ad hoc criminal tribunals will prolong the suffering in poor countries by supporting governments that will maintain foreign domination that seeks benefits that will worsen that condition.

The Violence And Division Within Yugoslavia Since The Collapse Of The Soviet Economy Was Caused By U.S.-Led Acts Designed To Balkanize The Federal Republic And Its Member Republics With The ICTY As Principal Weapon

The United States engaged in a decade-long effort aided by several European countries, to break-up and destroy the Federal Republic of Yugoslavia, causing the secession, (remember the American Civil War) of German-oriented Slovenia and Croatia with 500,000 Serbs purged from its borders. Then Bosnia was pried away from the Federal Republic of Yugoslavia and segregated into an unnatural three region religious apartheid, Muslim, Roman Catholic and Eastern Orthodox Christian. Now Macedonia is in turmoil nearing civil war from U.S.-stimulated and -supported aggression by the KLA terrorist organization. Thus Yugoslavia became former, losing half of its population and wealth and leaving only Serbia and Montenegro. Kosovo and Metohija, an historically precious part of Serbia, remains occupied by NATO forces after seventy-eight days of aerial bombardment in 1999.

U.S.-led aerial assaults inflicted billions in damages on civilian facilities, killed thousands of civilians throughout Serbia in the name of NATO. Thereafter the United States and NATO watched as 330,000 Serbs were forced out of Kosovo and Metohija and many hundreds murdered, emboldened by the United States. Violent efforts to remove all Serbs from Kosovo and Metohija continue. And the KLA has been empowered to attack Macedonia.

The ICTY was created at the insistence of the United States which had stimulated violence and secession in republics of Slovenia, Croatia, Bosnia and Herzegovina and Macedonia, and attempted division and conflict in the Serbian province of Kosovo and Metohija and in three municipalities in the South of Serbia and throughout the former six Republics. The U.S. intends to persecute and demonize leaders, who together with the people, by defending freedom and by resisting aggression of NATO war machinery, had defied its will, and at the same time make the people seem savage. Madeleine Albright, while U.S. Ambassador to the UN, was the driving force for creation of the ICTY. The U.S. Ambassador to the Tribunal, David Scheffer, concedes the ICTY is "supported, financed, staffed and provided information" primarily by the United States.

Now as the idea and existence of ad hoc tribunals are threatened by the treaty creating the International Criminal Court, the United States is exerting pressure to prevent nations from ratifying it. It is also pressing for new ad hoc Tribunals for the Democratic Republic of Congo, Sierra Leone, Sudan and elsewhere, to dominate those regions and defuse the drive for the International Criminal Court. The treaty, signed in Rome in 1998 by 120 nations, was ratified by the thirty-seventh nation, the Netherlands, in late July 2001.

The United States prefers to select nations for persecution while protecting itself, its allies and favored client states. Ad hoc tribunals, which are illegitimate, incapable of equal justice under law, by their nature unable to conduct fair trials, or provide due process and whose victims have long since been convicted in the United States-controlled media, are a U.S. weapon for establishing long term control and exploitation of targeted nations and regions. That is their globalization, that is new colonialism.

For these reasons, the so-called ICTY should be declared illegal and its prisoners, legally and illegally surrendered, should be released.

The Hague, August 30, 2001

A History of 'Legal' Oppression

R.M. Sharpe

History is replete with examples of trials conducted by colonial and imperialist powers against people who resist, or who in any way challenge the rule of the rich. Sometimes they just summarily execute their enemies with their superior force. But often the ruling class needs to hide its "might-is-right" approach to power behind the cloak of religion, public virtue or the trappings of an entrenched legal system. It needs to convince the mass of the people, and sometimes even itself, that its brutality and greed are legitimate.

The abduction of former Yugoslav President Slobodan Milosevic to stand trial before NATO's war crimes tribunal in The Hague is but the latest example. The Socialist Party of Serbia leader was kidnapped from a prison in Central Belgrade on June 28, 2001. The new NATO-backed Democratic Opposition of Serbia (DOS) regime, for close to three months, had held him without trial on allegations of corruption and abuse of power while in office.

A faction in the ruling DOS coalition headed by Serbian Prime Minister Zoran Djindjic manipulated Milosevic's transfer to the International Criminal Tribunal for the Former Yugoslavia (ICTY). The ICTY was initiated by Washington and illegally established under cover of the United Nations in May 1993. Milosevic was, furthermore, extradited against the wishes of the majority of the population and the parliament, and in defiance of an injunction issued by Yugoslavia's Constitutional Court.

This betrayal of Yugoslavia's sovereignty was in capitulation to the same forces that mercilessly bombed the country for seventy-eight days in 1999 when Milosevic was president. The handover followed demands by the United States and its European NATO allies that Milosevic stand trial for war crimes they claim were committed in Kosovo-Metohija when his administration defended the province against the murderous incursions of the CIA/NATO-backed "Kosovo Liberation Army."

The demands were openly linked to threats, coming loudest from Washington, to economically strangle Yugoslavia if the new DOS regime, whose rise to power was financed by the imperialist West, did not submit.

Inverting reality is crucial to setting the stage—in this case for a political show trial—which will deflect attention from the brutal crimes of the true aggressors. Milosevic's real, unspoken "offense" was to in fact defend Yugoslav sovereignty against big-business plunder—up to and including his administration's defense of Kosovo and its resistance to the NATO blitzkrieg that followed.

In order to justify NATO's devastating pounding of Yugoslavia—and polish their image as the great defenders of democracy and human rights—the U.S., along with its junior European NATO partners, first demonized Milosevic and then instigated his abduction to be tried in a kangaroo court.

This type of reality-turned-upside-down scenario, where the oppressor puts the oppressed on trial for resisting and thereby posing a threat to their unjust rule, is nothing new.

THE EASTER UPRISING IN IRELAND

In 1916 during World War I, for example, the British imprisoned Padraig Pearse, James Connolly, Roger Casement and scores of other Irish freedom fighters under the "Defense of the Realm Acts"—a measure originally aimed at German spies in the United Kingdom.

These activists were tried for their leading role in the heroic Easter Uprising against Britain's brutal 800-year colonial occupation of Ireland. The five-day insurrection involving some 2,000 people started in Dublin, the Irish capital, which the rebels took over. They then declared independence as well as a provisional government for the new Irish Republic.

After viciously crushing the resistance, "The British immediately brought the leaders of the uprising to trial before a field court-martial. Fifteen of the group, including Pearse, Connolly, and MacDonagh, were sentenced to death and executed by firing squad. Four others, including the American-born Eamon de Valera, received death sentences that were later commuted to life imprisonment, although de Valera and some others were granted amnesty the next year. Casement was convicted of treason and hanged. Many others prominently connected with the rebellion were sentenced to long prison terms."[1]

The executions caused such outrage among the population that it energized the struggle for a total end to British occupation—including of the northern counties. Consistent with its historic role as colonizer and imperialist predator, Britain is today a junior partner in the U.S.-led NATO alliance.

THE FIRST SUCCESSFUL SLAVE REVOLUTION: HAITI

France, another European NATO member, has its own bloody history of colonial terror.

In 1791, a slave uprising in Haiti sent shock waves through the forced-labor plantation system of the Western Hemisphere. This included the United States where slaves were treated most cruelly.

The rebellion started at a Voodoo ceremony in northern Haiti and spread rapidly. "Within six weeks 1,200 coffee estates and 200 sugar plantations had been burned, while 1,000 whites and 10,000 slaves had been killed. Compared with previous slave revolts, this was remarkable both in its scale and in the evident degree of organization. The slaves, initially led by Boukman, had coordinated their plans and succeeded in keeping them secret, so that the plantation owners were caught by surprise."[2]

The French beheaded Boukman after they were able to hunt him down. Before the end of the year Toussaint L'Ouverture joined the army of former slaves—first as a doctor, and then as a military commander who introduced guerrilla tactics into the struggle.

The insurrection sparked the Haitian revolution against domination, eventually decimated the mighty French colonial army, and later led to Haiti's independence under Jean-Jacques Dessalines.

France had abolished slavery in 1794. As a concession to the Haitian struggle, the French authorities allowed L'Ouverture to be appointed in 1796 as lieutenant governor of Haiti. Although L'Ouverture fought brilliantly to end slavery, his tenure as lieutenant governor saw no fundamental changes in Haitian property relations, and the former slaves remained landless and poor.

After seizing power in France in 1799, Napoleon Bonaparte renounced the ban on slavery, and in 1802 his army invaded Haiti. The troops of the French Empire made an example of L'Ouverture, who was the acknowledged leader of the first successful slave rebellion in history. He was seen as a threat that had to be eliminated since he had become a symbol of the fight against the colonial oppressors and their slave system. Napoleon succeeded in capturing L'Ouverture and exiled him to prison in France, where he met his death under uncertain circumstances.

JOHN BROWN AND THE ABOLITIONIST MOVEMENT

There have been many examples in the United States of people who fight oppression and exploitation being put on trial by the oppressing class.

Take for example John Brown, the white anti-racist abolitionist. Brown was born in 1800 in Connecticut, "just as the shudder of Haiti was running through all the Americas," wrote African-American historian W.E.B DuBois.[3]

Brown was a deeply religious man who hated all injustice, including slavery, which he condemned as "the sum of all villainies."[4] After learning first-hand of the brutality of the system, Brown declared his intention in 1839 to make war on slavery.

At first he worked to raise funds. Then in 1854 Brown and six of his sons joined the armed struggle in Kansas, where he played a pivotal role in keeping the state free from slavery. Brown worked tirelessly over the subsequent years for the anti-slavery cause—meeting people, raising funds and even setting up a military school in 1857.

The next year, Brown made a daring foray into Missouri to liberate some slaves. A price was put on his head—dead or alive—but this didn't stop him. Three months later, Brown landed the escapees in Canada.

On October 15, 1859, Brown's long-term strategy of armed struggle against slavery took shape in a bold plan to seize Harpers Ferry in Virginia. The town was strategically located with its arsenal, a retreat to the mountains and was the gateway to the southern slave states.

Because the delivery of weapons was delayed, many of Brown's fighters, who included freed slaves and whites, were killed or captured. The abolitionist refused to surrender but was taken prisoner after being gravely wounded.

Charged with murder, insurrection, and treason against the State of Virginia, Brown lay bandaged on a cot in the courtroom. His request that the proceedings be delayed by one day to allow time for his lawyer to arrive was denied. Brown was assigned counsel who, against Brown's wishes, set out to prove his client insane.

Brown rose from his cot to give his own statement:

> I believe that to have interfered as I have done—as I have always freely admitted I have done—in behalf of His despised poor, was not wrong, but right. Now if it is deemed necessary that I should forfeit my life for the furtherance of the ends of justice, and mingle my blood further with the blood of my children and with the blood of millions in this slave country whose rights are disregarded by wicked, cruel, and unjust enactments—I submit; so let it be done![5]

For the unthinkable "crime" of fighting to end slavery, John Brown was kept alive after being wounded, rushed to trial and hanged with federal complicity on December 2, 1859, less than two months after the attack on Harpers Ferry. The trial of Brown and the other fighters who seized Harpers Ferry got international coverage.

The State of Virginia tried to use the proceedings to prove that slavery was legal, just and godly. But Brown and the other defendants used their statements at the trial to condemn slavery and succeeded in arousing the abolitionist movement around the United States. Two years later, the Civil War started, which led to the emancipation of the slaves.

VESEY AND TURNER: SLAVE REBELLIONS

There was heightened security at Harpers Ferry when Brown's band struck due to the fact that slave conspiracies had been increasing in the South. Denmark Vesey, a South Carolina slave who had bought his freedom, shaped one of the most intricate and elaborate in 1822.

Vesey's plan reportedly involved thousands of people and was so far reaching, well organized and serious that "it frightened the South into hysterics."[6] Vesey, who consulted with leaders of the Haitian revolution, had planned to burn Charleston, the capital, and initiate a slave uprising. But the plot was betrayed, and 131 people were arrested and tried, forty-nine of whom were condemned to die. Twelve were finally pardoned, but thirty-seven, including Vesey, went to the scaffold for challenging the system.[7]

Before facing trial Vesey was demonized. One Charleston official—the equivalent of a mayor—attacked the former slave, calling him "ungovernable and savage."[8] He claimed Vesey was "impetuous and domineering in the extreme," and that this qualified him "for the despotic rule, of which he was ambitious."[9]

Vesey's scheme to free thousands of slaves was downplayed by the authorities, who were shaken to the core by its magnitude. As a result, the trials of the insurgents were held in deep secret, and records of the proceedings were long suppressed.

Robert P. Forbes of the Gilder Lehrman Center for the Study of Slavery, Resistance, and Abolition at Yale University reviewed one of the rare books recently published on the Vesey trials, entitled *Designs Against Charleston: The Trial Record of the Denmark Slave Conspiracy of 1822.*[10] Forbes asks:

> What does this transcript tell us? First and foremost...that the institution of slavery inverts the values of right and wrong. Kindness, loyalty, honesty, mercy: all of these are perverted into vices under the slave regime, while deceit, betrayal, cruelty and violence become virtues.[11]

Forbes also makes another important point in reference to the testimonies. He notes that at the "... trials, the delusion of paternalism falls away, and the state of war between master and slave that existed just below the surface of Southern life is graphically exposed."[12] In that war, the slave masters again and again tried to assert their moral and legal authority to own human beings, and for this they needed Vesey's trial.

There were many acts of resistance by the slaves after Vesey was hanged, including an uprising in 1831 led by Nat Turner in Virginia that "threw the slaveholding South into a panic, and then into a determined effort to bolster the security of the slave system."[13]

Turner had gathered supporters while moving from plantation to plantation, but most were captured after running out of ammunition. He eluded his pursuers for almost two months. While the troops of the slave state were chasing after Turner, they summarily executed hundreds, maybe thousands of slaves.

When caught, Turner was not immediately executed, but the slave masters made a point of putting him on trial before they hanged him. Though Turner had confessed to the rebellion, he pled "not guilty" because he believed his actions were just. As abolitionist Thomas Wentworth Higginson wrote:

> When Nat Turner was asked by Mr. T. R. Gray, the counsel assigned him, whether, although defeated, he still believed in his own Provdential mission, he answered, ... "Was not Christ crucified?"[14]

MARCUS GARVEY AND OTHERS

Jamaican-born Marcus Garvey was a symbol of Black racial pride, the unity of people of African descent, and economic self-reliance. In 1914 he founded the Universal Negro Improvement Association (UNIA). Prior to that, Garvey had used his skills as a journalist to organize his co-workers for better pay and working conditions. In 1916 he moved to the U.S. to raise funds for UNIA. Author Horace Campbell explains:

> Black workers in the USA at the end of World War I, chafing under the crudest forms of exploitation, forged organizations to struggle to better their lot and through their cultural outpourings they contributed to the intellectual development of the USA, in a period which is now known as the Harlem Renaissance.[15]

UNIA was the paramount organization of its time, growing to over five million members with 996 branches in forty-three countries. Its objective was to improve the socio-economic condition of Black people everywhere, and to promote African pride and unity.

When UNIA established the Black Star Line Shipping Company, launching four ships, the capitalist class moved against it. The enterprise, which was run cooperatively, was successfully sabotaged with help from petit-bourgeois elements inside the organization.

To crush this growing movement, the U.S. rulers used the full authority of their courts and media. A "Garvey Must Go" campaign was instigated in 1923 by the capitalists, steeped as they were in the rabid racism of the United States. It included Garvey's demonization and diplomatic pressure on the governments of countries where UNIA had branches.

Garvey was indicted on the spurious charge of mail fraud and put on trial. He served as his own defense counsel. He was convicted and imprisoned in Atlanta, Georgia, for five years, of which he served almost three. He was then deported to Jamaica, where he received a rousing welcome from the poor. Although Garvey died in 1940, today he remains a national hero and symbol of resistance.

There are many other examples where the rulers use the police and courts to suppress a rising movement by attacking individuals who in some way symbolize the struggle of the oppressed or of those who fight exploitation. Take Nicola Sacco and Bartolomeo Vanzetti, for example.

The two were framed for murder by the government in 1920, tried and executed. They were made examples for the many class-conscious immigrant workers, including many anarcho-syndicalists and communists, whom the U.S. rulers—in their fear of the Russian Revolution—wanted to deport and intimidate.

One of the clearest examples of using the courts to try leaders of workers organizing for their rights occurred even earlier. On May 4, 1885, a bomb was thrown into a rally at Haymarket Square in Chicago, Illinois, called by the leaders of the movement for the eight-hour workday. The bomb, which was probably hurled by an agent provocateur, killed seven policemen and injured scores. The cops fired on the crowd, slaying several people and wounding hundreds.

Eight anarchists were arrested and tried. But only one had been present at the rally and he was speaking when the device went off! Of the eight, Albert Parsons, August Spies, Adolph Fischer and George Engel were convicted and hanged by the state.

There's also the case of Lolita Lebron and the other Puerto Rican independence fighters who were tried and imprisoned for decades for demonstrating their opposition to Washington's colonization of their homeland, in a 1954 raid on the U.S. Congress.

Leonard Peltier, who defended Native American sovereignty at the Battle of Wounded Knee, was convicted without evidence for the 1975 deaths of two Federal Bureau of Investigation agents who had invaded the reservation. Today Peltier still remains a political prisoner.

Revolutionary journalist Mumia Abu-Jamal also comes to mind. The former Black Panther leader was convicted for the murder of a Philadelphia cop and sentenced to death in 1982. Today, years later, he remains on death row despite evidence pointing to his innocence. In April 1999, Abu-Jamal issued a statement against NATO's aggression on Yugoslavia and supporting a June 5 March on the Pentagon called by the International Action Center.

One doesn't have to be a revolutionary to become a target of the ruling class like Milosevic did. One simply has to resist domination by acting independently of big-business interests. President Manuel Noriega, for example, had collaborated with Washington before 1989. But when he stopped cooperating fully with U.S. plans he was targeted and hunted down by the Pentagon with a full invasion of Panama in December 1989 that killed thousands. Noriega was captured, tried for alleged involvement in transporting illegal drugs, and is still imprisoned in the U.S.

DIMITROV'S DEFENSE IN THE REICHSTAG FIRE TRIAL

Shortly after the Nazis took power in Germany in 1933, they attempted to use a fire set in the German Parliament building, the Reichstag, to open an all-out attack on the Communist Party. They charged Bulgarian Communist leader-in-exile Georgi Dimitrov, two other Bulgarians and one German communist with setting fire to the Reichstag.

Dimitrov faced centuries of authoritarian German ruling-class laws and an added enemy in the form of the new fascist dictatorship. To say the decks were stacked against him would be a wild understatement. He was refused counsel of his choice, but preferred to defend himself rather than accept a court-appointed lawyer.

Dimitrov turned the tables on the Nazis with a heroic defense. Despite being constantly told to shut up by the court, he was so determined in his questioning of witnesses that he reduced the Nazi leader Hermann Goering to hysteria.

In his final summary, an hours-long statement he had prepared while manacled in a Nazi prison, Dimitrov showed he understood the class character of the court and conducted his defense accordingly, saying:

> I have often been reproached for not taking the highest court in Germany seriously. That is absolutely unjustified.
> It is true that the supreme law for me as a Communist is the program of the Communist International, the Supreme Court—the Control Commission of the Communist International.
> But to me as an accused man the Supreme Court of the [German] Reich is something to be considered in all seriousness—not only in that its members possess high legal qualifications, but also because it is a highly important organism of state power, of the ruling order of society: a body that can dispose of the highest penalties.[16]

Even this Nazi-backed court was unable to find Dimitrov and his fellow defendants guilty. But it held them in prison until the Soviet Union traded captured German spies for them some months later, when they were finally freed.[17]

From slave owners to imperialist bankers, in different historic periods the ruling classes have never been satisfied to simply smash the oppressed on the field of battle. They have used the courts they created to uphold their rule over society, imposing special penalties on the leaders of oppressed peoples, in order to make examples of them. It is this open political use of the courts that makes the outcome of the case against former President Milosevic so important.

No one can predict with full certainty the outcome of the political show trial against Milosevic. But the Yugoslav leader has already begun by challenging the very legitimacy of the court and resisting NATO's feverish attempts to make him the scapegoat for every bloody conflict that has erupted in the Balkans since 1991. To continue this course will expose the tribunal for the unjust machine of repression and false propaganda that it is.

Those who oppose NATO's aggression in the Balkans have every right to continue their work by standing up and fighting the ICTY on every issue raised in Milosevic's trial. They can expose each charge that blames the Yugoslav president for the past ten years of turmoil in the Balkans as crimes really committed by the NATO powers in their drive to conquer and re-colonize Southeastern Europe.

One thing is certain. Even if Milosevic is found guilty by this victors' court, this won't be history's final judgment. In the examples provided above, no one remembers the names of the judges who presided over the unjust convictions of the leaders of the oppressed. Who will be remembered, who lives on in history, are those who stand up to the rule of the oppressors, and those who defy their courts. By their example, defendants at the ICTY can inspire the new struggles for freedom and independence that are sure to arise in the Balkans.

[1] http://www.attridge15.freeserve.co.uk/ireland/easter_rising.htm

[2] Latin America Bureau, Haiti Family Business, London, Great Britain, 1985, p. 15.

[3] W.E.B. DuBois, *John Brown a Biography*, M.E. Sharpe, Inc., Armonk, N.Y., 2nd edition 1997, p. 33.

[4] Quoted in DuBois, p. 59.

[5] Africans in America, http://www.pbs.org/wgbh/aia/part4/4h2943t.html, September 9, 2001

[6] DuBois, p. 37.

[7] Herbert Aptheker, *American Negro Slave Revolts*, 6th edition, 1993, International Publishers, New York, p. 271.

[8] Negro Universities Press, Slave Insurrections: Selected Documents, 1970, cited on www.pbs.org/wgbh/aia/part3/3h496.html., September 5, 2001.

[9] *Ibid.*

[10] Edward Pearson, ed., Chapel Hill: University of North Carolina Press. Cited in *The North Star*, Web edition, Spring 2000

[11] *The North Star*, Web edition, Spring 2000

[12] *Ibid.*

[13] Howard Zinn, *A People's History of the United States 1491-Present*, New York, Harper Perennial, 2nd edition 1995, p. 170.

[14] Thomas Wentworth Higginson, "The Confessions of Nat Turner, the Leader of the Late Insurrection in Southhampton, Va." *The Atlantic Monthly*, June 1861.

[15] Horace Campbell, *Rasta and Resistance From Marcus Garvey to Walter Rodney*, Africa World Press, Inc., Trenton, N.J., 1987, p. 53.

[16] Georgi Dimitrov, Minutes of Speech Before Court, December 16, 1933.

[17] Georgi Dimitrov, "Rulers of Bulgaria" www.Bulgaria.com., September 6, 2001.

II.
PROPAGANDA AND DEMONIZATION SET STAGE FOR WAR

Demonization and the Media Blitz

LENORA FOERSTEL

One has to wonder if it is possible for international public opinion to accept the prosecution of a democratically elected leader of a sovereign nation. "No citizen in the world would consider themselves fairly tried before a court that was paid for, staffed and assisted by private citizens or corporations which had a direct stake in the outcome of the trial and who were themselves, in practical terms, immune from the court."[1]

The United Nations Security Council under the control of the United States created the International Criminal Tribunal for the Former Yugoslavia (ICTY), which between 1994 and 1995 received $700,000 in cash and $2.3 million worth of computer equipment from the U.S. government. The Rockefeller Foundation provided $50,000 to the ICTY and the billionaire George Soros chipped in with $150,000. Soros' international foundation acts in coordination with U.S. agencies and he has significant business interests in the Balkans.

ICTY officials stated that this court's function is to prosecute war crimes and crimes against humanity, but it has chosen not to deal with the legal concept of "crimes against peace," established by Nuremberg Principle VI (a). This principle considers "Planning, preparation, initiation or waging of a war of aggression, or a war in violation of international treaties, agreements or assurances" as crimes against peace. If the Nuremberg principles were part of the ICTY the United States would itself be eligible to be brought to trial for its crimes against peace.

This section shows how the Western media, in cooperation with corporations, the Pentagon and the U.S. and other NATO governments, helped to make the corruption of international justice possible and took part in a crime against peace by laying the groundwork for war. Acting like a "second front," the media aids in the carrying out of a new form of colonization. NATO's incursion into Kosovo was carried out as the uncritical media passed on demonic lies issuing from NATO headquarters and NATO member states. "One of the great ironies of Operation Allied Force, NATO's brief 1999 war against Serbia, was that Yugoslavia's broadcasting facilities were bombed by NATO on the claim that they were a 'lie machine' serving the Yugoslav apparatus of war."[2]

In his paper "The Media and Their Atrocities," Michael Parenti documents the misinformation sent out by the Western media, especially the repeated lies about "mass graves" that were never found, as even the ICTY had to admit. More recently, we have learned that Bernard Kouchner, the United Nations chief administrator in Kosovo "had established close personal ties with the Kosovo Liberation Army (KLA) commander in chief Agim Ceku, who in a bitter irony was on the list of 'alleged War criminals of The Hague Tribunal.' "[3]

In their paper, "The Racak Massacre: Casus Belli for NATO", Doris Pumphrey and George Pumphrey describe how the so-called massacre was a hoax staged in order to pressure hesitant politicians and citizens of the NATO countries into accepting a war of aggression against Yugoslavia.

Thomas Deichmann's paper, "Scharping's Lies Won't Last," gives us a picture of how the German media made it possible for Germany to participate in dividing up Yugoslavia. Deichmann analyzes the attempt by the Social Democratic Defense Minister Rudolph Scharping to justify Germany's participation in the war against Yugoslavia. "The rhetoric of the Holocaust was deployed in Germany more than any other western country to endow the NATO attack on Serbia and German participation in it with moral legitimacy. Scharping followed up one horror story with another and constructed countless false analogies between Serbia and the Third Reich. Racism had always been used by those in power to divide communities and nations in order to gain economic control. The hatred of Slavic peoples nourished by Scharping and the Western press only repeats what Nazi Germany carried out in WWII."

Louis Dalmas, publisher and editor-in-chief of *Balkans-Info*, states that "the right of self-determination has its roots in an anti-colonialism meant to break up the huge British, French, German and other empires exploiting vast surfaces of the globe for their own profits: the supporters of 'self determination' did not struggle for the freedom of any specific ethnicity. Instead they sought to do away with the yoke on the backs of all the populations under foreign occupation."[4] Standing alone in the Balkans against an invasion by the world's wealthiest and most powerful nations, Yugoslavia asserted its right to independence and self-determination.

[1] Christopher Black, "An Impartial Tribunal? Really?" www.emperors-clothes.com/analysis/impartial.htm

[2] Emil Vlajka, "Demonization of Serbs: Western Imperialism and Media War Criminals." *REVOLT*, (Ottowa), 2000, p. 32.

[3] Michel Chossudovsky, "Macedonia: Washington behind Terrorist Assaults," July 2001, www.antiwar.com.

[4] Louis Dalmas, "From Territories to People: Nations Adrift," *Balkans-Info*, 20/3 - 20/4, 2001.

The Media and Their Atrocities

MICHAEL PARENTI

For the better part of a decade the U.S. public has been bombarded with a media campaign to demonize the Serbian people and their elected leaders. During that time, the U.S. government has pursued a goal of breaking up Yugoslavia into a cluster of small, weak, dependent, free-market principalities. Yugoslavia was the only country in Eastern Europe that would not dismantle its welfare state and public sector economy. It was the only one that did not beg for entry into NATO. It was—and what's left of it, still is—charting an independent course not in keeping with the New World Order.

TARGETING THE SERBS

Of the various Yugoslav peoples, the Serbs were targeted for de-monization because they were the largest nationality and the one most opposed to the breakup of Yugoslavia. But what of the atrocities they committed? All sides committed atrocities in the fighting that has been encouraged by the western powers over the last decade, but the reporting has been consistently one-sided. Grisly incidents of Croat and Muslim atrocities against the Serbs rarely made it into the U.S. press, and when they did they were accorded only passing mention.[1] Meanwhile Serb atrocities were played up and sometimes even fabricated, as we shall see. Recently, three Croatian generals were indicted by The Hague War Crimes Tribunal for the bombardment and deaths of Serbs in Krajina and elsewhere. Where were the U.S. television crews when these war crimes were being committed? John Ranz, chair of Survivors of the Buchenwald Concentration Camp, USA, asks: Where were the TV cam-eras when hundreds of Serbs were slaughtered by Muslims near Sre-brenica?[2] The official line, faithfully parroted in the U.S. media, is that Bosnian Serb forces committed all the atrocities at Srebrenica.

Are we to trust U.S. leaders and the corporate-owned news media when they dish out atrocity stories? Recall the 500 premature babies whom Iraqi soldiers laughingly ripped from incubators in Kuwait, a story repeated and believed until exposed as a total fabrication years later. During the Bosnian war in 1993, the Serbs were accused of pursu-ing an official policy of rape. "Go forth and rape" a Bosnian Serb commander supposedly publicly instructed his troops. The source of that story never could be traced. The commander's name was never produced. As far as we know, no such utterance was ever made. Even the *New York Times* belatedly ran a tiny retraction, coyly allowing that "the existence of 'a systematic rape policy' by the Serbs remains to be proved."[3]

Bosnian Serb forces supposedly raped anywhere from 25,000 to 100,000 Muslim women, the stories varied. The Bosnian Serb army numbered not more than 30,000 or so, many of whom were engaged in desperate military engagements. A representative from Helsinki Watch noted that stories of massive Serbian rapes originated with the Bosnian Muslim and Croatian governments and had no credible supporting evidence. Common sense would dictate that these stories be treated with the utmost skepticism—and not be used as an excuse for an aggressive and punitive policy against Yugoslavia.

The "mass rape" propaganda theme was resuscitated in 1999 to justify the continued NATO slaughter of Yugoslavia. A headline in the *San Francisco Examiner* (April 26, 1999) tells us: "Serb Tactic is Organized Rape, Kosovo Refugees Say." No evidence or testimony is given to support the charge of organized rape. Only at the bottom of the story, in the nineteenth paragraph, do we read that reports gathered by the Kosovo mission of the Organization for Security and Cooperation in Europe found no such organized rape policy. The actual number of rapes were in the dozens "and not many dozens," according to the OSCE spokesperson. This same story did note in passing that the UN War Crimes Tribunal sentenced a Bosnian Croat military commander to ten years in prison for failing to stop his troops from raping Muslim women in 1993—an atrocity we heard little about when it was happening.

A few dozen rapes is a few dozen too many. But can it serve as one of the justifications for a massive war? If Mr. Clinton wanted to stop rapes, he could have begun a little closer to home in Washington, D.C., where dozens of rapes occur every month. Indeed, he might be able to alert us to how women are sexually mistreated on Capitol Hill and in the White House itself.

The Serbs were blamed for the infamous Sarajevo market massacre. But according to the report leaked out on French TV, Western intelligence knew that it was Muslim operatives who had bombed Bosnian civilians in the marketplace in order to induce NATO involvement. Even international negotiator David Owen, who worked with Cyrus Vance, admitted in his memoir that the NATO powers knew all along that it was a Muslim bomb.[4]

On one occasion, notes Barry Lituchy, the *New York Times* ran a photo purporting to be of Croats grieving over Serbian atrocities when in fact the murders had been committed by Bosnian Muslims. The *Times* printed an obscure retraction the following week.[5]

The propaganda campaign against Belgrade has been so relentless that even prominent personages on the left—who oppose the NATO policy against Yugoslavia—have felt compelled to genuflect before this demonization orthodoxy, referring to unspecified and unverified Serbian "brutality" and "the monstrous Milosevic."[6] Thus they reveal themselves as having been influenced by the very media propaganda machine they criticize on so many other issues. To reject the demonized image of Milosevic and of the Serbian people is not to idealize them or claim that Serb forces are faultless or free of crimes. It is merely to challenge the one-sided propaganda that laid the grounds for NATO's aggression against Yugoslavia.

THE ETHNIC-CLEANSING HYPE

Up until the NATO bombings began in March 1999, the conflict in Kosovo had taken 2,000 lives altogether from both sides, according to Kosovo Albanian sources. Yugoslavian sources put the figure at 800. Such casualties reveal a civil war, not genocide. Belgrade is condemned for the forced expulsion policy of Albanians from Kosovo. But such expulsions began in substantial numbers only after the NATO bombings, with thousands being uprooted by Serb forces especially from areas where KLA mercenaries were operating.

We should keep in mind that tens of thousands also fled Kosovo because it was being mercilessly bombed by NATO, or because it was the scene of sustained ground fighting between Yugoslav forces and the KLA, or because they were just afraid and hungry. An Albanian woman crossing into Macedonia was eagerly asked by a news crew if she had been forced out by Serb police. She responded: "There were no Serbs. We were frightened of the [NATO] bombs."[7] I had to read this in the

San Francisco Bay Guardian, an alternative weekly, not in the *New York Times* or *Washington Post*.

During the bombings, an estimated 70,000 to 100,000 Serbian residents of Kosovo took flight (mostly north but some to the south), as did thousands of Roma and others.[8] Were the Serbs ethnically cleansing themselves? Or were these people not fleeing the bombing and the ground war? Yet, the refugee tide caused by the bombing was repeatedly used by U.S. war makers as justification for the bombing, a pressure put on Milosevic to allow "the safe return of ethnic Albanian refugees."[9]

While Kosovo Albanians were leaving in great numbers—usually well-clothed and in good health, some riding their tractors, trucks, or cars, many of them young men of recruitment age—they were described as being "slaughtered." It was repeatedly reported that "Serb atrocities"—not the extensive ground war with the KLA and certainly not the massive NATO bombing—"drove more than one million Albanians from their homes."[10] More recently, there have been hints that Albanian Kosovar refugees numbered nowhere near that number.

Serbian attacks on KLA strongholds or the forced expulsion of Albanian villagers were described as "genocide." But experts in surveillance photography and wartime propaganda charged NATO with running a "propaganda campaign" on Kosovo that lacked any supporting evidence. State Department reports of mass graves and of 100,000 to 500,000 missing Albanian men "are just ludicrous," according to these independent critics.[11] Their findings were ignored by the major networks and other national media.

Early in the war, the Long Island, N.Y., daily *Newsday* reported that Britain and France were seriously considering "commando assaults into Kosovo to break the pattern of Serbian massacres of ethnic Albanians."[12] What discernible pattern of massacres? Of course, no commando assaults were put into operation, but the story served its purpose of hyping an image of mass killings.

An ABC "Nightline" show made dramatic and repeated references to the "Serbian atrocities in Kosovo" while offering no specifics. Ted Kopple asked a group of angry Albanian refugees, what specifically had they witnessed. They pointed to an old man in their group who wore a wool hat. One of them reenacted what the Serbs had done to him, throwing the man's hat to the ground and stepping on it—"because the Serbs knew that his hat was the most important thing to him." Kopple was appropriately horrified about this "war crime," the only example offered in an hour-long program.

A widely circulated story in the *New York Times,* headlined "U.S. Report Outlines Serb Attacks in Kosovo," tells us that the State Department issued "the most comprehensive documentary record to date on atrocities." The report concluded that there had been organized rapes and systematic executions. But as one reads further and more closely into the article, one finds that State Department reports of such crimes "depend almost entirely on information from refugee accounts. There was no suggestion that American intelligence agencies had been able to verify, most, or even many, of the accounts ... and the word 'reportedly' and 'allegedly' appear throughout the document."[13]

British journalist Audrey Gillan interviewed Kosovo refugees about atrocities and found an impressive lack of evidence or credible specifics. One woman caught him glancing at the watch on her wrist, while her husband told him how all the women had been robbed of their jewelry and other possessions. A spokesman for the UN High Commissioner for Refugees talked of mass rapes and what sounded like hundreds of killings in three villages, but when Gillan pressed him for more precise information, he reduced it drastically to five or six teenage rape victims. But he had not spoken to any witnesses, and admitted that, "we have no way of verifying these reports."[14]

Gillan notes that some refugees had seen killings and other atrocities, but there was little to suggest that they had seen it on the scale that was being reported. One afternoon, officials in charge said there were refugees arriving who talked of sixty or more being killed in one village and fifty in another, but Gillan "could not find one eye-witness who actually saw these things happening." Yet every day western journalists reported "hundreds" of rapes and murders. Sometimes they noted in passing that the reports had yet to be substantiated, but then why were such unverified stories being so eagerly reported in the first place?

THE DISAPPEARING "MASS GRAVES"

After NATO forces occupied Kosovo, the stories about mass atrocities continued fortissimo. The *Washington Post* reported that 350 ethnic Albanians "might be buried in mass graves" around a mountain village

in western Kosovo. They "might be" or they might not be. These estimates were based on sources that NATO officials refused to identify.
Getting down to specifics, the article mentions "four decomposing bodies" discovered near a large ash heap.[15]

It was repeatedly announced in the first days of the NATO occupation that 10,000 Albanians had been killed (down from the 100,000 and
even 500,000 Albanian men supposedly executed during the war). No
evidence was ever offered to support the 10,000 figure, nor even to explain how it was arrived at so swiftly and surely while NATO troops
were still moving into place and occupied only small portions of the
province.

Likewise, repeatedly unsubstantiated references to "mass graves,"
each purportedly filled with hundreds or even thousands of Albanian
victims also failed to materialize. Through the summer of 1999, the media hype about mass graves devolved into an occasional unspecified reference. The few sites actually unearthed offered up as many as a dozen
bodies or sometimes twice that number, but with no certain evidence regarding causes of death or even the nationality of victims. In some cases
there was reason to believe the victims were Serbs.[16]

On April 19, 1999, while the NATO bombings of Yugoslavia were
going on, the State Department announced that up to 500,000 Kosovo
Albanians were missing and feared dead. On May 16, U.S. Secretary of
Defense William Cohen, a former Republican senator from Maine serving in President Clinton's Democratic Administration, stated that
100,000 military-aged ethnic Albanian men had vanished and might
have been killed by the Serbs.[17] Such widely varying but horrendous
figures from official sources went unchallenged by the media and by the
many liberals who supported NATO's "humanitarian rescue operation."
Among these latter were some supposedly progressive members of Congress who seemed to believe they were witnessing another Nazi Holocaust.

On June 17, just after the end of the war, British Foreign Office Minister Geoff Hoon said that "in more than 100 massacres" some "10,000
ethnic Albanians had been killed (down from the 500,000 and 100,000
bandied about by U.S. officials)."[18] A day or two after the bombings
stopped, the Associate Press and other news agency, echoing Hoon, reported that 10,000 Albanians had been killed by the Serbs.[19] No expla-

nation was given as to how this figure was arrived at, especially since not a single war site had yet been investigated and NATO forces had barely begun to move into Kosovo. On August 2, Bernard Kouchner, the United Nations' chief administrator in Kosovo (and organizer of Doctors Without Borders), asserted that about 11,000 bodies had been found in common graves throughout Kosovo. He cited as his source the International Criminal Tribunal for the Former Republic of Yugoslavia (ICTY). But the ICTY denied providing any such information. To this day, it is not clear how Kouchner came up with his estimate.[20]

As with the Croatian and Bosnian conflicts, the image of mass killings was hyped once again. Repeatedly unsubstantiated references to "mass graves," each purportedly filled with hundreds or even thousands of Albanian victims were publicized in daily media reports. In September 1999, Jared Israel did an Internet search for newspaper articles, appearing over the previous three months including the words "Kosovo" and "mass grave." The report came back: "More than 1,000—too many to list." Limiting his search to articles in the *New York Times*, he came up with eighty, nearly one a day. Yet when it came down to hard evidence, the mass graves seemed to disappear.

Thus, in mid-June 1999, the FBI sent a team to investigate two of the sites listed in the war-crimes indictment against Slobodan Milosevic, one purportedly containing six victims and the other twenty. The team lugged 107,000 pounds of equipment into Kosovo to handle what was called the "largest crime scene in the FBI's forensic history," but it came up with no reports about mass graves. Not long after, on July 1, the FBI team returned home, oddly with not a word to say about their investigation.[21]

Forensic experts from other NATO countries had similar experiences. A Spanish forensic team, for instance, was told to prepare for at least 2,000 autopsies, but found only 187 bodies, usually buried in individual graves, and showing no signs of massacre or torture. Most seemed to have been killed by mortar shells and firearms. One Spanish forensic expert, Emilio Perez Puhola, acknowledged that his team did not find one mass grave. He dismissed the widely publicized references about mass graves as being part of the "machinery of war propaganda."[22]

The *Washington Post* reported that 350 ethnic Albanians "might be buried in mass graves" around a mountain village in western Kosovo. Might be? Such speculations were based on sources that NATO officials refused to identify. Getting down to specifics, the article mentions "four decomposing bodies" discovered near a large ash heap, with no details as to who they might be or how they died.[23]

In late August 1999, the *Los Angeles Times* tried to salvage the genocide theme with a story about how the wells of Kosovo might be "mass graves in their own right." The *Times* claimed that "many corpses have been dumped into wells in Kosovo ... Serbian forces apparently stuffed... many bodies of ethnic Albanians into wells during their campaign of terror."[24] Apparently? Whenever the story got down to specifics, it dwelled on only one village and only one well—in which one body of a 39-year-old male was found, along with three dead cows and a dog. Neither his nationality nor cause of death was given. Nor was it clear who owned the well. "No other human remains were discovered," the *Times* lamely concluded. As far as I know, neither the *Los Angeles Times* nor any other media outlet ran any more stories of wells stuffed with victims.

In one grave site after another, bodies were failing to materialize in any substantial numbers—or any numbers at all. In July 1999, a mass grave in Ljubenic, near Pec (an area of concerted fighting), believed to be holding some 350 corpses, produced only seven after the exhumation. In Djacovica, town officials claimed that 100 ethnic Albanians had been murdered, but there were no bodies because the Serbs had returned in the middle of the night, dug them up, and carted them away, the officials seemed to believe. In Pusto Selo, villagers claimed that 106 men were captured and killed by Serbs at the end of March, but again no remains were discovered. Villagers once more suggested that Serb forces must have come back and removed them. How they accomplished this without being detected was not explained. In Izbica, refugees reported that 150 ethnic Albanians were executed in March. But their bodies were nowhere to be found. In Kraljan, eighty-two men were supposedly killed, but investigators found not a single cadaver.[25]

The worst incident of mass atrocities ascribed to Yugoslavian leader Slobodan Milosevic allegedly occurred at the Trepca mine. As reported by U.S. and NATO officials, the Serbs threw a thousand or more bodies down the shafts or disposed of them in the mine's vats of hydrochloric acid. In October 1999, the ICTY released the findings of Western forensic teams investigating Trepca. Not one body was found in the mine shafts, nor was there any evidence that the vats had ever been used in an attempt to dissolve human remains.[26]

By late autumn of 1999, the media hype about mass graves had fizzled noticeably. The many sites unearthed, considered to be the most notorious, offered up a few hundred bodies altogether, not the thousands or tens of thousands or hundreds of thousands previously trumpeted, and with no evidence of torture or mass execution. In many cases, there was no certain evidence regarding the nationality of victims.[27] No mass killings means that The Hague War Crimes Tribunal indictment of Milosevic "becomes highly questionable," notes Richard Gwyn. "Even more questionable is the West's continued punishment of the Serbs."[28]

No doubt there were graves in Kosovo that contained two or more persons (which is NATO's definition of a "mass grave"). People were killed by bombs and by the extensive land war that went on between Yugoslav and KLA forces. Some of the dead, as even the *New York Times* allowed, "are fighters of the Kosovo Liberation Army or may have died ordinary deaths"—as would happen in any large population over time.[29] And no doubt there were grudge killings and summary executions as in any war, but not on a scale that would warrant the label of genocide and justify the massive death and destruction and the continuing misery inflicted upon Yugoslavia by the western powers.

We should remember that the propaganda campaign waged by NATO officials and the major media never claimed merely that atrocities (murders and rapes) occurred. Such crimes occur in every war, indeed, in many communities during peacetime. What the media propaganda campaign against Yugoslavia charged was that mass atrocities and mass rapes and mass murders had been perpetrated, that is, genocide, as evidenced by mass graves.

In contrast to its public assertions, the German Foreign Office privately denied there was any evidence that genocide or ethnic cleansing was ever a component of Yugoslav policy: "Even in Kosovo, an explicit political persecution linked to Albanian ethnicity is not verifiable. ... The actions of the [Yugoslav] security forces [were] not directed against the

Kosovo-Albanians as an ethnically defined group, but against the military opponent and its actual or alleged supporters."[30]

Still, Milosevic was indicted as a war criminal, charged with the forced expulsion of Kosovar Albanians, and with summary executions of a hundred or so individuals, again, alleged crimes that occurred after the NATO bombing had started, yet were used as justification for the bombing. The biggest war criminal of all is NATO and the political leaders who orchestrated the aerial campaign of death and destruction. But here is how the White House and the U.S. media reasoned at the time: Since the aerial attacks do not intend to kill civilians, then presumably there is no liability and no accountability, only an occasional apology for the regrettable mistakes—as if only the intent of an action counted and not its ineluctable effects. In fact, a perpetrator can be judged guilty of willful murder without explicitly intending the death of a particular victim—as when the death results from an unlawful act that the perpetrator knew would likely cause death. George Kenney, a former State Department official under the Bush Administration, put it well: "Dropping cluster bombs on highly populated urban areas doesn't result in accidental fatalities. It is purposeful terror bombing."[31]

In sum, through a process of monopoly control and distribution, repetition and image escalation, the media achieve self-confirmation, that is, they find confirmation for the images they fabricate in the images they have already fabricated. Hyperbolic labeling takes the place of evidence: "genocide," "mass atrocities," "systematic rapes" and even "rape camps"—camps which no one has ever located. Through this process, evidence is not only absent, it becomes irrelevant.

So the U.S. major media (and much of the minor media) are not free and independent, as they claim, they are not the watchdog of democracy but the lapdog of the national-security state. They help reverse the roles of victims and victimizers, warmongers and peacekeepers, reactionaries and reformers. The first atrocity, the first war crime committed in any war of aggression by the aggressors is against the truth.

(This article is excerpted from Michael Parenti's book, *To Kill a Nation: The Attack on Yugoslavia,* published by Verso, October 2000.)

[1] For instance, Raymond Bonner, "War Crimes Panel Finds Croat Troops 'Cleansed' the Serbs," *New York Times*, March 21, 1999, a revealing report that has been ignored in the relentless propaganda campaign against the Serbs.

[2] John Ranz in his paid advertisement in the *New York Times*, April 29, 1993.

[3] " Correction: Report on Rape in Bosnia," *New York Times*, October 23, 1993.

[4] David Owen, *Balkan Odyssey*, p. 262.

[5] Barry Lituchy, "Media Deception and the Yugoslav Civil War," *NATO in the Bal kans*, p. 205; see also *New York Times*, August 7, 1993.

[6] Both Noam Chomsky in his comments on Pacifica Radio, April 7, 1999, and Alex ander Cockburn in Nation, May 10, 1999, describe Milosevic as "monstrous" without offering any specifics.

[7] Brooke Shelby Biggs, "Failure to Inform," *San Francisco Bay Guardian*, May 5, 1999, p. 25.

[8] *Washington Post*, June 6, 1999.

[9] See for instance, Robert Burns, *Associated Press* report, April 22, 1999.

[10] For example, *New York Times*, June 15, 1998.

[11] Charles Radin and Louise Palmer, "Experts Voice Doubts on Claims of Genocide: Little Evidence for NATO Assertions," *San Francisco Chronicle*, April 22, 1999.

[12] *Newsday*, March 31, 1999.

[13] *New York Times*, May 11, 1999.

[14] Audrey Gillan, "What's the Story?" *London Review of Books*, May 27, 1999

[15] *Washington Post*, July 10, 1999.

[16] See for instance, Carlotta Gall, "Belgrade Sees Grave Site as Proof NATO Fails to Protect Serbs," *New York Times*, August 27, 1999.

[17] Both the State Department and Cohen's figures are reported in the *New York Times*, November 11, 1999.

[18] *New York Times*, November 11, 1999.

[19] Associated Press release, June 18, 1999. Reuters (July 12, 1999) reported that NATO forces had catalogued more than one hundred sites containing the bodies of massacred ethnic Albanians.

[20] Stratfor.com, Global Intelligence Update, "Where Are Kosovo's Killing Fields?" Weekly Analysis, October 18, 1999.

[21] Reed Irvine and Cliff Kincaid, "Playing the Numbers Game," www. aim. org/mm/1999/08/03. htm.

[22] *London Sunday Times*, October 31, 1999.

[23] *Washington Post*, July 10, 1999.

[24] *Los Angeles Times*, August 28, 1999.

[25] Stratfor.com, Global Intelligence Update, "Where Are Kosovo's Killing Fields?" Weekly Analysis, October 18, 1999.

[26] Richard Gwyn in the *Toronto Star*, November 3, 1999.

[27] See for instance, Carlotta Gall, "Belgrade Sees Grave Site as Proof NATO Fails to Protect Serbs," *New York Times*, August 27, 1999.

[28] Richard Gwyn in the *Toronto Star*, November 3, 1999.

[29] *New York Times*, November 11, 1999

[30] Intelligence reports from the German Foreign Office, January 12, 1999 and October 29, 1998 to the German Administrative Courts, translated by Eric Canepa, Brecht Forum, New York, April 20, 1999.

[31] Teach-in, Leo Baeck Temple, Los Angeles, May 23, 1999.

The Racak 'Massacre':

Casus Belli for NATO

DORIS PUMPHREY AND GEORGE PUMPHREY

On January 16, 1999, the US-American head of the OSCE Kosovo Verification Mission (KVM), William Walker and journalists of the international press were led by members of the KLA to a gully at the edge of the village of Racak, where the bodies of some twenty persons were lying. Speaking in emotional terms to international media, Walker immediately accused Serbian security forces of having committed a frightful massacre of ethnic Albanian "unarmed civilians." He declared: "I don't hesitate to accuse the Yugoslav security forces of this crime."

According to the *Berliner Zeitung* (March 24, 2000): "The following day, the OSCE mission summarized in a 'special report' written under Walker's direction that proof of 'arbitrary arrests, killings and mutilation of unarmed civilians' had been found. The report listed details: twenty-three adult men in a gully above Racak, "many shot at extremely close range," another four adult men, who were apparently shot while fleeing, as well as eighteen bodies in the village itself. Among the last group were also a woman and a boy.

President Clinton condemned the "massacre" speaking of "a deliberate and arbitrary act of murder." The German foreign ministry proclaimed: "Those responsible have to know that the international community is not prepared to accept the brutal persecution and murder of civilians in Kosovo." For Joschka Fischer, Racak is a "turning point." NATO immediately convoked an emergency meeting. On January 19, 1999, Madeleine Albright called for bombing Yugoslavia as "punishment."

The Yugoslav government denied the allegation categorically, calling it a manipulation and accusing the KLA of having gathered corpses of their fighters, killed the day before in the battle between the Yugoslav police and KLA terrorists in Racak, and arranging them to resemble a mass execution of civilians.

The "Racak massacre" proved to be the "trigger" event making NATO's war against Yugoslavia appear ineluctable to the general public. *The Washington Post* (April 18, 1999) described Racak as having "transformed the West's Balkan policy as singular events seldom do." However, the facts that have come to light give grounds for a prima facie case that the "massacre of Racak" is a hoax, staged in order to pressure hesitant politicians and the populations of the NATO countries into accepting a war of aggression against Yugoslavia.

The version of events given by Walker, and subsequently broadcast around the world, was that Serbian police and military entered the village, kicked in doors, forced women to remain inside and gathered the men in the village center. They were then marched to the outskirts to a hill where they were systematically executed—shot in the back of the head and neck.

This Walker/KLA version forms the basis of the indictment The Hague Tribunal handed down May 24, 1999, against the government leaders of Yugoslavia. This was during the bombing of Yugoslavia, at a time when European governments were becoming very uncomfortable with the further escalation of the bombing campaign, the indictment appears designed to pressure European governments into accepting further blatant violations of human rights through deliberate targeting of civilians.

Almost immediately this version of events proved to have serious flaws. Doubt was cast that the Serb police had acted as a death squad commando and that the victims had been innocent civilians, and their deaths, executions.

A DEATH SQUAD OPERATION OF THE POLICE?

Only a few days following the incident in Racak the French daily press began publishing information that shed a different light on Walker's version of events.

Le Figaro correspondent Renaud Girard (Jan. 20, 1999) gave the following chronology of events:

> At dawn, intervention forces of the Serbian police [the legal police authority in Kosovo and the rest of Serbia] encircled and then attacked the village of Racak, known as a bastion of KLA (Kosovo Liberation Army) separatist guerrillas.
>
> 8:30 a.m., they invited a television team [two journalists of Associated Press TV working in Kosovo] to film the operation. The OSCE was also notified. Two cars with American diplomatic license plates were

sent to the scene, where observers posted on a hill overlooking the village watched throughout the day.

At 3 p.m., a police communique reached the international press center in Pristina announcing that 15 KLA "terrorists" had been killed in combat in Racak and that a large stock of weapons had been seized.

At 3:30 p.m., the police forces, followed by the AP TV team, left the village, taking with them one heavy 12.7 mm machine gun, two automatic rifles, two rifles with telescopic sights and about thirty kalashnikovs of Chinese fabrication.

At 4:30 p.m., one French journalist drove through the village meeting three orange OSCE vehicles. The international observers were chatting calmly with three middle-aged Albanians in civilian clothes. They were looking for possible civilian casualties.

At 6 p.m., the journalist returned to the village and saw the observers taking two very slightly injured old men and two women away. The observers, who did not seem particularly excited, did not mention any peculiarities to the journalist. They simply said that they were "unable to say what the battle toll had been."

Not until around 9 a.m. the following morning were journalists led by armed KLA soldiers to the scene of Albanian corpses in the ditch. Soon afterward OSCE observers arrived on the scene. At around noon, William Walker in person arrived and expressed his indignation.

Girard reports that "The most disturbing fact is that the pictures filmed by the AP TV journalists—which *Le Figaro* was shown yesterday—radically contradict the Walker/KLA version of events." According to the film:

> Racak had in fact been an empty village [*Le Monde*, Jan. 21, 1999, reported that smoke was rising from only two chimneys, the large majority of the inhabitants of the village having fled Racak during the summer of 1998 during the Serbian offensive] that the police entered in the morning, edging along close to the walls under intense fire coming from trenches dug into the hillside surrounding the village.
>
> The fighting intensified sharply when the security forces reached the hilltops above the village. Watching from below, next to the mosque, the AP camera team understood that the KLA guerrillas were trying desperately to break out of the encirclement. Aproximately twenty of them were able to escape, as the police also admitted.

Girard asks: "Did the KLA intelligently seek to turn a military defeat into a political victory? Could the KLA have gathered the bodies during the night, killed in fact by Serb bullets, to suggest a scene of a cold-blooded massacre?" And notes a disturbing fact: "Saturday morning the journalists found only very few spent cartridges around the ditch where the massacre supposedly took place."

Le Monde's correspondent in Kosovo, Christoph Châtelot, raises the question in his January 21, 1999, report, whether the Walker/KLA massacre version is not a bit too perfect. His own investigation led him to have considerable doubt about William Walker's version. He asks:

> How could the Serb police have assembled a group of men and led them calmly toward the execution site while they were constantly under fire from KLA fighters? How could the ditch located on the edge of Racak have escaped notice by local inhabitants familiar with the surroundings who had returned before nightfall? Or by the OSCE observers who were present for over two hours in this tiny village? Why so few cartridges around the corpses, so little blood where twenty three people are supposed to have been shot at close range with several bullets in the head? Or weren't the bodies of the Albanians killed in combat by the Serb police gathered and put into the ditch to create a horror scene which was sure to have an appalling effect on public opinion?

A Yugoslav press statement adds another detail about further developments following the battle in Racak.

> Immediately after the fighting, the police investigating team came to the scene, headed by Magistrate Danica Marinkovic of the Pristina District Court and the Deputy Public Prosecutor Ismet Sufta, but the KLA who were concentrated in the neighboring hillside opened fire and prevented further on-site investigation. The next day, January 16, 1999, the on-site investigation was again prevented because the OSCE KVM insisted that the investigating magistrate carry out the investigation without police presence, explaining that the fighting might be resumed. (Yugoslav Daily Survey, No. 2008, Belgrade, January 18, 1999)

This was not only a flagrant violation of Yugoslavia's and Serbia's sovereignty but, given the fact that the KLA had already retaken the village of Racak, also a direct threat to the life of the magistrate. But this insured that the scene would not be discovered before it became a scoop for the media.

No report was made of Walker or the KVM making any effort to secure evidence or research the circumstances under which these people died or how their bodies came to be at this site. *Le Figaro* journalist, Renaud Girard, rushed to the scene with the other journalists January 16, and observed Walker in action.

"Walker is a Profi [professional], when it comes to massacres," says Girard. "Every Profi knows what he has to do in such a case: He's supposed to close off the area, so that the evidence can be secured. Walker didn't do anything of the kind. He himself trampled all over the place and let the journalists fumble with the bodies, collecting souvenirs and destroying evidence." (*Berliner Zeitung*, March 24, 2000)

According to journalist reports, Walker spent over half an hour in secret consultations with KLA leaders in Racak, but he never went to the nearby Serbian police station to demand an explanation, the normal procedure for someone seeking to learn what really happened.

THE VICTIMS: 'UNARMED CIVILIANS'?

The OSCE Reports "Kosovo/Kosova: As Seen, As Told" (available at http://www.osce.org/kosovo/reports/hr/part1/p5sti.htm) shed light on the background leading to the police action and on the extent of the civilian nature of the inhabitants of the village of Racak. From a resumé of this report by Diana Johnstone one arrives at the following picture:

> Racak, a village strategically located only half a kilometer south of the crossroads town of Stimlje, where the main road between Kosovo's two main cities, Pristina and Prizren, connects to a southern turnoff to the important town of Urosevac on the road to the Macedonian capital of Skopje, had been abandoned by its 2,000 inhabitants and occupied by only about 350 people. Racak was unquestionably a KLA stronghold when attacked by Serb police on January 15, 1999. The KVM was quite aware of the KLA presence in Racak: "The KLA was there, with a base near the power plant." The village was surrounded by trenches, a common practice of the KLA which turned the villages it occupied into fortresses.
>
> The KVM also knew that the KLA had been carrying out armed ambushes, abductions and murders nearby for several months. "A number of Kosovo Serbs were kidnapped in the Stimlje region, mostly during the summer of 1998," the KVM report notes (p.353). Moreover, the local KLA regularly abducted Kosovo Albanians in an obvious effort to establish the rebels' power over the Albanian community.
>
> A month before the police raid, on December 12, 1998, the KLA "arrested" nine Albanians for various offenses: "prostitution," "friendly relations with Serbs" and "spying." Rather than release them, the KLA told the KVM that the kidnapped civilians were "waiting to be sentenced" and generously granted their families the right to send them gift packages. Subsequently, first six and then two more Albanians were ab-

ducted by the KLA for a total of seventeen missing persons. Little of this information was "newsworthy" for the "Western" media, only on the lookout for "atrocities"—real or imagined—committed by Serbs.

January 8, a KLA armed ambush on police vehicles left three policemen dead and one wounded. Three Kosovo Albanians in a passing taxi were wounded in the same ambush. "The ambush was well prepared: there was a camouflaged firing position for up to fifteen men, which had been occupied for several days, and small arms, heavy machine-guns and rocket-propelled grenades were fired at the police convoy," the KVM reported (p.354).

On January 10, yet another policeman was fatally wounded in an ambush south of Stimlje. It was at this point that the Serbian police prepared their operation against the KLA base in Racak.

During the battle that took place, several KLA fighters were killed. The *Berliner Zeitung* (March 24, 2000) reports:

Already on the morning of January 16, the KLA announced in an initial communique, that eight of its fighters fell in combat around Racak. The names of these casualties do not appear among the names listed by the Tribunal in The Hague. Just as strange: Also on January 16, the KLA gave the names of twenty-two people who had been executed in Racak. Of these only eleven of those listed, appear in the protocol of the Tribunal. Only the number twenty-two comes close to the number of those found on the hill behind Racak. ... KLA leader Hashim Thaci declared recently on the BBC: "We had a key unit in the area. It was a wild battle. We lost a lot of people. But the Serbs did also."

Serbian authorities have always insisted that the dead found in Racak were KLA fighters who were killed in battle. Since the autopsies carried out by a team of Serbian and Belarus pathologists were not considered "sufficiently credible" by western governments and their media, the European Union (EU) called in an "independent" team from Finland, which was accepted by the Yugoslav government.

EXECUTION—OR BATTLEFIELD DEATHS?

The final report of the EU's pathology expert team from Finland, which investigated the causes of death of the bodies found in Racak, was completed at the beginning of March 1999. It would take Helena Ranta, the team's coordinator, another two weeks before she would confront the press.

From information in the *Berliner Zeitung* (March 10, 16, and 19, 1999) and *Die Welt* (March 8, 1999) one can deduce the following picture:

The EU had the publication of the final report postponed repeatedly. March 5 became March 8, the date Ranta said she would submit the report to the German EU Council Presidency and added that "the German Foreign Ministry has taken responsibility for deciding whether the report would be made public or not." A spokesperson for the ministry announced that only after the report had been submitted would "there be further thought about what comes next, how and when it will be made public."

Even though Helena Ranta explained March 2, that no more than three days would be required to wrap up the finishing touches on the report, the March 8 submission of the report was also canceled. Because of "unsolved technical details" the expertise on Racak had to remain in the hands of the team of experts for at least another week, announced the Finnish Foreign Minister, Ms. Tarja Halonen.

According to circles within the OSCE, the Finnish expert report was at first withheld out of deference to the negotiations in Rambouillet. Only after repeated inquiry in Helsinki and Bonn and pressure from within the OSCE, did the German EU presidency concede that the report could be handed over March 17—possibly on the assumption that the Kosovo Conference's second round—originally planned to end by March 15—would in any case be over.

Just before the expert report was to be officially handed over, in an apparent attempt set the tone of the atmosphere, the *Washington Post* reported that the findings confirmed that there had been a massacre in Racak. As the *Berliner Zeitung* (March 19, 1999) observed: "Observers saw in this a direct link to the hard line followed by the U.S. during negotiations in Paris and were reminded of the propagandistic role played by this journal during the preparations of the Gulf War 1991."

"Whether there had been a massacre, no one wants to know anymore" was the German *Die Welt* headline. This was in the article that quoted an OSCE diplomat in Vienna as saying: "This report is a hot potato no one wants to touch." The head of the OSCE mission, William Walker, had again in February 1999 repeated, "It will be confirmed that there had been a massacre committed by the Serbs."

March 13, 1999, the *Berliner Zeitung* titled its article "OSCE representatives prove Walker wrong" and reported:

> The head of the OSCE Verification Mission in Kosovo, the U.S. American, William Walker, should be replaced as soon as possible—according to the wishes of several European states. As the *Berliner Zeitung* learned from OSCE sources in Vienna during the period leading up to the negotiations, Germany, Italy and Austria had demanded that Walker step down. According to these sources, high ranking European OSCE representatives have the evidence that the forty-five Albanians found in Racak in mid-January were not civilian victims of a Serbian massacre, as Walker alleges.

According to the OSCE, inside the organization it has been long since taken for granted that Racak "was a hoax set up by the Albanian side." This conclusion was reached through the examination of data from the communication center of the Kosovo Mission, in other words independently from the awaited expertise of Ms. Ranta's team of experts. "Most of the dead were gathered from a wide radius around Racak and relocated where they were later found." Most of the Albanians died in combat under fire from Serbian artillery. Many were "subsequently dressed in civilian clothes" according to a representative of the OSCE.

This evidence coincides with the Serbian version of events in Racak: that the Albanians were killed in combat between the KLA and Serbian units, and the scene of a massacre arranged afterward by the Albanians.

Right up to the end, Helena Ranta did not know if the results of her team's investigation would be made public, "The decision will be made at the last minute when we see what happens at the Kosovo Negotiations in Paris."

From the time Helena Ranta took on the job as head of the expert team, she was repeatedly under pressure, particularly from the German government, whose representative was acting president of the EU Council. Even at the March 17, 1999, press conference in Pristina, where the findings of the Finnish team were supposed to be transmitted to the German presidency of the EU Council and the Serbian Circuit Court, she had to follow the German ambassador's instructions when she answered journalist's questions. (*Berliner Zeitung*, March 18, 1999)

At the March 17 press conference, a written press statement was distributed that had been prepared by the German foreign ministry's press department in Bonn. The five-page statement announced that Dr. Ranta would transmit the Finnish forensic team's final report to the relevant Serbian officials the same day. The rest of the five pages are comments introduced as follows: "These comments are based upon the investigation of the EU team's forensic expert in Pristina, as approved by the Circuit Court of Pristina in accordance with the Yugoslav penal process standards. (...) The comments reflect the personal opinion of the author, Dr. Helena Ranta and do not represent an authorized statement from the Pathological Medicine section of the Helsinki University or the EU forensic experts."

These comments and the answers given by Helena Ranta during the press conference in Pristina, were kept so vague in the decisive points that no clear-cut conclusions could be arrived at. She declared, for example, that "the garments most probably had neither been changed nor removed" in response to the inquiry as to whether a number of the dead had not been originally wearing KLA uniforms, as the Serbian side claims. Just as inconclusive is the time of the victims' death. According to Ranta, "at best, it could be ascertained that the victims appear to have died at around the same time.

If it was a massacre, Helena Ranta does not want to answer, because "such a conclusion is not within the EU pathological team's competence. But she refuted the *Washington Post's* article, according to which the results of their investigation confirm that a massacre had taken place in Racak. Under pressure of persistent interrogation, she called the dead of Racak victims of a "crime against humanity." She did not want to exclude the possibility that the dead were inhabitants of Racak, who could have gotten caught in a cross fire between Serbian units and the KLA. Ranta also did not contradict the Yugoslavian and Belarus pathological experts, whose findings concluded that the victims had not been shot at close range.

The pathologist Branimir Aleksandric, at the University in Belgrade, stated after Helena Ranta's press conference that she had only spoken in her name as a private person and had not reflected the views of the Finnish team, led by the world renowned pathologist Antti Penttilä. From the medical standpoint, her answers were kept so vague that one could surmise that she wanted to avoid contradicting William Walker and those who pull his strings.

Her answers show also that she does not know about gunshot wounds. "She is a dentist by profession. Her expertise in forensic medicine is limited to identification. She is not competent therefore to give an opinion on the mechanics of inflicting injuries, which is what the Yugoslav, Belarus and Finnish pathologists were entrusted with doing in their medical examination of the Racak bodies." Her comments and answers along with the fact that her name was missing on the forty individual findings of the Finnish team shows that there is a gulf between the professional and the political in the Finnish team. (*Tanjug*, March 8, 1999)

Yugoslav and Belarus pathologists had already published the results of their investigations in February. These were carried out in accord with the Finnish pathologists, even though at the time the Finns did not sign these reports. To consider the refusal of the Finnish experts' signatures as resulting from a difference of opinion was repudiated by Helena Ranta, who insisted that on the professional level there was no problem in cooperation and that all had agreed on common methods and procedures. The difference lay apparently only in the time that the documents were signed. The Finnish team did not want to sign solely on the basis of the autopsy, but wanted first to submit the data to a comprehensive evaluation at the Section of Pathological Medicine at Helsinki University before signing.

A comparison of the findings performed by the Yugoslav/Belarus pathologists and those done by the Finnish pathologists shows no contradictions to one another. (Both autopsy reports are at our disposal.)

The following is a summary of the autopsy reports:

• The corpses show essentially no wounds other than gunshot wounds (some slight scratches and bruises etc.—only one elderly male showed traces of a violent blow to the face with a blunt instrument)

• Three corpses had been bitten postmortem by animals (on the head and neck)

• Gunshot wounds were the cause of death in all cases

• Both teams conclude: there is no evidence of wounds caused by contact discharge or close-range firing (only one corpse showed the possibility that one of two gunshot wounds could have been inflicted at a relatively close distance)

• In the reports of the Finnish team is repeated for each case: "Based on the verified autopsy of [classification number], the categorization of manner of death, as recommended by the World Health Organization, could not be determined. On the basis of external findings, the applicable alternatives are criminal homicide, war, or inconclusive."

- None of the findings showed evidence of an execution.

Strikingly, there was no mention of the results of examinations for traces of powder on the hands of the corpses. This would have furnished essential evidence about whether the victims were unarmed civilians, as The Hague indictment claims, or KLA guerrillas, who had recently fired a weapon before their death, in other words whether it was an execution or battlefield deaths. To this question posed by the *Berliner Zeitung* (March 24, 2000), Helena Ranta responded that the Finnish team had not even examined the hands for traces of powder.

The KVM Report refers repeatedly to Racak as the decisive event that determined the attitude of the "international community," but unlike William Walker, the report admits that the event in Racak remains a mystery. Five months following NATO's first attempt to destroy Yugoslavia, the *Berliner Zeitung* explains under the headlines: OSCE will re-open the case of Racak; European Union report about the tragedy remains secret (January 15, 2000):

The Organization for Security and Cooperation in Europe (OSCE) will again occupy itself with the case of the corpses found in the Kosovo village of Racak in January 1999. This was announced in Vienna by the new OSCE Chairman, Austria's Foreign Minister, Wolfgang Schuessel, in answer to a question posed by Willy Wimmer, Vice President of the OSCE Parliamentary Assembly. Wimmer raised the question before the Assembly's Standing Committee, where he referred to media reports concerning the Finnish Pathologist, Helena Ranta's return to Racak for new investigations, months following her having submitted her findings to the European Union—which are still being kept secret. Wimmer stressed the necessity for comprehensive clarity in the affair, in view of what a significance the discovery of the corpses in Racak had had for the further developments leading up to the Kosovo War. Schuessel promised to "examine the case."

The exact text of the final report, terminated in March 1999, has yet to be rendered public inside the EU. Germany's foreign ministry has placed this report, made to inform the European Union, under the stipulations of the German Archive Law to keep the findings secret even from the other member states of the European Union.

Yugoslavia, frustrated with the attitude of the OSCE mission, had begun to reinforce the troops on the ground in late 1998 and January 1999—in violation of the accords. The *Washington Post* (April 18, 1999) reported that Clinton's advisors had seen at that time no possibility of using this fact to mobilize the allies. "You're not going to get people to bomb over the specific number of troops."

The *Washington Post* explains that Ms. Albright realized that the galvanizing force of the atrocity would not last long. "Whatever threat of force you don't get in the next two weeks you're never getting," one adviser told her, "at least until the next Racak."

Madeleine Albright got what she wanted. The consequences will be felt for generations to come.

The skepticism concerning the "massacre" version became irrelevant in the rapidly changing events leading to a war, long since planned and prepared. Even though it should have been clear that Racak was needed to justify this aggression, there was no one on the political level willing to publicly demand a closer investigation—before NATO could start a war. The Walker/KLA version was allowed to predominate. This version prepared the next stage: the Rambouillet ultimatum.

Scharping's Lies Won't Last

THOMAS DEICHMANN

For the German political elite, the war against Yugoslavia signaled an important break with the past, as moral and political renunciation of militarism had characterized political culture in Germany for more than half a century since the end of World War II. Accepting a call to arms still was no routine occurance, especially since the attack was directed against a country that had suffered immensely from the brutal onslaught of German fascism sixty years ago. That this military campaign took place in violation of international law and the German constitution, both regulative foundations formulated in response to the crimes of Nazism, complicated matters even further. Moreover, the first marching orders for German soldiers came from parties commonly identified with the liberal traditions of the Federal Republic of Germany. The Social Democrat Rudolf Scharping and Green Party Foreign Minister Joschka Fischer took on the task of justifying German participation in this war of aggression. During the Bosnian war, Fischer, while still in the opposition, had argued against sending German troops into the Balkans, precisely by reference to the Holocaust.

The German Social Democratic Party (SPD) had fewer problems with pacifist attitudes in its ranks. It faced a different problem. After the German general elections in fall 1998, when the SPD and the Green Party (Buendnis'90/Die Gruenen) were setting out with their new coalition government, they were under harsh criticism. It became clear soon that the hype of the election campaign in 1998 had concealed a rather fumbling bunch of Chancellor Gerhard Schroeder's new government leaders. The war against Yugoslavia offered the government an ideal opportunity to leave its domestic problems behind and emerge with a new image. Certainly, the decision to enter the war was not made just with this goal in mind, but the disastrous condition of Schroeder's team was an important underlying consideration during the deliberations about the deployment of the Bundeswehr—the German armed forces.

This background led to overreactions that often not merely bordered fanaticism. The rhetoric of the Holocaust was deployed in Germany more than in any other Western country to endow the NATO attack on Serbia and German participation in it with moral legitimacy. Scharping followed up one horror-story with another and constructed countless false analogies between Serbia and the Third Reich.

A massive public relations campaign prepared and accompanied the German armed forces" participation in the NATO campaign. German Defense Minister Scharping became the tireless prime mover of this German war propaganda. His book *Wir duerfen nicht wegsehen. Der Kosovo-Krieg und Europa (We cannot look away. The Kosovo War and Europe,* 1999), which was published a few months after the conflict, quite openly discloses the scale of the lies and deception Scharping employed to justify the military campaign against Yugoslavia. For example, we find the following account in Scharping's 270-page work:

> Shall we overlook all the slaughter that is happening there? Are all the stories that people tell us no more than invention and propaganda: that corpses are destroyed with baseball-bats and that their limbs or heads are cut off? ... it seems that human beings in a frenzy can commit any bestiality, playing soccer with heads that were cut off, tearing apart corpses, cutting fetuses out of the womb of women who were killed. (p.125)

Many reports Scharping presented in this context even during the war could not stand up to scrutiny. Many allegations were, sooner or later, unmasked either as misrepresentation or attempts at manipulation – yet they are included in his book without the slightest amendment or qualification.

1. CONCENTRATION CAMPS IN PRISTINA

> Allegedly, Albanians are held in the stadium of Pristina. Parts of the stadium have a basement. There are several small shops below the spectator stands, which offer space for several thousand people. The first Albanians were reportedly brought into the stadium on April 1. (Entry of April 19, 1999, p.128)

At the outset of the war, Scharping mentions "serious evidence of concentration camps in Kosovo." He adds: "I say concentration camp on purpose." Scharping claims that the soccer-stadium of Pristina was converted into a Serb-run concentration camp holding 100,000 people. This claim originated from the KLA (as did the report that influential Kosovo-Albanian intellectuals were systematically killed by the Serb military). Scharping nonetheless treated it as though it were indisputable fact. Yet some days later, several persons who had allegedly been killed, reappeared. Pictures taken from German surveillance planes refute the claim that a concentration camp existed in the stadium of Pristina. Still, there were no retractions, and concentration camp stories continued to circulate.

2. OPERATION HORSESHOE

> From Joschka [J. Fischer, German Foreign Minister] I receive a paper that stems from intelligence sources and proves that "Operation Horseshoe' was prepared and executed by the Yugoslav Army... An evaluation of the operation-plan 'Horseshoe' exists. Now we have proof that a systematic cleansing of Kosovo and the deportation of the Kosovo-Albanians were already planned in December 1998. (Entries of April 5 and 7, 1999, pp.102 & 107)

While other German politicians showed some restraint in using the term *"genocide"* in relation to events in Kosovo, Scharping continues to repeat his thesis that a genocide in Kosovo was *"not only prepared,"* but systematically planned, and *"in fact is already happening"* (p.84). To support these claims, he presents dubious documents about an operation-plan allegedly named *"Horseshoe"* in early April, claiming that operation maps would prove that genocidal plans for the ethnic cleansing of Kosovo already existed in 1998 and were now awaiting final execution.

Some months later it was revealed that these documents were false. According to press reports they came from the German and the Austrian Secret Services. It is striking that Scharping's propaganda experts used the Croatian translation of the word *"horseshoe,"* which is Potkova, instead of its Serbian translation Potkovica, indicating that its source was not Serbian at all.

Yet in spring 2000 Mr. Scharping still insists on the authenticity of the documents in question and proudly explains to the press that he passed all evidence in his possession to the United Nations International War Crimes Tribunal (ICTY) in The Hague for use by the prosecution. But the ICTY stated in response to media inquiries that it would not allow Mr. Scharping's *"Operation Horseshoe"* documents as evidence, because of their unclear sources.

3. KILLING FIELDS AND MOUNTAINS OF CORPSES

> The brutality escalates, the refugees literally walk along mountains
> of corpses. An old fear comes to my mind: This criminal wants a cease-
> fire in the graveyard. (Entry of April 29, 1999, p.141)

The warring NATO-countries justify the ongoing bombing campaign
with the claim that it would stop "ethnic cleansing" in Kosovo. NATO
speaker Jamie Shea compares Kosovo with the "Killing Fields" of
Cambodia, and Mr. Scharping speaks of "mountains of corpses." Estimates of the numbers of Kosovo-Albanians allegedly killed and buried
in mass graves by Serbian soldiers increases continuously. In early
April, the U.S.-State Department puts out the figure of 500,000. On
April 18, David Scheffer, U.S.-Ambassador for War Crimes, says that
possibly up to 100,000 Albanians were killed. On the next day, James
Rubin, the spokesperson for the State Department, repeats this speculative number: "Based on past practice, it is chilling to think where those
100,000 men are." One month later, Defense Secretary William S.
Cohen guesses: "We've now seen about 100.000 military-aged men
missing... They may have been murdered" (*Washington Post*, May 17,
1999). At the end of the war, in early June, the number of alleged Kosovo-Albanian victims killed is drastically reduced to 10,000.

Immediately after NATO occupied Kosovo, approximately twenty
teams with experts from fifteen countries enter Kosovo on the orders of
the International Criminal Tribunal on the Former Yugoslavia to search
for mass graves. The teams numbered 500 experts altogether, including
some FBI officials. Indeed, hundreds of corpses are exhumed in a few
weeks. This seems to affirm the horrific expectations of genocide on a
mass scale. Yet the "success stories" come to an end soon. The FBI in-
vestigates in the British sector and finds no more than 200 corpses.

Finally, in the fall of 1999, a first report from the Chief Prosecutor of
the UN-Tribunal, Carla Del Ponte, reveals that the numbers given by
Western governments were gross exaggerations. The accusation that the
Serb military carried out genocide now appears to be sheer war propaganda. Of the 529 locations, where mass graves were suspected (according to witnesses), 195 were investigated between June and October
1999. The inspectors were ordered to start in those locations where the
investigations promised to be most successful. But by October, only

2,108 corpses were exhumed – they were mainly found in individual graves.

The UN investigators did not offer any information about age, sex, nationality, or probable time of death of these persons, among whom one suspects Kosovo-Albanian and Serb fighters as well as civilians from both sides. How many of these dead may have been killed by the NATO bombings was also not addressed. Del Ponte maintains, however, that many presumed gravesites were tampered with, and she speculates that there may still be as many as 10,000 victims. Further investigations during the year 2000 are supposed to prove this. But again this remains pure propaganda.

4. MASS GRAVES

> Our inquiry teams had learned that up to 200 persons were killed in the village of Izbica and buried. Soon afterwards, we had pictures that clearly showed fresh grave sites in Izbica as well as in the neighboring village of Krasnika. (Entry of May 25, 1999, p.182)

Scharping's claim is based on a report of the U.S. State Department, published on May 10, 1999, with the title "Erasing History: Ethnic Cleansing in Kosovo." Secretary of State Madeleine Albright says during its presentation that it proves "without any doubt" the existence of a horrible system of war crimes and crimes against humanity," including "systematic executions" and "organized rape." The report says that approximately ninety percent of Kosovo-Albanians were driven from their homes, a claim that was later exposed as a blatant lie. Moreover, it is said that approximately 150 Albanians were killed in Izbica. Satellite images, which are designed to prove a change in the surface of the soil, are presented and put onto the Internet. After the war ended, UN investigators find no corpses at the presumed grave-site near Izbica (*The Spectator*, November 20, 1999). However, they find evidence that allegedly points to the removal of signs of a mass grave by Serb security forces.

While it remains unclear whether there ever was a mass grave on the field near Izbica, other investigations at other sites have shown that similar claims were pure war propaganda. Immediately after the war, NATO officials referred to Ljubenic near Pec as the site of one of the largest mass graves. They state that retreating Serb units had buried 350 corpses there in a hurry. UN investigators go to the place and find exactly seven corpses (*Toronto Sun,* November 18, 1999). Moreover, the KLA also reports a huge mass grave in the Trepca mines, claiming that in one oven up to 100 persons were burned daily and the ashes thrown into the mine corridors. Approximately 6,000 Kosovo-Albanians allegedly lost their lives in the process. After the war ended, investigators expected to find at least the remains of 700 persons in the mine. In October, Kelly Moore, a speaker of The Hague Tribunal, reports that the investigators had "found absolutely nothing" (*New York Times,* October 13, 1999).

Emilio Perez Pujol, member of a Spanish team of pathologists, already made the following skeptical comments in September: "I calculate that the final figure of dead in Kosovo will be 2,500 at the most. This includes lots of mysterious deaths that can't be blamed on anyone in particular." The Spanish team was warned that it was going into the "worst zone of Kosovo," Istok. But at the end of their investigations, the pathologists had found 187 bodies. They do not find mass graves (*El Pais,* September 23, 1999).

5. SYSTEMATIC RAPE

> Satellite images show mass graves; women report to the OSCE about systematic rape; the UNHCR receives information about young women and men who are abused as human shields for an ammunition depot in Prizren. (Entry of April 27, 1999, p.137).

Scharping and his colleagues repeatedly mention reports of mass rape in Kosovo. Pictures of refugee convoys and comments by refugees are shown or presented almost daily in order to create moral concern among the population and to drown out discussion about the goals and legitimacy of the NATO war. Certainly, atrocities occurred during the war, but it is equally clear that corresponding information and speculation is used for propaganda purposes.

The situation in the camps is also described with distortions. Reinhard Munz, a German physician who worked in the Macedonian refugee camp Stenkovac, concludes in an interview: "The refugees were used for political reasons." He points out that "men of fighting age were the majority in our camp." This contradicts allegations by Scharping and others that children, women, and elderly lived in the camps, whereas masses of potential male fighters were victims of Serb soldiers. In reply to a question about the evidence of rape, Munz says: "During the whole time, we encountered no single case of a women who was raped. And we looked at 60,000 persons in Stenkovac I and II, as well as two smaller camps. Due to the rumors about systematic rape, we wondered in advance what to do about the raped women, but this situation did not arise. We have heard of no cases of rape, which of course does not mean that there were none at all." (*Die Welt*, June 18, 1999)

6. MASSACRE IN ROGOVO

> I feel sick when I look at these pictures... During the daily press conference I announce: "We will present to you pictures of a massacre that had already occurred on January 29, 1999 ... I advise you, however, to come well prepared, since these are original photographs taken by an OSCE observer. ... You will clearly see what was going on already in January." (Entry April 25 and 26, 1999, pp.132 and 136)

During a press conference on April 27, 1999, Scharping presents photographs of corpses to substantiate his claim that the Serbs had already committed massacres of civilians and begun systematic deportations of Kosovo-Albanians in January 1999. But journalists immediately recognized the pictures and replied that OSCE inspectors had already used them to refer, not to a massacre, but to combat between Serb soldiers and the KLA. When Scharping is confronted with these facts again during in a TV broadcast, he takes recourse to further speculation – allegedly, the skulls of the corpses were demolished with baseball bats (Bericht aus Berlin, April 30, 1999). Highly indignant, Scharping rejects all criticism of his behavior.

7. COLLATERAL DAMAGE

> The Serb media immediately use these tragic mistakes for their own propaganda, as proof of wanton destruction and deliberate attacks on the civilian population. Our media also spread these reports. (Entry April 6, 1999, p.192)

This is Scharping's entry, after a rocket had exploded in a residential neighborhood in the town of Aleksinac on April 5. Seventeen people had died. Later, "deliberate attacks" against civilians occur, for example, when the Radio and TV Station RTS, the Chinese Embassy, and the town of Korisa are attacked: On May 14, NATO airplanes fire ten bombs into the village Korisa in Kosovo, killing at least eighty-seven civilians. On the same day, NATO spokesperson Jamie Shea announces on BBC: "We have reports that soldiers died as well, not only civilians." During a press conference the following day, the German NATO General Walter Jertz insists that Korisa was a legitimate target, since there had also been military installations there.

Western information strategists manipulated so-called "collateral damage" evidence for their own propaganda, too. This becomes clear after a rocket-attack on April 12: During two subsequent sorties, a NATO fighter fired a rocket against a train as the train crossed a bridge near Grdelica. Two carriages are hit, at least twelve people die, and many more are wounded. On April 13, General Wesley Clark, the NATO Supreme Commander in Europe, speaks of a "freakish coincidence." At the end of the conference, he presents the cockpit-video of the plane, in order to emphasize that the pilot allegedly had no choice: "Look carefully at the target, concentrate on it, and you can see, if you focus like a pilot, that suddenly this train appeared."

In January 2000, it is revealed in Germany that NATO experts manipulated the tape before it was shown and thus deceived the international public. The tape was running five times faster than the real events, which gave the false impression that the train raced toward the bridge and the pilot could not detect it (Frankfurter Rundschau, January 20, 2000). NATO-speakers excused this as a "technical problem."

8. ROCKETS HIT REFUGEES

A convoy is hit near Djakovica, killing many people. It remains uncertain for days whether it was a civilian or a military convoy, whether the Serb military misused a civilian convoy as a shield, and whether it was a NATO attack at all. ... The probability that NATO pilots tragically mistook a group of refugees for a military convoy was another sad example that war without sacrifices among the civilian population does not exist. (Entry of April 14, 1999, p.121)

The rocket attack on the refugee convoy near Djakovica occurs on April 14. More than seventy people are killed. For days, Defense Minister Scharping and NATO speakers cast doubts on the NATO origin of the attack. Later, the event is excused with the high altitude of the plane and the pilot's confusion of "tractor-like vehicles" with Serb military vehicles. A few weeks later, the U.S.-based International Strategic Studies Association publishes the voice traffic between the USAF F-16 strike aircraft and his EC-130 Hercules AWACS:

> Pilot: Charlie Bravo to Mother. I am coming out of the clouds, still nothing in sight.
> AWACS: Mother to Charlie Bravo. Continue to the north, course 280.
> Pilot: Charlie Bravo to Mother. I am keeping 3,000 feet. Under me columns of cars, some kind of tractors. What is it? Requesting instructions.
> AWACS: Mother to Charlie Bravo. Do you see tanks? Repeat, where are the tanks?
> Pilot: Charlie Bravo to Mother. I see tractors. I suppose the Reds did not camouflage tanks as tractors.
> AWACS: Mother to Charlie Bravo. What kind of strange convoy is this? What, civilians? Damn, this is all the Serb's doing. Destroy the target.
> Pilot: Charlie Bravo to Mother. What should I destroy? Tractors? Ordinary cars? Repeat, I don't see any tanks. Request additional instructions.
> AWACS: Mother to Charlie Bravo. This is a military target, a completely legitimate military target. Destroy the target. Repeat, destroy the target.
> Pilot: Charlie Bravo to Mother. OK, copy. Launching. *(Defense & Foreign Affairs Strategic Policy,* Number 3, 1999)

The authenticity of this transcript of the mission radio traffic remains a matter of debate. But the statement of a Spanish F-18 pilot after he returned from the war at the end of May is clear proof that civilians were targeted deliberately. The pilot claims that he and his colleagues repeatedly received orders to attack civilian installations: "Our colonel went to his NATO heads several times and protested against the choice of targets that were not of a military nature. ... Once we received an encoded order from U.S. military officials to drop anti-personnel bombs over the towns of Pristina and Nis. Our colonel refused the order, and a few days later he was deposed" (*Articulo* 20, June 14, 1999).

The facts speak for themselves. During the war, thousands of anti-personnel bombs – so-called cluster-bombs against "soft targets" – were dropped on military as well as civilian installations in Serbia. For example, on May 7, two of them explode in Nis, killing thirteen civilians and wounding twenty-nine, some of them critically.

9. THE BOMBING OF RTS IN BELGRADE

> I am not satisfied with NATO's information policy. The information itself is reliable, but it comes much too late and allows too much time in between for speculation and disinformation. Why is it not possible to disseminate information in Brussels early in the morning, in order to counter images of Yugoslav TV? (Entry of April 4, 1999, p.99)

Evidently, other NATO officials shared Scharping's displeasure and did something about it. In the early morning hours of April 23, the central station of the Serb TV station RTS, located in the city center of Belgrade, is attacked. Sixteen journalists and technicians are torn to pieces, many more are wounded. At the same time, bombing raids on antennas and transmitter stations in the whole of Serbia increase from mid-April onwards, and in May satellite broadcasting by Yugoslav stations to Western Europe is interrupted. After the war, it is revealed that the attack on RTS was planned long in advance. During the *"NewsWorld"* media conference in Barcelona in October 1999, the head of CNN International, Easton Jordan, explains that he was informed about the imminent attack. He protested, and the NATO jets hence veered away during their first sortie (*Daily Telegraph*, November 7, 1999). Two days later, the attack is carried out, at a time when there were no foreign journalists in the RTS building and the CNN crew had removed its equipment to safety. Before the attack, the Serbian minister of information, Aleksandar Vucic, is invited into the RTS building for an interview during the live broadcast of a U.S. station. According to his own remarks, he escaped the attack only because he was late (*Le Monde,* August 13, 1999).

10. THE TARGETING OF THE CHINESE EMBASSY

> What a terrible disaster ... It will create great political difficulties, not only in terms of public opinion and growing impatience and uncertainties; this terrible mistake also threatens to ruin our political efforts. (Entry of May 8, 1999, p.154)

Scharping is worried after three rockets had hit the Chinese Embassy in the center of Belgrade on May 7. Three Chinese journalists are killed, and many officials are wounded severely. Scharping talks about *"imprecise target coordination"* and *"deficiencies of the information provided by intelligence services."* Months later, it is revealed that the CIA was responsible for the targeting process and that the building was not mistakenly hit. It is presumed that the embassy building was used to communicate intelligence information to the Serb military and that this was the reason for NATO's attack (*Der Spiegel*, 2/2000).

11. DEFENSE OF HUMAN RIGHTS

> Finally, we are not the aggressors, as we were so often before 1945, but we defend human rights. For the first time, the Germans are acting in cooperation with all Europeans, instead of against them. For the first time, the goal is not subjugation but human rights and their enforcement. (Entry of April 11, 1999, p.114)

Scharping's heroic justification of the German military campaign between March and June 1999 reiterates the delusion that motivated him before and during the war. On the eve of March 24, 1999, the opposite of Scharping's promise becomes reality within hours. With the start of the bombing campaign, the situation dramatically worsens – also for Kosovo-Albanian civilians. Members of aid organizations note that the NATO bombings led to the massive exodus from Kosovo. In the wake of the bombings, the conflict between Serb soldiers and the KLA escalates. Moreover, thousands of people from all ethnic groups flee their homes, because the ongoing air strikes make them fear for their life. An OSCE-report entitled "Kosovo/Kosova: As Seen, As Told," published on December 6, 1999, indicates that attacks against Kosovo-Albanians do occur, but the vast majority of them took place only after the NATO war began. Thanks to the NATO war, the basis for a peaceful life of the different groups in Kosovo, which was weak and previously damaged anyway, is destroyed for years, if not decades.

(Translated from German by Matthias Gockel.)

The U.S. Prison House

MONICA MOOREHEAD

The author gave this talk in New York at the June 10, 2000, International Tribunal for U.S./NATO War Crimes in Yugoslavia

The U.S. is the biggest human rights violator in the world. I stand before this tribunal to talk about another kind of war being waged by the same bloodthirsty ruling class that financed the war against the Yugoslav peoples. In this particular war, the victims are the poor and the oppressed inside the U.S.

This war takes the form of the fastest growing profitable sector of the U.S. economy — the prison industrial complex. There are presently two million people imprisoned in local, state and federal prisons—the figure is really about five million people trapped in the vicious cycle of the criminal justice system. This expanding sweatshop industry has become the second largest employer in the country with 523,000 employees—second only to General Motors. The value of goods produced by prison slave labor is well over $1 billion annually.

By the end of this year, $41 billion will have been invested by Wall Street into building more private prisons to help house twenty-five percent of the world's incarcerated. Since 1996, the U.S. government has spent more money to build prisons than universities. Working class and poor youth will have a greater chance of being "educated" inside of the walls than in a college.

The prison industrial complex is an outgrowth of "competitive globalization" that has deepened racist and class oppression.

The U.S. has executed more people, including juveniles, than any other industrialized country. The International Covenant on Civil and Political Rights states, "sentence of death shall not be imposed for crimes committed by persons below 18 years old." The Convention on the Rights of the Child includes the same stipulation, but the U.S. has refused to sign it. Almost half of the U.S. states, twenty-four, permit the execution of juveniles.

There are over 3,600 people on death row in the U.S. The majority of them are Black and Latino and a greater majority of them are poor.

Black and white people in the U.S. are murder victims in almost equal numbers but only five or six white people have been executed for killing a Black person while eighty-two percent of those executed were convicted of killing whites since the death penalty was reinstituted in 1977.

The application of the death penalty has nothing to do with fighting crime and everything to do with repression and super-exploitation. The federal prison population is expected to increase by fifty percent by the year 2006, from 130,000 to 200,000, due to the severity of prison sentences for non-violent drug convictions (including single mothers with children), the elimination of parole at the federal level, and the lack of drug rehabilitation. All of this means more cheap labor to super-exploit.

Sisters and brothers, there is a growing debate in this country over the use of the death penalty. Much of that debate is centered on the wrongfully convicted being executed. Many of those wrongfully convicted are political prisoners. Mumia Abu-Jamal is the most famous death row prisoner who is a revolutionary. Millions of people worldwide including inside the U.S. are demanding a new trial for Mumia in order to prove his innocence.

Even while fighting for his life, Mumia Abu Jamal made the following statement condemning the U.S. war on Yugoslavia.

From Death Row:

'NATO/U.S. Out of Yugoslavia!'

MUMIA ABU-JAMAL (APRIL 1999)

As a deadly rain of high-tech bombs falls on Yugoslavia, a deadening rain of propaganda falls on Americans—media-manipulated lies designed to prime the populace into supporting harsher military measures against a sovereign nation, in the name of protecting human rights.

NATO is but a fig leaf for American "interests," and the bombing of Yugoslavia is but a global demonstration of the ruthlessness of the American empire. A demonstration? The monstrous atomic bombing of Japan, after it was virtually beaten in World War II, was not a military necessity, but a political one, designed to demonstrate to the Russians that the U.S. was, and would ever be, boss. It was a massive, deadly demonstration.

So too, the Yugoslavia bombing treats Serbs as the U.S. treated Japanese during the war—as props to demonstrate the power of the empire.

Let us consider the claims that the U.S. is concerned about "human rights" or about the "rights of ethnic minorities," as the corporate press projects hourly. What of America's largest national minority—African Americans? The world-respected Amnesty International group, speaking through its secretary general, Pierre Sané, announced just days before the bombing, "Human-rights violations in the United States of America are persistent, widespread and appear to disproportionately affect people of racial or ethnic minority backgrounds."

Sané was critical of police violence and executions in the U.S. Further, internationally, let's see how the U.S. responds to "liberation movements" of the oppressed. When fighters for Puerto Rican independence began to raise their voices, the U.S. didn't support this "ethnic minority," they sought (and continue) to crush, incarcerate and silence them.

Consider the case of the Palestinians, the Kurds, the East Timorese, the Colombian rebels—who has the U.S. consistently supported, the oppressed or the U.S.-armed governments?

This isn't about "human rights." It isn't about "ethnic minorities." And it also isn't about "genocide." It's about establishing who's "boss" in the next century. It's about keeping Russia in its place. It's about keeping the European Union under the thumb of Wall Street.

The bombing of Serbia is an echo of the bombing of three other countries in the past six months—of Iraq, Sudan and Afghanistan. And for precisely the same reason—to show that it can be done, no matter what so-called "international law" states. It is to instill terror through out the world, in order for U.S. capital to institute what former President George Bush tried to do, but failed: to establish a New World Order.

Days before the bombing, NATO signed up Poland, Hungary and the Czech Republic as its newest members, thereby virtually isolating Russia. Only Serbia and the Yugoslav state have refused to join NATO—their bombing is their punishment.

Our brilliant, revered nationalist leader, Malcolm X, taught us to examine history. If we look at history, the bombing of Yugoslavia becomes clear.

Empires are maintained, not by reason, but by ruthless terror. It was so in Rome. It is so in the U.S. The brilliant revolutionary, Dr. Huey P. Newton, founder of the Black Panther Party, explained: "The United States was no longer a nation. ... We called it an empire. ... An empire is a nation-state that has transformed itself into a power controlling all the world's lands and people." (1973)

Huey was right then, and our response then was to oppose the empire. We must do that now.

Down with imperialism! Stop the bombing! NATO/U.S. out of Yugoslavia!

III. PHOTO SECTION
Introduction:
NATO Is Guilty of War Crimes

ELMAR SCHMAEHLING

Admiral Elmar Schmaehling's talk at the International Tribunal on U.S./NATO War Crimes against Yugoslavia in New York, June 10, 2000, is an extremely suitable introduction to this section—the editors.

May I introduce myself: I am a former rear admiral of the German navy. In 1990 I was dismissed after I had expressed my opposing views on NATO's nuclear strategy of first use and the irresponsible arms race between NATO and Warsaw Treaty Organization.

Since then I have been cooperating with peace and antimilitarist organizations nationally and internationally.

After the fall of the wall I observed and criticized the continuous change of NATO from a defense alliance to the offensive military arm of an aggressive type of Western capitalism. Its new strategic concept issued on April 24, 1999 stipulates these new terms of reference.

Within a militarized European Union, Germany's armed forces are taking the same path, from territorial defense only towards intervention. This means indeed a dramatic cut into Germany's after World War II tradition of a culture of peace.

The illegal war waged last year by U.S./NATO against the sovereign state Yugoslavia was the test for the U.S./Western Europe desired new world order.

When I studied and analyzed the course of actions during this war and its effects it became clear to me: NATO's heads of states and governments and the military leaders involved had deliberately pushed aside the customs and laws of war. They wanted to hit and destroy Yugoslav society in total by hitting and destroying the most important components of the civilian infrastructure and bases for life.

In order to hide their breaking of the humanitarian law they invented new terms unknown to the text of the law. They called civilian objects "high value targets" or "strategic targets" and defended their forbidden attacks as "legitimate". But the law does not foresee a third category "legitimate" besides "legal" and "illegal" when qualifying attacks during an armed conflict.

In the course of three visits to Yugoslavia I undertook as member of the preparatory committee for the European tribunal I had the opportunity of visiting target locations and talking to victims and eyewitnesses of attacks.

My statement before this court is the following:

All attacked civilian objects under scrutiny like the RTS-building, the USCE office-building in Belgrade, the heating plant in Novi Beograd and the chemical plants in Pancevo had no military function. They were civilian objects protected by the IV the Geneva Convention, 1949 and its additional protocol I.

The people killed or wounded during these illegal attacks were civilians also protected by the aforementioned humanitarian law.

By explicitly and systematically not only violating but even neglecting international humanitarian law NATO reintroduced medieval cruelty, inhumanity and the law of jungle into international relationship.

If not stopped this will change the world into a very unstable and dangerous place with new rounds of arms race, new and more dangerous weapons, even weapons of mass destruction, more terrorism, more hatred and mistrust.

The lesson to be learnt must be:

Stop this dangerous, inhumane and stupid avenue of U.S., NATO and European Union.

Abolish the criminal gang NATO.

Targeting civilians

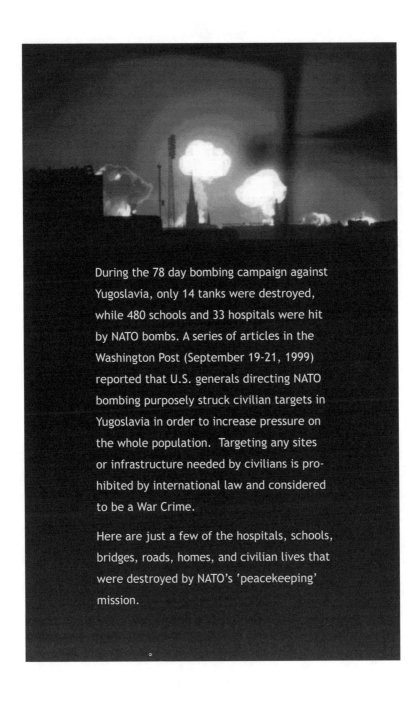

During the 78 day bombing campaign against Yugoslavia, only 14 tanks were destroyed, while 480 schools and 33 hospitals were hit by NATO bombs. A series of articles in the Washington Post (September 19-21, 1999) reported that U.S. generals directing NATO bombing purposely struck civilian targets in Yugoslavia in order to increase pressure on the whole population. Targeting any sites or infrastructure needed by civilians is prohibited by international law and considered to be a War Crime.

Here are just a few of the hospitals, schools, bridges, roads, homes, and civilian lives that were destroyed by NATO's 'peacekeeping' mission.

Destruction of residential areas

−Sara Flounders

The town of Aleksinac.

− *NATO crimes in Yugoslavia,* Vol. 1 p. 132

Clearing of debris on Kosovska St. where five members of the Gasi family were killed, April 7,1999.

—Strike on Yugoslavia CD

—NATO Crimes in Yugoslavia, Vol. II p.83

Bombed Podrimska Street in Prizen, Kosovo; about 50 houses owned by persons of Romani nationality have been demolished. Four people were killed and 20 were seriously injured, April 28, 1999.

Cluster bombs

—Strike on Yugoslavia CD

NATO dropped 35,000 cluster bombs and graphite bombs during its strike on Yugoslavia. A CBU-87 cluster bomb, described as one of the "most controversial weapons in the world," is used to kill people and disable armored vehicles. Each bomb sheds 200 bomblets the size of a soda can. Each bomblet produces 2,000 high-velocity shrapnel fragments.

—Strike on Yugoslavia CD

Cluster bombs are placed in canisters outfitted with a small parachute to allow the munition to float to the ground after it is released from an aircraft. The canisters are designed to open 50 feet off the ground. They send chunks of molten metal that can pierce armor and shrapnel that can slice through ¼ inch-plate or human flesh and bone. Many children worldwide are injured because they picked up or played with bright yellow unexploded cluster bombs.

Religious shrines

By violating all international conventions on the protection of cultural and historical heritage, NATO destroyed or damaged 365 monasteries, churches and other religious shrines. During frequent indiscriminate bombings not even cemeteries were spared. Currently, under NATO occupation the wholesale destruction of cultural, historic and religious sites has continued.

The Church of the Holy Virgin Hedegetria, built in 1315 in Musutiste before being destroyed.

The Church of the Holy Virgin Hedegetria after the destruction by the KLA.

Hospitals

Medical Complex – 'Dr. Dragisa Misovic' Neurology Hospital, Belgrade.

Medical Complex – 'Dr. Dragisa Misovic' Children's Lung Hospital, Belgrade.

Schools

Demolished new school building and damaged old school building,
Elementary School 'Djura Jaksic,' Bogutovac.

—*NATO Crimes in Yugoslavia*, Vol. I p. 198

The NATO aggression put a stop to the education of close
to one million pupils and students in Yugoslavia. More
than 480 schools, faculties and facilities for students
and children were badly damaged or destroyed.

Children in front of their bombed school in Novi Sad. —Sara Flounders

Aircraft fuel tank which fell into the courtyard of 'Misa Cvijovic' kindergarten in Prijepolje.

Children

Children made up 30% of all casualties, as well as 40% of the total number of the injured, while 10% of all Yugoslav children (approximately 300,000) suffered severe psychological traumas. For the most part, children have been victims of the sprinkle cluster bombs with delayed effect.

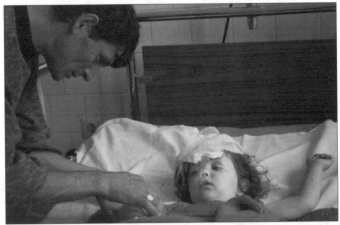

—*Stop the NATO occupation of Yugoslavia* CD

—*NATO Crimes in Yugoslavia*, Vol. II p. 13

Body of a baby killed in in the NATO bombing of refugee convoy in Kosovo. This child was one of many casualties. The number ten was used for identification.

Depleted Uranium radioactive weapons

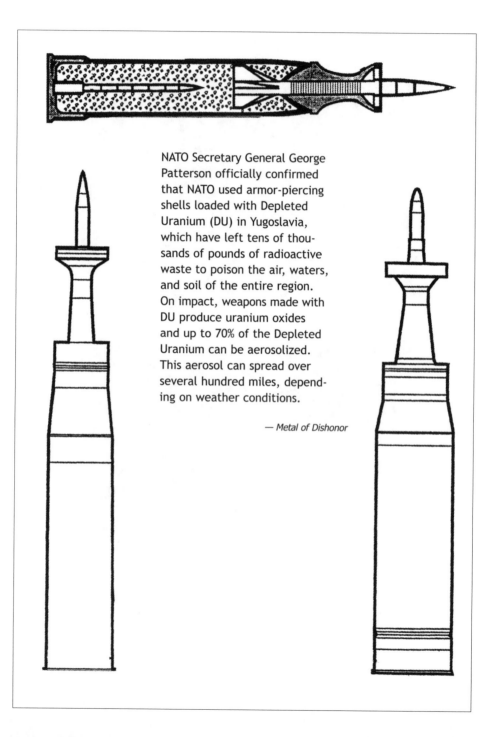

NATO Secretary General George Patterson officially confirmed that NATO used armor-piercing shells loaded with Depleted Uranium (DU) in Yugoslavia, which have left tens of thousands of pounds of radioactive waste to poison the air, waters, and soil of the entire region. On impact, weapons made with DU produce uranium oxides and up to 70% of the Depleted Uranium can be aerosolized. This aerosol can spread over several hundred miles, depending on weather conditions.

— Metal of Dishonor

Sites identified in Kosovo as being targeted by NATO ordinance containing Depleted Uranium during 1999.

o Sites targetted

YUGOSLAVIA

Serbia

Montenegro

Province of Kosovo

ALBANIA

MACEDONIA

UNEP

The Fairchild A-10A Thunderbolt II, also known as the Warthog, wields a GAU-8/A Avenger 30mm seven-barrel cannon capable of firing 4,200 DU rounds per minute. Each 30mm round contains a 300-gram DU penetrator.

U.S. Air Force Photograph — *Metal of Dishonor*

Environment

The United States is in violation of the 1949 Geneva Convention, which prohibits bombing not justified by a clear military necessity. As Ramsey Clark argues,

"Its attack on chemical plants, petroleum and natural gas refining, processing and storage facilities, fertilizer plants and other facilities and locations for the specific purpose of releasing and scattering toxic, radioactive and other dangerous substances and forces into the atmosphere, soil, ground water and food chain..." has poisoned the environment and injured the population.

19 Point Indictment of U.S. / NATO for War Crimes

—Sara Flounders

The destruction of petrochemical installations and warehouses in Pancevo, Novi Sad, Sombor, Baric and elsewhere, has caused wide-spread contamination of soil and air, as well as significant adverse effects on the health of the population of the former republic of Yugoslavia.

Destroyed water-pumping station 'Badovac' in the village of
Badovac—Pristina, May 2, 1999. —*NATO Crimes in Yugoslavia*, Vol. II p. 457

A July 14, 1999 New York Times news release describing the dire
effects of NATO's bombing on the population:

Farm workers, plunging their fingers into the earth, say they come
away with rashes that burn and blister. Those who eat the river fish
and vegetables or drink the tap water, which trickles out of faucets
because of the damage to the purification plant, come down with
diarrhea, vomiting and stomach cramps.

"View of the demolished 'Sarejevo' bridge in the Grdelica Gorge,
on the Leskovac-Vranje road, photographed on 29 April 1999
(Fourth Attack)   —*NATO Crimes in Yugoslavia*, Vol. II p. 337

The road and railway network of the Former Republic of Yugoslavia,
especially road and rail bridges suffered extensive destruction and
damage, which will necessitate substantial investments for their
reconstruction or repair. More than 60 road and rail bridges were
destroyed as well as the targeting of bus stations, railway stations
and transport companies.

— *Stop the NATO Occupation of Yugoslavia* CD

Hope for the future.

— *Strike on Yugoslavia* CD

Women dancing on the wing of a U.S. Stealth bomber shot down by Yugoslav forces.

— *Stop the NATO Occupation of Yugoslavia* CD

Women at 'Ground Zero' head back to work.

•The figures on destruction are taken from *The White Book on NATO Crimes in the Territory of the Federal Republic of Yugoslavia.*

See appendix for more extensive listing of civilian destruction.

IV.

CRIMES AGAINST PEACE: PRELUDE TO WAR

We Are Not an Instant Culture

NADJA TESICH

From a speech at the march on the Pentagon June 5, 1999, introducing section on the motivation and mechanics of U.S./NATO aggression.

Sisters and brothers,

With all this talk of peace one thing is clear—the struggle continues, *a luta continua,* or is about to start in earnest as the U.S. criminal government is getting ready to occupy Kosovo and will make attempts to seize other parts of the country and then comes the colonization. That's why they destroyed those factories right away.

When I can reach people in Belgrade under the bombs they shout on the phone, "Death to US fascism," "Death to NATO." "May they die." Our children will remember North Americans as the invisible monsters who tried to kill them from the sky.

We are not an instant culture. We have been there since the eighth century. We will remember for centuries, we will hate injustice for generations. And we will fight over and over again. Actually this system (U.S., who else) is worse than fascism because it sells freedom, democracy, human rights, together with Barbie dolls, Mickey Mouse while it kills, maims, poisons, occupies and dumps its culture like its garbage, like its bombs, all over the world.

Remember, these are not brave warriors but cowards with technology who kill for their salary and no more. In a real war our people, women and children included, could take care of them easily. The U.S. brags that it destroyed more in two months than the Nazis did in four years. Bridges, schools, hospitals, water supplies, small towns like mine, not in the papers, villages, national parks, churches, monuments against fascism.

Who will pay for all this, who will pay for lost lives, for the wounded who lost legs and arms? Who can ever pay for lost childhoods?

The U.S. is presently a menace to the entire world. It's mad as a mad dog, which means its end is near, says an Indian man.

That's why I remain optimistic. Nothing is forever; Rome fell too. *La lotta continua.* Even if they occupy us I can predict the next step, uprisings and wars of national liberation against U.S. tyranny but not just in

Yugoslavia. In other occupied countries around us, further north in Eastern Europe and Russia, and all over the world one, two, three, twenty and more that will alter the world in the next century. Even here in this country which will not be attacked by Iraq, Cuba, but will simply crumble because of its contradictions. It might happen sooner than you think.

Victory to the people of Yugoslavia! Victory to all of us united against the empire!

Washington's NATO Strategy

This chapter will concentrate on showing that for almost a decade those with authority in the U.S. government and its ruling circles, including influential think-tanks and global strategists, laid out the blueprints for the U.S.-NATO aggression against Yugoslavia that were eventually followed by the Clinton administration. These blueprints focused on expanding NATO's membership and its role as world cop. Washington was to use the NATO structure to maintain U.S. hegemony among its "allies" at a time when economic competition between the U.S. and Europe was growing ever more intense.

This economic rivalry was obscured during the Cold War period, when the European powers had no choice but to follow Washington's lead in confronting the USSR. In 1997-1999 the so-called banana war pitting the interests of U.S.-based Chiquita against European rivals,[1] the challenge to the dominant U.S. dollar from the Euro[2] gave evidence of this conflict. Later the collapse of World Trade Organization talks in Seattle in December 1999 and the attempt by the U.S. to corner the Latin American market with the Free Trade Association of the Americas exposed this increasingly bitter economic rivalry.

Despite claims of the "end-of-history" philosophers that the national state was withering away under worldwide capitalism, monopolies based in one or another of the major capitalist states have turned to their governments for help—including subsidies, pushing into markets and industrial spying. In the end, this competition means relying on force or the threat of force, which must be regularly demonstrated to be credible.

In the Balkans, the U.S. regime eventually sought a war where U.S. military technology, especially air power, would be decisive. In such a war Washington would not only prevail over the people of Yugoslavia, it would maintain its dominant position over its European rivals. By consciously planning for war and carrying out these plans, the U.S. government committed a crime against peace.

It is only possible to understand what NATO expansion and its war on Yugoslavia represent, if we consider these events from a class point of view. That is the only way to sort through the lies spewed out by the ruling class's trillion-dollar propaganda machine.

CLASS CHARACTER OF U.S. AND NATO

This propaganda machine sometimes writes of "U.S. interests." This term itself distorts reality. What it really means is the interests of the dominant group of bankers and industrialists who own and exploit much of the world's labor and natural resources. This group can be much better described as the U.S. imperialist ruling class.

To carry out foreign policies in their interest, this class employs politicians and officials in the national government, the Pentagon, CIA and State Department, and also a collection of think tanks from the Tri-Lateral Commission to the Soros Foundation, and world strategists like Henry Kissinger and Zbigniew Brzezinski and newspaper columnists like Thomas Friedman and William Pfaff. These politicians, strategists, managers and media flacks vie for the privileges and perks of representing the individual and collective interests of the class that owns and rules.

With the exception of Japan and Australia, NATO includes all the major imperialist powers: the United States, Germany, France, Britain, Italy and Canada. These six plus Japan make up the G-7 countries that set economic rules for the world.

Why call them imperialist countries? Because the corporate and financial ruling classes of these countries control the bulk of the world's capital, which they use to exploit labor throughout the world, both in the imperialist countries themselves and in the oppressed countries or the Third World. They export capital and import profits.

NATO also includes most smaller imperialist countries—like Spain, Belgium, the Netherlands, Portugal, Norway, Luxembourg, Iceland and Denmark. Greece and Turkey are also in NATO, and Poland, Hungary and the Czech Republic, formerly in the socialist camp, were admitted just before the war against Yugoslavia.[3]

These capitalist countries were the first to industrialize, they are now the most advanced in technology, they control the mass media, they manufacture the most powerful weapons and are the most heavily armed. They sell weapons to the world but keep the most powerful and advanced weapons systems for themselves. Despite claims that so-called globalization has diminished the importance of the national state, in each country the class that rules relies on the national state, and especially its military power, to advance its interests.

One of the most encouraging developments of the early twenty-first century has been the development of the anti-globalization movement that has targeted the leaders of the G-7, and which has the potential of developing into a militant anti-imperialist, anti-war movement.

The NATO powers include the big colonial powers of the nineteenth century—Britain and France—who directly ruled vast parts of the earth, and others that held colonies like Germany (Namibia, Tanzania), Italy (Eritrea, Somalia, Albania) the Netherlands (Indonesia), Portugal (Angola, Mozambique and Guinea-Bissau) and Belgium (Congo). Now there are few direct colonies, but through control of the world market, currency exchanges and banking and from their technological advantages they now indirectly control and oppress most of the world.

In 1878 it was essentially these same powers that met in Berlin and carved up the Balkans. In 1885 they met in Berlin and carved up Africa into spheres of influence. In 1999 they met in Bosnia and carved up Kosovo for so-called peacekeeping forces.

Of these countries, the United States, with the greatest single national economy, the dominant world currency and by far the strongest military power, is now the most dangerous to the rest of the world, spending more money on armaments than all its potential rivals combined.

1992 PENTAGON 'WHITE PAPER'

Since the defeat of the Soviet Union in 1989-1991, strategists in U.S. ruling circles have promoted the policy of expanding NATO and using that military pact as a world police force. This policy is first of all directed against smaller and weaker countries in Africa and the Middle East. It is aimed also at plundering Central Asia up to the Caspian Sea with its oil riches. But for U.S. strategists, it serves an additional purpose.

On March 8, 1992, *The New York Times* published excerpts from a forty-six-page document officially known as the "Defense Planning Guidance for Fiscal Years 1994-1999," leaked by Pentagon officials. At the time the current Republican Vice President Richard Cheney was secretary of defense. Current Deputy Secretary of Defense Paul Wolfowitz allegedly drafted this paper, which asserts the need for complete U.S. world domination in both political and military terms. It threatens other countries that even aspire to a greater role:

> First, the U.S. must show the leadership necessary to establish and protect a new order that holds the promise of convincing potential com-

petitors that they need not aspire to a greater role or pursue a more aggressive posture to protect their legitimate interests. Second, in the non-defense areas, we must account sufficiently for the interests of the advanced industrial nations to discourage them from challenging our leadership or seeking to overturn the established political and economic order.[4]

To put this more clearly: First, U.S. imperialism will remain the dominant power by far and will determine just how and to what proportion the world will be exploited and plundered. Second, the U.S. rulers should share enough of the plunder with their counterparts in Western Europe and Japan to make them believe it is not worth the effort and danger of challenging U.S. supremacy.

Other parts of the White Paper are directed at Iraq, Cuba, and North Korea, whose interests Washington doesn't pretend to take into account. But this part is clearly aimed at the European powers, especially Germany, and Japan. It also means Washington will not allow Russia—or China, India, Brazil or Nigeria, for that matter—to emerge as a truly competitive power, not even as a competitive capitalist power.

Regarding Europe, the document stated:

> **It is of fundamental importance to preserve NATO as the primary instrument** of Western defense and security. ... We must seek to prevent the emergence of European-only security arrangements which would undermine NATO.[5] [my emphasis—J.C.]

Looking back from the year 2001 it is obvious that U.S. officials carried out the strategy presented in this document. A short review of NATO's history shows why U.S. strategists make it the center of their plans.

WHAT IS THE SPECIFIC ROLE OF NATO?

After World War II ended, the class of plunderers and robbers who ruled the imperialist countries saw that while they had been fighting each other, a third of humanity had liberated itself from their grip. The Russian Revolution, which had ended World War I, survived Hitler's onslaught. World War II ended in Europe with the victory of the Yugoslav and Albanian revolutions and the Soviet Red Army's march to Berlin. By 1949 all mainland China was liberated and half of Korea. The Vietnamese people were winning against the French. There was revolutionary civil war in Greece. Colonial regimes were beginning to crumble around the world.

Only U.S. sabotage and bribery forced the French and Italian Communists, who had organized the workers' resistance to fascism, out of the governments there. Only British and U.S. intervention could set back the revolution in Greece.

So in 1949 the imperialist powers formed NATO in Europe as the military arm of their attempt to reverse these gains of the workers and oppressed. Only in 1955 did the Soviet Union and its allies form the Warsaw Pact to confront NATO and defend the socialist camp. From its beginning NATO was the military arm of capitalist counter-revolution directed at Eastern Europe and the USSR.

In 1949 the U.S. was by far the most powerful imperialist country—both militarily and economically—and NATO's structure reflected this U.S. hegemony. Even today NATO's structure favors rule from the Pentagon. In addition, Washington prefers working through NATO because—unlike in the United Nations—it doesn't have to win support from client regimes in the Third World, which are usually more unstable and subject to mass pressure.

1992 PLAN FOR AIR ASSAULT ON YUGOSLAVIA

Already toward the end of 1992 strategists began adapting the policy outlined in the "White Paper" to the developing crisis in the Balkans. Retired Air Force Chief of Staff General Michael J. Dugan and George Kenney of the Carnegie Endowment for International Peace wrote an opinion piece for *The New York Times* published Nov. 29, 1992, entitled "Operation Balkan Storm: Here's a Plan."

"A win in the Balkans would establish U.S. leadership in the post-Cold War world in a way that Operation Desert Storm never could," Dugan wrote, adding that massive air power should be used against Serbs in Bosnia and Serbia to destroy Serbia's electricity grid, refineries, storage facilities, and communications.[6]

General Dugan had been relieved of his command in September 1990 for candidly laying out U.S. plans for the massive assault on and destruction of Iraq before the Bush administration was ready to make them public. His scenario was also prophetic for the Balkans, although it was not fully carried out until 1999, and by NATO instead of some other coalition.

U.S.-Europe rivalries had already worked to extend the Bosnian war, however, which was ended by agreement only after the U.S. intervened militarily under the aegis of NATO. Washington had sabotaged earlier agreements signed by the same parties in Lisbon, Portugal, in March 1992 and the 1993 Vance-Owen plan, even though both contained virtually the same points as the 1995 Dayton Accords. The U.S. sabotage led to years more of bloody civil war. The main difference in the accords was that the earlier ones were negotiated under the leadership of the European Union, leaving the U.S. and NATO in a relatively minor role.[7]

In August and September 1995, the U.S. got its way. NATO launched a massive air war against positions of the Bosnian Serbs. The combination of these air raids with the NATO-enforced economic blockade led to the Dayton Accords of 1995—signed at Wright-Patterson Air Force Base in Dayton, Ohio, under U.S. sponsorship. As part of the agreement, 60,000 NATO troops, 20,000 of them U.S. soldiers, were sent into Bosnia under U.S. command. Although Clinton promised to bring the U.S. troops home by the end of 1996, and George W. Bush promised in his 2000 campaign rhetoric that he would remove them, the troops remain as of August 2001.

A large new NATO base was established in Hungary to facilitate troop deployment in Bosnia. The U.S. also established new bases in Macedonia and northern Albania.[8] The U.S. used the Bosnia operation as a wedge for the expansion of NATO into Eastern Europe.

After Dayton, while Washington backed anti-socialist forces inside Serbia, the German secret service began strengthening its ties with the so-called Kosovo Liberation Army, or KLA, following Berlin's historical connections with Albanian nationalism.[9] Washington also secretly backed the KLA, and by the middle of 1998, U.S. imperialism had thrown its weight and resources behind the reactionary KLA and looked to them to provide both the pretext for the next war against Yugoslavia and the ground troops for that war.

AUGUST 1998—ATTACK ON YUGOSLAVIA IN THE WORKS

By August 4, 1998, eight months before the bombing began, the Clinton administration confirmed that NATO had already developed detailed plans for an attack on Yugoslavia. Sources told *The New York*

Times that the focus is on "a variety of air-power options that could punish or intimidate."[10]

On July 29, 1998, the Albanian government had announced that seventy-six top NATO officers were in Tirana, the capital, to plan "joint Albania-NATO exercises" from August 17 to August 22, 1998, within fifty miles of the border with Kosovo. The maneuvers were to prepare NATO and Albanian troops for a "peacekeeping mission." Similar exercises were planned for Macedonia in September.[11]

These maneuvers were recommended in a March 20, 1998, position paper of the International Crisis Group, a think tank with White House ties headed by former Senate Democratic Leader George Mitchell. That report also recommended "an international force in Albania close to the borders of Kosovo to help prevent the conflict in Kosovo from spreading and ... facilitate rapid and effective action should an intervention become necessary."[12]

Meanwhile, Washington was pushing forward its plan to expand eastward both the membership of NATO and its area of intervention. This plan, however, was meeting resistance in European capitals where it was seen as increasing U.S. hegemony over its rivals.

An article in the November 28, 1998, *New York Times*, headlined "A policy struggle stirs within NATO," provided advance notice of U.S. plans to expand NATO's use beyond Europe. The article revealed that U.S. policy sees NATO as "an alliance of interests," and that those interests "may in some instances push the members into far-flung activities."[13] Washington wanted NATO forces ready to intervene not only in the Balkans and against countries like Iraq or Iran in the Middle East, or Libya, Sudan or Congo in Africa—but against any attempt at a popular revolution anywhere, from Russia to Indonesia.[14]

When U.S. officials speak of an "alliance of interests," they really mean the common need of the predatory ruling class in the United States and Europe to suppress any popular revolt that threatens their ability to plunder the raw materials and labor of the rest of the world. In the Balkans and Eastern Europe, they share the goal of turning that region back into a colony of the imperialist West, ripe for super-exploitation.

NATO'S WAR BURIES U.S.-EUROPEAN CONFLICTS

To say "alliance of interests," however, disguises the increasingly bitter economic and strategic competition among them. This competition fed the European rulers' opposition to NATO expansion,[15] and, as could be seen later, pushed them to search for an alternative, but not until the crisis in Yugoslavia had eased.

Within Europe, French imperialism has most often argued against NATO and for an independent European force. German imperialism has opposed the U.S. more quietly but just as bitterly—in the Balkans, for instance, where Berlin and the deutschemark predominate economically but U.S. military power gives Washington the last say.

In the period just before Washington launched the air war on Yugoslavia's people, the Clinton administration imposed 100-percent import duties on selected European-produced goods. This was a follow-up to the so-called banana war, the sharpest expression of U.S.-European economic rivalry.[16]

Washington had long decided to wage war against Yugoslavia. When this war began, on March 24, 1999, the competition with Europe was buried under the weight of U.S. air power. When Belgrade refused to sign the Rambouillet agreement, which was really no agreement but an ultimatum demanding Yugoslavia surrender its sovereignty, Washington used this pretext to launch a war against Yugoslavia with NATO backing.

In his 2001 book *Waging Modern Warfare*, NATO Commander General Wesley J. Clark admits that the war on Yugoslavia was a willful decision by the NATO powers. The Kosovo war, he writes, "was coercive diplomacy, the use of armed forces to impose the political will of the NATO nations on the Federal Republic of Yugoslavia, or more specifically, on Serbia. The NATO nations voluntarily undertook this war. In that regard," it "was much more like the interventions of an earlier era," before World War II, when the imperialist powers openly ruled colonies and protectorates.[17]

By the time the North Atlantic Treaty Organization celebrated its fiftieth anniversary on April 4, 1999, it had just made its first military assault beyond its borders and carried out the largest bombing in Europe since World War II. Washington used the war against Yugoslavia to impose its changes on NATO—changing it from a no-longer-needed anti-Soviet alliance to an intervention force ready to strike worldwide.

In addition, the U.S. government had recently succeeded in gaining NATO admittance for Poland, Hungary and the Czech Republic over the objection of other NATO members. It then pulled these three countries directly into the war. The brutal bombing of Yugoslavia gives the first example of how the U.S. wants to use the new, post-Cold War NATO to lead its European allies into battle.[18]

NATO powers met in late April 1999 in Washington to ratify U.S. expansion plans. Washington had hoped they would be meeting in triumph over a submissive Belgrade. But the heroic resistance of the Yugoslav population and its leadership had completely surprised them and created a near crisis in the NATO leadership. It took seventy-eight days of bombing of the Yugoslav infrastructure, destruction of its industry and environment, and threats of a full-fledged invasion before the NATO leaders were able to avoid a disaster for the aggressive alliance that the world's people would have welcomed.

Throughout the eleven-week assault on Yugoslavia by most of the world's biggest military powers, U.S. and European mainstream politicians of all political shades tried to give the impression that the NATO forces were united, whatever trade rivalries and military maneuvering were going on behind the scenes.

But no sooner had Yugoslavia agreed to terms than the European Union's leaders announced plans to emerge as a military power. Leaders from fifteen European countries announced the move on June 3, 1999— the same day that the Yugoslav leadership announced its acceptance of NATO's onerous terms. Their statement read: "The union must have the capacity for autonomous action backed up by credible military forces, the means to decide to use them, and a readiness to do so, in order to respond to international crises without prejudice to actions by NATO."[19]

Since World War II, Washington has bombed twenty-two countries in fifty-six years killing over four million people in Korea and another three million in Vietnam, Laos and Cambodia. It has also enforced an economic blockade against Iraq that has taken the lives of more than one and a half million people, half-a-million of them children under the age of five.[20]

U.S. military superiority is the key to U.S. global economic domination. A new military buildup is already under way, even though the United States today already spends more on its military than the rest of the UN Security Council combined. In 2001 the George W. Bush administration has proposed a military budget of $329 billion, a more than seven percent increase over the prior year.[21]

Washington also wants its allies to spend on the military. Then-U.S. Defense Secretary William Cohen showed this when he used an evaluation of the war against Yugoslavia to bully the NATO allies into accepting U.S. policies at an "informal meeting" of nineteen NATO defense ministers in Toronto September 21-22, 1999. Cohen wanted the European NATO countries to take the risks of wartime casualties and pay the costs, while Washington's control of strategic weapons and logistics gives it the final say. Cohen clearly expected NATO to fight future wars of a Kosovo size and bigger—and more distant from the United States or Western Europe.[22]

NATO's armies are strong, but they too have weaknesses. The greatest weakness of the U.S. military is the reluctance to accept casualties, a legacy of the U.S. defeat by a people's army in Vietnam. Gen. Wesley Clark complains of this weakness in the conclusions to his book.[23]

CONTINUED U.S.-EU RIVALRY

The European Union has proceeded to plan a "Rapid Reaction Force" of 100,000 professional troops, including the largest contingent of 18,000 from Germany, with the most modern weaponry and means of transport to function "out of area." Washington wants this force to be integrated with NATO and essentially under U.S. control. Those ruling the EU want their own imperialist intervention force, capable of intervening in, for example, Eastern Europe or Africa, without depending on U.S. logistical support or confronting U.S. reluctance to use ground troops.

How this "Rapid Reaction Force" is organized will be one axis of conflict between EU and U.S. imperialism. Driving this conflict will be economic competition under conditions of a downturn in the world economy. With a worsening world economy, it becomes less likely a dominant power like the U.S. will "account sufficiently for the interests of the advanced industrial nations to discourage them from challenging" U.S. leadership, as the *White Paper* quoted above puts it. There will simply be fewer spoils to share.

Washington still has overwhelming military predominance and the ability to ally with one or a few of the European imperialist states against the others. Under these conditions, for the near future it is likely the conflict among the imperialist powers will drive them to new military adventures against smaller, oppressed countries. Far less likely would be a major direct military conflict between the U.S. and Europe. As the first half of the last century showed, however, even the most horrific scenario is possible. Remember that while carrying out their rivalry for markets, colonies and raw materials in the first half of the twentieth century, these predatory states plunged the world into two world wars that together killed 100 to 200 million people—mostly workers, peasants and other toilers.

It is completely appropriate for workers' movements and governments of small states trying to defend their sovereignty to try to take advantage of any competition between the U.S. and Europe. But the world should never forget that—unlike the Cold War conflict between imperialism and the USSR—both sides of today's competition are predators and exploiters. Both sides are enemies of the working class and the oppressed nations.

Honest anti-war forces in both Europe and the United States have the responsibility of fighting to demilitarize the ruling class on both sides of the Atlantic. That means stopping the Rapid Reaction Force. It means, as the International Action Center has done, making the abolition of NATO—the real criminal force behind the war against Yugoslavia—a central demand of every anti-war action. They also have the duty to stand in solidarity with any oppressed people or nation from Congo to Colombia to the Balkans that has the courage to defy the U.S. and its NATO allies, as Yugoslavia did in 1999.

[1] Deirdre Griswold, "Chiquita aims to wipe out small banana farmers," *Workers World*, May 22, 1997.

[2] Andy McInerney, "The Euro, what change in global balance?" *Workers World*, January 19, 1999.

[3] John Catalinotto, "Why NATO is Washington's weapon of choice," *Workers World*, April 8, 1999.

[4] Sara Flounders, in "Introduction," *NATO in the Balkans — Voices of Opposition*, New York, IAC, 1998, pages 3-4.

[5] Ibid.

[6] Ibid.

[7] Ibid.

[8] Gary Wilson, "The Dayton Accords Reshape Europe," *NATO in the Balkans*, pages 144, 145.

[9] Matthias Kuentzel, *Der Weg in den Krieg* (The Road to War), Elefanten Press, 2000. pages 59 to 64.

[10] Steven Erlanger, *New York Times*, August 4, 1998, "NATO Readies Plan for Force in Kosovo."

[11] Albanian Telegraphic Agency, July 28, 1998.

[12] "Kosovo Spring," ICG Balkans Report, March 20, 1998

[13] Roger Cohen, "A policy struggle stirs within NATO," *New York Times*, Nov. 28, 1998.

[14] John Catalinotto, *Workers World*, Dec. 10, 1998, "U.S. plans expanded role for NATO."

[15] William Pfaff, *Los Angeles Times*, Dec. 5, 1998, "Washington's New Vision for NATO Could Be Divisive."

[16] John Catalinotto, *Workers World*, March 18, 1999. "Top gun, bananas and executions."

[17] Gen. Wesley J. Clark, *Waging Modern Warfare*, Westview Press, 2001. page 418.

[18] John Catalinotto, *Workers World*, April 18, 1999, "Why NATO is Washington's weapon of choice."

[19] Background Document, European Council Declaration on Strengthening the Common European Policy on Security and Defense, Cologne, June 3-4, 1999. www.weu.int/eng/info/d990603a.htm

[20] William Blum, *Killing Hope, U.S. Military and CIA Interventions Since World War II*. Common Courage, 1995

[21] *Washington Post*, July 11, 2001.

[22] John Catalinotto, *Workers World*, October 7, 1999, "Pentagon imposes U.S.-led expansion on NATO allies."

[23] Gen. Wesley J. Clark, ibid, page 438.

Controlling Oil and Gas Routes[*]

MICHEL COLLON

> The oil fields of Kazakhstan, the gas fields of Turkmenistan and the
> enormous off-shore reserves of black gold in Azerbaijan constitute an
> area that could acquire, in the next fifty years, an importance equal to
> that of the Gulf region today. (*Die Zeit*, Germany's largest daily news-
> paper)[1]

It has often been said that the war in Yugoslavia dragged on because
there was no oil there and therefore the great powers were not interested.
This is false.

Yugoslavia and the Balkans cannot be isolated from the surrounding
regions. What was at stake in the Gulf War was controlling the Middle
East and its oil. However, two areas are decisive in controlling the
Mediterranean route to that oil. The Balkans and Turkey have always
been regions of strategic importance to the various Great Powers for the
Drang nach Osten (eastward expansion) as German imperialism stated
it, the passage to the East and the Middle East.

Today the major struggle is for control of the ex-USSR and its enormous wealth in raw materials, particularly Caspian and Kazakh oil. Production in the former Soviet Union is actually about forty percent of that
of the Middle East, but certain analysts consider the resources to be as
significant as those of Saudi Arabia. Many think that Siberia, with its
wealth of mineral reserves, will become a region of decisive importance
in the twenty-first century. As *Le Monde Diplomatique* has written,
American, Japanese and European firms are already confronting each
other there:

> The most important gold mine in the world—estimated production is
> fifty tons of ore per year—is found in Uzbekistan, north of Afghanistan.
> To the northeast, Tajikistan sits on the largest deposit of silver on the
> planet. Even further north, the underground strata of Kazakhstan hold a
> quarter of the world's known oil reserves. Ever since they arrived in
> 1990, large western companies have been waging a "take no prisoners"
> battle there. Chevron has already invested ten billion dollars in the coun-
> try. As for AGIP (Italy) and British Gas, they are confronting a Russian
> consortium for control of gigantic Kazakh natural gas reserves. One ru-

---

[*] This chapter is from Michel Collon's *Poker Menteur*, 1998, to be published by
the International Action Center in 2002 under the title, *Liar's Poker*, pages 129-134.

mor speaks of the existence of uranium in Gorno-Badakhstan (Tajiki-stan) and in Kirghistan. No holds are barred to secure contracts.[2]

No holds barred, including war. Which European country—Germany in particular—or the United States will control these strategic regions? These are the high stakes at risk in the crises and wars of this entire period, from Sarajevo to Chechnya via Macedonia, the breakup of Czecho-slovakia, Georgia, the war in Armenia and Azerbaijan.

SIBERIA—THE ELDORADO OF THE 21ST CENTURY...

Accounting for twenty percent of world industrial production, the former USSR represents a decisive target for the multinationals. It was the world leader in production of the following products: oil, coal, iron ore, cast iron, steel, lumber, mineral by-products, cement, butter, sugar... It was the second largest producer of gold, almost on par with South Africa.

Between the Ural Mountains and the Pacific Ocean stretch immense territories that are still severely under-exploited. The exceptional deposits of oil and gas, along with enormous hydroelectric resources, mean that Siberia will become the Eldorado of the twenty-first century. Numerous minerals are in abundance: copper, lead, zinc, tin, manganese, nickel. And precious metals: chromium, tungsten, molybdenum, vanadium.[3]

Now independent, four central Asian republics share the largest part of the wealth in oil and gas: Azerbaijan, Turkmenistan, Uzbekistan, and Kazakhstan (as well as the reserves in Astrakhan, in Russia). Besides producing 435,000 barrels of oil per day, Kazakhstan also has important deposits of coal, cheap and very useful for large industrial consumers (aluminum smelters, chemical refineries). As for Azerbaijan, it is one of the oldest oil producers. The petroleum center of Baku has been coveted by the imperial powers for a century. Today the industry is moving to the off-shore zone, to the Caspian Sea itself.

Within these diverse republics, the local bourgeoisie that emerged after the fall of the USSR face often catastrophic blows to their economies: collapse of production, unemployment, budgetary deficits, and social unrest. This of course pushes them to flaunt their riches to western multinationals even more. One of the first acts of the "independent" Azerbaijan was to open its doors in the summer of 1991 to the multinational company, Amoco, in order to exploit the offshore reserves of the Caspian Sea.

Any country that links its survival to a sole export, however, instantly becomes dependent on "the market," i.e., the multinational corporations and their speculations. These new producing countries also tried to enter into the market at an unfavorable time, because the West had succeeded in breaking the front organized by Third World producers. Under the direction of the U.S., the Organization of Petroleum Exporting Countries (OPEC) was systematically sabotaged and weakened. The Gulf War worked against them, as well, since Western control was imposed on the price of oil and the quantities sold.[4]

Western multinationals profit from the divisions between these small new countries by bringing them into competition with each other. When the USSR was still united, it negotiated with Chevron for four years. The latter wanted a thirty percent return on investment. The Soviets said that was too much. The newly "independent" Kazakhstan took only a few months to sign up.[5] Chevron promised to invest $10 billion and bring production up to six or seven hundred thousand barrels per day by the end of the century. It has to be stated that this could bring them revenues of up to $5 billion per year.

THOSE WHO CONTROL OIL CONTROL THE WORLD

Is all this Central Asian oil, deeper than that of the Middle East and, therefore, more costly to extract, really so interesting from an economic point of view? Isn't there an abundance of weak countries, who are desperately competing to attract foreign investment for the Western multinationals, to choose from?

In the short-term, maybe, but oil is a long-term question. First, the West has an interest in diversifying its supplies to diminish dependence on the Middle East. The stability of the region—namely, Western domination—is not guaranteed forever. Second, there is no question of letting Third World nations develop in an independent fashion; no, a firm grip must be kept on their wealth in order to control the world market.

Last, and most important, the Great Powers are competing with each other to insure access to strategic primary resources. The oil industry earns two billion dollars per day: more than most of the world's countries. It follows that whichever Great Power controls oil supplies can say to the others, "You will not get any except under my terms." This particular Great Power will control the world. In preparation for a confrontation between major powers, each one wants at its disposal an industrial complex and the natural resources that cover all the needs of equipment and arms. The two world wars have shown it: the battle to gain access to raw materials—and depriving others of them—knows no limits.

The U.S., weaker economically than Germany and Japan, compensates with the fact that it is the sole superpower. This allows it to control access to oil. We saw it in the Gulf War: the U.S. tightened its grip on the Middle East. The French firms Elf and Total, firmly established in Iraq, were deliberately penalized by Washington's policy. Japan depends entirely on the United States for its supply of oil. That is the very problem Germany wants to escape. F.W. Christians, president of the administrative council of Deutsche Bank, expressed German concerns in the crudest possible terms: "Baku is a petroleum center of great importance in the eyes of Germany. In the area of raw materials, we must be on the offensive."[6]

Despite official "alliances," the rivalry between the Great Powers over access to oil is sharpening. The "D'Amato Bill" is an example of this. Signed into law by Clinton in August 1996, it seeks to punish non-American firms that invest in the gas and oil industries in three countries: Iran, Iraq, and Libya. These were three "terrorist" countries, claimed Washington, and it declared an embargo on them.

Who, by chance, are the main buyers of Libyan and Iranian crude? The great rivals, Europe and Japan. The French Total Corporation was the first to sign an oil contract with Iran after the revolution of 1979. U.S. Senator Alfonse D'Amato threatened openly, "... Any business deal that helped Iran develop its energy sector was considered a 'direct threat to U.S. national security.' " "... The European Union is discussing possible retaliation against U.S. economic interests.... Japan added its voice to the criticism of the U.S. sanctions law..."[7] Are these "allies" or enemies?

AS IF BY CHANCE, NATIONALIST CONFLICTS...

Kazakhstan, Azerbaijan, Turkmenistan, Uzbekistan, all these oil-producing nations are competing for a place on the world market. "Analysts inform us that in contesting Azeri domination of the Caspian Sea as well as their industrial capacity, Kazakhstan has taken the initiative by starting construction of an industrial port and a petrochemical complex in the city of Aktan on the north shore of the Caspian. This new port, and the one in Krasnovodsk in Turkmenistan, are seeking to compete with Baku."[8]

Are all means acceptable to unbridled capitalist competition? "Azerbaijan, these same analysts write, seems to have a long lead over its neighbors, but the country has also been wedged into a painful armed conflict with Armenia."[9] Is it a coincidence?

Nationalist tensions, systematically encouraged by the West to weaken the USSR, are re-surfacing and erupting with even more strength in the republics hit by economic crises. Especially since they are provoked by outside agitators. The fortune in petroleum has attracted many concerned "protectors." Various neighboring states are competing to be the godfather of the region: Russia, Turkey, Saudi Arabia, Iran and even Pakistan. Ultimately, all the large Western powers, even if they are now waiting in the wings, are coveting the black gold.

Each has its protégés: Russia is trying to make Kazakhstan a dependency, while Turkey is betting on Azerbaijan. But there is no shortage of means to ignite fires in order to destabilize a troublesome competitor. Nagorny-Karabakh, the Armenian enclave inside of Azerbaijan, is one trouble area. Uzbekistan, hit by massive unemployment, is also experiencing strong nationalist tensions. First of all, between the Uzbek majority and Russians (seventeen percent), but also between the Turkish minority. Serious confrontations have already occurred. In Turkmenistan, the Russian minority represents ten percent of the population, but that figure jumps to forty percent in urban areas.

Meanwhile, Kazakhstan is where the population breakdown is most favorable for explosive manipulations: forty-two percent Kazakh, thirty-nine percent Russian and twenty percent various other nationalities. It is a situation that evokes Bosnia... The Russians, who arrived at the end of the nineteenth century, are vilified by Kazakh nationalism; this also extends to the Jewish and Uighuri minorities. Add the presence of one million distant descendants of German immigrants, and it is already clear who will find a pretext to intervene when the time comes.

TURKEY, SAUDI ARABIA, IRAN: ISLAMIC RIVALRIES

Three Islamic powers are competing to control the region. Iran is using Islam to "unite" all the Muslims of Asia. Saudi Arabia is influencing marginal Islamic groups. In contrast, Turkey is more often than not playing the "cultural" card. Turkish universities are opening special offices to admit students from the countries of the ex-USSR. Ankara has sent thousands of typewriters there in an attempt to proliferate the Roman alphabet. The Saudis have responded by sending tons of copies of the Koran. Betting on the expansion of the Turkish language, Ankara has proposed a common market consisting of all the Turkish-speaking countries of the ex-USSR. A project condemned by the Kazakh poet Suleimanov: "A political union of Turkish-speaking peoples would represent the return of the Ottoman empire."[10]

Iran has established a mass transit company with Kazakhstan, but it remains Turkey who exerts a dominant influence in the region. A cooperation treaty signed by Azerbaijan dates back to 1991. The president of Kirgistan has compared Turkey to "the polar star, which must be observed for direction."[11] As for the president of Uzbekistan, he stated that, "There is no other route to follow but Turkey."[12]

Ankara therefore plays a key role. But its limited economic power does not allow it to act alone. In fact, Turkey is more of an intermediary. Germany, for example, is using Ankara to help set up markets in central Asia and the Caucasus.

TWO PIPELINES: ONE TOO MANY

Who can export the six billion tons of oil located beneath the Western Caspian? Since the beginning of the 1990s, two pipeline routes have been proposed for this colossal contract. The shortest passes through Russia via Chechnya. The other travels through Turkey (via Georgia) and ends at the Ceyhan terminal. Hence the violent confrontation between Moscow and Ankara. Russia is threatening Azerbaijan with a boycott. Finally in the fall of 1995, the Western company exploiting the Azerbaijani oil decided to use… two pipelines! It is, in effect, a proposal put forth by Clinton, who, at least for now, does not want to upset either Turkey or the Yeltsin camp.[13] It must be noted, however, that all along the two routes, civil wars are multiplying. As if by chance.

(Translated by Milo Yelesiyevich)

NATO's STRATEGIC STAKES IN THE BALKANS

Stake No. 1

Control of Oil and Gas Routes

• The Balkans and Turkey are two strategic regions that provide access to Middle Eastern oil (Saudi Arabia, Iraq, Kuwait).

• But they also provide access to the enormous oil reserves of the ex-USSR (Kazakhstan and the Caspian Sea). Notably, access via the highly coveted pipe-lines that supply, or will supply, Europe.

• Who will control these reserves? Moscow, Washington or Bonn?

Stake No. 2

Domination of Eastern Europe

Bringing Poland, Hungary, the Czech Republic, Rumania, etc. back to the capitalist fold, which constitute for Western multinationals rich reservoirs of

• Raw materials   • Cheap labor   • Export markets

Stake No. 3

Weaken and Control Russia

• Eliminate Russia's influence in the Balkans, and weaken Russia to prevent it from becoming an imperialist rival.

• Which power will dominate the ex-USSR, its markets and raw materials?

Stake No. 4

Insuring the Establishment of Military Bases

• To prepare NATO for "re-establishing order" in case of revolt in Eastern Europe or Russia.

• Also to prepare NATO to intervene (against Russia or any other rival) to control strategic oil and gas wealth.

• Since 1991, the United States has acquired a number of military bases or important positions in Albania, Macedonia, Bosnia, Hungary, the Czech Republic. They are thus establishing an "iron curtain" blocking the entire southern flank of Europe and the ex-USSR. No power will have access to this region without their approval.

Three Decisive European Routes

Yugoslavia occupies a strategic location in relation to Balkan lines of communication. It is on the crossroads of three decisive European routes:

• The Danube (see p. 137).

• The only large North-South route across the Balkan mountains.

• The only large East-West route across these same mountains. These last two routes are controlled by Macedonia, a small republic pushed towards secession by the United States since 1992. The United States has sent numerous military "advisors" there.

[1] *Die Zeit* (Germany), March 1996.

[2] *Le Monde Diplomatique*, November 1996, p. 22.

[3] Rudi Borremans, La richesse économique de l'ex-URSS (unpublished), Bruxelles, 1995.

[4] Regarding this point, see *Attention, médias!* (chapter 4) and also *La Guerre du pétrole*, both published by Éditions EPO, Bruxelles.

[5] Pinar, in *Politiques Economiques* (France), December 1994.

[6] Quoted by Stefan Eggerdinger, Antikriegstag, 1995, Munich (unpublished).

[7] *International Herald Tribune* (Paris), July 8, 1996.

[8] Pinar, op. cit.

[9] Pinar, op. cit.

[10] Pinar, op. cit.

[11] BBC, Summary of world broadcasts, February 25, 1992.

[12] Turkish press, January 1992.

[13] *NCR Handelsblad* (Holland), 10.10.95; *International Herald Tribune* (Paris), March 9, 1996.

The Hidden Hand

GARY WILSON

On June 25, 2001, U.S. KFOR forces in Macedonia were surrounded by angry workers and farmers trying to block several busloads of mercenaries who had been terrorizing the region. The terrorist force of the so-called National Liberation Army had been defeated and was about to be captured (or killed if any resisted capture).

The U.S. forces were on a rescue mission, not to rescue the Macedonian workers and farmers who had been terrorized, but to rescue the defeated National Liberation Army mercenaries.

The United States government's "Radio Free Europe" described the confrontation with the U.S. military. "Angry crowds blocked the convoy and forced it to split up into at least three sections," RFE reported the next day.

The convoy "did not make it to the intended goal, the village of Lipkovo in the northern border zone. A group of around 10 buses was held up" by a thousand angry civilians in the village of Umin Do.[1]

Why were U.S. military paratroopers rescuing a band of mercenary terrorists? Col. David H. Hackworth, a retired U.S. Army officer and syndicated columnist, says the operation was undertaken because the seventeen lead officers of the mercenary force were all former U.S. military officers working under contract to the Pentagon.[2]

Hackworth is a supporter of George W. Bush who he says is simply cleaning up a mess created by Bill Clinton and his administration.

While the Clinton administration was certainly up to its eyeballs in intrigue and worse in the Balkans, the covert operations began during the previous Republican administration of the first President George Bush.

Both Democratic administrations and Republican administrations have shared an obsession with the Balkans since the successful Yugoslav socialist revolution following World War II that is not unlike their obsession with Cuba.

This obsession has involved both open and hidden operations against both Yugoslavia and Cuba, including military attacks using mercenary forces recruited from the exile communities in the U.S. The obsession had nothing to do with any alleged threat from the Balkans or from

Cuba. It came from Washington's fear and hatred of the successful socialist revolutions in both places.

In March 1960, President Dwight Eisenhower secretly approved a CIA plan to invade Cuba. The idea was to use U.S.-trained Cuban mercenaries as a cover for the invasion. Once the attack began, U.S. military planes would arrive to "help" the mercenaries, who were called Cuban liberation fighters in the U.S. media. The Cuban revolutionary leaders soon knew of the plan. They publicly warned the people that an invasion was coming. The people of Cuba rallied together and put down the CIA-planned mercenary invasion.

While the Bay of Pigs invasion failed, something similar played out in the Balkans, but with a very different ending.

Yugoslavia was targeted for the 1990s version of the Bay of Pigs, including a mercenary army recruited from exiles in the United States. In the war on Yugoslavia, the so-called Atlantic Brigade was a special U.S.-trained mercenary force.[3]

The operation did not begin during the Clinton years, however. The U.S. openly began its move to support counter-revolution in Yugoslavia during the first Bush administration. The operation went into high gear with the collapse of the Soviet Union in 1991.

A detailed account of the key role the NATO powers played in the breakup of Yugoslavia in the 1990s can be found in the book *NATO in the Balkans*, published by the International Action Center.[4]

The Balkans version of the Bay of Pigs came with the U.S.-led NATO bombing campaign in 1999 that was justified in the media by claims to be supporting Albanian freedom fighters, the Kosovo Liberation Army. This KLA is also the core of the National Liberation Army that was rescued by U.S. forces in Macedonia.

What is left out of almost all of the media stories is the role of the CIA in building up the KLA, just as it built up the Cuban counter-revolutionary mercenary force for the Bay of Pigs invasion. The buildup to the U.S.-NATO war began almost a decade before, however. The bombing was launched because of Yugoslav resistance to a takeover by the capitalist powers, particularly the United States and Germany.

During much of the Cold War, Washington's policy toward Yugoslavia was aimed at trying to prevent any Yugoslav alliance with the Soviet Union and the other socialist countries. With the collapse of the Soviet Union, this policy ended. Washington's new agenda was the destruction of socialist Yugoslavia.

The leaders of Yugoslavia immediately saw when this shift in policy began. The League of Communists, Yugoslavia's communist party, was not prepared for the change in Washington's policy. The Yugoslav leadership had become soft in the years when Washington was showering Yugoslavia with favors.

But the League of Communists had a revolutionary history and had led the partisan victory over the Nazi invasion during World War II. It also had the allegiance of the workers in all the republics that made up Yugoslavia.

The Yugoslav party had never abandoned its socialist goals and when Washington's policy shifted, a new political leadership emerged that was prepared to defend the revolutionary gains made in Yugoslavia.

On January 25, 1991, a remarkable document was read to military units all across Yugoslavia. It has become known as the "General's Manifesto" because the authors were leading generals in the Yugoslav military.[5]

The manifesto is an assessment of the world situation and an exposure of the expected attacks by the NATO powers. It was a call for unity in Yugoslavia and for preparations to fight to defend the socialist revolution.

It begins with a statement that a new period had begun, and an assessment of the developments in the Soviet Union. As long as the USSR remained, the manifesto states, the Western powers' ability to act against Yugoslavia is limited. But the Soviet Union was in turmoil and its future was uncertain at that time.

The manifesto continued: "In Yugoslavia, socialism has not yet been finished off, brought to its knees. Yugoslavia has managed to withstand, albeit at a high cost, the first attack and wave of anti-communist hysteria. Real prospects of maintaining the country as a federative and socialist community have been preserved."

At that time, most of the socialist states in Eastern Europe had fallen.

"Western planners have achieved considerable success in the realization of their basic strategic orientation—the destruction of communism and the socialist option—but not their ultimate aim. They have not succeeded in overthrowing communism in any country where the revolution had been authentic," the manifesto continued

"The West has realized that the Yugoslav idea and socialist option have much deeper roots than they had envisaged, so that the overthrow of socialism in Yugoslavia is not the same thing as in other countries. This is why we can expect that they will modify the method of their action and move to an even stronger attack. It would be very important for them to achieve complete success in Yugoslavia. For they would be cutting into a country where revolution had been authentic."

The manifesto assesses the multiple fronts of attack that were developing. It notes the CIA's declaration that "Yugoslavia will fall apart in eighteen months." This declaration, the manifesto says, reveals the CIA's intentions.

"The same is true of the State Department declaration of December 25, 1990" that the U.S. will intervene to support the "democratic processes," code words that mean the U.S. is preparing to openly intervene to overturn the government. "The essence of the message is quite clear: they will overthrow socialism in Yugoslavia even at the price of its disintegration," the manifesto states.

There have been many accounts that have revealed the role of the NATO powers in the subsequent breakup of Yugoslavia, particularly by U.S. and German operations. In the end it took a full-scale war, a massive bombardment of Yugoslavia that was reminiscent of the Nazi bombardment of Yugoslavia during World War II. Only a full-scale war had the possibility of crushing socialism in Yugoslavia.

To justify that war, however, the NATO powers could not openly declare that their goal was to kill the last kernel of a revolutionary socialist state in Europe. Like many aggressors in the past, the United States presented a humanitarian pretext for launching the war. In this case, it was to protect the Kosovo Liberation Army, presented as the defenders of Albanian national rights.

In the U.S. and Western European media. the Kosovo Liberation Army were painted in the most glowing terms. They were the new freedom fighters defending the Albanian peoples from oppression. The African National Congress and its guerrilla military, Umkhonto we Sizwe, never received such favorable coverage in all its years of fighting apartheid in South Africa. That's because the ANC and Umkhonto we Sizwe really were revolutionary freedom fighters.

The KLA was like the right-wing Cuban "freedom fighters" who were acting on behalf of the CIA. The core of the KLA was the so-called Atlantic Brigade, mercenaries recruited mostly from the anti-Communist

Albanian exile community in the United States. It was trained in the U.S. and armed with U.S. provided equipment.

The CIA's role in training and arming the KLA began at least a year before NATO's bombing of Serbia and Kosovo, and probably as early as 1996.

The *Intelligence Newsletter* reported shortly after the NATO bombing began on March 24, 1999:

> Sources close to the German intelligence agencies say the CIA and BND [Germany's spy organization, the Federal Information Service] are both working to provide support for the Kosovo Liberation Army through a series of front companies located mainly in Germany. The companies are used to pump money into accounts in Switzerland held by Albanian sympathizers.
>
> In the field, KLA guerrillas are armed chiefly with light weapons that the CIA has drawn from stocks accumulated covertly in Albania.[6]

The Scotsman, a newspaper from Scotland, was more specific about the covert role of the U.S. government:

> The rag-tag Kosovar Albanian rebels were taken in hand by the Virginia-based company of professional soldiers, Military Professional Resources Incorporated. An outfit of former U.S. marines, helicopter pilots and special forces teams, MPRI's missions for the U.S. government have run from flying Colombian helicopter gunships to supplying weapons to the Croatian army.[7]

In 1995, MPRI armed and trained the Croatian army for "Operation Storm," a brutal campaign that forced over 200,000 Serbs out of their long-time homes in the Krajina region of Croatia.

The Scotsman says that following Operation Storm (and well before the U.S.-NATO war), the MRPI was arming and training the KLA. As reported in *The Scotsman:*

> MPRI subcontracted some of the training program to two British security companies, ensuring that between 1998 and June 1999 the KLA was being armed, trained and assisted in Italy, Turkey, Kosovo and Germany by the Americans, the German external intelligence service and former and serving members of Britain's 22 SAS Regiment.

Col. Hackworth reported in his column that the seventeeen military commanders rescued in Macedonia in June 2001 were all from MPRI and that seventy percent of the equipment used by the mercenaries was U.S. made.

Here is how Hackworth describes the role of MPRI:

[The seventeen were] members of a high-ticket Rent-a-Soldier outfit called MPRI—Military Professional Resources Incorporated—that operates in the shadow of the Pentagon and has been hired by the CIA and our State Department for ops in ex-Yugoslavia. The company, headed up by former U.S. Army Chief of Staff Gen. Carl E. Vuono, is filled with former U.S. Army personnel, from generals to senior sergeants, all of whom draw handsome wages on top of their Army retired salaries. ...

This is the same outfit that in the early 1990s trained Croatian soldiers for Operation Storm—which resulted in the brutal ethnic cleansing of 200,000 unarmed Serb civilians—as well as bringing Croatian Gen. Agim Ceku up to speed. Ceku, who played a central role in the slaughter, is alleged to have killed thousands of other Serb civilians before joining the KLA in 1999, where he again received training and assistance from CIA and State Department contractors operating overtly and covertly throughout ex-Yugoslavia and around the globe.[8]

In another report in *The Scotsman* headlined "CIA aided Kosovo guerrilla army," the opening sentence declares that "American intelligence agents have admitted they helped train the Kosovo Liberation Army before NATO's bombing of Yugoslavia."[9]

In fact, the so-called cease-fire monitors from the Organization for Security and Cooperation in Europe (OSCE) headed by U.S. Ambassador William Walker was really a front for a CIA support operation for the KLA, *The Scotsman* reports. It continues

Central Intelligence Agency officers were cease-fire monitors in Kosovo in 1998 and 1999, developing ties with the KLA and giving American military training manuals and field advice on fighting the Yugoslav army and Serbian police. ... American policy made air strikes inevitable.

The Scotsman report continues: "Some European diplomats in Pristina, Kosovo's capital, concluded from [William] Walker's background that he was inextricably linked with the CIA."

The report adds a quote from a CIA source: "[The OSCE monitors were] a CIA front, gathering intelligence on the KLA's arms and leadership. ... [They would advise the KLA on] which hill to avoid, which wood to go behind, that sort of thing."

The Scotsman report says that the CIA operation in building up the KLA actually began in 1996, the first year of KLA operations in Kosovo.

Another report, this one in the *Ottawa Citizen*, published in Canada's capital, also details how the "CIA trained Kosovo rebels."[10]

The *Ottawa Citizen* report says the U.S. intelligence agents have admitted that they trained the KLA well before NATO's bombing. The report also identifies the OSCE's observor team headed by William Walker as a CIA front.

The *Ottawa Citizen* reports that when the OSCE monitors left Kosovo a week before air strikes began, "many of its satellite telephones and global positioning systems were secretly handed to the KLA, ensuring that guerrilla commanders could stay in touch with NATO and Washington. Several KLA leaders had the mobile phone number of Gen. Wesley Clark, the NATO commander."

[1] Radio Free Europe/Radio Liberty broadcast transcript, June 26, 2001, www.rferl.org

[2] July 9, 2001, column by Col. David Hackworth, King Syndicate, www.hackworth.com

[3] See the *Philadelphia Inquirer's* "Crisis in Kosovo" report for a description of the arrival of the Atlantic Brigade; www.philly.com/specials/99/kosovo/Raw/KLA0418.asp

[4] *NATO in the Balkans: Voices of Opposition*, International Action Center, New York, www.iacenter.org

[5] "The General's Manifesto" was reprinted in newspapers across Yugoslavia. An English translation of excerpts from the version printed in the Zagreb, Croatia, newspaper Vjesnik on Jan. 31, 1991, appears in *The Destruction of Yugoslavia* by Branka Magas, Verso, 1993.

[6] *Intelligence Newsletter*, April 18, 1999, www.indigo-net.com

[7] "Private U.S. firm training both sides in Balkans," *The Scotsman*, March 2, 2001, www.scottsman.com

[8] Hackworth, op. cit.

[9] "CIA aided Kosovo guerrilla army," *The Scotsman,* March 12, 2000, www.scottsman.com

[10] "CIA trained Kosovo rebels," *The Ottawa Citizen*, March 12, 2000, www.ottawacitizen.com

Kosovo: Winter 1998-1999

The security situation within Kosovo on March 19, 1999, as reported by the Organization for Security and Cooperation in Europe (OSCE) was calm but tense. In addition, the alert status remained at "one," a "potentially" deteriorating environment, but not actually deteriorating, and there was no direct threat to OSCE personnel. This had been the reported situation: general stability throughout Kosovo for the weeks and months prior to March 20, 1999. It was also the situation that Field Station, Kosovo Polje had experienced since its establishment in mid-February.

Yet, on March 20, the OSCE Kosovo Verification Mission (KVM) was ordered to evacuate Kosovo by the then OSCE Chairman in Office, the Norwegian foreign minister. This was the penultimate Western move to force Yugoslavian compliance to accept the Rambouillet-Paris ultimatum and to surrender its sovereignty. It did not change the political stand off, however.

The result was an anticipated air strike of a few days, that ended in an eleven-week air bombardment, creating directly, or indirectly, a full scale civil war, along with a vast humanitarian disaster, combined with destruction throughout Yugoslavia. Given its length and consequences, this aerial war was ill-conceived and planned. It could and should have been avoided!

So what led to this breakdown of the peace process and were there alternatives?

Historical grievances existed within the Kosovo ethnic communities. These had been exacerbated by the political destabilization and a loss of local Kosovo autonomy within Yugoslavia, itself exacerbated by Western interference in Yugoslavia's 1990s wars of secession. The resulting increasing tensions in Kosovo led to the commencement of an armed insurrection in February 1998 by the UCK, or Kosovo Liberation Army (KLA). The Yugoslav Ministry of the Interior Police (MUP), supported by the Yugoslav Army (VJ), reacted to impose security and counter the terrorist threat.

The resulting destruction of numerous villages, with some 2,000 fatalities, including some 600 Serbs, along with the displacement of some

200,000 residents, as well as 50,000 refugees who fled the province, led to the creation of a significant, but mostly Internally Displaced Population (IDP).

Once again, international interference had help create destabilization which threatened the Balkans. Under United Nations Security Council Resolution 1199 of September 1998, the international community called for a Kosovo cease-fire, a withdrawal of belligerent contact and a limitation of the military and security forces and their weaponry. This "peace, stability and cooperation" was to be verified by the OSCE international observer mission, along with the KVM of up to 2,000 OSCE verifiers, whose unarmed monitoring presence was agreed to by Special Envoy Richard Holbrooke, representing the western Contact Group, and Slobodan Milosevic, representing the Federal Republic of Yugoslavia (FRY), on October 16, 1998. This was to hopefully end the previous eight months of internal conflict and its humanitarian consequences.

Given its international composition, the KVM was organized and deployed quite slowly, and it was not fully operational, even on a partial basis, until early in 1999.

Also, given its composition, its myriad of verifier experience, and its limited administrative support, the KVM international observer teams did manage to provide a degree of calming stability by monitoring cease-fire compliance or non compliance, investigating cease-fire violations and security road blocks, and assisting humanitarian agencies. It was restricted, however, by its very limited presence to vehicle road patrols, and its numerous liaison meetings with both the security forces, the insurgents and various groups of inhabitants.

These limitations, however, enabled the 1,300 verifiers to monitor the security forces, who were attempting to maintain security within the major communities and the internal lines of communication, better than they could monitor the KLA factions. Consequently, they [KLA] were left in control of much of the hinterland unchallenged. The KLA also generally ignored the cease-fire, provoking and inhibiting the security forces, while it consolidated and built its strength in preparation for a military solution, hopeful of NATO military support.

The result was inevitable: the low intensity conflict at the end of 1998 increasingly evolved into a mid-intensity insurrection, with ambushes, kidnappings of security forces, and with the encroachment of critical lines of communication in a series of incidents leading to government casualties. The security force response was also inevitable, as they struck back, and thereby also exceeded their restrictions on the application of force.

So, with no desire for further diplomacy, NATO had its war, and only after seventy-eight days of air bombardment was it suspended. Yugoslav forces withdrew from Kosovo, and NATO ground forces occupied the province, establishing a UN-administered protectorate. With the reversal of power, the 800,000 Kosovar refugees, created by the war, returned, supporting the KLA's policy of reverse intimidation and atrocities. This all but ethnically cleansed the majority of the 270,000 Kosovo Serbs and other minorities from the province.

Thus, once again foreign intervention exacerbated Yugoslavian political problems, and it will likely increase Albanian regional ambitions. This could also potentially result in a Serbian irredentist movement, which will only destabilize the surrounding Balkan nations and European security even further.

The disastrous Kosovo war could and should have been avoided. Further diplomacy and increased international monitoring may well have restored human rights and reestablished stability, cooperation and peace. This could and should have been attempted. NATO went to war ostensibly to prevent a humanitarian disaster, with the expulsion of the majority Albanians; however, the war caused their displacement to occur, and then it created the circumstances for the reverse expulsion of Kosovo Serbs. By all accounts, the result of this unprovoked, unnecessary and illegal NATO war has been a disaster. There were alternatives and it could and should have been avoided. It was a colossal failure of international diplomacy!

Austria's Role in the Aggression

Gregor Kneussel

Since the world already knows too well the crimes committed by Austrian soldiers and politicians against the Balkans sixty years ago, this chapter will concentrate on summarizing the role of Austrian politicians in Yugoslavia between 1990 and 2000, plus a little about the popular resistance to that policy.

Austria declared a state of neutrality after the Second World War. That meant, according to the Austrian Constitution, that the country was not supposed to join any military alliance and not to side with any other country in a war.

Nevertheless the Austrian government has played a crucial rôle in the disintegration of Yugoslavia. In 1991 the U.S. government was still thinking that the secession of Slovenia and Croatia from Yugoslavia was not in its interest. This was clearly expressed by James Baker in a meeting in Belgrade in June 1991. The German and Austrian govern-ments on the other hand were already trying to get their share of the Balkans at that time. Just three days after Slovenia and Croatia declared they had seceded from Yugoslavia, several Austrian politicians of the ruling Social Democrats (SPÖ) and Christian Conservatives (ÖVP) went to Ljubljana, the capital of Slovenia, to demonstrate support for this se-cession. Slovenian politicians were received as representatives of an independent country long before even just one single country in the world had recognized Slovenia as a separate state. Representatives of the Christian conservative People's Party, members of parliament argued that Slovenia could become a part of Austria.

Later on, in 1992, Alois Mock, the Austrian minister of foreign affairs, actively tried to convince the government of the United States and other countries to launch a military intervention in the conflict in Bosnia.

All these actions were of course clear violations of the Austrian Constitution and the Neutrality Law.

In August 1998 the Austrian government once more took part in the actions against Yugoslavia. Wolfgang Petritsch was the Austrian ambassador in Belgrade at that time, and he was sent to Kosovo to represent the European Union in the Contact Group that was supposed to solve the conflict in Kosovo. Together with the U.S. representative in that Contact Group, Christopher Hill, he actively prepared the Rambouillet negotiations, held in France in February-March 1999. He specifically delivered the ultimatum that came out of Rambouillet to the Yugoslav government.

In fact NATO had already threatened to bomb Yugoslavia in October 1998, five months before the Rambouillet negotiations started. The so-called Rambouillet agreement was signed by the Albanian side and also by Wolfgang Petritsch, but the Yugoslav and the Russian representatives did not sign it.

In March 1999, the content of the so-called Rambouillet agreement and the Appendix B as NATO and EU proposed it was not known at all to the public. Wolfgang Petritsch made it quite clear in an interview with the German *Spiegel* that it was meant as an ultimatum against Yugoslavia. He said:

> Eighty percent of our demands will just be rushed through. Two things are definitely forbidden [for the Yugoslav delegation]: press contacts and leaving before a conclusion. They all remain interned in a conclave. In the end it is going to be tough and the final result will probably be dictated by us. But I guarantee one thing: By the end of April either the Kosovo conflict will be formally resolved, or NATO will bomb [Yugoslavia].

On March 18 the Yugoslav side explained to the press why they refused to sign that military annex, but the Western media just refused to report on that. Six days later [March 24] NATO forces started to bomb Yugoslavia.

In April 1999, during the NATO bombings, I joined a delegation to Yugoslavia to see the effects of the NATO air raids; we witnessed the destruction of civilian targets—bridges, factories, schools and apartment houses in Belgrade, Novi Sad, Niš and Aleksinac. The most shocking experience for us was Aleksinac, a very small town with no industry whatsoever. NATO had bombed several apartment blocks and small houses there, as well as the local polyclinic. In Belgrade we also met Vladimir Stambuk who had been a member of the Yugoslav delegation to Rambouillet. He gave us a copy of the Rambouillet ultimatum as Petritsch and the other western envoys had delivered it. Only then did we learn about the Annex B the Yugoslav representatives had refused to sign.

During the seventy-eight days of NATO attacks, we Austrian anti-war activists in alliance with the large Yugoslav community were on the streets of Vienna every single day. We had smaller demonstrations during working days and big meetings and demonstrations every weekend. When the NATO bombings were over we still thought that it was very important to continue our activities. It became clear that there is an embargo against Yugoslavia, and we had seen what an embargo meant to Iraq and to other countries. In Iraq more than a million people died due to the embargo. Therefore we founded the Austrian-Yugoslav Solidarity Movement (JÖSB), and we go on organizing meetings and we go on informing people in Austria about what's going on in Yugoslavia.

On December 4, 1999, we held the Vienna Tribunal against the Austrian government's aiding and abetting the NATO aggression against Yugoslavia. The Tribunal in Vienna found that the Austrian Federal Government, as well as Alois Mock, the former minister of foreign affairs, as well as Ambassador Wolfgang Petritsch, the European Union special envoy to Kosovo, all bear responsibility for the NATO aggression against Yugoslavia.

The Rambouillet Accord:

Declaration of War Disguised as Peace Agreement

RICHARD BECKER

Who was responsible for the wars that tore apart Yugoslavia? According to the "conventional wisdom" in Washington and the other NATO capitals, blame for the four Yugoslavia wars of the 1990s can be placed squarely and exclusively on the shoulders of one person: former Yugoslav President Slobodan Milosevic. To say that this kind of "analysis" is simplistic and self-serving is to engage in the most restrained form of understatement.

The extreme demonization of Milosevic (and by inference the Serbian people as a whole) is used as a shield by the U.S. and other NATO leaders to fend off any inconvenient questions about their own crucial roles in the bloody destruction of the Yugoslav federation. The International Action Center and others have documented the key part played by the U.S., Germany, and other European imperialist powers in the Slovenia, Croatia and Bosnia wars of the early 1990s.

In 1998-1999, these same powers presented themselves once again as "peacemakers," this time in regard to the conflict in the southern Serbian province of Kosovo. In February 1999, U.S. Secretary of State Madeleine Albright convened a "peace conference" in Rambouillet, France. Albright and NATO demanded that the leaders of the Federal Republic of Yugoslavia, the Republic of Serbia, the western-backed and armed Kosovo Liberation Army, and other parties sign a U.S.-written agreement.

The Rambouillet Accord, presented in the U.S. and other Western corporate media as a bonafide attempt to negotiate a resolution to the crisis in Kosovo, was, in fact, a declaration of war disguised as a peace agreement.

In explaining why they launched the devastating seventy-eight-day bombing war against Yugoslavia, President Clinton, Secretary of State Albright and other U.S. and NATO leaders repeatedly attempted to place the blame on the Belgrade government for refusing to negotiate and failing to sign the Rambouillet agreement.

In a major speech on March 23, 1999, justifying the war that the U.S. was about to initiate, Clinton told the American Federation of State, County and Municipal Employees national convention, *"President Milosevic refused even to discuss key elements of the agreement."*

The reality was very different. NATO presented the Rambouillet Accord to Yugoslavia as an ultimatum. It was a *"take it or leave it"* proposition as Albright and other officials often emphasized in February 1999. There were, in fact, no real negotiations at all.

The accord provided Kosovo with a very broad form of autonomy. A province of Serbia, one of two republics (along with Montenegro) which make up present-day Yugoslavia, Kosovo would have its own parliament, president, prime minister, supreme court and security forces under Rambouillet. The new Kosovo government would be able to negate laws of the federal and Serbian republic legislatures and conduct its own foreign policy. The agreement was to be enforced by 28,000 NATO troops.

The Yugoslav government indicated its willingness to accept the autonomy part of the agreement. It rejected the occupation of Yugoslavia by NATO as a violation of its sovereignty, but indicated its willingness to consider alternative international *"peacekeeping"* forces.

The U.S. rejected any negotiation on this point. On February 21, 1999, Secretary of State Madeleine Albright declared in Rambouillet: *"We accept nothing less than a complete agreement, including a NATO-led force."* Asked on CNN the same day: *"Does it have to be [a] NATO-led force, or as some have suggested, perhaps a UN-led force or an OSCE force? Does it specifically have to be NATO-run?"* she replied: *"The United States position is that it has to be a NATO-led force. That is the basis of our participation in it."*

Two days later, Albright repeated this position at a press conference: *"It was asked earlier, when we were all together whether the force could be anything different than a NATO-led force. I can just tell you point blank from the perspective of the United States, absolutely not, it must be a NATO-led force."*

Over the next month, this position was repeated many times by State Department officials. The U.S. refused to allow the Serbs to sign the political agreement until they first agreed to a NATO-led force to implement it.

"The Serbs have been acting as if there are two documents but they can't pick and choose," Albright said, according to a *French Press Agency* report of March 13, 1999. "There is no way to have the political document without the implementation force that has to be NATO-led.... If they are not willing to engage on the military and police chapters, there is no agreement." (FAIR Media Advisory, May 14, 1999)

In a *New York Times* article dated April 8, 1999, Steven Erlanger wrote: "Just before the bombing, when [the Serbian Parliament] rejected NATO troops in Kosovo, it also supported the idea of a United Nations force to monitor a political settlement there."

The NATO leaders were clearly fixed on war and dismissive of anything that might interfere with their military plans. On March 24, 1999, the day the bombing started, State Department spokesperson James Rubin was asked at a press conference about the Serbian parliament's offer to consider an international force:

> QUESTION: Was there any follow-up to the Serbian Assembly yesterday? They had a two-pronged decision. One was to not allow NATO troops to come in; but the second part was to say they would consider an international force if all of the Kosovo ethnic groups agreed to some kind of a peace plan. It was an ambiguous collection of resolutions. Did anybody try to pursue that and find out what was the meaning of that?
>
> RUBIN: Ambassador Holbrooke was in Belgrade, discussed these matters extensively with President Milosevic, left with the conclusion that he was not prepared to engage seriously on the two relevant subjects. I think the decision of the Serb Parliament opposing military-led implementation was the message that most people received from the parliamentary debate. I'm not aware that people saw any silver linings.
>
> QUESTION: But there was a second message, as well; there was a second resolution.
>
> RUBIN: I am aware that there was work done, but I'm not aware that anybody in this building regarded it as a silver lining.

PROVISIONS OF RAMBOUILLET

In addition to its publicized aspects, the Rambouillet Accord contained many provisions that are extraordinary in their intrusiveness and violation of Yugoslavia's sovereignty. Most of these provisions have never been mentioned in the mainstream media in the United States. A brief (and non-comprehensive) survey of some of the accords' articles follows.

Chapter 4a, Article I – "The economy of Kosovo, shall function in accordance with free market principles." Kosovo, it should be noted, is rich in mineral resources like gold, silver, mercury, molybdenum and other ores. Most of the mines were state-owned or joint ventures. Why it was necessary to stipulate the character of Kosovo's projected new economy has never been publicly explained.

Chapter 5, Article V—"The Chief of the Implementation Mission (CIM) shall be the final authority in theater regarding interpretation of the civilian aspects of this Agreement, and the Parties agree to abide by his determinations as binding on all Parties and persons." The CIM is to be appointed by the European Union countries.

Chapter 7, Article XV—"The KFOR [NATO] commander is the final authority in theater regarding interpretation of this Chapter and his determinations are binding on all Parties and persons." This chapter refers to all military matters.

Together, the CIM and the NATO commander were to be given complete dictatorial powers, the right to overturn elections, shut down organizations and media, and overrule any decisions made by the Kosovo, Serbia or federal governments.

APPENDIX B

Appendix B, the "Status of the Multi-National Military Implementation Force," includes even more intrusive provisions for Yugoslavia as a whole.

> Section 6a. NATO shall be immune from all legal process, whether civil, administrative, or criminal.
>
> Section 6b. NATO personnel, under all circumstances and at all times, shall be immune from the Parties, jurisdiction in respect of any civil, administrative, criminal or disciplinary offenses which may be committed by them in the FRY (Federal Republic of Yugoslavia).
>
> Section 7. NATO personnel shall be immune from any form of arrest, investigation, or detention by the authorities in the FRY.

Together, Sections 6 and 7 comprise the old colonial concept of "extra-territoriality," under which the colonizers were immune from being tried by the courts of the occupied country.

What followed next was even more intrusive, and indeed, must be seen as the **key section of the entire agreement**:

> Section 8: NATO personnel shall enjoy, together with their vehicles, vessels, aircraft, and equipment, free and unrestricted passage and unimpeded access throughout the Federal Republic of Yugoslavia including associated airspace and territorial waters. This shall include, but not be

limited to, the right of bivouac, maneuver, billet and utilization of any areas or facilities as required for support, training, and operations.

This astounding provision, for NATO to occupy not just Kosovo, but all of Yugoslavia, was never reported in the corporate media here during the period leading up to the war.

> Section 11: NATO is granted the use of airports, roads, rails, and ports without payment of fees, duties, dues, tolls, or charges occasioned by mere use.
>
> Section 15: The Parties (Yugoslav government) shall, upon simple request, grant all telecommunications services, including broadcast services, needed for the Operation, as determined by NATO. This shall include the right to utilize such means and services as required to assure full ability to communicate and the right to use all of the electromagnetic spectrum for this purpose, free of cost.
>
> Section 22: NATO may, in the conduct of the Operation, have need to make improvements or modifications to certain infrastructure in the FRY, such as roads, bridges, tunnels, buildings, and utility systems.

The Rambouillet accord required that Yugoslavia allow NATO unfettered access to any and all parts of the country's territory, with all costs to be borne by the host country.

The accord blatantly violated Yugoslavia's sovereignty in so provocative a manner that it could not have been accidental.

Clearly, U.S. policymakers never intended for Yugoslavia's leadership to sign this document. It was just another step in the preparation for war. The role of Rambouillet in this process was to put the onus on the Yugoslav side for the failure to achieve a peaceful resolution, in order to justify the massive bombing of the entire country.

In the June 14, 1999, issue of *The Nation*, George Kenney, a former State Department Yugoslavia desk officer, wrote:

> An unimpeachable press source who regularly travels with Secretary of State Madeleine Albright told this [writer] that, swearing reporters to deep-background confidentiality at the Rambouillet talks, a senior State Department official had bragged that the United States *"deliberately set the bar higher than the Serbs could accept."*

Kenney's account was supported by Jim Jatras, a foreign policy aide to Senate Republicans. Jatras reported in a May 18 speech at the Cato Institute in Washington that he had it *"on good authority"* that a senior administration official told media at Rambouillet the following: "We intentionally set the bar too high for the Serbs to comply. They need some bombing and that's what they are going to get."

In an interview on Pacifica Radio's *Democracy Now* program on June 2, 1999, Kenney said that the "senior State Department official" in his article was Secretary of State Albright.

Both Kenney and Jatras state that they have seen the reporter's notes with exact quotes.

The other leading NATO powers have collaborated with the U.S. administration in planning the war of aggression against Yugoslavia, a country that had not threatened any other state. As one example, the German Foreign Ministry, headed by Green Party leader Joschka Fischer, justified its intervention in Kosovo by references to a "humanitarian catastrophe," "genocide" and "ethnic cleansing" occurring in the year prior to March 24, 1999. Yet, intelligence reports from its own Foreign Office, and from various regional Administrative Courts in Bavaria, Baden-Wurttemberg, Munster, Mainz and elsewhere in Germany, during the year before the start of NATO strikes, repeatedly and amply testify to the lack of any such dire circumstances. (*Junge Welt*, April 24, 1999).

Moreover, all of the NATO leaders collaborated with the U.S. State Department in blocking any real negotiations at Rambouillet.

U.S./NATO – GUILTY OF WAR CRIMES

U.S. leaders never tire of accusing governments that refuse to bow to Washington's will of violating international law. At the same time, the U.S. and the other NATO powers, which, through war, colonialism, genocide and slavery, have inflicted so much death and destruction on the world, are seemingly exempt from any international sanction.

The Principles of the Nuremberg Tribunal, adopted by the International Law Commission of the United Nations in 1950, defines Crimes against Peace in Principle VI:

> a. Crimes against Peace:
> i. Planning, preparation, initiation or waging of a war of aggression
> or a war in violation of in-ternational treaties, agreements or assurances;
> ii. Participation in a common plan or conspiracy for the accomplishment of any of the acts mentioned under (i).

The Nuremberg Final Declaration in 1946 stated that a "crime against peace is not only an international crime, it is the supreme international crime." The death sentences of several Nazi leaders, including

Hermann Goering, were based upon their convictions for crimes against peace.

The conduct of the "negotiations" prior to March 24, 1999 (the beginning of the U.S./NATO bombing of Yugoslavia), and the content of the proposed Rambouillet Accord, indicate that the governments of the United States and its NATO allies are guilty of Crimes against Peace under the above sections.

V.

WAR CRIMES COMMITTED DURING U.S./NATO WAR

Lawless War

MICHAEL RATNER

On March 24, 1999, U.S. Armed Forces, along with military forces from the North Atlantic Treaty Organization (NATO) began massive air strikes against the sovereign nation of the Federal Republic of Yugoslavia. President Clinton asserted that he ordered United States forces into action "pursuant to my constitutional authority to conduct U.S. foreign relations and as Commander-in-Chief and Chief Executive." Neither President Clinton nor NATO articulated authority for the bombing under the United Nations Charter. Rather, they claimed NATO had authority itself and, at least implied that the war was undertaken for humanitarian purposes to stop ongoing human-rights violations.

As is set forth in this chapter, none of the legal justifications claimed by Clinton, NATO or others for the war against Yugoslavia are valid. The war was flatly illegal, contrary to U.S. domestic law, the UN Charter and international law. Under U.S. domestic law, war without authorization from Congress, constitutes an impeachable offense; under international law, aggressive war and war in violation of the UN Charter is a crime against the peace–a crime defined at Nuremberg as the most serious international law violation. Nor can the illegality of the war be escaped by arguing "humanitarian intervention." Not only do the facts on the ground not support this argument (as discussed elsewhere in this book), there is no such doctrine in law. History has demonstrated that a rule permitting such intervention would be used as a pretext by countries acting in their own interest. That is precisely what occurred in the war against Yugoslavia.

Unfortunately, few commentators, journalists, human rights groups and international lawyers have addressed the clear illegality of the war. They have failed to understand the seriousness of what the U.S. and NATO did, not only to the people of Yugoslavia, but to the post-World War II legal order that gave protection against unilateral war making. The UN Charter, as will be explained, prohibited war except in self-defense or when authorized by the Security Council. While this is still part of the Charter, it is part, as far as the U.S. is concerned, in name only. It is apparently open season on any country the U.S. chooses to attack and the Charter be damned. The U.S. as the only superpower calls the shots. Similarly, the U.S. Constitution and the War Powers Resolution (WPR) require that Congress affirmatively consent to war.

War should not be made without consent of the people of the Untied States through their representatives. Congress never gave such authority; in fact, it refused to vote for the war. Yet the president went ahead anyway, shredding both constitution and statute. It is a dangerous time for the peoples of the world; institutions and the legal framework built to protect us all from the scourge of war are in eclipse. There is neither another superpower nor law (that will be obeyed) to hem in the power and aggrandizement of the United States.

VIOLATIONS OF THE U.S. CONSTITUTION AND WAR POWERS RESOLUTION

The analysis begins with the violations of U. S. domestic law: the Constitution and the War Powers Resolution. The U.S. Constitution in Article 1, Section 8, grants the power to initiate war solely to Congress. That section states that Congress has the power to "declare war." Only Congress can decide to go to war except where the president acts in an emergency to repel an enemy attack. This means that both the Senate and the House of Representatives must affirmatively approve the initiation of a war.

The framers were opposed to giving one person–the president–the power to initiate war. They were familiar with the abuses of the war power by the monarchy in England and wanted to insure that war would be fought in the national interest and not for the self-aggrandizement of the president. James Madison spoke of war as "among the greatest of national calamities," while Thomas Jefferson desired an "effectual check to the Dog of War," and George Mason was "for clogging, rather than facilitating war." As a representative to the U.S. House, Abraham Lincoln, in opposing U.S. intervention in Mexico, argued that the Constitution's intent was "that no one man should hold the power of bringing this oppression [war] upon us." The U.S. courts have unanimously reaffirmed this requirement that a decision to wage a war requires prior congressional approval except in response to an enemy attack. (Although, the courts repeatedly state this rule of law in their opinions, they have never yet ordered an end to an illegal war.)

Wars requiring such congressional approval are not only conflagrations on the scale of World War II, but include the commitment of significant numbers of American armed forces to sustained combat against a foreign government. Under this or any other sensible definition of the term "war," the hostilities against Kosovo were a war that required congressional consent. Professor John Basset Moore, one of the most prominent international law professors of the first half of the Twentieth Century, strongly criticized the view that the president could go to war based on what he thought was right and pointed to the dangers of such a belief:

> There can hardly be room for doubt that the framers of the Constitution, when they vested in Congress the power to declare war never imagined that they were leaving it to the executive to use the military and naval forces of the United States all over the world for the purpose of actually coercing other nations, occupying their territory and killing their soldiers and citizens, all according to his notions of the fitness of things, so long as he refrained from calling his actions war or persisted in calling it peace.

Of course, even if the war had had congressional consent, this would not have represented a true democratic decision. It is well understood that the current Congress does not represent the mass of people of the United States. Millions are disenfranchised and elections are dominated by big wealth. What is interesting is that even with a Congress so skewed by power and money, President Clinton could not get consent to the war against Yugoslavia.

The constitutional requirements are clear. Congress had to affirmatively and explicitly authorize the war against Yugoslavia. Congressional silence would not be sufficient; approval is necessary. Such approval should have been given before the war began, for once a war starts there is strong pressure on Congress to "rally around the troops." The president never even tried to obtain such approval from the House of Representatives prior to the war. Presumably, he knew the House would not give its approval to the war. However, once the war began, he did seek such approval and failed to get it. Amazingly, on April 28, 1999, the House of Representatives rejected a resolution that would have authorized the president to conduct military air operations and missile strikes in cooperation with NATO against Yugoslavia. It did so by a tie 213-213 vote, the result of which was in doubt until the very last moment.

The significance of this vote should not be underestimated. This was the first time in U.S. history that a Congress had actually voted to deny a president the authority he requested to fight a war. But the vote made no difference to the president. He continued to fight the war and ignored the action that the House of Representatives had taken. A more unconstitutional and blatantly illegal act is difficult to imagine. During this same period Congress was considering impeachment charges against the president regarding the Monica Lewinsky matter; what it should have been doing was drafting articles of impeachment for his subversion of the Constitution with regard to his unilateral war against Yugoslavia.

The Constitution was not all that was pushed to the side in the war. The War Powers Resolution met its final and ignominious end–although it is still supposed to be the law of the land. Despite a clear violation of that statute by the president, Congress did absolutely nothing about it; most members of Congress and the president acted as if the statute did not exist.

The WPR was passed in the wake of the Vietnam War in an effort to insure that no president acting alone could drag the United States into a war. It was passed, over President Nixon's veto, to prevent war by presidential fiat and to protect the constitutional power of Congress to declare war. The statute requires the president to submit a report to Congress in any situation in which United States Armed Forces are introduced into hostilities. The submitting of this report triggers the key provision of the statute–the sixty-day rule. Under that rule, all U.S. forces must be withdrawn from hostilities within sixty days unless Congress affirmatively approves of the troop commitment. In other words, if the president does not get congressional approval within sixty days, he must withdraw all U.S. forces. This is known as the automatic termination provision. Congress need do nothing. The burden, as the Constitution requires, is on the president to get the authority from Congress to continue a commitment of U.S. armed forces in combat or war.

In its brief twenty-four-year history since the statute was passed in 1976, the sixty day provision had never been invoked. Either no war or commitment of troops had lasted for more than sixty days or Congress, as it did in the 1991 war against Iraq, had given approval. The war against Yugoslavia was to be the first time since 1976 that a war continued for over sixty days and did not have the approval of Congress.

All of the statutory requirements needed to trigger the automatic termination provision of the WPR were met. On March 26, 1999, the president submitted the report required under the WPR to Congress; he stated that on March 24, "U.S. military forces...began a series of air strikes in the Federal Republic of Yugoslavia." This report began the running of the sixty-day clock after which all hostilities against Yugoslavia would have to cease unless Congress gave its approval. Thus by approximately May 25, 1999, the war should have been over unless Congress gave its specific approval.

Prior to the sixty days expiring, Representative Tom Campbell, a Republican, introduced various resolutions that would require a congressional vote on whether to approve the war. It was his view that the Constitution and WPR had to be complied with and if they were not, all troops had to be withdrawn. As was stated earlier, none of these resolutions passed; the key resolution, which would have given the president authority to continue the war past sixty days failed to pass by a tie 213-213 vote. Thus, as the war continued it was clear that the president did not have the constitutional authority to have initiated the war, nor the statutory authority to keep fighting past the sixty-day limit by which the WPR mandated termination.

The sixty-day termination date passed almost unnoticed by the press, Congress and the pundits. Only Representatives Tom Campbell, Dennis Kucinich and a few others brought up the issue and no one paid attention. It was a remarkable moment. Here was a statute, the WPR, which had been written because of the debacle of Vietnam; it was meant to keep the U.S. out of wars that did not have congressional approval. One could say the statute was literally written in the blood of the Americans and Vietnamese who died in that war. And now the statute was treated as naught, as if nothing was learned from the Vietnam War. The bombing of Yugoslavia was continuing; people were being killed and the country was being destroyed; and it was all a clear violation of U.S. law.

A few courageous members of Congress decided to take the issue of the illegality of the war to the federal courts. The leader of this group was Representative Tom Campbell and he gathered a dozen or so Republicans to join with him. He asked the Center for Constitutional Rights (CCR) to bring the litigation on his behalf. [The author, along with Jules Lobel, James Klimaski, Joel Starr, Franklin Siegel and H. Lee Halterman were the attorneys in this lawsuit.] The CCR had brought a number of lawsuits previously challenging illegal uses of U.S. military force in Grenada, El Salvador, Nicaragua, Panama, and Iraq.

All of these suits had been against Republican presidents and the majority if not all of the congressional plaintiffs had been Democrats. Now that the shoe was on the other foot, and a Democratic president was unilaterally going to war, Democratic plaintiffs were hard to come by. Many Democrats did not like the war, thought it was illegal, but did not want to buck the president and say so publicly whether by way of speeches or by joining a lawsuit. It was an amazing demonstration of political opportunism. On the issue of should the U.S. go to war, probably the most fundamental and important decision a politician can make, these Democrats sold out. The only two Democrats to join the suit were Dennis Kucinich and Marcy Kaptur.

Even though the illegality of the war was clear both on constitutional and statutory grounds, the attorneys for the members of Congress knew it would be difficult to win. Courts did not like these lawsuits and had developed various legal doctrines so they could avoid dealing with the merits of such controversies. In other words, with regard to the issue of war making the courts have consistently refused to play the role the U.S. Constitution assigned to them–that of determining the proper allocation of power between the president and the Congress. Of course, without the courts as a check on an overreaching president and with Congress silent, there is simply no mechanism to prevent a president from going to war when and how he wishes. The bankruptcy of the constitutional system of checks and balances could not be more clear.

While the attorneys knew the case would be difficult, in many ways the legal claims were better than those of any prior litigation. This time there was a violation of the sixty-day WPR termination provision and no one was doing anything about it. President Clinton was blatantly violating the law. If the court did not act there was no remedy. Were laws simply meaningless?

The case was argued in the federal district court in Washington, D.C., and eventually in the United States Court of Appeals for the District of Columbia. The members of Congress lost in both courts. They did not lose on the merits; the courts never reached the merits. Instead, the judges found that members of Congress did not have the right to bring the lawsuit, or as the court said they did not have standing. While not unexpected, it was a big blow. Prior to this litigation, the attorneys still believed it was possible to litigate the legality of unilateral presidential war making. That is no longer the case.

From a domestic legal point of view, the country is back to business as usual with regard to presidential war making. It's as if the Vietnam War never occurred. Checks and balances, if they ever worked, work no longer. The war against Yugoslavia was not the first unilateral presidential war since Vietnam. Presidents, Democratic and Republican, have frequently employed military force without the consent of Congress. To name a few recent examples: the 1998 air strikes against Afghanistan and Sudan, the 1998 air strikes against Iraq, the 1995 air strikes against the Bosnian Serbs, the 1994 military invasion planned against Haiti, the 1989 invasion of Panama, the 1995 air strikes against Libya and the 1983 invasion of Grenada.

But although these wars have been carried out by the president, Congress should not be let off the hook. It does have the power to stop presidential war making, but has failed to do so. It can vote to stop wars, it can cut off funds and finally it can impeach a president. So the problem is not simply one of presidential overreaching. There is obviously a consensus among most politicians and members of the elite that such wars are to be fought. Certainly, the president, Congress and the courts cannot be depended upon to keep the U.S., out of war. Without a strong anti-war and peace movement in this country and elsewhere, the future is bleak. More Yugoslavia-type interventions will be the order of the day.

VIOLATIONS OF THE UN CHARTER AND INTERNATIONAL LAW

The violations of domestic law were serious, but they pale in comparison to NATO's violations of the UN Charter and international law. By treating as a nullity key provisions of the Charter, the U.S. and NATO have undermined the most important legal restraints on war making. They have effectively nullified legal prohibitions on war, passed in the wake of World War II, that were critical to world peace. Now it is a free for all, where might is right. Any country can choose to follow the path of the Untied States and make war without the authority of the UN. Of course, it is the more powerful countries, those that have U.S. and NATO approval, that will use this awful precedent. It is indeed a dangerous time for the peoples of the world. As twenty members of the

Greek Council of State (Greece's Supreme Administrative Court) stated during the war:

> The truth is that NATO's attack on Yugoslavia inaugurates a period of lawlessness in international relations. We are returning to the era of the Holy Alliance and the Axis, against which humanity, and the Greeks in particular, fought with such great sacrifices.

The UN Charter, a treaty binding on the United States and all of the NATO countries, states in its stirring preamble that its purpose is "to save succeeding generations from the scourge of war," and "to bring about by peaceful means...settlement of international disputes ... which might lead to a breach of the peace." Military force was to be relied upon only as an extreme last resort. The Charter clearly prohibits nations from attacking other states for claimed violations of human rights. Article 24, the central provision of the Charter, prohibits the "threat or use of force against" another state. There are only two exceptions to this prohibition. Article 51 allows a nation to use force in "self-defense if an armed attack occurs against" it or an allied country. The Charter also authorizes the Security Council to employ force to counter threats to or breaches of international peace. This has been interpreted to allow individual nations to militarily intervene for humanitarian reasons, but only with the explicit authorization of the Council. This occurred in Somalia, Rwanda, Haiti and Bosnia.

What is critical about the Charter and represented a major break with the past is that war or the use of military force was made illegal unless specifically approved by the Security Council under Article 42. These provisions were the cornerstone of efforts to insure that the world would not again be drowned in blood. So important have they become in the fifty plus years since the Charter's ratification that they have achieved the status of what international law scholars refer to by the Latin term jus cogens or fundamental customary international law–the highest and most binding form of law. A violation of this law is an international crime against peace.

Prior to the war, the Security Council was dealing with the situation in Yugoslavia. It had passed resolutions in efforts to end the conflict in Kosovo and was actively engaged in attempting to bring peace to the area. But what it has not done and has never done is pass a resolution granting authority to any country to use force against Yugoslavia. The

United States and NATO did not even go to the Council to obtain such authority. On their own, and without the sanction of the Security Council, they went to war against Yugoslavia. In doing so, these countries violated the central provisions of the Charter and committed an international crime. There is simply no valid argument that supports the actions of the U.S. and NATO. Fundamental international law required them to obtain authority from the Security Council.

THE WAR CANNOT BE JUSTIFIED BY CLAIMS OF HUMANITARIAN INTERVENTION

Some scholars, particularly in the United States, have argued that there is a right to humanitarian intervention when genocidal crimes are being committed within a state. But of course, that was not the situation in Kosovo. There has been absolutely no proof that genocide was going on or was planned.

Most countries and scholars, however, have rejected any doctrine of unilateral humanitarian intervention. The purported good that might come from allowing countries to intervene without UN authority would be outweighed by the dangers that would arise from weakening the Charter's restraints on the use of force. The proponents of humanitarian intervention assume that great powers such as the U.S. will act with humanity's interest in mind. History, the current geopolitical context and the war against Yugoslavia indicate otherwise; they act in their own interest.

The history of humanitarian military intervention is replete with invocations of humanitarian intentions by strong powers or coalitions to conceal their own geopolitical interests. This historical record led the International Court of Justice to conclude in 1949 that a right of forcible intervention in the name of international justice "has, in the past, given rise to most serious abuses. . . . [F]rom the nature of things, it would be reserved for the most powerful states."

The United States often asserted humanitarian reasons to justify military interventions that served its own geopolitical interests. President McKinley justified U.S. militarily intervention against Spain by invoking the cause of humanity. President Johnson claimed that U.S. intervention in Vietnam and the Dominican Republic were undertaken for humanitarian reasons. President Reagan asserted that the interventions against Nicaragua and Grenada were designed to restore freedom and human rights for those people.

The actual history of so-called humanitarian interventions therefore leaves one deeply suspicious of any doctrine that would allow powerful states or even coalitions of allied nations a right to intervene in the affairs of other states. It is a right that would only be employed against small states. Permitting individual or coalitions of states to attack other nations based upon their own determinations of human rights abuses would eviscerate the international legal restraints against the use of force.

The Kosovo crisis illustrates the danger of bypassing the Security Council and lends credence to those who argue that the intervention was not for humanitarian purposes. The U.S. never went to the Council. Had it done so, it is possible that the final settlement that ended the air war could have been achieved without the use of force. The Council might have insisted on more negotiations, a more flexible approach to the Rambouillet proposal, and altered U.S. insistence that the negotiator be from the U.S. Moreover, the destructiveness of the war and its aftermath—100,000 Roma people and over 200,000 Serbs have been forced to flee Kosovo—undermines the humanitarian claims of the U.S. and reemphasizes the reasons the Charter's framers chose peace as its central tenet.

CONCLUSION

The unsanctioned and illegal war against Yugoslavia was a watershed event that is a harbinger of an insecure future for countries and peoples that find themselves in disagreement with the policies and aims of the United States and its NATO allies. Apparently, the United States and NATO now believe international restraints on force and the United Nations can be dispensed with. When and where to use military force will be decided by the United States and NATO. The world can look forward to more killings and devastation, like that in Yugoslavia, all in the name of human rights. It is not a pretty picture and represents a major retreat from the hopes that we could one day grow up in a world free from war.

On the domestic front, the retreat from the principle that the people, through Congress, should control the use of military force, appears complete. We now face the prospect of war at the behest of one person—the president.

There is an obvious parallel in terms of what has occurred domestically and internationally. Those institutions, the Congress and the Security Council (imperfect as they are), that were required to approve the use of military force have been bypassed. To the extent they made the decision to use force more democratic and more difficult, that is no longer true. We have entered a very dangerous period. Power and might rule.

NATO's Civilian Targets[*]

SARAH SLOAN

The way in which NATO's war was carried out is indicative of the lies and the priorities of those who waged it. U.S./NATO bombs destroyed only fourteen tanks in Yugoslavia. But they hit at least 480 schools.

I would like to enter for the record that list of schools.

This was not an accident, it was a matter of military policy. As such this entire policy is a violation of law regarding war crimes. This truth about the war against civilians has been fully revealed in recent weeks.

The May 15, 2000, issue of *Newsweek* described "The Kosovo Cover-Up." This article, based on an internal suppressed U.S. Air Force report, described in detail the discrepancy between Defense Secretary William Cohen's lie that Yugoslav military forces were "severely crippled" and the fact—which the U.S. policy makers knew all along—that only fourteen tanks were actually destroyed.

This report reveals that the Pentagon decided early in the campaign they could not quickly win the war and avoid large U.S. casualties by direct engagement with the Yugoslav army. Not only could they not find Yugoslav army targets from the air, the U.S. dreaded direct engagement because U.S. casualties would make the anti-war movement in the U.S. an irresistible force, as it was in Vietnam.

This report shows that they opted for Plan B. What was Plan B? And it's possible it was actually Plan A. They targeted the civilian population, they terrorized the people, they bombed schools, hospitals, petrochemical plants, irrigation ducts, auto factories, bridges, residential neighborhoods.

I quote from *Newsweek*:

> Air power was effective in the Kosovo war not against military targets but against civilian ones. Military planners do not like to talk frankly about terror-bombing civilians ("strategic targeting" is the pre-

---

[*] The following are three short reports on NATO's civilian targets in Yugoslavia, gathered from various sources but all available in the Yugoslav *White Book*, which we have summarized in the Appendix. The reports are from talks given at the June 10, 2000, final tribunal hearing in New York on NATO's War Crimes Against Yugoslavia.

ferred euphemism), but what got Milosevic's attention was turning out the lights in downtown Belgrade. Making the Serb populace suffer by striking power stations—not "plinking" tanks in the Kosovo country-side—threatened his hold on power.

There are additional examples that demonstrate this truth.

In October 1999, Clinton announced his opposition to allowing emergency heating oil to be supplied to Yugoslavia for the winter months after the war. Clinton and Secretary of State Albright said they hope to increase "discomfort" among Yugoslavs in an effort to incite the hoped for overthrow of Yugoslav President Slobodan Milosevic and his administration.

It was mid-December—a time in Yugoslavia when temperatures frequently fall below zero degrees Fahrenheit. Much of Yugoslavia's oil reserves were destroyed in the bombing. This means U.S. government policy was to freeze Yugoslav people.

Systematic attacks on civilian populations have been repeated ever since the Iraq war. The civilian infrastructure of a country--meaning the arteries of that country, its ability to provide electricity and transportation and other basic necessities of life—are systematically destroyed. This is designed to combine bombing with economic sanctions for maximum impact.

The heating system is bombed. Sanctions are enforced so that it cannot be rebuilt. And the intended, unavoidable, the calculated suffering to the civilian population is designed for one objective: the overthrow of a government by imperialism. It's a new form of colonialism: Countries that are thriving, that have the potential to be regional powers, like Yugoslavia and Iraq, consciously are being un-developed—taken backwards—by U.S. imperialism.

The military establishment is carrying out a war against people abroad, against human beings who dare to defy the dictates of the IMF and the World Bank. This war was carried out in our name, but we say here before the whole world that the young people and the working people of Yugoslavia are not our enemies.

Our enemy, the enemy of working people, isn't in Novi Sad or Belgrade or Nic or Pristina, it's those who carry out the most vicious war crimes and crimes against humanity in the pursuit of corporate profit. Clinton, Cohen, Albright, Wesley Clark should be arrested and stand trial for their crimes, and with them we should and will indict the bankers and robber barons on Wall Street, whose lust for profit and exploitation drives them to ever new military adventures.

The only way to make the world safe, really safe, the only way to guarantee lasting peace is to remove the system that breeds war. This is our task: to abolish NATO. And moreover to abolish the Pentagon, and to build a new society to meet people's real needs—jobs, education, health care, child care and human relations based on international solidarity rather than wars of aggression.

Bombing the Hospitals

ELLEN CATALINOTTO

Perhaps the simplest way to present the evidence of NATO war crimes against the people of Yugoslavia would be to read this list of the thirty-three hospitals and other health care facilities that were bombed last year, but just to name them all would take longer than the few minutes I have been allotted. The main sources for the information we now present are *Associated Press, Reuters, BBC* and *Agence France Presse* news releases.

From the first days of the bombing, when the Hospital and Medical Center and Gerontological Center in Leskovac were hit on March 25, 1999 and the Pristina dental station on March 29, destruction of these civilian structures occurred with regularity too great to be smart bombs gone astray.

The Dragisa Misovic medical center in Belgrade, bombed on May 19, 1999, is a complex of twenty separate buildings half a kilometer from the nearest military facility. The Neurological Institute was hit, killing three people and wounding many more, and the nearby maternity section suffered damage. At the time of the attack four deliveries were taking place. The windows were shattered and two mothers recovering from Cesarian sections suffered cuts to their faces. Women in labor, mothers who had just delivered and their newborns had to be evacuated to another maternity hospital.

At the Institute for Prematurely Born Infants in Belgrade, electricity was lost after a NATO attack on the nearby power plant on May 2, 1999. In spite of emergency generators, there was not enough power to supply the respirators and nurses had to ventilate their tiny patients by hand. Seventy of the 111 babies in the hospital were in incubators that operate on electricity to supply the warmth these frail infants need to survive.

Because the bombing of chemical factories released many toxins and possible teratogens–agents which cause birth defects–women in Yugoslavia have been advised not to become pregnant for now.

Zeroing in on China

JUDI CHENG

Thirteen months ago, hundreds of thousands of Chinese people took to the streets in China protesting the criminal bombing of the Chinese Embassy in Belgrade. Their fury and anger included the trashing of the U.S. Embassy in Beijing. They felt that the direct hit of the Chinese Embassy in Belgrade by three cruise missiles, which killed three journalists and wounded many more, was not an accident but a deliberate act of mass murder aimed at punishing China for its opposition to the NATO bombing of Yugoslavia. China and Yugoslavia had enjoyed friendly relations and naturally the Pentagon must have considered China an "ally of Yugoslavia."

The May 7 U.S./NATO attack on the embassy was described by the Clinton administration as an accident based on CIA/Pentagon mapping errors. They asserted that the targeting plans mistakenly used old road maps of downtown Belgrade. Is this believable? Is this even slightly credible?

The British newspaper *The Observer*, on Sunday, October 19, 1999, reported based on widespread investigation and quoting unnamed senior military and intelligence sources in Europe and in the United States that NATO did deliberately bomb the Chinese Embassy in Belgrade.

What precisely would the job of the Central Intelligence Agency in Belgrade be if not to carry out daily, systematic surveillance of all the embassies, and specifically the Chinese Embassy. U.S. Defense Department officials in fact attended events at the Chinese Embassy in Belgrade in recent years. Moreover, *The Observer* reported that the CIA and other NATO intelligence agencies had routinely monitored communications traffic from the Chinese Embassy since it moved to its current site in 1996.

It is illegal to bomb government embassies, even in the case of the embassy belonging to an enemy in a declared war. In the case of Yugoslavia, the war was undeclared. China was not part of the conflict.

We charge that the Pentagon deliberately and flagrantly violated international law by bombing the embassy of China on May 7, 1999. This brazen act of terrorism was meant to create exactly the feeling that it did create. Namely, the United States wanted China and all governments in the world to know that should they fail to follow the absolute dictates of U.S. policy, they will become the targets of terror and high tech violence. It is part of an aggressive strategy to use military power as the principle method of imposing U.S. hegemony not just on Yugoslavia, but on all those countries that seek to be independent of U.S. imperialism.

Ecology and Health:

Consequences of the NATO Bombings of Pancevo

JANET M. EATON

This chapter provides evidence that the NATO bombings of Pancevo and other related industrial complexes created an environmental catastrophe which poses a serious threat to human health, the immediate environment and ecosystems of the broader Balkan region; that NATO's aggressive actions were carried out with full awareness of the impact they would have on the environment and peoples of the region; and that NATO flagrantly violated international agreements put in place to protect human rights, and the environment during war and in general.

'ECOLOGICAL CATASTROPHE'

Within the first few weeks of the NATO war against Yugoslavia informed scientific warnings of a pending "ecological catastrophe" echoed through cyberspace and continued throughout the war to alert the public to possible long term destruction of the environment, the eco-destruction of Yugoslavia, ecocide, a great environmental catastrophe for the entire Balkan region, ecocide and indeed the possible risk to all of Europe.

Why did the NATO bombings exact such a degree of dire ecological concern and outcry?

A July 15, 1999, review and analysis of over eighty news releases, articles and papers compiled and summarized in "Ecological Catastrophe and Health Hazards of NATO Bombings"[1] suggested that the alarming outcry of "Ecological Catastrophe" was related to two major causes among others: the bombing of chemical, petrochemical and pharmaceutical plants releasing thousands of tons of noxious contaminants into the atmosphere, soils, ground water and rivers, and NATO's confirmed use of depleted uranium (DU) weapons.[2]

That these were the significant reasons for the perception of an ecological catastrophe was further confirmed by Green Cross International President Mikhail Gorbachev. In a June 13, 1999, *Guardian* article entitled "Poisons in the Air: The Environmental Cost of the Kosovo Conflict," Gorbachev stated that "strikes against certain industries and infrastructure, such as nuclear power stations and some chemical and petrochemical plants must be prohibited." He noted that weapons whose use may have "particularly dangerous, long-term environmental and medical consequences, in particular weapons containing depleted uranium, should be banned. ..."[3]

BOMBING PANCEVO WITH INTENT

When reports emerged that NATO was bombing industrial complexes in major urban centers, news releases began to emerge which resounded with horror and disbelief. An innocent civilian population, the environment and indeed entire ecosystems of one of the most biodiverse regions of all Europe would be threatened, potentially for generations to come, with volumes of toxic materials known to be highly hazardous to human health and devastating to the integrity of ecosystems and to biodiversity. In particular the bombing and subsequent burning of the sprawling Pancevo Petrochemical Complex, on April 18, 1999, which unleashed a dense, massive, toxic black cloud which drifted for days across the Balkans provided incontrovertible incriminating evidence of NATO's abhorrent actions.

A media release by the Serbian Ecological Society describing the final destruction of the Pancevo complex which included an oil refinery, a fertilizer processing plant and a vinyl chloride monomer (VCM) plant stated:

> We are faced with a serious ecological catastrophe. According to all the terms and rules of warfare accepted and followed so far, the plants of chemical process industries of this type have never been military targets and objects of strikes. The range of products of 'HIP Petrohemija' d.p. Pancevo is of a primarily civilian nature and bombardment of these plants represents the worst war crime and it reveals genocidal intentions of the aggressor.[4]

Indeed targeting an industrial complex, even one classified as a military target, located in the midst of a large urban population, would seem beyond conscience and humanitarian convention when the hazardous effects on so many civilians and the environment can be so readily and scientifically deduced. Even more egregious would be the intentional targeting, in urban centers of industrial chemical complexes known to be primarily civilian in nature. But indeed that is what transpired when NATO bombed and destroyed Pancevo on the night of April 18, 1999.

That NATO strategists were well informed of the layout and design of Pancevo is well known. As several news reports and analyses of the war have noted the Pancevo complex had been built with the assistance of a U.S. multinational company, which specialized in petrochemical and polymer plants. That NATO bombed with the intent to create an environmental disaster and to threaten Belgrade into submission can also be further inferred from damning evidence unearthed by Professor Michel Chossudovsky. In his post-war visit to Pancevo, Professor Chossudovsky spoke with the Pancevo plant manager and saw and gathered first hand evidence that NATO selectively bombed holding tanks, which contained highly toxic chemicals of a non-military nature. Meanwhile, NATO bombers ignored those tanks that workers had emptied to avoid combustion from bombing attacks.[5]

Thermal-sensitive satellite imagery along with smart bombs make possible such precise targeting. Conversely, such targeting would have allowed NATO to disable the plant without the devastating consequence to the environment and human health. Instead NATO bombed with an intent to threaten the entire population of the Pancevo/Belgrade area and beyond. Indeed but for a quirk of meteorological fate, which blew the thick dense mile-long black cloud from the Pancevo bombings in a northwesterly direction, the entire city of Belgrade would have been subject to the deadly black cloud of toxins that hovered just above the city.

These actions can be considered all the more egregious when one recalls that the Pentagon, in an April 12, 1999, Department of Defense briefing, assured the world that NATO was engaging in precise targeting using sophisticated weaponry to avoid "collateral damage" including environmental hazards.

The purposeful targeting of these bombings with full knowledge of the implications and consequences for both the civilian population and the life sustaining ecosystems of the Balkan region reveal the duplicity of the words of NATO leaders, the ecocidal and genocidal intent, and the criminal nature of their actions.

Whereas the final destruction of Pancevo was the single most brutal assault on the human environment, there were daily attacks on the chemical industry all over Serbia. These bombings caused uncontrolled spilling, spreading, evaporation and sublimation of huge quantities of toxic substances as well as the burning, combustion, and incomplete combustion of inflammable materials. All told huge volumes of carcinogenic, allergenic, mutagenic, and teratogenic toxic substances were transmitted into the environment and ecosystems of Yugoslavia.

HUMAN HEALTH CONSEQUENCES

Dr. Radoje Lausevic, of the University of Belgrade and the Serbian Ecological Society in his "Overview of Ecological Consequences of NATO Bombing of Yugoslavia" recorded the following chemicals and substances which were released into the atmosphere, water and soil: oils and petroleum products, polychlorinated biphenyles (PCBs), ammonia, ethylene dichloride, natrium hydoxide, hydrogen chloride (1,000 tons released into the river), vinyl chloride monomer (1,000 tons released), phosgene, nitrogen oxides, hydrofluoric acid, heavy metals, as well as products from incomplete combustion such as carbon monoxide, aldehydes, and soot and particulates. In this comprehensive overview Dr. Lausevic also reviewed the health consequences and known limits for human tolerance of each of the substances.

Polluting substances endanger the population directly through several mediums: air, water and food; one should not neglect the indirect influence stemming from the chemical transformation of pollutants, which can result in the increase or in the reduction of their toxicity, as well as from the fact that they tend to accumulate—most often in geological formations or in the biosphere.[6]

After the April 17 and 18 bombings, thousands of people fled the city, coughing and complaining of burning eyes, stomach pain and choking. A report in the Budapest-based Regional Environment Center's Bulletin "After the War" noted that according to Yugoslav estimates some 70,000 people were endangered locally — poisoned, injured and /or evacuated.[7] An International Action Center background research paper citing the health risks caused by NATO's assault against Yugoslavia, reported that in Pancevo the risks were considered so great that physicians have recommended that all women who were in town during the bombing avoid pregnancy for at least two years.[8]

Atmospheric measurements made immediately after the bombings of Pancevo in particular showed levels of many toxic chemicals in the air at several thousand times the tolerable limits for humans. In the case of the highly hazardous vinyl chloride monomer, a concentration of 10,600 times above permitted levels was recorded near Pancevo, according to a press release from Belgrade's Institute of Public Health.[9]

A July 14, 1999, *New York Times* news release further echoed the dire effects of the NATO bombings on the human population:

> Farm workers, plunging their fingers into the earth, say they come away with rashes that burn and blister. Those who eat the river fish and vegetables or drink the tap water, which trickles out of faucets because of the damage to the purification plant, come down with diarrhea, vomiting and stomach cramps. ... Children still suffer headaches and dizziness. ... There are twice as many miscarriages as during this period last year, doctors here said. [10]

Professor Mico Martinovic, a hydrologist, said the array of toxic chemicals released in the region is unique in world history: "What was done against Pancevo was a crime against humanity. ... I never thought NATO or the Americans would bomb the petrochemical plant. I thought they were more civilized."[11]

And Pekka Haavisto, Finland's former environmental minister and head of the UNEP/UNCHS (Habitat) Balkans Task Force team investigating the environmental damage in Yugoslavia, stated in a July 8, 1999 media release: "This is also a question of people who are very concerned about their health in the area. They are afraid of radioactivity. They are afraid of toxic materials. The damage to Yugoslavia is tremendous."[12]

More recently "A Report of Current Cancer Epidemiology in Serbia Based on Available Data" published by the Cancer Foundation of Yugoslavia in December of 1999 reported that the destruction of petrochemical and fertilizer factories, refineries and electro-energetic systems released carcinogens into the air: sulfur dioxide, nitrogen hydroxide, hydrocarbons, pyralene, vinylchloride monomer and lead, and that many carcinogens have polluted water flows. The report also states that for a number of reasons, including the carcinogens released by the bombings, it is reasonable to expect a much higher trend of increase of malignant diseases, both in terms of incidence and mortality. They report though that long-term effects won't be visible for five to fifteen years.[13]

CONSEQUENCES FOR THE ENVIRONMENT, ECOSYSTEMS AND BIODIVERSITY

The chemicals that were released into the atmosphere, water, and soils by the NATO bombings pose a serious threat not only to human health but also to the environment, ecological systems and the biodiversity of Yugoslavia and the broader Balkan and European region as well. Scores of mainstream news releases, as well as numerous reports from and studies by regional and international agencies and NGOs, and special publications like *War in Europe: Ecocide*[14] and The Regional Environment Center's special Bulletin on "After the War"[15] have explored the extent and consequences of these problems from an ecosystem and trans-boundary perspective.

That air pollution was a devastating consequence of the bombings is evident from the testimonies of the effects on human health above. Other airborne impacts were the acid rains, which were measured in several adjacent countries, for indeed such widespread contamination knows no boundaries.

Dr. Luka Radoja, an agronomist and member of the New Green Party in Belgrade, highlighted the consequences of NATO's destruction of fuel storage depots: "By burning down enormous quantities of naphtha and its derivatives more than a hundred highly toxic chemical compounds that pollute water, air and soil are released." He also noted that these poisons endanger all life forms, not only on the territory of Yugoslavia but the territory of neighboring countries as well as the wider region of Europe, because the winds and water-flows are directed right to Central Europe, the Aegean Sea and the Black Sea region.[16]

Soil contamination directly from chemical spills and indirectly from the settling out of substances carried in the black clouds also threatened the environment. The Regional Environment Center (REC) for Central and Eastern Europe in their post-war study Assessment of the Environmental Impact of Military Activity During the Yugoslav Conflict reported that 2.5 million hectares of land (one hectare is about 2.5 acres) were pulled from production to prevent corn, sunflower, soy, and sugarbeet crops from being contaminated by petrochemical clouds and other pollutants created when oil refineries and fertilizer plants were hit in Pancevo, Sombor and Novi Sad.[17]

In addition the Swiss-based humanitarian and scientific group FOCUS conducting independent investigations in the region estimated that mercury spills at Pancevo had contaminated an area of 20,000 square miles including 4,000 cubic meters of soil around the catchment's channel area.

In addition to air and soil pollution, the contamination of water supplies was a major cause for concern from the earliest days of the war. In an April 7, 1999, Environmental News Service release, Branko Jovanovic, a leader of the Yugoslavian New Green Party, said that NATO bombing of Yugoslavia was endangering the entire environment of Europe. "I warn you that Serbia is one of the greatest sources of underground waters in Europe and that the contamination will be felt in the whole surrounding area all the way to the Black Sea."[18]

On May 7 the World Wildlife Fund for Nature (WWF), Danube/ Carpathian program director Philip Weller expressed concern that long-term damage to the environment in both Yugoslavia and surrounding Balkan countries will only increase problems in the region. He noted that the release of these toxics into the Danube, which is the source of drinking water for up to 10 million people, could have serious consequences for people as well as for aquatic organisms and the ecosystem. He also warned of the build-up of toxins in the food chain and possible inability to reproduce among some species.[19]

Furthermore an October 1999 Symposium on the Danube, "A River of Life," noted that Europe's greatest river was already threatened by profound problems demanding immediate redress — its pollution, the future of its wetlands and living ecology, the management and control of this huge waterway passing through many sovereign states and its impact on the Black Sea. A summary statement from a Symposium Workshop on "War and the Environment" illuminates the seriousness of NATO's bombing effects on the already beleaguered Danube river system: "Armed conflicts have a devastating impact on the environment. ...Weapons and military equipment tear apart the earth, saturate it with chemicals, destroying at the same time plant and animal life."[20]

FORMAL ASSESSMENT OF ENVIRONMENTAL EFFECTS
AND RELATED ISSUES

A June 27, 1999, press release from the UN Inter-Agency Needs Assessment Mission noted that throughout the Federal Republic of Yugoslavia, the 11 weeks of NATO air strikes that ended June 10 have had "a devastating impact" on the environment. It also noted that "land, air, rivers, lakes and underground waters as well as the food chain and public health are affected."[21]

The Mission team's report repeatedly called for "urgent" specialized environmental assessment and remedial action focused on the environment and noted that Pancevo may pose a serious threat to health in the region, as well as to ecological systems in the broader Balkans European region. In addition, other environmental agencies in the region—including the WWF, Green Cross International and the Regional Environment Center for Central and Eastern Europe—called for some or all of the following: the need for effective immediate assessment of the entire region, the need for immediate and effective cleanup operations, the need for ecologically sound reconstruction and the need for NATO countries to take responsibility for assisting in the multi-billion dollar price tag already determined to be needed to set things right.[22]

Instead there was limited and inadequate official investigation and assessment. The Balkans Task Force set in motion by the United Nations to examine the environmental consequences of NATO's military actions, although composed of many expert scientists from around the world, was very limited in duration, lacked breadth and scope, failed to have within its mandate assessment of the impact on human health and lacked the cooperation of NATO authorities to either locate or assess the impact of depleted uranium weapons in spite of widespread concern and warnings about the ecological and health implications.

As if to add insult to injury, the UNEP team's final reporting of their limited investigations down-played and minimized the ecological effects of the bombings as evidenced in the press releases accompanying the completion of their investigation:

"Hot Spots in Balkans but No Eco-Catastrophe,"[23] a parallel short-term study by the WWF, in sharp contrast offered the following summation: "WWF analysis shows toxic contamination in Yugoslavia is spreading," highlighting the broader trans-boundary and ecosystem implications of the highly toxic chemicals.[24] And the independent Swiss based FOCUS team of humanitarians and scientists that spent June to September 1999 assessing post-war damage in Serbia and Kosovo-Metohija offered a less politically constrained assessment as well: "Destruction of many potentially dangerous objects on FRY territory caused the threat of ecological catastrophe."[25]

However, the Balkans Task Force did recognize that pollution detected at four hot spots (Pancevo, Kragujevac, Novi Sad, Bor) was serious and posed a threat to human health.[26]

GLOBALIZATION AND MILITARISM

As the many popular tribunals in many countries over 1999-2000 have shown, and as much post-war analysis has demonstrated, the broader political economic rationale for the NATO bombings finds its context in the geo-political machinations of neo-liberal economic globalization.

This post-cold war era has been heralded as the "end of history" and the "triumph of glorious capitalism" over socialism. Meanwhile a form of corporate economic globalization has been transforming ideological mantras of free trade, privatization, deregulation and commodification into a series of "vested interest economic agreements" while often ignoring, sidestepping, denying, clawing back and/or violating fifty years of United Nations progress in developing international universal public trust agreements. It has also become more evident during the past year how militarism and globalization are inextricably linked. Indeed the NATO bombings in Yugoslavia contributed to that greater awareness as people all over the world began to see through the transparent guise which attempted to justify economic aggrandizement as "humanitarian intervention" and deliberate ecocidal and genocidal bombings as "collateral damage."

If there was ever any doubt, the words of Thomas Friedman, U.S. foreign-affairs journalist and author of *The Lexus and the Olive Tree: Understanding Globalization*, rendered the relationship transparent.

> For globalism to work, America can't be afraid to act like the almighty superpower that it is. ... The hidden hand of the market will never work without the hidden fist—McDonald's cannot flourish without McDonnell Douglas, the designer of the F-15. And the hidden fist

that keeps the world safe for Silicon Valley's technologies is called the
United States Army, Air Force, Navy and Marine Corps.[27]

What also has become more evident is that just as communism's industrial development practices ignored the environment with devastating
results, both globalization and militarism are also contributing to the
devastation of the environment and ecosystems of the planet. A new
comprehensive study commissioned by the United Nations, involving
UNEP, UNDP, World Resources Institute and the World Bank, as part
of the Pilot Analysis of Global Ecosystems, and recently previewed in
Time's Special Earth Day Edition, leaves little doubt about the broad decline of the worlds' ecosystems given the present economic course.

Indeed the title of this study "People and Ecosystems: The Fraying
Web of Life" prepares us for one of its major conclusions that the broad
decline of the world's ecosystems must be reversed or there could be
devastating implications for human development. In fact so dire is the
threat that the heads of UNEP, UNDP, the World Resources Institute
and the World Bank have confirmed their commitment to making the
viability of the world's ecosystems a critical development priority for
the twenty-first century.[28]

What was not referred to in the preview of this landmark integrated
study of all the earth's ecosystems was the contribution of militarism to
the over all devastation to the environment. However, Professor Asoka
Bandarage in her seminal text *Women, Population and Global Crisis: A
Political-Economic Analysis* sheds light on the issue:

> Given that the global economy is a military economy, an examina-
> tion of the relationship between industrial capitalist development and
> environmental destruction must be expanded to include militarism. Evi-
> dence shows that global expansion of weapons production and military
> activities may be far more responsible for resource depletion and envi-
> ronmental destruction than human population.[29]

Indeed the devastation wreaked upon the environment in Yugoslavia
by NATO further serves to illuminate the words of Professor Bandarage.

Awareness of the devastating extent of environmental deterioration
should further highlight the imperative for NATO countries to commit
to their obligations and comply with international conventions, treaties
and UN General Assembly resolutions particularly at this period in history when the world is caught in a relentless spiral of violence and self-

destruction on a planet desperately out of balance, where all the world's ecosystems are rapidly collapsing around us, where millions of people are dying of hunger, disease and war, and where nation states and communities and families are breaking apart.

VIOLATION OF INTERNATIONAL LAW

Instead the unprovoked and illegal NATO bombings of Yugoslavia have violated the fundamental provisions of humanitarian law, the principles of environmental protection enshrined in numerous international agreements as well as in other UN instruments and General Assembly resolutions put in place to protect the planet from the "scourge of war."

The extent of these violations has been brought to light by the many testimonies and tribunals during the past year, the numerous cases assembled by lawyers of conscience all over the world and by numerous research papers on the legal consequences. Joan Mcqueeny Mitric writing on the "Cascading Human Consequences of NATO's War in the Balkans" for the spring volume of the *Mediterranean Quarterly: A Journal of Global Issues*, interviewed defense specialist William Arkin whose reflections also shed light on the issue under consideration here.

Arkin said that while current interpretations of international law require the military to consider how many civilians are likely to be hurt, killed and affected by a specific military target being selected, international law has not evolved to force the military to consider microenvironment effects. He went on to suggest, however, that when systemic or massive cascading effects on the human environment are predictable the military would be remiss not to consider the human outcomes of such targets.[30]

With regard to the violation of international agreements put in place to protect the environment, the NATO countries committed blatant violations of treaties and conventions relating to the protection of the Mediterranean Sea against pollution; the Convention on Trans-boundary Pollution; the Convention on the Cooperation in the Field of the Protection and Sustainable Use of the Danube River; the Convention on Climate Changes; the Convention on Protection of the World's Cultural and Natural Heritage; the Ramsar Convention; the Convention on Conservation of European Wildlife and Natural Habitats; the Convention on Conservation of Migratory Wild Animals; the Basel Convention on Trans-boundary Movements of Hazardous Wastes; among others. NATO also violated Principle 24 of the Rio Declaration on the Environment and Development which was adopted at the UNCED Conference in 1992 which declares that states shall respect international law which enables the protection of the environment during war and conflict.

CONCLUSION

In conclusion, there is overwhelming evidence that NATO's bombings of Pancevo and other related industrial chemical complexes created an environmental disaster which has seriously threatened not only the immediate environment, but also ecosystems, biodiversity and health of human populations in the region now and for generations to come; considering that NATO's aggressive actions were planned and executed with full awareness of the harmful and hazardous impact they would exact on environment and peoples; and that the NATO countries turned a blind eye to humanitarian conventions and the ecosystems of this planet in blatantly violating international agreements set in place to protect citizens, their health and the environment during war and at all times.

Readers are invited to join the writer in condemning NATO's actions and flagrant violations and to commit themselves to end the "scourge of war" and in so doing to truly make human rights, peace, and the viability of the world's ecosystems a priority for the new millennium. For indeed the manner in which these unconscionable and illegal actions and their consequences are addressed will determine the fate, not only of the environment, ecosystems and peoples of the Balkans but may well determine the fate and future of humanity and this planet.

[1] Eaton, Janet M. 1999. Ecological Catastrophe & Health Hazards of the NATO Bombings: an Annotated URl Referenced List of Internet Articles, News, Press Releases. (Part 6) (Compiled by Dr. Janet M. Eaton, July 15, 1999)
http://www.flora.org/flora.mai-not/12608

[2] Eaton, Janet M. 1999. Ecological Catastrophe — NATO Bombings in the Balkans. Commissioned by: The Regional Environmental Center for Central and Eastern Europe, Szentendre, Hungary. For the BULLETIN, Quarterly Magazine, Volume 8,Number 4. Submitted: July 7, 1999 http://www.flora.org/flora.mai-not/12864

[3] Gorbachev, Mikhail. 1999. "Poison in the air: The environmental costs of the Kosovo conflict must be exposed," *The Guardian,*(June 18, 1999).
http://www.newsunlimited.co.uk/comment/story/0,3604,59107,00.html

[4] VCM over our heads. Serbian Ecological Society Media Release Belgrade, April 18, 1999, 10:00 http://www.flora.org/flora.mai-not/10989

[5] Personal Communication, Michel Chossudovsky, Professor of Economics, University of Ottawa, Canada. Since this testimony was given Professor Chossudovsky has published an article on his observations entitled "NATO willfully Triggered an Environmental Catastrophe in Yugoslavia." Poverty, Third World Network, Penang, Zed Books, London, 1997. Complete article at:
http://emperors-clothes.com/articles/chuss/willful.htm

[6] Lausevic, Radoje. Overview of Ecological Consequences of NATO Bombing of Yugoslavia [until] May 20, 1999. May 23, 1999. Full report available as a zip file wordperfect document:
http://www.BalkanPeaceNetwork.freeserve.co.uk/Environment.htm

[7] "The Bombing of Pancevo. Regional Environment Center for Central and Eastern Europe." *Bulletin* Volume 8 No. 4, August 1999.

[8] Mark Fineman, *Los Angeles Times*, July 6, 1999

[9] Serbian Town (Pancevo) Bombed by NATO Fears Effects of Toxic Chemicals By : Chris Hedges, *New York Times,* July 14, 1999.

[10] *ibid*

[11] Uli Schmetzer, "Serbs Allege NATO Raids Caused Toxic Catatrophe Bombed Refineries,Plants Spewed Stew of Poisons they Say," *Chicago Tribune*: July 14, 1999

[12] UN Environmental Team Asks NATO About Kosovo Targets, *Reuters*, Central Europe Online, July 8, 1999.

[13] Cancer Foundation of Yugoslavia. A Report of Current Cancer Epidemiology in Serbia Based on Available Data."Bežanijska kosa" Medical Center Expert Group Belgrade, December 1999. .(Cancer Foundation Yugoslavia, 11080 Belgrade)

[14] War in Europe: Ecocide. *Tehnokratia Volume 2*, July 1999 (with CDROM) http://www.flora.org/flora.mai-not/13040

[15] The Regional Environmental Center for Central and Eastern Europe, Szentendre, Hungary. For the BULLETIN, Quarterly Magazine, Volume 8,Number 4. Submitted: July 7, 1999 http://bulletin.rec.org

[16] Environment News Service (ENS) End Eco-destruction Yugoslav Scientists Plead April 14, 1999 http://ens.lycos.com/ens/apr99/1999L-04-14-03.html

[17] Regional Environment Center for Central and Eastern Europe. Assessment of the Environmental Impact of Military Activity during the Yugoslav Conflict. http://www.rec.org/REC/Announcements.yugo/contents.html

[18] Environment of Europe at Risk from NATO Bombing Environment News Service (ENS) Belgrade, Yugoslavia, April 7, 1999 http://ens.lycos.com/ens/apr99/1999L-04-07-04.html

[19] Danube River Ecosystem Caught in Balkan War Environmental News Service Vienna, Austria, May 7, 1999 (ENS) http://www.flora.org/flora.mai-not/11352

[20] Symposium III. Religion, Science & The Environment "A River of Life" Down the Danube to the Black Sea October 1999

[21] Damage to Yugoslav Environment "Immense" UN Team Reports, Environmental News Service, New York, June 29, 1999 http://ens.lycos.com/ens/jun99/1999L-06-29-02.html

[22] UNEP BTF Team concludes work -downplays risk- 4 items. Internet post coining four press releases from UNEP, United Nations Wire and Environmental News Service. Posted by: Janet M. Eaton, September 15, 1999 http://www.flora.org/flora.mai-not/13675

[23] *ibid*

[24] World Wide Fund for Nature's Danube Carpathian Programme. 1999 WWF analysis shows toxic contamination inYugoslavia is spreading September 14, 1999 , Gland, Switzerland http://www.panda.org/news/press/news.cfm?id=460 Background Information: WWF Mission to Yugoslavia and Results http://www.panda.org/crisis/background.html

[25] FOCUS Executive Summary and Final Report. PHARMA, Aug 18-28. http://www.focus-initiative.org

[26] United Nations Environment Program and United Nations Centre for Human Settlements (Habitat). Kosovo Conflict: The Environmental Consequences. Nairobi, Kenya. 1999. http://www.grid.unep.ch/btf/final/index.html

[27] Thomas Friedman, *New York Times*, March 28, 1999.

[28] Condition Critical: The Fraying Web of Life. *Time Magazine*. Special Edition. Earth Day Spring, 2000. http://www.time.com/time/reports/earthday2000/assessment01.html "People and Ecosystems: The Fraying Web of Life": http://www.wri.org/wri/wrr2000.

[29] Asoka Bandarage. *Women, Population and Global Crisis: A Political -Economic Analysis*. London: Zed Books, 1997.

[30] Joan McQueenay Mitric. "Cascading Human Consequences of NATO's War in the Balkans." *Mediterranean Quarterly: A Journal of Global Issues*. Volume 11 Number 2 Spring 2000.

Depleted Uranium

Carlo Pona

From a presentation to the June 10, 2000 International Tribunal for
U.S./NATO War Crimes in Yugoslavia held in New York City.

During its criminal aggression against Yugoslavia, NATO used armor-piercing shells loaded with depleted uranium. This was officially confirmed in a letter from NATO Secretary General George Robertson to the UN Secretary General Kofi Annan. During the aggression there was an unofficial confirmation by U.S. Department of Defense spokesman Major General Chuck Wald during a press briefing on May 3, 1999.

Depleted uranium (DU) is essentially a byproduct of the cycle of production of nuclear fuel and of the weapons-grade enriched uranium used to build nuclear bombs. It is also used to produce plutonium. The U.S. has retained stockpiles of DU since the inception of its nuclear weapons program in the 1940s. The costs associated with storing such an extraordinary quantity of material, estimated to be something like 700,000 metric tons, as UF6 (Uranium Flouride), are a very heavy burden for the U.S. Department of Energy. The employment of DU in ammunitions thus became a viable method of reducing storage costs.

The problem is that DU is both radioactive and toxic. To dispose of it as a nuclear waste is extremely expensive, and hence the Department of Energy itself is promoting its commercial use in many ways. They say that other uses of DU (including weapons) constitute a "benefit for humanity." DU is used in ammunitions, counterweights, shielding, and now commercial concrete (DUCRETE).

DU is 1.7 times denser than lead. Shells made of it can penetrate tank armor or concrete. The various types of DU munitions include the following: 7.62 mm, 20 mm (180 grams), 25 mm (200 grams), 30 mm (280 grams), 105 mm (3,500 grams), and 120 mm (4,500 grams) penetrators and the ADAM and PDM cluster bombs. DU is also present in Tomahawk III cruise missiles.

DU is dangerous as a weapon, but it is more dangerous after it has been fired. Upon impact, indeed, the DU core partially vaporizes producing uranium oxide in particulates between 0.5 and 5 microns in size.

This aerosol can spread over several hundred miles, depending on weather conditions. DU emits alpha, beta, gamma and X-ray radiation, and can present a hazard to the human body both externally and internally. The external radiation hazard would arise from close proximity to DU and is made up mainly of beta, gamma and X-ray radiation. The main external radiation hazard from DU is from contact with bare skin. The current dose limit to the skin is exceeded if the skin remains in continuous contact with DU for more than 250 hours per year.

The main internal radiation hazard is from the inhalation of the aerosol particles. The alpha and beta radiation from the retained material could, over a long period of time, cause damage to the lung tissue. The inhalation of 80 mg of insoluble DU would result in the dose limit being exceeded. Upon ingestion, the uranium oxides are mostly metabolized to uranyl ion ($UO2++$), and, if dissolved in the blood, up to ninety percent of it may be excreted by the kidneys in the urine. Excretion takes approximately three days if DU is dissolved.

When uranium reaches other organs, such as bones, it may never be excreted. A particular example, which occurs very frequently following the use of DU as a weapon, is that DU fragments wind up embedded in the muscle of civilian victims close to battlefields. In this case even a small particle of DU can cause high level of DU contamination in the urine for the rest of the victim's life. One "hot particle" in the lungs is equivalent, for the nearest cells, to exposure to an X-ray every hour of every day for the rest of the victim's life.

Besides being radioactive, DU is also highly poisonous. DU's high toxicity presents ever more danger to human health in the short time after exposure, affecting mainly the kidneys. The uranium oxides go into the soil as well. DU in the soil is incorporated in vegetables and the meat and milk of farm animals, and can contaminate humans via the food chain.

The International Criminal Tribunal for the Former Yugoslavia (ICTY) said in May 2000 that there is no worldwide agreement on the dangers of DU, and that it is not forbidden as a weapon. Maybe they forgot, or would like to forget, that National Lead Industries in New York was shut down during the 1980s because it accidentally released into the environment only 375 grams of DU, the same amount that is contained in only one of the munitions rounds fired by the U.S. and

NATO in Kosovo and Yugoslavia. Of course the U.S. government and the ICTY deny that there is anything harmful about depleted uranium that should prevent its use in a battle situation anywhere.

Numerous independent experts say depleted uranium is deadly and will permanently pollute those areas contaminated by the munitions. The Military Toxics Project, a non-governmental organization that has been tracking depleted uranium for years, has published an update. Author Dan Fahey draws primarily on declassified government documents and public statements, concluding with a sort of rough indictment of irresponsibility.

During the 1999 war against Yugoslavia, the Pentagon brought out a Rand Corporation think-tank study to prove once again that DU is harmless. Once more independent experts protested. As a consequence the World Health Organization (WHO) was asked to investigate. A fact sheet on DU was announced as in the works, and then it was cancelled. An initial UN mission to Yugoslavia in May produced a report of serious contamination by DU. The report's sponsor, United Nations Environmental Program (UNEP) director Klaus Toepfer suppressed it under pressure from Washington. The UNEP's Balkan Task Force produced a big study in October 1999, but the section on DU was dramatically reduced in the final version. The task force had tried to involve the WHO, but the International Atomic Energy Agency (IAEA), did not allow it. Measurements were done using Geiger counters incapable of detecting the particular alpha radiation and nothing was found.

In the meantime, in August 1999, the WHO announced that a study of DU was under way. In March 2000 it become known that the study was under the responsibility of an electro-magnetic field expert who has delegated it to a British geologist. Faced with the IAEA's opposition to studying radiation and health, the WHO has opted to study DU only as a heavy metal pollutant. So it comes as no surprise that in these circumstances the ICTY would say that there is no international agreement on the dangers of DU.

NATO admitted to having fired 31,000 of such rounds over a small area of Kosovo. We know now that DU was also used outside Kosovo, including Belgrade and Novi Sad. In a comprehensive report entitled Consequences of NATO Bombing on the Environment of the Federal Republic of Yugoslavia, the Yugoslav Ministry for Development, Science and Environment of the Federal Republic of Yugoslavia pointed to the use of DU outside Kosovo, in seven sites in Serbia and one in Montenegro.

It is not the first time the U.S. or other NATO powers have used DU in the battlefield. It happened already in Iraq in 1991 (from 300 to 700 tons of munitions) and Bosnia in 1995. The U.S. Army routinely uses DU on the small island of Vieques, off the coast of Puerto Rico. In April 1999, the U.S. Navy accidentally fired hundreds of DU rounds there. Similar events happened recently in South Korea and in Japan, where Marines fired DU bullets on an uninhabited island, prompting apologies from U.S. defense officials.

The Department of Defense itself published a lot of books and essays regarding DU that justify the concern about its use. They admit DU is a chemical and radiological hazard. DU is also one of the possible causes of the so-called Gulf War Syndrome, which affects thousands of U.S. and British Gulf War veterans, and for the increase of genetic malformations among the newborn in southern Iraq.

Many Iraqi pediatric oncologists claim that childhood leukemia has risen 600 percent in the areas where DU was used. Stillbirths, births or abortion of fetuses with monstrous abnormalities, and other cancers in children born since 1991 have also been found. And in 1996 the UN itself in the framework of the Subcommission on Preservation of Minorities, "urged all States to curb the production and spread of weapons of mass destruction or with indiscriminate effects," including explicitly, among others, depleted uranium.

The recent NATO confirmation of DU use in Kosovo, complete with a map, somehow alarmed the public, especially in Italy, because the most exposed area is right where there are Italian KFOR soldiers. The head of the Balkan Task Force mission, Pekka Haavisto, declared that there is no reason for serious concern. But the UN High Commissioner for Refugees, the main coordinator of aid to Kosovo, has quietly decided to refrain from sending pregnant staff to Kosovo, to offer those assigned there the option of going elsewhere and to put a note into the personnel files of those sent there to facilitate compensation claims for illnesses that might develop from DU contamination.

The German and Dutch Governments, whose occupation zones coincide with the areas hit, have ordered their soldiers not to eat anything outside their posts, especially not from the surrounding countryside. Dutch soldiers had to hand in all clothing and equipment, which was shipped back to the Netherlands, sealed in heavy-duty plastic. The government claims these measures are due to asbestos contamination, but a Dutch military source points to DU, noting that the vehicles, also sent back, ended up in a radiation decontamination plant. And, as far as Italy is concerned, there is the news that two Italian soldiers sent to the Serbian part of Bosnia, bombed with DU munitions by NATO in 1995, in the framework of the "peace force" SFOR, have died of leukemia. In this case there have been arguments because the time elapsed between exposure to DU and the death, only a couple of years, seems to be too short. An important Italian oncologist said in a popular TV documentary that in some cases a very short onset time for cancer is not impossible.

In conclusion, we cannot have any doubt that using DU as a weapon is a war crime and that DU must be banned forever.

VI.

U.S./
EUROPEAN UNION
INTERVENTION
SINCE
NATO
OCCUPIED KOSOVO

Belgrade: The Struggle Continues

GLORIA LA RIVA

At the end of March 1999, after the war had begun, I was fortunate to travel to Yugoslavia with Ramsey Clark, the former U.S. attorney general and current human rights fighter. It was from the fifth to the ninth day of the brutal U.S. and NATO bombing. It was evident even early in the war that the Yugoslav people were the intended targets of NATO. We saw schools, bridges, homes, heating plants and factories destroyed. Dozens of people had already been killed.

Then in May as the bombing reached an unprecedented level of savagery, Clark and I returned to Yugoslavia, along with Sara Flounders of the International Action Center (IAC) national office.

Traveling there to oppose the destruction and terror brought by U.S.-NATO pilots, we also witnessed the great courage of the people of Yugoslavia as they used all their means to resist.

Images of people standing night after night on bridges to keep them from being bombed, or thousands rallying in daytime outdoor concerts, inspired millions internationally. Pinning targets on themselves to mock the NATO forces, the Yugoslavs made an unforgettable impression with their courage.

Today, it is apparent that the refusal of the vast majority of the Yugoslav people to surrender their country to NATO domination is the real reason that Yugoslavia—the people and former leaders—remain targets of U.S. imperialism and its Western allies. When NATO bombs stopped falling on Yugoslavia two years ago in June 1999, the war didn't end. If anything, it intensified, continuing in a different form.

The war changed form but the aim was the same: divide and conquer, destroy not only Yugoslavia but Serbia itself. Even through summer 2001, U.S.-NATO knives continue to carve up the Balkans. Witness the NATO troop invasion of Macedonia, and unfolding plans to rip the northern province of Vojvodina from Serbia.

All these plans could be defeated with the kind of unity and determination that existed during the NATO bombing war. That was the greatest asset that the Yugoslav people had in their struggle. In the war, the enemy was easily identifiable and any illusion about "Western democracy" suddenly disappeared when NATO's barbaric killing began.

In our discussions with Yugoslavs during the war they may have had different political opinions but they agreed on one thing. They were united in struggle against the U.S. and NATO. Also clear was that the people and Yugoslav army were not defeated. They were prepared to resist as long as necessary.

Often they referred back to their brave history in resisting Nazi Germany's attacks. If they could defeat Nazi Germany, they reasoned, they could defeat NATO too.

People from all walks of life played their part in defending the country. In April 1999 in the midst of a huge daily concert in Republic Square, thousands of people, young and old, joined together to defy one more day of bombing.

I asked a 12-year-old, "Why are you here?" She replied, "Because no child in the world should have to go through this, and we want to show that this is wrong, and that we can fight, even with music, but we can fight." At first parents stayed home with their children but as the war continued and parents had to return to work to survive, the youth took care of the younger children, taking them to the shelter when alarms rang.

Workers at the Nis tobacco factory, second largest in Europe, went to work even though their workplace was heavily bombed. One man said, "Every day we hear planes in the sky, there is no place that is safe here, only in the basement." I remarked, "But still you come to work." He replied, "We must work, we want to work, there is no life without work."

Rescue workers, firefighters and medical personnel risked their lives daily. With the knowledge that NATO bombers would return to newly bombed sites fifteen minutes later to bomb again, the rescue workers still rushed to the scene. They knew they were the intended targets of the second bombing run, but they heroically carried out their duty to help others.

We met one such hero in the Clinical Center of Serbia, a 40-year-old man whose legs were blown off only days before. He was barely able to whisper to us as he said, "I'm in terrible pain but I still have great motives to go on living."

His physician, Dr. Sonja Pavlovic, said, "These men are truly our heroes because they know of the second bombs and still rush to the scene to recover the wounded and dead."

When the enemy was clear, unity was easier.

Then the war ended, and it ended in extremely difficult conditions for Yugoslavia. First, Kosovo, historically the heart of the Serbian nation, was now occupied by the five principal NATO forces.

The German deutschemark became the local currency in Kosovo. And the armed right-wing groups coordinated by the Kosovo Liberation Army beat, killed and drove Serbs, Roma, and other nationalities of Yugoslavia out of their towns and Kosovo itself, while NATO troops stood by and watched.

Two factors worked to create discontent and frustration among the population in post-war Yugoslavia: the demoralization that set in after the end of the war with the developments in Kosovo, and the intense pressure and damage to the economy by U.S.-UN sanctions.

In the cold hard winter that set in after the war, NATO forces led by the United States and their banks offered bribes and made threats, taking advantage of the dire situation. Major heating plants had been bombed, leaving people vulnerable to the weather. The U.S. offered oil only to the cities that actively opposed the Milosevic socialist government. The others that resisted these machinations could freeze.

In the year 2000 Washington led an intense destabilization campaign aimed at the upcoming September national elections. It and the European Union poured in over $100 million to those parties backing an opposition candidate to then-President Milosevic.

Vojislav Kostunica came forth to run for election against Milosevic. He was groomed by the U.S. and presented himself as a great defender of Serbia, who had even criticized Milosevic for losing Kosovo to NATO. It seems ironic that the United States backed Kostunica even though he demanded that Kosovo remain part of Serbia. But as long as Kostunica was willing to play a strategic role in defeating the Socialist-led government and splitting the population he would have served his purpose to U.S. and NATO.

The internal counter-revolution to overturn what remained of the socialist system in Yugoslavia began with Kostunica's coup on October 5, 2000, after his "Democratic Opposition of Serbia (DOS)" supporters refused to accept a run-off election. The run-off was required since neither he nor Milosevic had won fifty percent of the vote in the first round on September 24, 2000.

With Kostunica in office, and the counter-revolutionary DOS in power, a rapid dismantling of socialist property is now underway. Along with the privatization schemes and resulting economic difficulties, people are finding that the "democratic opposition" is not so democratic after all.

In fact, during our third visit to Yugoslavia, in June 2001, a common graffiti in the streets referred to the DOS as "Democratic Occupation of Serbia." Many people complained to us that the media is now one sole viewpoint, a pro-U.S., pro-capitalist stance. Repression against progressive activists is growing daily. We could see on this visit that the sentiment against NATO and their puppets Kostunica and Djindjic is growing.

In addition to living miserably because Kostunica and Djindjic have been unable to solve the country's economic woes, now the people have witnessed the servile attitudes of Serbian Prime Minister Zoran Djindjic and Yugoslav President Vojislav Kostunica towards the U.S. rulers. What complacency and confusion that may have existed in recent months is turning into anger and action again. The outrageous act by Djindjic in flouting Yugoslavia's constitutional court decree and suddenly handing over Milosevic to NATO war criminals sparked widespread anger in the country.

And the circumstances of that extradition, in exchange for a $1 billion "loan" promise, made the crime particularly odious to the Yugoslav people. The U.S. had said, "Milosevic must be in our hands by Friday, June 29 or there will be no money. "

Milosevic was in NATO's prison Thursday evening, June 28, 2001. As news of the kidnapping reached people, thousands rallied in downtown Belgrade and throughout the country within hours.

Ramsey Clark and I arrived Friday morning.

We experienced the profound change the moment Clark and I landed at the Belgrade airport on June 29, 2001, just one day after Milosevic was illegally extradited to The Hague. Clark originally intended to arrive before Milosevic's kidnapping to assist in preventing the extradition but the regime in Belgrade had sabotaged his efforts.

Trying to enter the country was itself a struggle. We had already been denied visas by the new Yugoslav ambassador in Washington but decided to fly to Belgrade without visas anyway. As we approached the visa booths in Belgrade's airport to request permission, the police officers at the windows closed the booths.

As members of the Republic of Serbia police force, they were under orders of the Djindjic government. When they saw we were the last people from the plane, they closed the visa windows and transferred to the booths where passengers were to enter the country.

Because of his reputation in Yugoslavia and because they had received their orders, they knew who Clark was. They immediately said no, no entry without a visa. Instead, we were told we had to board the plane and return to Rome.

"We need to make one phone call. Can we please make one call?" we asked. We needed to contact friends of the IAC in Belgrade for their help.

"No, no phone calls," they answered. They turned down repeated requests.

Clark told the immigration officer who approached us, "I'm Ramsey Clark and ..."

"We know who you are. You can't stay."

Then suddenly, a policewoman came up to us and intervened. She took Clark's passport and left the room. Another police officer came into the scene and led me upstairs to a busy shopping area. After he dialed the phone number I had requested, he left me on my own.

Twenty minutes later we were given our visas by the policewoman who had spoken to Clark. She told him her brother had been wounded in the war, and she deeply appreciated Clark's opposition to NATO's bombing. As we shook her hand, she said, "I'll see you tonight at the rally."

The rally was the second mass gathering in as many days. Only twenty-four hours before, Milosevic had been flown out of the country, handcuffed and with a hood over his head.

We were told by many people that in the post-war period, the U.S. and NATO forces are directing the new Serbian and Yugoslav governments to identify the sources of wartime resistance and root them out. These include leaders and members of the Socialist Party of Serbia, and other activists. One particular group that was purged from their jobs is media workers who defied NATO bombs to broadcast the crimes of the U.S. and western powers.

The media workers and directors who transmitted the daily broadcast of NATO's deadly war used every means to keep the news alive. Each reporter, each production person, each worker knew they were a military target. NATO had declared them so. They defied NATO's bomb threats and reported the truth without fail, even after sixteen workers were murdered as U.S. rockets hit Serbian TV in Belgrade April 23, 1999.

What price have the survivors paid since then? Dragan Milanovic is one example. During the war he was director of the Serbian TV and worked in the tall TV station building in downtown Belgrade which was crushed by NATO bombs. He was recently imprisoned for four months by the new pro-U.S. Serbian government of Djindjic, because as they put it, he knew NATO would bomb the TV station, but "did nothing to prevent it."

The new regime was charging the victims with not stopping casualties from a criminal bombing, while the bombers were feted in banquets. Indeed, at the same time Milanovic was in prison, Zoran Djindjic was hosting Javier Solana at a banquet in Belgrade. Solana, who was secretary general of NATO during the war, was responsible for the strategy that targeted Yugoslavia's media. He is the one who belongs in prison.

Yet no matter how self-assured he may have sounded before, Zoran Djindjic is fearful that his plans for the wholesale economic privatization of Yugoslavia's wealth could be doomed. He admitted as much when he expressed doubts about his government's future if the $1.28 billion promised by NATO for Milosevic's handover does not materialize.

In an interview in the German weekly, *Der Spiegel* in July 2001, Djindjic said:

> We are trying here to reform the country and propagate a pro-western course in spite of the NATO bombardment. ...
>
> *Der Spiegel*: Can you explain this in detail?
>
> Zoran Djindjic: In August we should be getting the first installment, 300 million Euro. Suddenly we are being told, that 225 million euro will be withheld for the repayment of old debts, which in part were accumulated during Tito's time. Two-thirds of that sum are fines and interests, accrued because Milosevic refused for ten years to pay back these credits. We shall get the remaining seventy-five million euro in November at the earliest. Such are the principles in the west, we are being told. This means: A seriously ill person is to be given medicine after he is dead. Our critical months will be July, August and September.

Der Spiegel: Do you fear a collapse of the government?

Zoran Djindjic: If we do not immediately get a financial injection we will have demonstrations in September at the latest together with social unrest, since we could not fulfill our promises. 330,000 families live on an income of forty DM a month; 600,000 refugees are a great burden for our budget and 100,000 will lose their jobs as a consequence of the transformation of the economy which was set as a precondition for credits by Western donors.

There is no investment, there is no work, no construction. On the other side Milosevic's Socialists are still in important positions in the economy and want the country to sink into chaos.

Der Spiegel: The Socialists are obviously regaining terrain. Can they again become a danger for the government coalition of the DOS-democrats?

Zoran Djindjic: Socialists and radicals could certainly count on an increase of their votes if there were elections. Add to that Yugoslav President Kostunica with his skeptical attitude towards the West and constant warnings that the promised moneys will not arrive .

Der Spiegel: ...and who calls you a putschist for having extradited Milosevic and thus having brought shame over the country.

Zoran Djindjic: ...There is a danger however that through such quasi-patriotic statements anti-West anger will be reawakened in the population. ...

When I was in the opposition the EU had promised us 3 billion DM for the overthrow of Milosevic. Where is this money?

Der Spiegel: You offered to resign if the extradition of Milosevic to the Tribunal failed. Will you throw down everything if the western finance ministers do not give in?

Zoran Djindjic: I cannot constantly speak to our population about western aid if we do not see any signs of it here. Thus I'm losing my credibility and cannot stabilize the country.

In reality the program of the "Democratic Opposition" of Serbia—the DOS—could never solve the problems of the Yugoslav people. It will in fact destroy Yugoslavia's national economy because their program is patterned after the countless IMF-style austerity plans, complete with selling off of the country's socially-owned wealth, and gutting of social programs.

Imperialist loans and privatizing socialized wealth spells disaster. Just ask the Mexican people, who have been saddled with a debt impossible to pay thanks to U.S.- and IMF-engineered "rescues."

Djindjic and Kostunica are not long on history's stage. They are useful puppets for the U.S. and NATO, and they may be wreaking economic and political havoc, but sooner or later the people will fight back.

Understanding and support for Yugoslavia's people is needed from the people of the United States more than ever. Our greatest challenge in the U.S. progressive movement is overcoming the media and U.S. government's demonization of Milosevic and the Yugoslav people.

If a U.S. worker's only source of news about the Balkans is a biased report in the big-business media, this worker can hardly resist accepting the outrageous lies as truth, leaving the real war criminals in Washington, London and Berlin off the hook. Only an independent press and movement that are free of the interests of the NATO powers, only a progressive movement that is free of their influence can explain what is really happening in Yugoslavia, and rally the masses to fight for their true interests.

Since the war against Yugoslavia, and under the impact of that war, a new movement against corporate globalization has grown up inside the United States and the other imperialist centers. The threat from corporate globalization is not only from the bank's strangling economic plans, but also from the war plans of the imperialists, especially the United States, as carried out against the Yugoslav people. It will be important for this movement to understand how progressive it is to defend the Yugoslav leader, and by extension the people of Serbia, from NATO's court in The Hague.

When the International Action Center made the decision to send the delegations to Yugoslavia that I described above, it was not just for the temporary show of solidarity, as important as that was. It was also to carry out a vital task, that of establishing a movement center within the United States that is free of the influence of the corporate media and the government officials who plan and carry out aggression worldwide.

This is essential if we are going to have any hope of building a world finally free of war, poverty and oppression.

Pentagon Enforces Globalization

BRIAN BECKER

When I give food to the poor, they call me a saint. When I ask why the poor have no food, they call me a communist—Dom Helder Camara, Brazilian archbishop

The late Brazilian Archbishop Helder Camara's now famous utterance took on a new poignancy with the announcement that Quebec's archbishop plans to criticize the official activities of the Summit of the Americas set for Quebec City, in Quebec, Canada, starting April 17, 2001, and to speak instead at the alternate conference.

Summit planners want this summit meeting to confirm the next step in the "globalization" of both North and South America by backing the Free Trade Area of the Americas.

The bankers and corporate barons are unhappy that Quebec Archbishop Maurice Couture refuses to limit his intervention to simply praying for the victims of "globalization." Instead, the archbishop has chosen to show solidarity with tens of thousands of students and workers protesting the forced layoffs, union busting, wage slashing, land theft and privatization of vital social services that are the heart of the proposed FTAA treaty.

BEWARE OF CERTAIN WORDS

If it has excelled at anything, modern-day corporate culture has become the master at advertising and political propaganda. A handful of corporate media monopolies that dominate the airwaves and newspapers can mass produce and widely distribute carefully chosen words, phrases and slogans, using them to distort the realities that they describe.

The word "globalization" sounds neutral, benign or even democratic. But globalization is in fact a form of class war by the rich and powerful against the poor. It is a form of corporate violence against working people and their labor unions. On the environmental front, globalization is a systematic assault to eliminate anti-pollution regulations imposed on the oil, mining and logging industries.

Globalization is also a war against the development strategies of the so-called Third World countries that have nationalized and "protected" home industries so that they would not be overrun or destroyed by more powerful transnational corporations from the United States, Britain, Japan, Germany, France, Italy or Canada.

Globalization is not simply an economic policy that favors corporate profit over workers' rights and the environment. It is also economic domination enforced by war and the threat of war.

LINK BETWEEN GLOBALIZATION AND IMPERIALIST WAR

The U.S./NATO demonization of Yugoslav President Slobodan Milosevic and attack on Yugoslavia best show how economic imperialism is organically linked to military imperialism. This is what is most important to really understanding the phenomenon of globalization.

> For globalization to work, America can't be afraid to act as the almighty superpower that it is ... The hidden hand of the market will never work without the hidden fist—McDonald's cannot flourish without McDonnell Douglas, the designer of the F-15. And the hidden fist that keeps the world safe for Silicon Valley's technologies is called the United States Army, Air Force, Navy and Marine Corps.

These are the words of a leading advocate of globalization, *New York Times* columnist Thomas Friedman, explaining the real but unstated reason for NATO's war against the Yugoslav government (*New York Times,* March 28, 1999).

Milosevic was the leader of the Socialist Party of Serbia. His government had cooperated with the International Monetary Fund's globalization program in the late 1980s. In the early 1990s, after the collapse of the USSR and the other socialist governments in Eastern Europe, Milosevic changed economic strategies. He began taking steps to slow down and resist the wholesale privatization of the state-owned or socialized industry, banking and trade that were demanded by the IMF and the World Bank. This made him the target of all-out hostility from the globalizers on Wall Street.

Anti-Milosevic rants in the Western corporate media reached new levels of fury by 1994. The propaganda focused public attention on alleged "ethnic cleansing" by Serbs in Bosnia and later Kosovo. But that was to fool the public into thinking that the coming war against Yugoslavia was for humanitarian purposes.

The real story was located in the fine print.

"Milosevic is harking back to the political control promised by that old communist star on his presidency building ... he is revoking some privatization and free market measures," the *Christian Science Monitor* wrote on June 6, 1996. A month later, the July 18, 1996, *New York Times* complained about Milosevic's determination to "keep state controls [of industry] and his refusal to allow privatization."

"Milosevic failed to understand the message of the fall of the Berlin Wall ... while other communist politicians accepted the Western model ... Milosevic went the other way," was the even more explicit message carried in the August 4, 1996, *Washington Post.*

The globalizers are driven to militarily crush those who dare resist their demands to privatize the industries, collective farming lands, and service sectors of their economies. "War is merely an extension of politics, but by other means," according to the famed dictum of the nineteenth century Prussian military theorist Carl Von Clausewitz. And the politics of the current era is the concentrated economic interests of the biggest transnational corporations and banks.

Resistance to these policies could be contagious among the poor and downtrodden, who make up the majority of the world's people. That's what Thomas Friedman meant when he wrote that "the hidden hand of the market will never work without the hidden fist" of the Pentagon war machine.

NATO eventually dropped 23,000 bombs and missiles on Yugoslavia during the 1999 war. U.S. and NATO troops took over Kosovo in June 1999. Then the United States and the European Union promised to lift economic sanctions on Yugoslavia and Serbia only if the people "unelected" Milosevic and replaced his government with a pro-IMF administration. The Clinton administration and the European Union poured in $100 million for the electoral opposition during the Yugoslav presidential campaign of September 2000. Surprise, surprise, Milosevic lost his plurality and the election to a pro-IMF candidate.

The campaign against Yugoslavia was designed as a clear message to any who resist the IMF's "globalization" conditions. If poor countries dare resist they will encounter every form of pressure.

The U.S. government and the IMF announced that the Yugoslavs would have economic sanctions lifted and be eligible for new IMF loans to rebuild their war-torn country only if Milosevic was arrested by

March 31, 2001. On March 30, masked police and elite commandos arrived to arrest him. His supporters resisted, but he was finally arrested early April 1 in Belgrade—it was still March 31 in Washington.

The U.S. government later announced that if Milosevic were not turned over to the International Criminal Tribunal for the Former Yugoslavia (ICTY) by the start of a June 29, 2001, "donors' conference," Yugoslavia would not receive $1.3 billion in aid and loans. Despite it being an unconstitutional act, the new pro-West Yugoslav regime illegally turned him over on June 28, 2001.

CAPITALISTS WAGE CLASS WAR

It is no wonder that tens of thousands of workers and students protested globalization outside the Summit of the Americas April 18-22, 2001, in Quebec City. Or that close to 300,000 people braved vicious police attacks to protest the summit meeting of the G-8—the seven most powerful imperialist countries plus Russia—in Genoa, Italy, July 19-22, 2001.

Globalization is a form of class warfare. It is violence by the rich and powerful against everyone else.

The consequences are staggering. Karl Marx's prediction in "The Communist Manifesto" that the rich will get richer while the poor will get poorer is confirmed in today's statistics.

The top 200 transnational corporations have almost twice the economic clout of the poorest four-fifths of humanity. The combined revenues of just General Motors and Ford—the two biggest automobile companies in the world—exceed the combined Gross Domestic Product for all of sub-Saharan Africa.

Transnational corporations hold ninety percent of all technology and product patents worldwide. The top 200 corporations' combined sales are bigger than the combined economies of 182 countries. That's all the countries of the world minus the biggest nine imperialist countries.

The ten richest people in the world own wealth equivalent to the total production of the fifty poorest countries. The top 447 billionaires and mega-millionaires have fortunes greater than the income of half of humanity, or the three billion poorest people.

The three richest capitalists in the United States—Bill Gates, Warren Buffet and Paul Allen—have wealth equal to the combined income and savings of the world's 600 million poorest people.

Globalization in the hands of the capitalist class does not simply mean the spread of uniform high technology, computers and industry throughout the world. It means the strengthening of the power of finance capital over working people.

It is the stranglehold of a peculiar institutional structure that entitles a tiny handful to amass great fortunes. This tiny handful privately possesses the products that are created by the collective labor of working people in society.

Workers get wages, while the corporate capitalists privately hold and own the products and thus the profits created by the collective work performed by others.

Resistance to a system that accumulates wealth at one pole and misery at the other is inevitable. The class warfare of the bosses and bankers must be answered with the class resistance of working people.

The property used to produce wealth in society can either be privately owned for the benefit of the owners and investors or it can be publicly owned. The two systems represented by these two different kinds of property are diametrically different.

The former—privately owned means of production—serves the capitalists. The latter—publicly owned means of production—is free to meet society's needs.

Will the priority be corporate profits or people's needs? In its basic form this is the question: What direction for society—capitalism or socialism?

The Destabilization of Macedonia

Heather Cottin

In the summer of 2001, civil war descended upon Macedonia. Stories appeared in the Western media clearly reminiscent of the hysterical tales that propelled the public into supporting NATO intervention in the Balkan wars of the 1990s. Macedonian "government troops pounded the ethnic Albanian village of Ljuboten," wrote the *Washington Post,* on August 13, 2001.[1] "Ten Macedonian soldiers killed by rebels, threatening peace moves,"[2] read one headline, as "Albanian rebels" intensified their terror campaign against the Macedonian government. "Albanian rebels" attacked water pipelines, military barracks, naval vessels,[3] "ethnic Albanian rebels kidnapped five Macedonian civilians."[4] Suddenly Macedonians were labeled "Slavs," and the press began to portray the former Yugoslav republic as an aggressor under siege by the media-legitimized "oppressed Albanian minority."

It was not enough that Macedonia had declared its independence from Yugoslavia ten years previously. NATO had to develop a pretext to intervene, and the Kosovo Liberation Army was born again as the National Liberation Army (KLA/NLA) in Macedonia. Once again, it was fighting for the "liberation" of Albanians in a region once part of Yugoslavia. Once again, the KLA received help from NATO.[5]

As if there were two licit sides, the NATO powers inserted themselves into the crisis. Calling their intervention, "Operation Essential Harvest," NATO leaders reassured Macedonia of their concern. But their words were belied by their actions. "NATO's doors are always open to Albania,"[6] said NATO Secretary-General Lord George Robertson, visiting Tirana in July 2001. NATO pressed for a peace agreement that August; former NATO secretary general and current European Union foreign policy chief Javier Solana and Robertson smiled as they left Skopje in August 2001, with a cease-fire accord that was broken the moment it was signed. "Robertson insisted the accord constituted a 'great step forward,' a very proud day for this country."[7]

The war in Macedonia pits a U.S.-sponsored government against the U.S.-sponsored National Liberation Army.[8] As bizarre as that appears, it is true, and was part of a NATO project which aimed at destabilizing another Balkan republic and strengthening the drug-running, slave-trafficking kleptocracy whose aim was to establish "Greater Albania."

Over 120,000 refugees fled the intensified fighting between NLA/KLA terrorists and the Macedonian armed forces in the summer of 2001.[9] The NLA/KLA forces followed a pattern that had already been seen in Kosovo in 1998 and 1999. They first preyed on defenseless villages. When FYROM (Former Yugoslav Republic of Macedonia) forces came to the rescue, the NLA/KLA would withdraw. In June of 2001, when these terrorists were actually threatened with a major loss, according to the *Christian Science Monitor,* NATO sent buses to rescue 500 of the terrorists, and they were transported with their weapons to safety.[10]

NATO cautioned the Macedonian government not to fight back, urging instead that it submit to a "Peace Plan" that remarkably resembled the Dayton Accords. These accords, signed in November 1995, robbed Yugoslavia of Bosnia. They also resembled the Rambouillet Agreement that proceeded the seventy-eight-day bombing attack on Yugoslavia and announced NATO's intention of destroying the sovereignty of Yugoslavia.

The people of Macedonia stormed the government buildings in Skopje in their fury at the weakness of their government's response. With some important exceptions, the FYROM government was impotent or silent. Macedonia's President Boris Trajkovski was in the pocket of the U.S. government and NATO,[11] but Prime Minister Ljubko Georgievski accused U.S. envoy James Pardew of "forcing Macedonia to cave in to demands from Albanian guerrillas."[12] Georgievski also accused the West of siding with Albanian insurgents, saying their terrorist actions were "performed with logistical support from so-called western democracies."[13]

The U.S. government played both ends against the middle. Allowing the infamous Military Professional Resources Inc. (MPRI) mercenaries to help "both sides," the United States guaranteed money and contracts for this Virginia-based guns-and-generals-for-hire outfit.[14] It didn't matter whether both sides received equal help, because the United Nations supplied financial assistance to and supported the KLA/NLA fighters. The UN financed the leader of this army, Agim Ceku, who was responsible for the ethnic cleansing in 1995 in the Krajina region of Croatia. Ceku became leader of the KLA in Kosovo in 1999, and then was hired as a salaried UN employee even as his KLA forces opened attacks on Macedonia.[15] The BBC readily admitted, "Western forces were training guerrillas," and opening a "new front in Southern Serbia (Presevo Valley) and Macedonia."[16]

This scenario was an exact replica of U.S. policy in Bosnia and Kosovo. In fact the KLA/NLA, like the Bosnian Moslem army in the early 1990s or the KLA army in the late 1990s could win no battles without U.S./NATO intervention. Here is how they carried out their actions: The NATO-sponsored and -equipped militants would attack a village, provoking an armed response from the state in power. The terrorists would then appeal to the international press, which reacted in sympathy with the terrorists against the horrible "repression" of the government. Declaring their commitment to peace, the terrorists demanded control of the area and the West agreed. The Western media then accuses the sovereign government of "ethnic cleansing" in Kosovo and Macedonia of Albanians who live in that nation.

Public relations for this scenario was carried out by Human Rights Watch and George Soros spindoctors, through the Open Society Institute, which support "alternative media," and key duplicitous nationals, willing to sell out their nation, in the case of Macedonia, with World Bank financing.[17] Then the U.S./NATO created a phony "peace agreement."

"What we have on the table is a document tailored to break up Macedonia," Prime Minister Ljubco Georgievski said. He called the draft a blatant violation of Macedonia's internal affairs.[18]

But the plot gets thicker. In the fall of 2000, at a meeting between the Turkish Minister of Defense Ismet Sezgin and Albania's Prime Minister Fatos Nano, the Turkish government announced it was "ready to be engaged in restructuring the Albanian army." Turkey's aid to the Albanian military in 2001 amounted to $120 million, with more on the way in the coming years. Turkish officials have called their country a "regional superpower in the Balkans." Turkey is a NATO member and the most powerful military force locally in the region, both in the Aegean and the Balkans.[20]

The Bulgarian government is purportedly offering "assistance" to Macedonia, hoping to annex what's left of the region. In March of 2001, the Bulgarian regime gave NATO troops free access to all of Bulgaria. [21] While all this was happening, a new terrorist army began organizing; the Liberation Army of Chameria. With a structure just like the KLA/NLA, the LAC is planning a war against Greece for Thrace, which the Albanians call Chameria, in Greece's north. "Greater Albania" terrorists claim that one million Albanians who live in this region "must enjoy their rights" and "an armed struggle will get underway" as the terrorists turn against the Greek minority in the region.

FYROM news agency, which reported this, notes that many pro-KLA websites end with the phrase, "Greece is the next country from which we will take back our land."[22] Thus Greece is facing hostility from its neighbors on both sides, Turkey and Albania.

Although the Greek government under Prime Minister Andreas Papandreou originally supported Yugoslavia in the war in Bosnia, the Greek state was passive during the Seventy-eight-day bombing attack and subsequently accepted NATO's dictates in Yugoslavia. The great majority of the Greek people and even individuals within the armed forces, however, have consistently defied NATO intervention and resist calls for the creation of Greater Albania.

What is Washington's stake in all of this? Why is the United States backing the KLA in Albania and Kosovo, the group that is by all accounts responsible for most of the drug and sex-slave trafficking in Europe,[23] bringing unimaginable poverty and corruption to the Albanian people while attacking and ethnically cleansing the Serbs, Rom and Macedonian people? Why is the U.S. secretly backing the Greater Albanian project? Why is Turkey NATO's favorite weapon in the region? And why have NATO troops intervened in yet another part of the former Yugoslavia?

The most repressive dictatorship in Asia Minor rules Turkey, whose war against its Kurdish minority has cost 37,000 Kurdish lives. Political prisoners languish and die in Turkey's prisons, but since the Truman Doctrine in 1947, the U.S., British and Federal German governments have developed close military and economic ties with Turkey and never find fault with its human rights abuses.

A NATO member, Turkey plays a key role in the oil-transport business, and expects the Baku oil transshipments to pass though Turkish land and water. Turkey is pressing for a Baku-Ceyhan pipeline. Looking to collect a tariff on the pipeline that bypasses the Straits of Bosporus, Turkey's rulers also want to profit from tankers using the Bosporus for oil transport.[24] Thus, "Greater Albania" in control of the region from Kosovo through Macedonia to Thrace and the Aegean Sea and Turkey on the Black Sea and the Mediterranean would be the key players in the oil business in the region. United States oil corporations will be the major beneficiaries of this development.

"Greater Albania" would be possible only with the intercession of the U.S./NATO; and though they give no official credence to it, NATO may have its reasons for supporting the project. The idea of a "Greater Albania" goes back to the Albanian fascists of World War II, but the United States is no stranger to helping ex-fascists regain power.[25] The KLA/NLA "Greater Albanian" criminals expect to annex Kosovo,[26] with U.S. government support. The U.S. and NATO have established a military protectorate in Bulgaria, and could give their Bulgarian client territory stolen from Macedonia, a policy that also hearkens back to Nazi geostrategy. Thus, with Turkey's army as the United States' puppet bully in the south and U.S.-supported "Greater Albania" and Bulgaria to the north, the U.S. would dominate southern Europe and the Caspian, Black, Adriatic, Aegean, and eastern Mediterranean Seas. U.S. access to the oil and gas fields and pipelines from the Caspian region would be guaranteed.

A look at a map of oil conduits proposed by U.S.-dominated Albanian-Macedonian-Bulgarian Oil (AMBO) shows every region the KLA/NLA operates or has plans to operate in, including a key town in Thrace that the Turks call Janina, as routes for the AMBO pipeline, due to open in 2005. Every major American oil company is involved in

AMBO.[27] This Trans-Balkan pipeline gets money from the Export-Import Bank and the World Bank.[28]

But the war in Macedonia and the machinations of the United States and NATO in the Balkans are not just about oil. At issue is the market for American goods, and the labor power of the people of Eastern Europe. NATO and NATO compradors will try to prevent trade unions from winning decent wages for workers, better conditions for the people of the region, from social services to freedom to live where they want. The pattern of creating ethnic rivalries has done the very opposite of creating what Soros' bogus "human rights" organizations call "civil society."

The poverty, corruption, fear and warfare that has characterized the Balkans since the breakup of Yugoslavia began in 1989 is intensifying. Society in the former Yugoslavia is anything but civil, and enhances the lives of the bourgeoisie at the expense of the vast majority of the Croatian, Bosnia, Serb, Albanian and Rom people, who are poor, unemployed and at the mercy of NATO-sponsored governments. The conditions of all of the workers and farmers of Eastern Europe have deteriorated since NATO invaded the region.[29] The civil war in Macedonia represents NATO's cynical maneuver to ensure the dominance of Washington, Wall Street and London in the Balkans.

Once again militarism accompanied a media campaign of deception. Once again the goal was economic and political hegemony. In *The Grand Chessboard,* Zbigniew Brzezinski wrote of a long-term strategy for Eurasia. He urged the United States to establish "global hegemony," and warned that there were only ten to twenty years to take control "before the door is closed."[30] Brzezinski wrote of controlling the Eurasian corridor, from the Balkans to Xinjiang and Tibet. By invoking this, Brzezinski, a member of the Council on Foreign Relations, has resuscitated Adolf Hitler's "Geopolitics" theory—taboo for a generation—which goads those who would seek world dominance to control "Eurasia."

As the economic systems of the Great Powers contract and inter-imperial rivalries grow, the risk of war increases. The United States and Britain are fearful of the shift to the euro currency in January 2002, which will mark "a clash between Europe and America for 'colonial control' over national currencies."[31] Since German banking represents the financial strength behind the Euro, the "quest by Wall Street's financial establishment—in alliance with the oil giants, to destabilize and discredit the deutschemark (and the euro)" is a move to "impose the U.S. dollar as sole currency in the region."[32] Profits made from the sale of U.S. weapons and mercenary services in the Balkans and Eastern Europe will increase if NATO has its way.

NATO is planning wars to wrest the entire Eastern European and Caspian Sea region, rich in oil and natural gas and cheap labor power, from its people. The U.S. and Britain are working together, to the chagrin of France, Germany and of course Russia. Inter-imperial rivalries are burgeoning, especially between the U.S. and Germany, both wishing to dominate and exploit the region. The threat of war among the imperialist powers hovers.

The late Sean Gervasi, political analyst and economist, asked a profound and prescient question. In 1996 he wrote:

> The Western system is experiencing a profound economic, social and political crisis. And Western leaders apparently see the exploitation of the East as the only large-scale project available which might stimulate growth, especially in Western Europe. They are therefore prepared to risk a great deal for it. The question is: will the world accept the risks of East-West conflict and nuclear war in order to lock into one region economic arrangements which are already collapsing elsewhere?[33]

[1] Misha Savic "Clashes continue as Macedonia set to sign peace accord," http://www.washingtonpost.com/wp-dyn/articles/a3881-2001aug13.html.

[2] "Ten Macedonian soldiers killed by rebels, threatening peace moves," *Agence France Presse* Aug 8, 2001

[3] "Yugoslav Naval Boat is Fired on From Albania," *Agence France Presse* July 19, 2001, "Albanian Guerrillas Attack Military Barracks in Tetovo," *Agence France Presse* August 10, 2001.

[4] "Ethnic Albanian Rebels Abduct Five in Macedonia" *Agence France Presse* August 8, 2001.

[5] Marjorie Cohn, Pacification for a Pipeline: Explaining the U.S. Military Presence in the Balkans, Thomas Jefferson School of Law, JURIST@law.pitt.edu.

[6] "Robertson Praises Albania's Election, Regional Policy," *Deutche Presse Agenteur*, July 13, 2001.

[7] "NATO, EU envoys arrive for Macedonia peace signing" *Agence France Presse*, August 13, 2001.

[8] Renate Flottau, Olaf Ihlau, Susanne Koelbl and Alexander Szandar, "Macedonia: The Double Game of the Americans," *Der Spiegel*, (Hamburg), July 30, 2001.

[9] Yuri Kovalenko, Ria Novosti Sofia, July 28, 2001.

[10] *Christian Science Monitor*, 27 June 2001. As quoted in Michel Chossudovsky, "Washington Behind Terrorist Attacks in Macedonia," http://emperorsclothes.com/articles/choss/behind.htm July 23, 2001.

[11] "Press Background Briefing on the President's Meeting with Macedonian President Trajkovski by Senior Administration Officials," The White House, Office of the Press Secretary, May 2, 2001.

[12] Aleksandar Vasovic, "Macedonia Rejects U.S.-EU Backed Plan," *Associated Press* July 18, 2001.

[13] *Ibid.*

[14] "Fact Sheet: U.S. Assistance to FRY Macedonia, United States Mission to the European Union, Brussels, April 12, 2001, and. Marjorie Cohn, *op.cit.*

[15] *London Sunday Times*, June 10, 2001, (from Chossudovsky, *op cit.)*

[16] *BBC World News*, January 29, 2001. (from Chossudovsky, *op.cit.*)[18]

[17] World Bank, Kosovo Foundation for an Open Society (KFOS) World Bank, World Bank Launches First Kosovo Project, Washington, November 16, 1999 from Michel Chossudovsky, *op.cit.*

[18] Vasovic, *op.cit* .

[19] ATA, Tirana, "Turkish Government is Ready to be Engaged in Restructuring of Albanian Army," September 13, 2000.

[20] Stratfor, "Turkey to Aid Albanian Military-Mixed Blessing for NATO" *Strategic Forcasting* 2001.

[21] "Bulgaria Offers to Give NATO a Helping Hand in its Possible Operations in Macedonia," *Pravda RU* June 22, 2001.

[22] Alabanian Extremists Threaten to Take Action in Greece," *Macedonian Press*

Agency, Skopje, May 30, 2001.

[23] James Pringle, "Sex Slave Trade Thrives Among Kosovo Troops," *The Times* (London), February 5, 2000.

[24] Ronald Soligo and Amy Jaffe, "The Economics of Pipeline Routes: the Conun drum of Oil Exports from the Caspian Basin" Baker Institute at Rice University, 1998.

[25] George Thompson, "KLA-Resurgent Nazis Under Nato's Wing," http://www.Srpska_Mreza.com

[26] "Greater Albania or not, Kosovo Effect Worries Macedonia," *Agence France Presse,* September 20,2000

[27] Karen Talbot, "Former Yugoslavia: The Name of the Game is OIL! And the Prize is Profits," *People's Weekly World,* May 18, 2001. Please note: Map of pipeline found at http://www.scarabee.com/EDITO2/070699htm

[28] "Trans-Balkan Pipeline Planned," *Pipeline and Gas Journal,* October 2000, from the Governments of the Republic of Bulgaria, Macedonia, Albania and the Board of Directors of AMBO. (AMBO CEO E.L. Ferguson was vice president of Dick Cheney's old company, Halliburton. (Karen Talbot, *op cit.*)

[29] "Poverty Deepening in Former Communist Countries" *The Associated Press London,* October 11, 2000.

[30] Zbigniew Brzezinski, *The Grand Chessboard.* Basic Books 1998.

[31] Michel Chossudovsky, "America at War in Macedonia," June 14, 2001. http://emperors-clothes.com

[32] *Ibid.*

[33] Sean Gervasi, "Why is NATO in Yugoslavia?" A Paper Delivered to the Conference on the Enlargement of NATO in Eastern Europe and the Mediterranean," Prague, Czech Republic, January 13-14, 1996.

U.S./EU Manipulate Elections:

Promote Coup to Cause Upheaval

GREGORY ELICH

For one long decade, the West waged a fierce campaign to subjugate Yugoslavia. Every means was utilized: support for violent secessionists, the imposition of severe sanctions, a seventy-eight-day bombardment, followed by forcible occupation of the region of Kosovo. The Yugoslav Federation withstood it all, but it was Western covert operations that finally brought disaster.

Flagrant Western interference distorted the political process in Yugoslavia. U.S. and Western European funds were channeled to right-wing opposition parties and media through such organizations as the National Endowment for Democracy and George Soros' Open Society Institute. The National Democratic Institute (NDI) is yet another of the myriad semi-private organizations that have attached themselves like leeches on Eastern Europe. The NDI opened an office in Belgrade in 1997, hoping to capitalize on opposition attempts to bring down the government through street demonstrations. By 1999, the NDI had already trained over 900 right-wing party leaders and activists on "message development, public outreach and election strategy." NDI also claimed to have provided "organizational training and coalition-building expertise" to the opposition.[1]

The New Serbia Forum, funded by the British Foreign Office, brought Serbian professionals and academics to Hungary on a regular basis for discussions with British and Central European "experts." The aim of the meetings was to "design a blueprint for post-Milosevic society." The Forum developed reports intended to serve as "an action plan" for a future pro-Western government. Subjects under discussion included privatization and economic stabilization. The Forum called for the "reintegration of Yugoslavia into the European family," a phrase that translated into the dismantling of the socialist economy and turning it over to Western corporations.[2]

Western aims were clearly spelled out in the Stability Pact for Southeastern Europe of June 10, 1999. This document called for "creating vibrant market economies" in the Balkans, and "markets open to greatly expanded foreign trade and private sector investment." One year later, the White House issued a fact sheet detailing the "major achievements" of the Pact. Among the achievements listed, the European Bank for Reconstruction and Development (EBRD) and the International Finance Corporation were said to be "mobilizing private investment," and the Pact's Business Advisory Council was "visiting all of the countries of Southeast Europe" to "offer advice" on investment issues. Another initiative was Hungarian involvement with opposition-led local governments and opposition media in Serbia leading up the September 24, 2000, election in Yugoslavia.

On July 26, 2000, the Overseas Private Investment Corporation (OPIC) inaugurated an investment fund to be managed by Soros Private Funds Management. The Southeast Europe Equity Fund "will invest in companies in the region in a range of sectors." Its purpose, according to the U.S. Embassy in Macedonia, is "to provide capital for new business development, expansion and privatization." In March 2000, Montenegro signed an agreement permitting the operation of OPIC on its territory.

Billionaire George Soros spelled out what all this means. U.S. involvement in the region, he said, "creates investment opportunities," and "I am happy to put my money where they are putting theirs." Bluntly put, there is money to be made.

George Munoz, President and CEO of OPIC, was also clear. "The Southeast Europe Equity Fund," he announced, "is an ideal vehicle to connect American institutional capital with European entrepreneurs eager to help Americans tap their growing markets. OPIC is pleased that Soros Private Funds Management has chosen to send a strong, positive signal that Southeast Europe is open for business."

The final text of the Stability Pact for Southeast Europe suggested that a Yugoslavia that would "respect" the Pact's "principles and objectives" would be "welcome" to become a full member. "In order to draw the Federal Republic of Yugoslavia closer to this goal," the document declared, Montenegro would be an "early beneficiary." Western leaders expressed hope that a future pro-Western Yugoslavia would, as had the rest of Eastern Europe, be "eager to help Americans" make money.[3]

Western leaders yearned to install a puppet government in Belgrade, and placed their hopes in the fragmented right-wing opposition parties in Serbia. In 1999, American officials encouraged these parties to organize mass demonstrations to overthrow the government, but the rallies quickly fizzled. When Yugoslav federal and local elections were announced for July 24, 2000, American and Western European officials met with leaders of Serbian opposition parties, urging them to unite behind one presidential candidate, Vojislav Kostunica.

At the beginning of August 2000, the U.S. opened an office in Budapest specifically tasked to assist opposition parties in Yugoslavia. Among the staff were at least thirty psychological warfare specialists, some of whom had earlier been engaged in psychological warfare operations during NATO's war against Yugoslavia and against Iraq in the Gulf War.[4] Members of the student opposition group, Otpor, were invited to attend ten-day courses, beginning August 28, and again on September 11, 2000, at the American embassies in Bulgaria and Romania. The courses, conducted by CIA personnel and propaganda experts, focused on political and public-image techniques.[5]

In Bulgaria, the Western-financed Political Academy for Central and Southeastern Europe established a program for training the Serbian opposition. The academy was tied to Vojislav Kostunica's Democratic Party of Serbia, Otpor and various opposition groups. Another Bulgarian-based and Western-financed organization, the Balkan Academy of Leading Reporters, gave "financial, technical and expert assistance" to Yugoslav opposition media prior to the election.[6]

On August 13 through 15, 2000, CIA Director George Tenet visited Bulgaria. In a series of extraordinary meetings, Tenet met with Bulgarian President Petur Stoyanov, as well as the prime minister, interior minister and defense minister. Officially, the purpose of Tenet's visit was to discuss the problem of organized crime and narcotics. However, Tenet spent a combined total of only twenty minutes at the headquarters of the National Security Service and the National Service for Combating Organized Crime. Unnamed diplomatic sources revealed that the proposed oil transit pipeline from the Caspian Sea was also topic of discussion.

The driving motivation for Tenet's visit, though, was to discuss Yugoslavia. According to an unnamed diplomatic source, Montenegrin secession from Yugoslavia topped the agenda. Following the meeting between Tenet and Major General Dimo Gyaurov, Director of the National Intelligence Service, a public statement was issued which stressed their "commonality of interests." Reports in the Bulgarian press revealed that various options were discussed with Bulgaria's president and prime minister.

Leaked information from the meetings indicated that Tenet's preferred option was the removal of the Yugoslav government, either as a result of the September 24 election, or by street demonstrations or an internal coup. Another alternative Tenet discussed was a NATO military assault that would install a puppe government. The third option was Montenegrin secession from Yugoslavia. Were open warfare to break out over Montenegro's secession from Yugoslavia, then the United States planned to wage a full-scale war. Sofia's *Monitor* reported that the "CIA coup machine" was forming. "A strike against Belgrade is imminent," it warned, and "Bulgaria will serve as a base."[7]

In preparation for possible military action, the Italian army signed a lease contract to conduct training exercises beginning in October 2000, at the Koren training ground, near Kaskovo in southeast Bulgaria. The French army signed a similar agreement, in which French soldiers and tanks would train at the Novo Selo grounds in central Bulgaria from October 11 to December 12, 2000. Plans called for the U.S. military to lease the Shabla training grounds in northeastern Bulgaria. All could have served as a launching pad for a NATO strike.[8] An amphibious training exercise with Croatian and U.S forces was conducted near Split, Croatia immediately following the Yugoslav election, and fifteen British warships were sent to the region.[9]

Tenet's third option, the secession of Montenegro from Yugoslavia, would follow the well-tested model of swallowing Yugoslavia, bite by bite. The paths of Yugoslavia's two republics had sharply diverged. Only Serbia stood in the way of the West's grand scheme to integrate the Balkans into an economic model in which the region's economies would be subordinated to Western corporate interests. Serbia's economy included a strong socialist component, and large- and medium-sized firms were socially owned. In contrast, Montenegro had embarked on a program to place its entire economy at the service of the West.

November 1999 saw the introduction in Montenegro of the German mark as an official currency and the passage of legislation eliminating socially owned property. One month later, several large firms were publicly offered for sale, including the Electric Power Company, the 13th July Agricultural Complex, the Hotel-Tourist firm Boka and several others.[10] The republic's privatization program for 2000 called for privatization of most state-owned industries, and included measures to "protect domestic and foreign investors."

In early 2000, the U.S. signed an agreement to provide Montenegro $62 million, including $44 million from the U.S. Agency for International Development (USAID). According to the agency, it would also undertake "assistance programs to support economic reform and restructuring the economy ... to advance Montenegro toward a free market economy." U.S. policy advisor on the Balkans James Dobbins indicated that the U.S. viewed the "market-oriented reforms of the Djukanovic regime as a model and stimulus for similar reforms throughout the former Yugoslavia." The U.S. also offered guarantees for private investors in the republic. Additional aid was provided by the European Union (EU), which approved $36 million for Montenegro. "From the first day," admitted Djukanovic, "we have had British and European consultants."[11]

The Center for International Private Enterprise, an affiliate of the U.S. Chamber of Commerce, provided support to the Center for Entrepreneurship (CEP) in Montenegro. According to the CEP's executive director, Petar Ivanovic, the organization "focuses on elementary and high schools," establishing entrepreneurship as a new subject to be taught in schools. As Ivanovic explained it, "Introducing young people to the concept of entrepreneurship will make them less resistant to the private sector." The CEP also intends to "educate government officials about the potential rewards of the private sector," and to help them "understand the benefits of economic reform and privatization."[12] According to Djukanovic, when he met with President Clinton on June 21, 1999, the U.S. president gave the privatization process a shove by telling Djukanovic that the U.S. planned to "stimulate the economy" by "encouraging U.S. corporations and banks to invest capital in Montenegro."[13]

Djukanovic moved steadily toward secession from Yugoslavia, indicating that he would push for separation if President Milosevic were reelected in the September 24 election. In a phone call to Djukanovic in July 2000, Madeleine Albright promised that the U.S would provide him with an additional $16.5 million. That same week, Djukanovic blurted out that Montenegro "is no longer part of Yugoslavia." He also made the astonishing claim that he considered it a "priority" for Montenegro to join NATO, the organization that had bombed his country only the year before. The next month, Albright announced that she and Djukanovic "try and talk to each other and meet on a regular basis," and that the "United States is supportive of the approach that President Djukanovic has taken in terms of democratic development and his approach to the economic reforms also."[14]

Western support for secession extended beyond Albright's meeting and talking with Djukanovic. More than half of the population of Montenegro opposed secession, and any such move was likely to explode into violence. In preparation for a rift, Djukanovic built up a private army of over 20,000 soldiers, the Special Police, including units armed with anti-tank weapons and mortars. Sources in Montenegro revealed that Western special forces trained Djukanovic's private army.

Prior to the election, Djukanovic requested that NATO establish an "air shield over Montenegro." One member of the Special Police, named Velibor, confirmed that they had received training from the British SAS. "If there is a situation where weapons will decide the outcome, we are ready," he said. "We are training for that." At a press conference on August 1, 2000, Information Minister Goran Matic declared that the "British are carrying out part of the training of the Montenegrin special units. It is also true," he added, that the Special Police "are intensively obtaining various kinds and types of weapons, starting with anti-aircraft and anti-helicopter weapons and so on, and they are also being assisted by Croatia, as the weapons go through Dubrovnik and other places."

Furthermore, Matic pointed out, "[L]ast year, before and after the aggression, a group from within the Montenegrin MUP [Ministry of Interior Affairs] structure left for training within the U.S. police structure and the U.S. intelligence structures." In August 2000, two armored vehicles bound for Montenegro were discovered in the port of Ancona, Italy. One of the vehicles was fitted with a turret suitable for mounting a machine gun or anti-tank weapon. Italian customs officials, reported the Italian news service *ANSA*, were "convinced" that arms trafficking to Montenegro was "of far greater magnitude than this single episode might lead one to believe." Reveling in anticipation of armed conflict, Djukanovic bragged that "many will tuck their tails between their legs and will soon have to flee Montenegro."[15]

A violent conflict in Montenegro would have provided NATO with a pretext for intervention. As early as October 1999, General Wesley Clark drew up plans for a NATO invasion of Montenegro. The plan envisioned an amphibious assault by more than 2,000 Marines storming the port of Bar and securing the port as a beachhead for pushing inland. Troops ferried by helicopters would seize the airport at Podgorica, while NATO warplanes would bomb and strafe resisting Yugoslav forces. According to U.S. officials, other Western countries had also developed invasion plans.[16] Richard Holbrooke, U.S. Ambassador to the UN declared, "We are in constant touch with the leadership of Montenegro," and warned that a conflict in Montenegro "would be directly affecting NATO's vital interest."[17] NATO General Secretary George Robertson was more explicit. "I say to Milosevic: watch out, look what happened the last time you miscalculated...."[18]

What the U.S. truly wanted, though, was all of Yugoslavia, not merely another piece. U.S. Secretary of State Madeleine Albright expected and demanded street demonstrations to topple the government if the election result did not satisfy her. At meetings held in Banja Luka in spring 2000, Albright expressed disappointment with the failure of past efforts to overthrow the legally elected Yugoslav government. Albright said that she had hoped sanctions would lead people to "blame Milosevic for this suffering." An exasperated Albright wondered, "What was stopping the people from taking to the streets?" Indicating that the U.S. was casting about for a pretext for intervention, she added, "Something needs to happen in Serbia that the West can support."[19]

The multifaceted U.S. destabilization campaign planned for every contingency. In the end, George Tenet's preferred scenario unfolded. An electoral process distorted by Western intervention, combined with street action, finally toppled the government of Yugoslavia. The U.S. pumped $35 million into the pockets of the right-wing opposition in the year preceding the September 24, 2000, election. This haul included transmitters for opposition radio, and computers, telephones and fax machines for several organizations. Right-wing media received an additional $6 million from the European Union during this period.

Two organizations under the umbrella of the National Endowment for Democracy, the National Democratic Institute and the International Republican Institute, provided $4 million for a door-to-door campaign and get-out-the-vote programs.[20] U.S. officials assured opposition media "not to worry about how much they're spending now," because much more was on the way.[21] Immediately following the election, the U.S. House of Representatives passed by voice vote a bill authorizing an additional $105 million for right-wing parties and media in Yugoslavia.[22]

The week before the election, the European Union issued a "Message to the Serbian People," in which it announced that a victory for opposition candidate Vojislav Kostunica would result in lifting of sanctions. "Even if Milosevic were to be returned by democratic vote," stated one EU official, sanctions would remain. This was a powerful inducement for a population impoverished and devastated by years of Western sanctions.[23]

Before the election even took place, Western officials were accusing the Yugoslav government of electoral fraud, planting the seeds for disruption. Throughout election day and the days that followed, the Democratic Opposition of Serbia (DOS) coalition proclaimed their candidate's victory. American officials encouraged the opposition to call for mass demonstrations, even before official results were announced. Virtually every day, DOS claimed a different percentage for their candidate. At one point they claimed fifty-seven percent. Two days after the election, on September 26, DOS claimed Kostunica won 54.66 percent of the vote, based on 97.5 percent of the ballots processed, but that 130,000 votes "and the votes from Kosovo and Montenegro" had yet to be processed by DOS.

The next day, DOS announced that Kostunica led with 52.54 percent of the vote. The tally, they said, was based on 98.72 percent of the ballots counted. This time, DOS Electoral Staff spokesman Cedomir Jovanovic changed his tune, claiming that unprocessed ballots were from soldiers and mail-in ballots.

According to Jovanovic, on September 26, 5,093,038 ballots out of a total of 5,223,629 were processed for a total of percentage of 97.5. Based on the total given by Jovanovic, that would have meant less than 64,000 ballots were counted the following day, when he claimed a count of 98.72 percent. Assuming that Kostunica lost every single one of those votes, his percentage would have dropped to 52.75 percent, higher than the announced 52.54 figure. Also on September 26, Jovanovic announced that President Milosevic trailed with 35.01 percent, then the following day that he had only 31.01 percent.

Given Jovanovic's total, if Milosevic had also lost every single one of the remaining votes, his percentage would have dropped only to 34.1 percent. DOS disposed of this awkwardness by issuing significantly different totals. On September 26, Jovanovic announced that Kostunica led with 2,783,870 votes, yet on the following day he claimed that when all votes were counted, "Kostunica will have 2,649,000 votes." Then on October 2, opposition spokesman Zoran Sami announced 2,414,876, for a percentage of 51.34. Later, Sami claimed the final result showed 2,377,440 votes and a percentage of 50.35 for Kostunica.

Excluded from these counts were the votes from Kosovo and refugees from Kosovo. Western media treated DOS's claims uncritically, proclaiming them to be based on precise and meticulous tallying of ballots, and loud cries of fraud were leveled against the Yugoslav government. Clearly there was fraud. The figures given out by DOS itself indicate who was perpetuating the fraud.[24]

Despite claims made to the contrary in the Western media, the official vote count was publicized widely in Yugoslavia. Vojislav Kostunica won 48.96 percent of the vote, falling just short of the 50 percent required for outright victory. President Milosevic trailed with 38.62 percent of the vote. A second electoral round for the two top candidates was called for October 8.[25] Backed by Western officials, Kostunica and DOS refused to participate in the second round, claiming that they had already won. DOS filed a complaint with first the Federal Election Commission, and then the Constitutional Court. They demanded, among other things, the annulment of votes by refugees from Kosovo, and from Kosovo itself, where President Milosevic led by a wide margin.

The Constitutional Court upheld the proposal by Milovan Zivkovic, a member of the Federal Election Commission, for returns from all voting districts to be reexamined so as to dispel doubts.[26] It was the threat of a recount that motivated the almost daily reduction in the number and percentage of votes claimed by DOS for their candidate. The final percentage DOS announced was close to the official result. However, DOS refused to include votes cast in Kosovo and by many refugees from Kosovo, ostensibly because polls in Kosovo closed at 4:00 PM, rather than 8:00 PM. According to DOS, the scheduled early closing time invalidated all of the ballots cast by these voters. Only by discounting votes from Kosovo residents and refugees could DOS claim a 50-percent victory for Kostunica.

Over 200 international observers from fifty-four countries monitored the election. The observers attended every stage of the election, including vote counting and correlation of results. One of the observers, Greek Foreign Minister Carolos Papoulias, concluded, "Those who had announced widespread fraud, like [EU foreign policy chief] Javier Solana have been proved wrong," and that the vote had been conducted in "an impeccable manner."

Atila Volnay, an observer from Hungary, said his delegation had visited several polling stations and confirmed the presence of opposition representatives in electoral commissions, and that "there could be no anomalies." A three-person delegation from Great Britain's Socialist Labour Party declared that the Federal Electoral Commission "did everything in its power to ensure that people were able to cast their votes without intimidation and in an orderly manner," but that irregularities were observed in Montenegro. "We received many first-hand reports from people who stated that they had been threatened [by Djukanovic supporters] with the loss of their jobs if they turned out to vote."

The delegation also noted that "countless refugees from Kosovo had been deliberately excluded from the electoral lists in Montenegro," and that the delegation "could only conclude that these tactics of intimidation and disenfranchisement were designed to benefit the so-called Democratic Opposition." The head of the Russian delegation, Konstantin Kosachev, said that they "were satisfied that virtually no large-scale falsification of the election in Yugoslavia was possible." A final statement by the observers declared that "the voting process overall was orderly and smooth" and that, "in the opinion of many, was equal or superior to the ones in their own countries."[27]

Given his lead in the first electoral round, a Kostunica victory in the runoff on October 8 was a near certainty. Why then, did Kostunica refuse to participate in the runoff? As a result of the September 24 election, the left coalition won seventy-four out of 137 seats in the Chamber of Citizens and twenty-six out of forty seats in the Chamber of Republics. The left-led coalition already held a majority in the Serbian Parliament, whose seats were not up for election until the following year. It would have been impossible for DOS to implement their program, as the president's duties are rather limited. Only a coup d'etat would allow DOS to bypass legal constraints and govern unopposed.

Kostunica's campaign manager, Zoran Djindjic, called for a general strike. "We shall seek to paralyze all institutions, schools, theaters, cinemas, offices," and "call everyone onto the streets."[28] DOS supporters throughout the country heeded his call, bringing segments of the economy to a standstill, while mass demonstrations sprang up throughout Serbia. Madeleine Albright's cherished scenario became reality, as demonstrators demanded the removal of the government. According to opposition sources, as many as 10,000 armed DOS supporters joined the final mass demonstration in Belgrade. The assault on the Federal Parliament and Radio Television Serbia was led by a group of specially trained squads of former soldiers.

Velimir Ilic, opposition mayor of Cacak, led the assault. "Our action had been planned in advance," he later explained. "Our aim was very clear; take control of the regime's key institutions, including the parliament and the television." Ilic also arranged prior contacts with turncoat policemen, who assisted Ilic's soldiers.[29] It is probable that the CIA was involved in the planning of the well-coordinated attacks. After armed squads forced their way into the Federal Parliament, they were followed by a drunken mob of DOS supporters, who rampaged through the building, smashing furniture and computers and setting the Parliament ablaze. In the streets, police were beaten and drunken gangs, many armed with guns, roamed the streets. Ambulances taking injured police to hospitals were stopped by DOS activists, who demanded that the injured policemen be turned over to them.

After Radio Television Serbia in Belgrade was seized, it too was torched. Throughout Serbia, offices of the Socialist Party of Serbia and Yugoslav United Left were demolished. Socialists were threatened and beaten, and many received threats over the telephone. In Kragujevac, ten Socialists were tied and abused for hours. DOS thugs forced their way into the home of Zivojin Stefanovic, president of the Socialist Party in Leskovac. After looting and smashing Stefanovic's belongings, they set his house afire.[30]

While roving gangs overturned and burned police vehicles, vandalized buildings and beat people, Kostunica announced, "Democracy has happened in Serbia. Communism is falling. It is just a matter of hours."[31] Establishing their democratic credentials, DOS activists systematically seized left-oriented media throughout Yugoslavia. Left-wing newspapers, radio and television stations were reoriented in support of the right. A formerly rich and diverse media culture, representing the entire political spectrum, took on overnight a hue of uniformity, churning out praise for DOS.

Gangs of DOS thugs forcibly removed management at state-run factories and enterprises, universities, banks and hospitals in towns and cities all across Serbia. Government ministers were pressured to resign, and DOS established a crisis committee to perform government functions, circumventing Parliament and government ministries. DOS officials openly threatened to call forth more street violence as a means of pressuring the Serbian Parliament to agree to a new election, one year ahead of schedule.

Western officials couldn't hide their glee. American and European corporations were waiting to snatch up state enterprises. The economic program for DOS was drawn up by an organization named Group 17 Plus. Their plan, called Project for Serbia, calls for a rapid transition to a full market economy. Immediately following the coup, the European Bank for Reconstruction and Development promptly announced plans to open an office in Belgrade. "It's important that we be there quickly," explained the bank's spokesman Jeff Hiday. "We suspect there will be a lot to do with privatization and restructuring."[32]

Days before the coup, President Milosevic warned that DOS was an instrument in NATO's campaign to impose neocolonial control over Yugoslavia. Milosevic pointed out that neighboring countries already under Western dictate "have speedily become impoverished in a manner destroying all hope for more just and humane social relations," and that Eastern Europe had seen a "great division into a poor majority and a rich minority." Inevitably, he said, "That picture would also include us."[33]

Alone and isolated, Yugoslavia resisted imperial domination, withstanding Western-backed secessions, sanctions, war, and covert operations. Against all odds, they remained committed to social ownership and independence. The most powerful forces on the planet were arrayed against them, and yet they held out for a decade. The NATO-backed coup swept all that away. In one of his first acts as president, Kostunica joined the Balkan Stability Pact. The privatization minister, Aleksandar Vlahovic, announced a plan for the privatization of 7,000 firms. "I expect that four years from now socially-owned property will be completely eliminated," he explained.[34] The millions of dollars that the West stuffed into the pockets of DOS officials will pay handsome dividends.

[1] "NDI Activities in the Federal Republic of Yugoslavia (Serbia-Montenegro)," NDI Worldwide Activities, www.ndi.org

[2] "Britain Trains New Elite for Post-Milosevic Era," *The Independent* (London), May 3, 2000. The New Serbia Forum, http://ds.dial.pipex.com/town/way/glj77/Serbia.htm

[3] "Final Text of Stability Pact for Southeast Europe," June 10, 1999.

"Southeast Europe Equity Fund Launched July 26," U.S. Embassy, Skopje, Macedonia, July 27, 2000.

"The Stability Pact for Southeast Europe: One Year Later," White House Fact Sheet, July 27, 2000.

[4] "Federal Foreign Ministry Sends Memorandum to UN Security Council," *Tanjug* (Belgrade), October 4, 2000.

"U.S. Anti-Yugoslav Office Opens in Budapest," *Tanjug* (Belgrade), August 21, 2000.

[5] "CIA Training Resistance Members in Sofia, Bucharest," *Tanjug* (Belgrade), August 25, 2000.

[6] Elena Staridolska, "Daynov Academy Trains Serbian Opposition," *Standart News* (Sofia), August 29, 2000. Konstantin Chugunov, "We Report the Details: Our Little Brothers Have Bent in the Face of NATO," *Rossiyskaya Gazeta* (Moscow), August 23, 2000.

[7] "Bulgaria – Press Review" *BTA* (Sofia), August 12, 2000

"Bulgaria – Us CIA Director's Visit," *BTA* (Sofia), August 15, 2000

"CIA Did Not Tell Us the Most Important Thing," *Trud* (Sofia), August 16, 2000

"Bulgaria – Press Review," *BTA* (Sofia), August 14, 2000

"Bulgaria – Press Review," *BTA* (Sofia), August 16, 2000

[8] Mila Avramova, "Italians Lease Training Ground for 400,000 Leva," *Trud* (Sofia), August 9, 2000.

Michael Evans, "Balkans Watch for 'Invincible'," *The Times* (London), August 26, 2000.

[9] "U.S. Forces Travel to Croatia for Amphibious Exercise," Office of the Assistant Secretary of Defense (Public Affairs), September 12, 2000.

"U.S. War Game in Adriatic, U.K. Navy in Mediterranean," *Reuters*, September 16, 2000.

[10] Ljubinka Cagorovic, "Montenegro Assembly Scraps Socially-Owned Property," *Reuters,* November 13, 1999.

"Montenegrin Government Prepares to Privatise Economy," *Tanjug* (Belgrade), December 25, 1999.

[11] Central and Eastern Europe Business Information Center, "Southeastern Europe Business Brief," February 3, 2000.

Central and Eastern Europe Business Information Center, "Southeastern Europe Business Brief," April 27, 2000.

Anne Swardson, "West Grows Close to Montenegro," *Washington Post*, May 24, 2000.

[12] Petar Ivanovic, "Montenegro: Laying the Foundation of Entrepreneurship," Center for International Private Enterprise.

[13] Statement by Montenegrin President Milo Djukanovic, "Important Step in Opening New Perspectives For Montenegrin State Policy," *Pobjeda* (Podgorica), June 22, 1999.

[14] "Albright Renews Montenegro Support," *Associated Press*, July 13, 2000.

"Montenegro Wants to Join NATO and the EU," *Agence France-Presse*, July 10, 2000.

Office of the Spokesman, U.S. Department of State, "Secretary of State Madeleine K. Albright and Montenegrin President Milo Djukanovic," Press Stakeout at Excelsior Hotel, Rome, Italy, August 1, 2000.

[15] "Montenegro Ahead of Elections: Boycott and Threats," *BETA* (Belgrade), August 9, 2000.

"Montenegro and Elections – Boycott Becomes Official," *BETA* (Belgrade), August 17, 2000.

Phil Reese, "We Have the Heart for Battle, Says Montenegrin Trained by SAS," *The Independent* (London), July 30, 2000.

"Yugoslav Information Minister Says U.S. Behind Dutch 'Mercenaries'," *BBC Monitoring Service*, August 1, 2000.

"Yugoslavia Says British SAS Trains Montenegrins," *Reuters*, August 1, 2000.

"Information Minister Sees Montenegrin Arms Purchases, Croatian Assistance," *BETA* (Belgrade), July 31, 2000.

"Foreign 'Dogs of War' Training Montenegrin Police to Attack Army," *Tanjug* (Belgrade), August 9, 2000.

"Montenegro: Camouflaged Military Vehicles Seized in Ancona," *ANSA* (Rome), August 21, 2000.

"Montenegro: Traffic in Camouflaged Armored Vehicles: Investigation into Documentation," *ANSA* (Rome), August 22, 2000.

"SAS Training Montenegrin Police," *The Sunday Times* (London), October 1, 2000.

[16] Richard J. Newman, "Balkan Brinkmanship," *US News and World Report*, November 15, 1999.

[17] "'Clinton Warns Milosevic 'Remains a Threat to Peace'," *Agence France-Presse*, July 29, 2000.

[18] "NATO's Robertson Warns Milosevic on Montenegro," *Reuters*, July 27, 2000.

[19] Borislav Komad, "At Albright's Signal," *Vecernje Novosti* (Belgrade), May 18, 2000.

[20] George Jahn, "U.S. Funding Yugoslavian Reformers," *Associated Press*, September 29, 2000.

Jane Perlez, "U.S. Anti-Milosevic Plan Faces Major Test at Polls," *New York Times*, September 23, 2000.

"U.S., EU Generous to Foes of Milosevic," *Associated Press*, October 1, 2000.

[21] Steven Erlanger, "Milosevic, Trailing in Polls, Rails Against NATO," *New York Times*, September 20, 2000.

[22] "U.S. House Votes to Fund Yugoslavia's Opposition Movement," *CNN*, September 25, 2000.

[23] Geoff Meade, "Cook Backs EU Over Oust Milosevic Message," *London Press Association*, September 18, 2000.

[24] "DOS Claims Kostunica Leading Milosevic with 54.66 to 35.01 Percent of Vote," *BETA* (Belgrade), September 26, 2000.

"DOS Announces Kostunica Clear Winner with 98.72 Percent Data Processed," *BETA* (Belgrade), September 27, 2000.

"Federal Electoral Commission – DOS Election Staff Misinformed Public," *Tanjug* (Belgrade), October 3, 2000.

"Who Lies Kostunica?" statement by the Socialist Party of Serbia, October 11, 2000.

[25] Federal Republic of Yugoslavia web site, www.gov.yu "Total Election Results," and "The Federal Eections Commission Statement." Both statements were removed following the coup.

"Final Results of FRY Presidential Election," *Tanjug* (Belgrade), September 28, 2000.

[26] "Yugoslav Constitutional Court Holds Public Debate on DOS Appeal," *Tanjug* (Belgrade), October 4, 2000.

"DOS Requests Annulment of 142,000 Kosovo Votes," *BETA* (Belgrade), September 29, 2000.

[27] "Contrary to EU Claims, Yugoslav Elections a Success: Greece," *Agence France-Presse*, September 26, 2000.

"210 Observers from 53 States Commend FRY Elections," *Tanjug* (Belgrade), September 27, 2000.

"Foreign Observers Say Elections Democratic and Regular," *Tanjug* (Belgrade), September 25, 2000.

"Yugoslav Elections – a Lesson in Outside Interference," Socialist Labour Party statement. Broadcast, Mayak Radio (Moscow), October 2, 2000.

"'A Fair and Free Election,' International Observers Say," statement by international observers.

[28] Misha Savic, "Milosevic Will Take Part in Runoff," *Associated Press*, October 5, 2000.

[29] Richard Boudreaux, "A Mayor's Conspiracy Helped Topple Milosevic," *Los Angeles Times*, October 10, 2000.

"Cacak Mayor Says He Led Assault on Yugoslav Parliament," *Agence France-Presse*, October 8, 2000.

Jonathan Steele, Tim Judah, John Sweeney, Gillian Sandford, Rory Carroll, Peter Beaumont, "An Outrage Too Far," *The Observer* (London), October 8, 2000.

Gillian Sandford, "Army Units Claim Credit for Uprising," *The Guardian* (London), October 9, 2000.

[30] "Information for the Public," statement by the Socialist Party of Serbia, October 7, 2000.

"Group of Demonstrators Demolished the House of the District Head," *BETA* (Belgrade), October 6, 2000.

[31] "Protesters Storm Yugoslav Parliament," Associated Press, October 5, 2000.

"Good Evening, Liberated Serbia," *The Times* (London), October 6, 2000.

"Milosevic's Party HQ Ransacked by Protesters," *Agence France-Presse*, October 5, 2000.

[32] Jelena Radulovic, "Yugoslavia's Kostunica Sets Economic Goals for New Government," *Bloomberg*, October 7, 2000.

"Brains Behind Kostunica Have a Plan," *Sydney Morning Herald*, October 2, 2000.

Stefan Racin, "Yugoslavia's Opposition Outlines Economic Plans," *UPI*, September 27, 2000.

[33] "Yugoslav President Milosevic Addresses the Nation," *Tanjug* (Belgrade), October 3, 2000.

[34] Beti Bilandzic, "Serbia Eyes New Privatization Law by April," *Reuters*, January 28, 2001.

Economic Terrorism

MICHEL CHOSSUDOVSKY

In Yugoslavia, the IMF has become the steadfast financial bureaucracy of the Western military alliance, working hand in glove with NATO and the U.S. State Department.

The International Monetary Fund (IMF) is known to bully developing countries, imposing strong doses of "deadly economic medicine" while saddling governments with spiraling external debts. In complicity with Washington, the IMF often meddles in cabinet appointments in debtor countries. In South Korea in the turmoil of the 1997 Asian crisis, the finance minister —sacked for allegedly "hindering negotiations" with the IMF— was replaced by a former IMF official.[1] In Turkey, also in the wake of an IMF-style financial meltdown (March 2001), the minister of economy was substituted by a vice-president of the World Bank.[2]

But what has occurred in Yugoslavia sets a new record in the abusive practices of the Washington-based international financial bureaucracy: the arrest of a head of state of a debtor nation —demanded by its main creditors— has become "a precondition" for the holding of loan negotiations.

While March 31, 2001, was Washington's deadline date for the arrest of President Slobodan Milosevic by the "Democratic Opposition of Serbia" (DOS) government, another ultimatum was set for transferring the former head of state to the jurisdiction of the NATO-sponsored International Criminal Tribunal for the Former Yugoslavia at The Hague (ICTY). In the words of Secretary of State Colin Powell: "The U.S. administration's support for an international donors' conference where Yugoslavia is hoping for up to $1 billion to help rebuild would depend on continued progress in full cooperation with the [Hague] tribunal."[3]

A State Department spokesman further clarified "that the United States has the power to stop the conference from going ahead in the early summer if Washington is not satisfied."[4] Meanwhile, The Hague Tribunal has threatened to take the matter before the UN Security Council, if President Milosevic is not rapidly transferred to its jurisdiction.[5] [Milosevic was transferred June 28, 2001.—editor]

WITHHOLDING FINANCIAL "AID"

Very timely. At the height of the Yugoslav presidential elections (September 2000), "enabling legislation" was rushed through the U.S. House of Representatives. Washington had forewarned Kostunica — pursuant to an Act of Congress (HR 1064)— that unless his government fully complied with U.S. diktats, financial "aid" would be withheld. The IMF and the World Bank had also been duly notified by their largest shareholder, namely the U.S. government, that:

> [T]he U.S. Secretary of the Treasury [would] withhold from payment of the United States' share of any increase in the paid-in capital of [the IMF and World Bank] an amount equal to the amount of the loan or other assistance [to Yugoslavia].[6]

Meanwhile, Washington had demanded the setting up of an office of the ICTY in Belgrade as well as modifications to the legal statutes of Yugoslavia. The latter—to be rubber-stamped by the Parliament— would place the ICTY above the jurisdiction of Yugoslavia's national legal system. It would also allow the ICTY to order on NATO's behest, the arrest of thousands of people on trumped up charges.

RELEASING KLA TERRORISTS

U.S. officials had also intimated that the prompt release of Kosovo Liberation Army (KLA) "freedom fighters" serving jail terms in Serbia was to be regarded as an "additional pre-condition" for the granting of financial assistance:

State Department officials later told the UPI news agency that among other steps the United States was looking for were Yugoslav President Vojislav Kostunica to begin returning Albanians captured during the 1999 Kosovo conflict to Kosovo and for an acceptance of the war crimes tribunal's jurisdiction inside Serbia, where numerous indicted suspects still enjoy immunity.[7]

An "Amnesty Law" was rushed through the Yugoslav parliament barely a month before Washington's March 31, 2001, deadline.[8] While the victims of the war are persecuted and indicted as war criminals, the Kostunica regime—on Washington's instructions—has released KLA criminals linked to the drug mafias who committed atrocities in Kosovo.

Meanwhile, these criminals have rejoined the ranks of the KLA, now involved in a new wave of terrorist assaults in southern Serbia and in neighboring Macedonia. The evidence amply confirms that these terrorist attacks are supported and financed by Washington.[9]

'ECONOMIC NORMALIZATION'

Without further scrutiny, the Western media touts the holding of a donors' conference as "a necessary step" towards "economic normalization" and the "reintegration" of Yugoslavia into the "family of nations". Public opinion is led to believe that the "donors" will "help" Yugoslavia rebuild. The term "donor" is a misnomer. In fact the donors' conference is a meeting of bankers and creditors mainly from the countries that bombed Yugoslavia. Their intent is to not only to collect money from Yugoslavia, but also to gain full control and ownership of the Yugoslav economy.

Meanwhile, national laws have been revised to facilitate sweeping privatization. Serbia's large industrial complexes and public utilities are to be restructured and auctioned off to foreign capital. In other words, rather than "helping Yugoslavia", the donor conference—organized in close consultation with Washington and NATO headquarters in Brussels—would set the stage for the transformation of Yugoslavia into a colony of the Western military alliance.

Yugoslavia's external debt is in excess of $14 billion of which $5 billion are owed to the Paris Club (i.e. largely to the governments of NATO countries) and $3 billion to the London Club. The latter is a syndicate of private banks, which in the case of Yugoslavia includes some 400 creditor institutions. The largest part of Yugoslavia's commercial debt, however, is held by some sixteen mainly American and European banks that are members of an "International Coordinating Committee" (ICC) headed by America's Citigroup and Germany's giant West-Deutsche Landesbank. Other big players in the ICC include J.P. Morgan-Chase and Merrill Lynch.

The ICC—which operates discretely behind the scenes—ultimately call the shots regarding debt negotiations, privatization and macro-economic therapy. In turn, the IMF bureaucracy acting on behalf of both the commercial and official creditors has called for "a restructuring of FRY's external debt on appropriate terms," underscoring the fact that fresh money can only be approved "following the regularization of arrears."[10] What this means is that Belgrade would be obliged to recognize these debts in full as a condition for the negotiation of fresh loans as well as settle pending succession issues regarding the division of the external debt of the FRY with the "successor republics."

FICTICIOUS MONEY

While token "reconstruction" loans are envisaged, vast amounts of money and resources will be taken out of Yugoslavia. In fact, most of the promised "reconstruction" money is totally fictitious.

A $208 million "bridge loan" granted by Switzerland and Norway in January 2001 was used to reimburse the IMF. In turn, the IMF had granted $151 million to Belgrade in the form of a so-called "post-conflict assistance" loan. But this "aid" was tagged to reimburse Switzerland and Norway, which had coughed up the money to settle IMF arrears in the first place:

> The [IMF] Board approved a loan [of] ... $151 million under the IMF's policy on emergency post-conflict assistance in support of a program to stabilize the FRY's economy and help rebuild administrative capacities. Of this amount, the [Belgrade] authorities will draw ... $130 million to repay the bridge loans they received [from Switzerland and Norway] to eliminate arrears with the IMF.[11]

The illusion is conveyed that "money is coming in" and that "the IMF is helping Yugoslavia." In fact, what remains after the IMF "has reimbursed itself" is a meager influx of $21 million. And broadly the same fictitious money arrangement has been put in place by the World Bank, which has ordered that $1.7 billion in arrears "be cleared" before the granting of fresh loans.

In this regard, Belgrade will be granted a so-called "loan of consolidation" from the World Bank to reimburse the $1,7 billion debt it owes to the World Bank. Little or no money will actually enter the country. In the words of Central Bank governor Mladan Dinkic:

> [this] will pave the way for Yugoslavia's return to the World Bank. 'In the first three years, we will receive the so-called AIDA status, which the World Bank gives to the poorest countries ... [this] is the most favorable arrangement possible, with a longer grace-period and minimum interest, which will allow our economy to pay off the [$1.7 billion] debt and create conditions for receiving new loans.[12]

More generally, the "reconstruction" money will line the pockets of international creditors and multinational corporations (with trinkets for DOS cronies) while putting the entire Yugoslav economy on the auction block. Assets will be sold at rock-bottom prices under IMF-World Bank supervision. The meager proceeds of forced privatization, in which only foreign "investors" will be allowed to bid, will then be used to pay back the creditors, who happen to be the same people who are buying up Yugoslavia's assets.

And who will appraise the "book value" of Yugoslavia's industrial assets and supervise the auction of state property? The large European and U.S. merchant banks and accounting firms, which also happen to be acting on behalf of their corporate clients involved in bidding.

DEADLY ECONOMIC MEDICINE

Fictitious reconstruction money, however, is only granted on condition Yugoslavia implements economic "shock therapy." The donor-sponsored program is predicated on "destruction" rather than "reconstruction". Under the disguise of "economic normalization," the IMF, the World Bank and the London-based European Bank for Reconstruction and Development (EBRD) have been given the mandate to dismantle through bankruptcy and forced privatization what has not yet been destroyed by the bombers.

In this process, political terror and "economic terror" go hand in hand. The evidence amply confirms that the IMF-World Bank's lethal economic reforms imposed in more than 150 developing countries have led to the impoverishment of millions of people. In a cruel irony, bitter economic medicine and token financial assistance are presented as "the rewards" for transferring President Milosevic to the jurisdiction of the ICTY.

While the present IMF program is a "continuation" of the deadly economic reforms first imposed on federal Yugoslavia in the 1980s (and then on its "successor republics"), it promises to be far more devastating.[13]

The Group of 17 economists (G-17) —which controls the Ministry of Finance and Yugoslavia's Central Bank (NBJ)—is in permanent liaison with the IMF, the World Bank and the U.S. Treasury. A "Letter of Intent" outlining in detail the economic therapy to be imposed on Yugo-

slavia by the DOS government had in fact been drawn up in secret negotiations with the creditors before the September 2000 presidential elections. Mladjan Dinkic, who now holds the position of governor of the
National Bank of Yugoslavia (NBJ—Central Bank), had stated that one
of the first things they would do under a Kostunica presidency would be
to implement economic "shock therapy":

> Immediately after taking the office, the new government shall abol-
> ish all types of subsidies... This measure must be implemented without
> regrets or hesitation, since it will be difficult if not impossible to apply
> later, in view of the fact that in the meantime strong lobbies may appear
> and do their best to block such measures. ... This initial step in economic
> liberalization must be undertaken as a "shock therapy" as its radical na-
> ture does not leave space for gradualism of any kind.[14]

The G-17 does not hide the fact that one of its main objectives consists in breaking social resistance to the economic restructuring program:

> Any future democratic regime is likely to face substantial public re-
> sistance to privatization and the socio-economic reforms that will ac-
> company it. In the short term, the insolvency and restructuring of Ser-
> bian enterprises is likely to generate unemployment or wage cuts for
> many employees ... The servicing of debts and fiscal adjustments are
> likely to require cuts in public expenditure and the introduction of poten-
> tially unpopular new taxes and levies. The purchase of Serbian firms by
> wealthy domestic and foreign investors may also generate resentment,
> especially as it will represent a radical break with the former Yugoslav
> tradition of workers' or "social" ownership. Nationalist and anti-
> reformist groups are likely to mobilize popular resistance by exploiting
> these problems. This form of political opposition would limit the scope
> for introducing effective economic reform and privatization.[15]

FREEZING WAGES

The IMF program—put into full swing in the wake of the September
2000 elections—calls for the adoption of "prudent macroeconomic policies and bold structural reforms." In IMF lingo, "bold" invariably means
the application of "shock treatment" while "prudent" means carefully
designed and uncompromising austerity measures.[16] Upon assuming office, the Kostunica government, under IMF instructions, has deregulated
the prices of basic consumer goods and frozen the wages of working
people.[17] A new Labor Law setting the minimum wage at thirty-five

percent of the average wage was rubber-stamped by the Yugoslav parliament. In other words, with rising prices coupled with the deindexation of wages ordered by the IMF, the new legislation allows the real minimum wage to slide to abysmally low levels.[18]

Credit has been frozen to local businesses and farmers. Interest rates have already skyrocketed. With the end of the economic sanctions, the IMF has also demanded that import barriers be removed to facilitate the dumping of surplus commodities on the domestic market leading to the bankruptcy of domestic producers. In turn, energy prices are to be totally deregulated prior to the privatization of public utilities, state oil refineries, coal mining and electricity.

In turn, drastic cuts in the social security and pension funds of the Republic of Serbia are envisaged, which would virtually lead to their collapse. The restructuring of social programs is a carbon copy of that imposed in neighboring Bulgaria, where pensions paid out to senior citizens plummeted in 1997 to as low as $3 as month.[19]

ENGINEERING THE COLLAPSE OF THE DINAR

The most lethal component of the IMF program, however, is the so-called "managed float" of the exchange rate, which—according to IMF Deputy Managing Director Stanley Fischer—is implemented "to better reflect market conditions".[20]

Yugoslavia's central bank foreign exchange reserves are of the order of $500 million, the external debt is in excess of $14 billion. Under agreement with the IMF, money (in the form of a "precautionary loan") would be granted to replenish the foreign exchange reserves of the Central Bank with a view to supporting the dinar. Moreover, following the Brazilian pattern, the dinar would also be artificially propped up by extensive government borrowing from private banking institutions at exorbitant interest rates, thereby fuelling the internal public debt.[21]

In the absence of exchange controls restricting capital flight, central bank foreign exchange reserves would eventually be depleted. In other words, when the "borrowed reserves" are no longer there to prop up the currency, the dinar collapses. In the logic of the "managed float," the dollars borrowed under an IMF precautionary fund arrangement would be reappropriated by international creditors and speculators once the dinar slides, leading to a further expansion of Yugoslavia's external debt.

In fact, this policy is largely instrumental in triggering hyperinflation. The national currency would become totally worthless. In other words, prices would go sky high following the collapse of the national currency. In turn, wages would be frozen on IMF instructions as part of an "anti-inflationary program" and the standard of living would plummet to even lower levels. And Yugoslavs are already impoverished with two-thirds of the population (according to UN sources acknowledged in the IMF report) having a per capita income below $2 a day.

It's the same financial scam that the IMF applied in South Korea, Indonesia, Russia, Brazil and more recently Turkey.[22] In this process, various speculative instruments (including "short selling" of currencies) were applied by international banks and financial institutions to trigger the collapse of national currencies. In South Korea, debts spiraled in the wake of the currency crisis. As a result, the entire economy was put on the auction block and several of South Korea's powerful conglomerates were taken over by U.S. capital at ridiculously low prices.

In Russia, the ruble became totally worthless following the implementation of an IMF program. The float of the ruble applied in 1992 under IMF advice led in less than a year to a one-hundred-fold (9,900 percent) increase in consumer prices. Since nominal earnings increased tenfold (900 percent), the collapse in real wages in 1992 was of the order of eighty-six percent. In subsequent years, real earnings continued to plummet, precipitating the descent of the vast majority of the Russian people into extreme poverty.[23]

More generally, the IMF program creates a framework for collecting as well as enlarging the debt through the manipulation of currency markets. It is worth mentioning, in this regard, that barely a few weeks before the arrest of President Milosevic, Turkey was subjected—following the destabilization of its currency—to the most brutal economic reforms leading virtually over night to the collapse of the standard of living. Under IMF ministrations, interest rates in Turkey had shot up to a modest 550 percent.

WAR DAMAGES

The IMF has acknowledged in its report that the damage caused by NATO bombings is of the order of $40 billion.[24] This figure does not take into account the losses in Yugoslavia's Gross Domestic Product

(GDP) resulting from years of economic sanctions, nor does it account for the loss of human life and limb, the human suffering inflicted on an entire population, the toxic radiation from depleted uranium and the environmental devastation amply documented by Yugoslav and international sources.[25] Ironically, this study on war damages was coordinated by G-17's Mladjan Dinkic and Miroslav Labus, who now hold key positions in the DOS government. Since his appointment to the position of central bank governor, Dinkic has not said a word about "war damages" in his discussions with Western creditors.[26]

LUCRATIVE RECONSTRUCTION CONTRACTS

No "compensation" for war damages let alone debt relief has been contemplated. In a cruel twist, a large part of the fresh loans—which Yugoslavia will eventually have to reimburse—will be used to rebuild what was destroyed by the bombers. Moreover, under the World Bank-European Bank for Reconstruction and Development (EBRD) system of international tender, these loans are in fact tagged to finance lucrative contracts with construction companies from NATO countries:

> [T]he big winners [are the Western] telecommunications companies, construction firms, banks and shipping concerns who can rebuild the Danube River bridges, power plants and refineries destroyed by NATO air strikes. ... While European companies, already busy with Balkan projects, have a home-court advantage, U.S. companies such as infrastructure specialists Brown & Root [a subsidiary of Vice President Dick Cheney's company Halliburton Oil], AES and General Electric could get a piece of the action.[27]

And what will these companies do? They will sub-contract with local firms and/or hire Yugoslav engineers and workers at wages below $100 a month. In other words, the borrowed money promised to Belgrade for "reconstruction" will go straight back into the pockets of Western banks and multinational corporations (MNCs). In turn, the so-called "prioritization of expenditures" imposed by the IMF means that the state (i.e. Yugoslavia's own money) would be footing the bill for clearing the Danube and rebuilding the bridges, essentially "subsidizing" the interests of foreign capital. Moreover, IMF "conditionalities"—which require drastic cuts in social expenditures—would prevent the government from allocating its budget to rebuilding schools and hospitals hit during the bombing campaign.

THE COSTS OF THE AIR CAMPAIGN

Accusing the Serbian people and the former head of state of the crimes committed by the aggressor is intended to instill a sense of fear and collective guilt on an entire nation.

But there is something else which has so far not been mentioned: Washington's design is to hold President Milosevic responsible for the war not as an individual but as the country's head of state, with a view to eventually collecting war reparations from Yugoslavia.

In other words, if the former head of state were to be indicted by the ICTY, the country could be held "legally responsible" not only for the costs of NATO's "humanitarian bombs," but for all the military and "peacekeeping" expenses incurred since 1992.

In fact, at NATO's behest, an army of accountants and economists has already evaluated the costs of the air campaign and the various "peacekeeping operations." In this regard, the U.S. share of the costs of the bombing, "peacekeeping" and "refugee assistance" solely in fiscal year 1999 was estimated at $5.05 billion. The amounts allocated by the Clinton Administration to pay for the war and the refugees in Fiscal Year 1999 were of the order of $6.6 billion. So-called "emergency funding" appropriated by Congress for operations in Kosovo and other defense spending in FY 1999 totaled $12 billion. Moreover, the Department of Defense estimates the costs of deployment of American occupation forces and civilian personnel stationed in Bosnia and Kosovo since 1992 to be of the order of $21.2 billion.[28]

In other words, indicting President Milosevic on trumped up charges raises a fundamental question of legitimacy. It sanctions the bombings as a humanitarian operation. It not only absolves the real war criminals, it also opens up the avenue for the indictment of Yugoslavia as a nation.

The former head of state is indicted; the people are collectively indicted. What this means is that NATO could at some future date oblige Yugoslavia to pay for the bombs used to destroy the country and kill its people.

There is nothing fundamentally new in this process. Under the British Empire, it was common practice not only to install puppet regimes but also to bill the costs of gunboat operations to countries that refused to sign a "free trade" agreement with Her Majesty's government. In 1850, Britain threatened to send in its "gun boats" —-equivalent to today's humanitarian air raids— following the refusal of the Kingdom of Siam (Thailand) to sign a free trade treaty with Britain (equivalent to today's "Letter of Intent" to the IMF). While the language and institutions of colonial diplomacy have changed, the similarity with contemporary practices is striking. In the words of British envoy Sir James Brooke (equivalent to today's Richard Holbrooke):

> The Siamese Government is hostile—its tone is arrogant—its presumption unbounded... Should these just [British] demands firmly urged be refused, a force should be present, immediately to enforce them by a rapid destruction of the defenses of the river. ... Siam may be taught the lesson which it has long been tempted, ... a better disposed king placed on the throne, and an influence acquired in the country which will make it of immense commercial importance to England. ... [Note the similarity in relation to Yugoslavia] Above all, it would be well to prepare for the change and to place our own kind on the throne ... This prince [Mongkut] we ought to place on the throne and through him, we might, beyond doubt, gain all we desire.... And the expense incurred [of the military operation] would readily be available from the royal treasury of Siam.[29]

Replace the head of state, impose "free" trade, bill the country for the military operation!

PRECEDENTS OF WAR REPARATIONS: VIETNAM AND NICARAGUA

In fact in the case of Vietnam—which won the war against U.S. aggression—Hanoi was nonetheless obliged to pay war reparations to the United States, as a condition for the lifting of economic sanctions in 1994.

Although the historical circumstances were quite different to those of Yugoslavia, the pattern of IMF intervention in Vietnam was in many regards similar. The decision to lift the sanctions on Vietnam was also taken in the context of a donors' conference.

Some two billion dollars of loans and "aid" money had been pledged in support of Vietnam's IMF-sponsored reforms, yet immediately after the conference another separate meeting was held, this time "behind closed doors," in which Hanoi was obliged to fully reimburse the debts incurred by the U.S.-installed Saigon military government.[30]

By fully recognizing the legitimacy of these debts, Hanoi had in effect accepted to repay loans that had been utilized to support the U.S. war effort. Moreover, Hanoi's acceptance had also totally absolved Washington from paying war reparations to Vietnam totaling $4.2 billion as agreed at the Paris Peace Conference in 1973.[31]

NICARAGUA: 'FREEDOM FIGHTERS' AND IMF ECONOMIC MEDICINE

Similarly the $12 billion "reparations" that the U.S. had been ordered to pay to Nicaragua by The Hague International Court of Justice (ICJ) were never paid. In 1990, following the installation of a pro-U.S. "democratic" government, these reparations—ordered by the ICJ—were erased in exchange for "normalization" and the lifting of sanctions. In return, Washington approved a token $60 million in "emergency aid" which was of course conditional upon the payment of all debts and the adoption of the most deadly IMF economic shock therapy:

> The United States ... provides severance pay to government workers fired under the U.S.-mandated [IMF structural adjustment] program to reduce the size of Nicaragua's government. Among the results: Nicaragua's social security budget has been slashed from $18 million to $4 million while unemployment has risen to about forty-five percent. Health spending has dropped from $86 per person [per annum] five years ago to $18 [in 1991 in the year following the elections]. Pensions for disabled war veterans have been frozen at $6.50 per month while food prices have risen [1991] to nearly U.S. levels ... In the words of a State Department official, "The U.S. is committed to rebuilding Nicaragua, but there's only a limited amount you can do with development aid."[32]

Yet the U.S. did not hesitate in spending billions of dollars to finance nine years of economic embargo and war in which Washington created and funded a paramilitary army (the Contras) to fight the Sandinista government. Heralded by the Reagan administration and touted by the media as "freedom fighters," the Contras' insurgency was financed by drug money and covert support from the CIA. And in fact the same pattern of covert support using drug money was applied to financing the KLA with a view to destabilizing Yugoslavia. William Walker, head of the Organization for Security and Cooperation in Europe (OSCE) mission to Kosovo in the months preceding the 1999 war, was responsible together with Col. Oliver North for channeling covert support to the Contras, which ultimately led to the downfall of the Sandinista government and its defeat in "democratic" elections in 1990.

THE ROLE OF THE UNITED NATIONS COMPENSATION COMMISSION

Another case is that of Iraq, which in the wake of the Gulf War was obliged to pay extensive war reparations. The United Nations Compensation Commission (UNCC) was set up to process "claims" against Iraq. Thirty percent of Iraqi oil revenues in the "oil for food program" are impounded by the UNCC to pay war reparations to governments, banks and corporations. The UNCC "has awarded more than $32 billion [in claims], and more than $9.5 billion has been paid out under the food-for-oil regime."[33]

These precedents are important in understanding the war in Yugoslavia. Although no official statement has been made by NATO, the framework and bureaucracy of the UNCC could at some future date be extended to collecting war reparations from Yugoslavia. The UNCC's claim procedures are based on a 1991 UN Security Council resolution, which establishes Iraq's liability for the Gulf war under international law.

In the case of Yugoslavia, President Milosevic is accused by The Hague Tribunal for "crimes against humanity and violations of the laws or customs of war."[34] Following the Iraqi precedent, a decision of The Hague Tribunal concerning President Milosevic could constitute the basis for the formulation of a similar UN Security Council Resolution establishing the liability of the government and people of Yugoslavia for the "direct loss, damage ... to foreign governments, nationals and corporations," including "the costs of the air campaign."[35]

REWRITING HISTORY

Recent events have shown how realities can be turned upside down by the aggressor and its propaganda machine. NATO's intent is to blatantly distort the course of events and manipulate the writing of modern history. It is therefore essential that the Yugoslav people remain united in their resolve. It should also be understood that the "demonization" of the Serbian people and of President Slobodan Milosevic alongside the triggering of ethnic conflicts is intended to impose the "free market" and enforce the New World Order throughout the Balkans.

Internationally, the various movements against IMF-World Bank-WTO reforms must understand that war and globalization are interconnected processes. Applied around the world, the only promise of the "free market" is a world of landless farmers, shuttered factories, jobless workers and gutted social programs with "bitter economic medicine" under IMF-WB-WTO custody constituting the only prescription. Moreover, militarization increasingly constitutes the means for enforcing these deadly macro-economic reforms.

Yugoslavia's struggle to preserve its national sovereignty is at this particular juncture in its history a part of the broader movement against the New World Order and the imposition throughout the world of a uniform neo-liberal policy agenda under IMF-World Bank-WTO supervision. Behind these organizations—which routinely interface with NATO—are the powers of the U.S. and European financial establishments and the Western military-industrial complex.

[1] *Agence France Presse*, November 19, 1997.

[2] Quest Economics Database. West LB Emerging Trends, March 8, 2001, *Agence France Press*, March 16, 2001.

[3] Statement of Secretary of State Colin Powell quoted *in International Herald Tribune*, Paris, April 4, 2001

[4] *International Herald Tribune*, op. cit.

[5] B 92 News, Belgrade, May 3, 2001.

[6] U.S. House of Representatives, Bill HR 1064, section 302, September 2000, at http://www.house.gov/house/Legproc.html., click 106th Congress and enter bill number.

[7] UPI, April 2, 2001

[8] *New York Times*, February 27, 2001.

[9] See Michel Chossudovsky, "Washington Finances Ethnic Warfare in the Balkans," *Emperors Clothes*, April 2001.

[10] See IMF, IMF Approves Membership of Federal Republic of Yugoslavia and $151 Million in Emergency Post-Conflict Assistance, http://www.imf.org/external/np/sec/pr/2000/pr0075.htm.

[11] See IMF, IMF Approves Membership of Federal Republic of Yugoslavia and $151 Million in Emergency Post-Conflict Assistance, http://www.imf.org/external/np/sec/pr/2000/pr0075.htm.

[12] Government of Serbia, *Serbia Info*, Belgrade 2 May 2001, http://www.serbia-info.com/news/2001-05/03/23335.html.

[13] For further details see Michel Chossudovsky, "Dismantling Former Yugoslavia, Recolonising Bosnia," *Covert Action Quarterly*, Spring 1996, available at http://www.ess.uwe.ac.uk/Kosovo/Kosovo-controversies4.html or http://www.emperors-clothes.com/articles/chuss/dismantl.htm.

[14] See Group of 17 "Program of Radical Economic Reforms," Belgrade 1999 at http://www.g17.org.yu/english/programm/program.htm.

[15] New Serbia Forum, "Privatization," Budapest, March 13-15, 2000, http://www.newserbiaforum.org/Reports/privatisation.htm.

[16] The full text of the IMF program is available at http://www.imf.org/external/pubs/cat/longres.cfm?sk&sk=3875.0 The Government's commitment under the IMF program is outlined in Federal Republic of Yugoslavia, "Economic Reform Program for 2001" Belgrade, December 9, 2000, http://www.seerecon.org/FRYugoslavia/erp2001.htm, see also "Synthetic View" of main economic policy measures at http://www.seerecon.org/FRYugoslavia/epmeasures.pdf.

[17] See Michel Chossudovsky, "Kostunica Coalition Drives Up Prices and Blames...Milosevic," October 2000, http://emperors-clothes.com/articles/chuss/triples.htm.

[18] See B 92 News, May 3, 2001 at http://www.b92.net/archive/e/index.phtml.

[19] IMF Program, op cit. On Bulgaria see "The Wind in the Balkans," *The Economist*, London, February 8, 1997, p.12 and Jonathan C. Randal, "Reform Coalition Wins, Bulgarian Parliament," *The Washington Post*, April 20, 1997, p. A21. (See IMF Program, op cit)

[20] See the Statement of IMF Deputy Managing Director Stanley Fischer, December 2000 at http://www.imf.org/external/np/sec/pr/2000/pr0075.htm.

[21] See Michel Chossudovsky, "Brazil's IMF Sponsored Financial Disaster," *Third World Network*, 1998 at http://www.twnside.org.sg/title/latin-cn.htm.

[22] For details see Michel Chossudovsky, Financial Warfare triggers Global Financial Crisis, Third World Network at http://www.twnside.org.sg/title/trig-cn.htm.

[23] See Michel Chossudovsky, *The Globalization of Poverty*, Zed Books, London 1997, chapter 12.

[24] The IMF quotes the G-17 study, "Economic Consequences of NATO Bombardment," Belgrade 2000 at http://www.g17.org.yu/english/index.htm.

[25] See Michel Chossudovsky, NATO Willfully Triggered an Environmental Catastrophe in Yugoslavia, June 2000, at
http://emperors-clothes.com/articles/chuss/willful.htm.

[26] See G-17, "Economic Consequences of NATO Bombardment," Belgrade 2000 at http://www.g17.org.yu/english/index.htm.

[27] *USA Today*, October 10, 2000.

[28] GAO : Briefing report to the Chairman, Committee on Armed Services, House of Representatives, RPTno: gao/nsiad-00-125br, Washington, April 24, 2000.

[29] Quoted in M. L. Manich Jumsai, *King Mongkut and Sir John Bowring*, Chalermit, Bangkok, 1970, p. 21.

[30] See Michel Chossudovsky, *The Globalisation of Poverty*, op cit., Chapter 8.

[31] A. J. Langguth, The Forgotten Debt to Vietnam, *New York Times*, November 18, 2000, see also Barbara Crossette, Hanoi said to vow to give MIA Data, *New York Times*, October 24, 1992.

[32] *The Houston Chronicle*, December 8, 1991. To consult the International Court of Justice 1986 Judgement on "Nicaragua v. United States of America" see: "Military and Paramilitary Activities in and against Nicaragua."

[33] *UPI*, December 7, 2000.

[34] See the text of 1999 indictment of President Milosevic by The Hague Tribunal at http://www.un.org/icty/indictment/english/mil-ii990524e.htm.

[35] See the text of UNSC resolution 687 (1991) pertaining to Iraq at http://www.unog.ch/uncc/introduc.htm.

VII.

CRIMES AGAINST HUMANITY:

KOSOVO UNDER NATO OCCUPATION

Cultural Genocide:
The Destruction of Serbian Orthodox Monasteries

MILOS RAICKOVICH

From a talk presented at the June 10, 2000 Tribunal on U.S./NATO War Crimes in New York City

The official name of the Serbian province under NATO occupation is not simply *Kosovo,* as it is referred to by the mainstream media, but rather *Kosovo and Metohija.* Sometimes, *Kosovo and Metohija* is abbreviated as a compound word, *Kosmet.* The word *Kosovo* comes from Serbian, *Kosovo Polje,* or *The Field of the Blackbirds*, while *Metohija* means *The Land of the Monasteries.* This is extremely important. By dropping *Metohija* from the region's name, NATO propaganda and the mainstream media are concealing the fact that this is the land where 1,400 Serbian medieval churches and monasteries are to be found. These shrines are masterpieces of European and Byzantine architecture, as well as fresco painting. In other words, Serbs and other ethnic groups are not only being expelled from Kosmet, but the genuine historical name of the region, Kosovo and Metohija, is being erased.

This kind of oversimplification is an imperialist game. Once the truncated name, Kosovo or, as the "Kosovo Liberation Army" (KLA) calls it, *Kosova,* is introduced, next comes the concept of the *Kosovars.* By falsely naming Albanians after the region, NATO propaganda suggests that the Albanians in Kosovo and Metohija are the only historical people of the region, and that they hold an exclusive claim to it. As in Krajina and in Bosnia and Herzegovina, Serbs are once again presented as foreigners in their own homeland.

The imperialist occupation has brought with it cultural genocide. Hundreds of thousands of Serbs, Roma, Jews, Turks, Egyptians, Goranis, Slavic Muslims, pro-Yugoslav Albanians and others have been expelled from Kosovo and Metohija under NATO supervision. In order to erase all trace of Serbs, the terrorist KLA launched a systematic campaign to destroy Serbian churches and monasteries by first robbing and looting them of icons, manuscripts and other relics, then by desecrating, burning and mining these monuments and houses of worship, until they are finally demolished.

To this day, the number of shrines that have been destroyed is unknown, because many are located in areas to which Serbian clergy has no access, due to the reign of terror imposed by the KLA and NATO. The number of documented cases of destruction, according to the evidence collected as of May 2000, was approximately 100 churches and monasteries destroyed and desecrated. Most of these shrines were destroyed in the U.S., Italian and German zones, while the rate of destruction is slightly less in the zones controlled by the British and French. To sum up, more Serbian Orthodox churches and monasteries were destroyed in the first year of NATO occupation than during 500 years of the Ottoman Empire's occupation of Serbia.

NATO propaganda often suggests that the presence of the KFOR troops is the only guarantee for the protection of cultural sites in Kosovo and Metohija. Sheer hypocrisy! NATO bombs struck some of these holy sites directly, and NATO bombs fell close enough to others to shake their foundations. NATO also brought "KLA" terrorists into Kosovo and Metohija. This is an ongoing crime against the whole region and its people. It is cultural genocide.

The only way to stop the destruction is by the restoration of a multicultural society under the protection of the Serbian and Yugoslav authorities. Let us hope that Vietnam will not be repeated here, and that NATO, KFOR, SFOR, UNMIC and the "KLA" terrorists will disband and withdraw from the region before they are all defeated and expelled by the people of the Balkans.

Long live multicultural Serbia and all of its twenty-seven minorities! Long live Yugoslavia!

Interviews with Refugees

BARRY LITUCHY

From a presentation to the June 10, 2000, International Tribunal for U.S./NATO War Crimes in Yugoslavia held in New York City.

As you know, the United Nations Convention on Genocide specifically mentions five actions which, when carried out against a national, ethnic, racial or religious group, in a deliberate attempt to destroy that group in full or in part, fall under the definition of crimes of genocide.

Those actions are:

(1) killing members of that group;

(2) causing grievous bodily or spiritual harm to members of that group;

(3) enforcing living conditions designed to exterminate that group;

(4) preventing births from that group;

(5) removing the children of that group and transferring them to another group.

We have evidence that shows that all of the above actions pertain to NATO/KFOR''s occupation and aggression in Kosovo and Yugoslavia.

Your Honors, today we are presenting evidence that specifically shows that NATO forces—especially American and British NATO forces attached to the so-called KFOR occupation army in Kosovo—carried out, either by themselves or in collaboration with the KLA, numerous acts that fall under the United Nations' definition of crimes of genocide against members of the Serbian, Roma, Egyptian, Gorani, and Turkish national minorities in Kosovo.

Last August [1999] I led a two-week independent delegation to Yugoslavia that conducted its own investigation of NATO war crimes against the civilian population in Kosovo and Serbia. We collected testimonies of victims of these crimes. In numerous instances these victims directly accused KFOR soldiers and officers of participating in these crimes.

My colleague Gregory Elich, who will be speaking next, and I, will be presenting detailed evidence today documenting numerous cases of KFOR involvement in crimes of genocide, including forced expulsions. Many other types of crimes in addition to the ones discussed here today are documented in our book, *Interviews and Testimonies, An Investigation of US and NATO War Crimes in Yugoslavia* [unpublished].

Exactly one year ago in the days immediately following the military agreement and United Nations resolution that ended the war, Europe witnessed the single worst chapter of ethnic cleansing and crimes of genocide since World War II. As many as 500,000 Serbs, Romas, Goranis, Turks, Egyptians, and pro-Yugoslav Albanians, as well as other national minorities, were racially cleansed or murdered by the KLA. These many hundreds of thousands have received little or no aid from the very same international agencies and NGO's which precipitated the war in the first place by their calls for "humanitarian intervention."

Of the dozens of interviews we conducted with Serbian, Roma, Egyptian, Turkish and pro-Yugoslav Albanian refugees from Kosovo last August, a full one-third of the cases testified to some level of NATO/KFOR involvement in the crimes committed against them. Among these crimes are included crimes of murder, kidnapping, rape, torture, expulsion, and terror.

Allow me now to briefly review a few of the individual testimonies we collected and which we are now submitting as evidence to this tribunal.

First, there is the case of Adan Berisha, a Roma of 270 Jugbogdan Street in Obilic. Mr. Berisha's father and son were both murdered by the KLA in separate episodes. In both cases this was done under the eyes of KFOR with their knowledge. Also with the knowledge of KFOR Mr. Berisha was tortured and later expelled by the KLA. Despite full knowledge of these crimes KFOR also did nothing subsequently to apprehend the perpetrators, whom they knew were the Krasniqi brothers who also lived on Jugobogdan Street in Obilic. Mr. Berisha currently is very ill and lives in the outskirts of Belgrade.

There is the case of Rada Rakipi, a Roma from Glagovac in Kosovo. On June 26, 1999, his family was expelled from his home with the full knowledge of KFOR.

There is the case of Rakmani Elis, a Roma of 163 Moraska Street in Pristina, who was expelled from Kosovo with KFOR's full knowledge.

There is the case of Ajsha Shatili, a Roma of 55 Goldberg Street in Pristina. Her family was tortured and injured—including her children— by KLA terrorists with the actual presense, involvement and aid of British KFOR soldiers. They were then expelled with the knowledge of the same KFOR soldiers.

There is the case of Hasim Berisha, a Roma of 290 Proletarian Street in Pristina whose family was ordered—yes, actually ordered!—to leave their home by British KFOR soldiers on June 15th, 1999. When they returned to their home the next day, June 16, 1999, they found it burned to the ground and they were forced to flee Kosovo.

There is the case of Abdullah Shefik, a Roma from Svechanskaya Street in Urosevac. His family was pulled over by American KFOR troops in a road block. During this pull-over, right in front of the American KFOR soldiers and with their apparant participation, the Shefik family was robbed of its car, its van, and all of its property and personal belongings by KLA soldiers.

There is the case of Biljana Lazic, a Serb from Suva Reka in Kosovo, whose brothers were kidnapped with the knowledge of William Walker and the then OSCE observers in Kosovo in 1998.

There is the case of Dostena Filipovic, a Serb from Lesanje in Kosovo, whose entire family was arrested and abused by a joint unit of KLA and KFOR soldiers on June 14, 1999.

All of the cases I have just mentioned are documented in our book *Interviews and Testimonies, An Investigation of US and NATO War Crimes in Yugoslavia.* All of these cases are also documented on videotape.

At this time I also would like to submit as evidence the following excerpt from our videotaped testimonies of two of the Romas previously mentioned who directly accuse British and American KFOR soldiers respectively of involvement in crimes of genocide: Mrs. Ajsha Shatili from Pristina and Mr. Abdullah Shefik from Urosevac.

(Showing of the videotaped testimonies of Ajsha Shatili and Abdullah Shefik where they accuse British and American soldiers of war crimes with some explanation by the presenter)

Your honors, on behalf of my delegation I submit these testimonies and additional documents contained in our book as evidence for this tribunal of crimes of genocide against Serbs, Romas, Egyptians, pro-Yugoslav Albanians, and indeed against all of the twenty-eight nationalities of the Federal Republic of Yugoslavia. On behalf of all of the victims of KLA and NATO terror and genocide I plead with you to do everything in your power to seek restitution, reparations, repatriation, expulsion of NATO and the KLA from Kosovo, and the arrest and punishment of the perpetrators of these crimes of genocide.

We shall never forget these crimes. And we shall never cease in our struggle to achieve justice for the victims. Thank you.

The editors would like to add a transcript of one of the video interviews done by Lituchy and others in his group, which was published in the document "If They Find Me, They Will Kill Me."

INTERVIEW WITH CORIN ISMALI

(Questions by Barry Lituchy, Iman El-Sayed and Joe Friendly)

Lituchy: Tell us your name, and what town you're from, and also what your position was in the Albanian community in Kosovo.

Ismali: Corin Ismali, from Stimlje, near Lipljan.

Lituchy: What position did you have in the Albanian community?

Ismali: I was under-secretary in the Executive Council in Kosovo for national social questions, and also secretary for the party.

Lituchy: Would you tell us what happened after the bombing stopped in Kosovo?

Ismali: After the NATO bombing stopped, we had to leave Kosovo because KFOR did not guarantee us freedom, or peace, or the possibility to walk in the evening without being afraid of KLA soldiers.

Lituchy: Did you speak with KFOR at any time and ask for their protection?

Ismali: We wanted to speak with Mr. Kouchner, but we could not meet with him. We don't know the reason. No one told us why. [Dr. Bernard Kouchner was Head of the United Nations Interim Administration Mission in Kosovo.—editor]

Lituchy: Are you a refugee from Kosovo?

Ismali: Yes, we had to leave Kosovo.

Lituchy: Why did you leave Kosovo?

Ismali: Because I was not safe in Kosovo.

Lituchy: Were you threatened by anyone in Kosovo?

Ismali: Yes, because I supported Yugoslavia, and I opposed secession. That is why I had to leave Kosovo.

Lituchy: Why did, or do, Albanians support Yugoslavia?

Ismali: Because we want to live with other ethnic groups in Yugoslavia. We do not want to live in a country that has only one ethnic group.

El-Sayed: Do Albanians in Kosovo want to live in Yugoslavia, but they are forced to listen to the KLA?

Ismali: Yes. They are forced by the KLA to leave Kosovo because they don't want to join the KLA.

Lituchy: Why did some Albanians join the KLA? Why do you think?

Ismali: We don't know, because that is their own opinion.

Lituchy: What percentage of the people in Kosovo of Albanian background do you think would have been happy to stay in Yugoslavia without the KLA?

Ismali: Almost all of us want to return to Kosovo, to live in Kosovo with other ethnic groups, if someone could guarantee our safety. About eighty percent of refugees want to return. But we are afraid of the KLA.

Lituchy: When you left Kosovo, what did you leave behind?

Ismali: I left approximately one million Deutsche Marks in Kosovo: houses, property, fields, cars, furniture, everything.

Lituchy: What kind of government do you expect the KLA will establish, now that they've gained power?

Ismali: They want a mono-ethnic government.

Lituchy: Was any member of your family threatened, injured or killed?

Ismali: No, because we left Kosovo in time.

Lituchy: What day did you leave Kosovo?

Ismali: We left Kosovo on the 16th of June [1999].

Lituchy: And you haven't been back?

Ismali: No. I left my municipality fourteen months ago, because they threatened me to leave Stimlje. Then I moved to Brecovica, and I left Brecovica on the 16th of June.

Lituchy: Would you like to return to Kosovo?

Ismali: Yes, of course. Why not?

Lituchy: Under what conditions do you think you might be able to return to Kosovo?

Ismali: If our army and police return to Kosovo, I will go the same day. The reason is that I must have peace, freedom, and no one to threaten me before I can return to Kosovo.

El-Sayed: Do you think the United States created the KLA?

Ismali: They had support, but I cannot say whether the United States formed the KLA.

Lituchy: Why do you think the United States intervened in Kosovo? Why did it want to break up Yugoslavia?

Ismali: They have their interests, and they wanted to install their military bases in Kosovo.

Lituchy: Is there anything you would like to say to the American people about what the United States government has done in Kosovo?

Ismali: I want to say to the American people not to intervene in our Yugoslav problems. We will solve these ourselves.

Friendly: Does the KLA give any indication of their interest in democracy, or do they tend to be more totalitarian?

Ismali: I think it won't be democracy.

On September 3, 2001, Ismali was shot down and murdered in front of his family in Gornje Godance, fifteen miles from Pristina. KLA killers are suspected.

The Persecution of Roma

SHANI RIFATI

All over Western Europe a new generation of Roma are arriving, in flight from persecution, discrimination, ethnic cleansing and/or other hardships in Eastern Europe. The reemergence and acceleration of genocidal attacks on Romani populations in Eastern Europe, since the collapse of Socialism, have lead Roma into forced flight and migration.

In Western Europe too, skinhead and mob attacks against Roma [who are called Gypsies] are on the rise. International organizations have done virtually nothing to help this group of people, a population who both historically and currently bore no responsibility for initiating or voluntarily participating in ethnic conflicts or wars. This is the situation faced by tens of thousands of Roma who have fled from Kosovo during and in the aftermath of the NATO bombing which ended in June, 1999.

International human rights monitors are busily debating whose rights come first and whose needs are greater. Some argue that economic, social and cultural rights should come before civil and political rights; a person's right to eat is more important than another person's freedom of expression. Others argue that civil and political rights are most important, and only when these are achieved will people be insured of their economic, social, and cultural rights.

The fact is that all human rights are interdependent. The daily reality confronting the Romani people across Europe is that they do not enjoy any of these rights, nor do they have anyone advocating on their behalf. In general, Roma have received little or no help from the community of international human rights organizations and nongovernmental organizations, prior to the NATO bombing of Kosovo.

Now there are a few, precious few, humanitarian organizations helping Roma in and from Kosovo. But the occupation of Kosovo by Western governmental institutions and NGOs, whose purposes are supposedly the benign offering of economic and humanitarian aid to the people there, is compounded by Western jingoism. There are often political motivations, far less benign than they are made out to be, underlying the distribution of humanitarian aid.

Who receives this aid and how the aid distribution is publicized, indicates the needs of many of these international institutions to show the world how great they are and how politically correct they are; in other words, a self-serving public relations game. In the meantime, even the NGOs and governmental bodies themselves admit that what aid is reaching the people of Kosovo is pathetically meager, and not equitably distributed amongst the different ethnic groups in and from the region.

Only a handful of Romani organizations have begun to tackle the enormous task of making the world aware of their invisible people's plight; a people facing a "New Age Holocaust." The lack of world attention for what Roma in Europe are currently facing is analogous to what befell the Romani victims of the Holocaust after WWII. Very few Holocaust spokespeople have ever mentioned that there are estimates that more than 1.5 million Roma were the victims of the Third Reich's extermination campaign.

This Romani invisibility is still going on, with very few NGOs advocating for and providing aid to Roma inside and out of the former Yugoslavia. Roma are dying in cities and villages throughout the country they used to call home; prior to the war, 1.2 million Roma lived in the former Yugoslavia. The only victims of the turmoil there who receive ongoing and persistent public attention are the Bosnians, Croats and Kosovo Albanians.

Why does this division exist between the recognition of Kosovo Albanian, Bosnian Muslim, and Croatian refugees and the Romani refugees? The first three ethnic groups are seen as political refugees, in strong opposition to the Serbian regime of the former Yugoslavia, with ties to extreme nationalist movements, former fascist collaborators, and eager to ally themselves to the interests of Western Capitalism.

Roma, on the other hand, are a people with no historical or current territorial claims within the former Yugoslavia. They have no political representation, are economically weak, have no leadership, and lack organizational structure due to their place at the bottom of the economic scale. Their energies are entirely consumed by the struggle for survival. The reason why Roma are overlooked is that they are completely irrelevant to the explicit and implicit goals of the Western powers, whereas the other groups of "political refugees" support, encourage, and embrace the Westernization of the former Yugoslavia.

BACKGROUND ON THE FLIGHT OF ROMANI REFUGEES

Since the end of the U.S./NATO bombing of Kosovo, ethnic Albanians forced thousands of Roma to flee at gunpoint, with only the clothes on their backs. Most Romani neighborhoods in Kosovo have been burned and destroyed, with a few of the nicer houses left intact, now occupied by Albanians in front of the eyes of occupation KFOR forces in Kosovo and the United Nations High Commisioner of Refugees (UNHCR).

In fact, some of the Albanians now occupying the homes of Roma who were ethnically cleansed, are reportedly renting their former homes to Western NGO representatives and workers. Since July 1999, thousands of Roma have made the perilous eighteen-to-twenty-four hour journey from Bar, in Montenegro, to Brindisi, Italy, crammed onto small fishing boats from which the boat captains jumped ship one to two hours out to sea.

Ships carrying hundreds of people and riding dangerously low in the water have been reportedly arriving in Italy regularly since shortly after the entry of KFOR troops and the return of the refugees from Albania and Macedonia. The Italian daily *Il Manifesto* reported on July 7, 1999 that 700 Roma had arrived in Puglia.

On August 3, 1999, *Il Manifesto* reported that 1,010 Roma from Kosovo had arrived by ship from Montenegro on July 31. A ship with 300 refugees arrived in the Italian port of Brindisi, according to *Reuters* on August 18, followed by another large ship with 1,120 Roma arriving in Bari on August 19, according to the same source.

Sources in Kosovo and Montenegro told the European Romani Rights Center that smugglers charged between 1,500 and 3,000 German Marks (approximately $1,000 to $1,700 at the time) per person.

The Italian weekly newspaper, *Panorama,* wrote on July 22, 1999 that the Italian consulate in Bar, Montenegro had refused as many as 3,000 Romani applicants for political asylum. Roma reportedly make the illegal crossing in very poor conditions. The Montenegrin daily *Vijesti* reported on August 26, 1999, that the bodies of thirty-six Roma had been found in the Adriatic Sea by the Montenegrin Coast Guard. The Roma were refugees from Kosovo who were being smuggled into Italy when their ship sank on August 20.

Many of the refugees who traveled to Italy in this way have reported that the Kosovo Albanian mafia organizes this illegal, lucrative method of smuggling Romani refugees. Further, these refugees claim that the Albanian Mafia is working in conjunction with Milo Djukanovic, the leader of the Montenegrin opposition [to Milosevic] and secession movement, who is openly sponsored by Western countries. Needless to say, this story has received virtually no coverage in the international press.

Upon reaching Italy, Roma have been put in locked camps for "illegals," where the lucky ones have waited two weeks to a month for temporary (usually thirty-day) permits to remain in Italy. From here, some Romani refugees have traveled to various overcrowded ghetto settlements in Italian cities.

According to United Nations High Commisioner for Refugees reports and documentation from the European Roma Rights Center, there are currently 5,000-6,000 Roma remaining in Kosovo, the majority of whom are living in makeshift camps and receiving nominal aid and protection from the international agencies operating on the ground there.

A recent survey conducted by an independent researcher, Paul Polansky, placed the number of Roma currently in Kosovo at approximately 30,000. In his report he stated:

> Since the arrival of KFOR forces and the return of ethnic Albanians to Kosova, more than 14,000 Roma homes have been burnt. It is not only the local Albanians who are discriminating against the Roma, but also the major aid agencies in Kosova. In many districts I found Mother Teresa Society openly refusing to deliver food to Gypsies. Islamic Relief also seems to have a policy of not providing aid to Gypsies although the Roma are Muslim.
>
> Even at Oxfam, which has done more for the Roma than any other aid agency in Kosova, deliveries to minorities are sometimes delayed for long periods by local Albanian staff. Urgent requests for food aid for hungry Gypsy families made to several major aid agencies months ago have gone unfulfilled. Although the Roma are the second largest minority in Kosova (and may soon be the largest minority at the rate the Serbs are leaving) no aid agency including UNHCR and the Office of Security and Cooperation in Europe have hired a Kosovar Rom, although many Roma speak passable English.

Throughout the seventy-eight days of NATO bombings, many Roma remained in Kosovo, while others fled to Serbia, only to find themselves in equally life-threatening circumstances in Belgrade, Nis, and other Serbian cities. Many Roma attempted to flee to Macedonia or Albania, only to be turned back at the border, or to be refused assistance at refugee camps inside these countries by Albanian officials who falsely accused them of being allied with the Serbs. Those that remained in Kosovo, and those that returned or tried to return to their homes there after the bombing ended in June, found their lives threatened once again by the now triumphant ethnic Albanians.

Thousands of Roma were forced to flee at gunpoint, with only the clothes on their backs. Estimates range from 125,000 to 200,000 Roma from Kosovo who have fled to other parts of Serbia, or sought refuge in other European countries from the southern tip of Italy to the Scandinavian countries. Paul Polansky's survey concludes:

> As seen by the results of this survey, most Roma have left Kosova to save their own lives. They are not economic emigrants as some UNHCR staffs depict them, but people desperately trying to survive. From my interviews in the refugee camps in Macedonia and Montenegro, most want to return when it is safe to do so. It is in their culture, their heritage and their tradition that Roma are buried in the homeland of their ancestors. For at least 700 years, Kosova has been their homeland.

Many of the thousands of Roma who have fled to Italy are often coerced into registering as Albanians in order to receive assistance and documents. This not only requires them to adopt the identity of the very people who have driven them out of their homeland, but once again makes them invisible in the eyes of the international help organizations and the media. When released with temporary papers, many have gone to join friends or family at overcrowded ghetto settlements in various Italian cities, where living conditions are appalling and the new arrivals are under constant threat of deportation.

Other Romani refugees from Kosovo are awaiting uncertain outcomes to their political asylum claims, in locked camps with poor food and housing situations in Austria, Hungary, Germany, Holland, etc. This is taking place fifty years after the adoption of the Universal Declaration of Human Rights, whose promise of the right to seek and enjoy asylum from persecution certainly rings hollow for the Roma from Kosovo.

Women Are Enslaved

LESLIE FEINBERG

An imperialist occupation army brings with it rape, prostitution, and extreme and brutal forms of oppression of women. This has been true throughout history. The strength of a liberation army can be directly measured by its role in freeing women from oppression.

When the U.S. ordered the bombing war on Yugoslavia, U.S. and NATO leaders posed as liberators. The people of the Balkans knew this was a lie.

Now, with the Pentagon and other NATO "peacekeepers" hunkered down in Kosovo, what has emerged are conditions that are no different from other imperialist occupations. Most particularly revealing of the near-colonial state that has been imposed on Kosovo by the United States and NATO are the conditions for women in the occupied territory.

Rape, prostitution, brutality and murder—and the literal enslavement of thousands of women—are the documented reality in just over one year of imperialist occupation.

"The sex-slave traffic in East European women, one of the major criminal scourges of post-communist Europe, is becoming a major problem in Kosovo, where porous borders, the presence of international troops and aid workers, and the lack of a working criminal-justice system have created almost perfect conditions for the trade," reported the April 24, 2000, *Washington Post.*

This report of the nightmare condition for these women was admitted by the very imperialist forces that ushered in this lucrative profit industry: NATO occupiers, United Nations police officials and capitalist "aid" agency personnel.

"The first case of sex-slave trafficking came to light in October [1999]—four months after NATO-led peacekeepers entered the province," admitted the April 24, 2000, *Washington Post* report.

"In the last 10 years, according to women's advocacy groups," the article continued, "hundreds of thousands of women from the former Soviet republics and satellites have been trafficked to Western Europe, Asia and the United States."

Recall the media hoopla, the Pepsi Cola commercials, all hailing the "liberation" of Eastern Europe from socialism? Yet on October 22, 1999, UNICEF released a report on the plummeting standard of living for the 150 million women and 50 million girls of Central and Eastern Europe.

IMPERIALIST MILITARY OCCUPATION

What has the reintroduction of the capitalist profit-driven economy meant for women and girls in these former workers' states? Widespread unemployment, loss of free health care and education, the rise of drug and alcohol abuse, and anti-woman violence. This has helped created fertile ground for the emergence of a large-scale prostitution industry.

What created the conditions for Kosovo to be the hub of a sex-slave industry?

"Kosovo, which had some local prostitution but no trafficking problem before the peacekeepers arrived after the Kosovo war ended last June, is just another new market," officials said.

According to a few women lucky enough to escape their confinement, the *Post* noted, "Peacekeeping troops—including Americans—also were customers."

The women and girls—some in their early teens—are lured with lies or outright kidnapped from Moldavia, Ukraine, Bulgaria and Romania. They are reportedly robbed of their passports.

The *Post* referred to a report, recently released in France, that the women are frequently taken to slave-breaking stations in Albania where they are repeatedly raped and beaten in an attempt to crush their spirit. Although many people forced into prostitution are paid very little, these women are literally held as chattel.

"These women have been reduced to slavery," conceded Col. Vincenzo Coppola, commander of the national police in Kosovo.

Who is profiting? According to the *Washington Post* report, the women and girls "were transported along a well-established organized-crime network from their East European homelands to Macedonia, which borders Kosovo to the south. There, they were held in motels and sold at auction to ethnic Albanian pimps for $1,000 to $2,500.

"The pimps work under the protection of major crime figures in Kosovo, officials said, including some with links to the former anti-Serbian rebel force, the Kosovo Liberation Army."

Liberation army? The KLA began as a mercenary force covertly armed and uniformed by Germany and the United States. Even the *New York Times*—an avowed enemy of the Yugoslav government—reported March 28, 2000, that many of the leaders of the KLA trace their roots to a fascist unit set up by the Italian occupiers during World War II.

The KLA's stated aim is an "ethnically pure," Albanian-only Kosovo. KLA leaders insisted on the U.S.-NATO occupation of the multi-ethnic province of Yugoslavia.

That's under whose protection these crime bosses work. No industry can function in Kosovo today without U.S.-NATO approval and collusion.

What has the Pentagon-NATO war of bloodshed brought to the Balkans? Ethnic peace? The post-war military occupation has provided the cover for murderous pogroms against Serbs, Roma and other peoples in Kosovo.

Freedom and democracy? Ask the women and girls being sold on the auction block for NATO armies and KLA crime bosses.

VIII.

APPENDIX

International Panel Finds
U.S./NATO Leaders Guilty

A panel of sixteen judges from eleven countries at a people's tribunal meeting in New York June 10, 2000, attended by 500 people, found U.S. and NATO political and military leaders guilty of war crimes against Yugoslavia in the March 24-June 10, 1999, assault on that country.

Former U.S. Attorney General Ramsey Clark, the lead prosecutor at the International Tribunal on U.S./NATO War Crimes Against Yugoslavia, urged those present and those they represented from twenty-one countries participating to fight to abolish NATO.

Ben Dupuy, former ambassador from Haiti, Rev. Kiyul Chung of Korea, and auto worker Martha Grevatt, who heads the AFL-CIO's organization Pride at Work, read the three parts of the verdict.

Participants taking the witness stand included eye-witnesses, researchers who visited Yugoslavia, renowned political and economics analysts, historians, physicists, biologists, military experts, journalists and lay researchers.

Many of these witnesses have in the past fifteen months presented to audiences worldwide a complete picture of the war NATO waged against Yugoslavia. For the tribunal, however, all limited themselves to a single area of expertise that made up a single part of the evidence against the political and military leaders of the United States and the other NATO countries.

Taken together, the judges decided, each single part contributed to construct a proof that the accused were guilty beyond a reasonable doubt, just as the proper placing of single tiles can build a mosaic.

The witnesses' presentations were accompanied in many cases by slides and videos displayed on a large screen on the stage of the auditorium at Martin Luther King Jr. High School in Manhattan. This screen was easily visible to the judges, who sat on the stage, and to the hundreds in the audience.

In addition to hearing nine hours of testimony, judges and audience saw pictures and videos on display in the hall outside the auditorium, and had access to documentary evidence in books and research papers.

The International Action Center, founded by Clark in 1992, organized this final session of the tribunal. Participants included those who had organized similar tribunal hearings in Germany, Italy, Austria, Russia, Ukraine, Yugoslavia and Greece.

In addition to the witnesses, there were also important guest presentations from representatives of the governments Yugoslavia and Cuba. Ismael Guadalupe from Vieques, Puerto Rico showed in a powerful speech how the practice runs against his small island laid the basis for U.S./NATO aggression around the world.

There were also representatives of the Roma people—often referred to by the derisive term "gypsy." Shani Rifati, a Roma witness who was born in Pristina, capital of Kosovo, told how NATO occupation has led to the expulsion of 100,000 Romas. He pointed out that the verdict condemned the persecution of Roma people, the first time this has happened in any international tribunal.

FINAL JUDGMENT OF THE COMMISSION OF INQUIRY TO INVESTIGATE U.S./NATO WAR CRIMES AGAINST THE PEOPLE OF YUGOSLAVIA

Final Judgment

The Members of the Independent Commission of Inquiry to Investigate U.S./NATO War Crimes Against the People of Yugoslavia, meeting in New York, having considered the Initial Charges and Complaint of the Commission dated July 31, 1999, against President William J. Clinton, Gen. Wesley Clark, Secretary of State Madeleine Albright, Prime Minister Tony Blair, Chancellor Gerhard Schroder, President Jacques Chirac, Prime Minister Massimo D'Alema, Prime Minister Jose Maria Azmar, the Governments of the United States and the other NATO member states, former Secretary General Javier Solana and other NATO leaders, and Others with nineteen separate Crimes Against Peace, War Crimes and Crimes Against Humanity in violation of the Charter of the United Nations, the 1949 Geneva Conventions, other international agreements and customary international law;

Having the right and obligation as citizens of the world to sit in judgement regarding violations of international humanitarian law;

Having heard the testimony from Commissions of Inquiry and Tribunals held within their own countries during the past year and having received reports from numerous other Commission hearings which recite the evidence there gathered;

Having been provided with documentary evidence, eyewitness statements, photos, videotapes, special reports, expert analyses and summaries of evidence available to the Commission;

Having access to all evidence, knowledge and expert opinion in the Commission files or available to the Commission staff;

Having been provided by the Commission, or otherwise obtained, various books, articles and other written materials on various aspects of events and conditions in Yugoslavia and other countries in the Balkans, and in the military and arms establishments;

Having considered newspaper coverage, magazine and periodical reports, special publications, TV, radio and other media coverage and public statements by the accused, other public officials and public materials;

Having heard the presentations of the Commission of Inquiry in public hearing on June 10, 2000, and the testimony, evidence and summaries there presented;

And having met, considered and deliberated with each other and with Commission staff and having considered all the evidence that is relevant to the nineteen charges of criminal conduct alleged in the Initial Complaint, make the following findings:

Findings

The Members of the International War Crimes Tribunal find the accused Guilty on the basis of the evidence against them and that each of the nineteen separate crimes alleged in the Initial Complaint has been established to have been committed beyond a reasonable doubt. These are:

1. Planning and Executing the Dismemberment, Segregation and Impoverishment of Yugoslavia.

2. Inflicting, Inciting and Enhancing Violence Between and Among Muslims and Slavs.

3. Disrupting Efforts to Maintain Unity, Peace and Stability in Yugoslavia.

4. Destroying the Peace-Making Role of the United Nations.

5. Using NATO for Military Aggression Against, and Occupation of, Non-Compliant Poor Countries.

6. Killing and Injuring a Defenseless Population throughout Yugoslavia.

7. Planning, Announcing and Executing Attacks Intended to Assassinate the Head of Government, Other Government Leaders and Selected Civilians in Yugoslavia.

8. Destroying and Damaging Economic, Social, Cultural, Medical, Diplomatic—including the Embassy of the People's Republic of China and other embassies—and Religious Resources, Properties and Facilities throughout Yugoslavia.

9. Attacking Objects Indispensable to the Survival of the Population of Yugoslavia.

10. Attacking Facilities Containing Dangerous Substances and Forces.

11. Using Depleted Uranium, Cluster Bombs and Other Prohibited Weapons.

12. Waging War on the Environment.

13. Imposing Sanctions through the United Nations that are a Genocidal Crime Against Humanity.

14. Creating an Illegal Ad-Hoc Criminal Tribunal to Destroy and Demonize the Serbian Leadership. The Illegitimacy of this Tribunal is Further Demonstrated by Its Failure to Bring Any Case Regarding the Oppression of the Romani People, Who Have Suffered the Highest Rate of Casualties of Any People in the Region.

15. Using Controlled International Media to Create and Maintain Support for the U.S. Assault and to Demonize Yugoslavia, Slavs, Serbs and Muslims as Genocidal Murderers.

16. Establishing the Long-Term Military Occupation of Strategic Parts of Yugoslavia by NATO Forces.

17. Attempting to Destroy the Sovereignty, Right to Self-Determination, Democracy and Culture of the Slavic, Muslim, Roma and Other Peoples of Yugoslavia.

18. Seeking to Establish U.S. Domination and Control of Yugoslavia and to Exploit Its People and Resources.

19. Using the Means of Military Force and Economic Coercion in Order to Achieve U.S. Domination.

The Members hold NATO, the NATO states and their leaders accountable for their criminal acts and condemn those found guilty in the strongest possible terms. The Members condemn the NATO bombardments, denounce the international crimes and violations of international humanitarian law committed by the armed attack and through other means such as economic sanctions. NATO has acted lawlessly and has attempted to abolish international law.

Recommendations

The Members urge the immediate revocation of all embargoes, sanctions and penalties against Yugoslavia because they constitute a continuing crime against humanity. The Members call for the immediate end to the NATO occupation of all Yugoslav territory, the removal of all NATO and U.S. bases and forces from the

Balkans region, and the cessation of overt and covert operations, including the "International Criminal Tribunal for the Former Yugoslavia" in The Hague, aimed at overthrowing the government of Yugoslavia.

The Members further call for full reparations to be paid to the Federal Republic of Yugoslavia for death, injury, economic and environmental damage resulting from the NATO bombing, economic sanctions and blockades. Further, other states in the region which have suffered economic and environmental damage due to the NATO bombing and economic sanctions on Yugoslavia must also be awarded reparations. The Members condemn the threat or use of military technology against life, both civilian and military, as was used by the NATO powers against the people of Yugoslavia.

The Members urge public action and mobilization to stop new and continued sanctions and aggressions by the U.S. and other NATO powers against Iraq, Cuba, North Korea, the countries of Eastern Europe and the former Soviet Union, Puerto Rico, Asia, Sudan, Colombia and other countries. We ask for the immediate cessation of overt/covert activities by the U.S. and NATO in such countries.

The Members believe that the interests of peace, justice and human progress require the abolition of NATO, which has proved itself beyond any doubt to be an instrument of aggression for the dominant, colonizing powers, particularly the United States. The Pentagon, the central and key element of NATO and the greatest single threat to the people of the world, must be disbanded.

The Members urge the Commission to provide for the permanent preservation of the reports, evidence and materials gathered to make them available to others, and to seek ways to provide the widest possible distribution of the truth about the U.S./NATO war on Yugoslavia.

We urge all people of the world to act on recommendations developed by the Commission to hold power accountable and to secure social justice on which lasting peace must be based.

Done in New York this 10th day of June, 2000.

European Tribunal

Concerning the NATO War against Yugoslavia

Verdict

June 3, 2000:

This Tribunal has reached the following unanimous decision:

The defendants are found guilty, as charged, of committing serious violations of International Law through their aggression from March 24 to June 10, 1999 against the Federal Republic of Yugoslavia:

1) Of violating the categorical prohibition of the use of force as formulated in the UN Charter, Article 2, Number. 4; of violating the territorial sovereignty of a state, as formulated in the Principles of the Declaration of Peaceful Coexistence of States and in the interdiction of aggression as contained in the UN General Assembly Resolution 3314.

NATO states—without themselves having been attacked by the Federal Republic of Yugoslavia and while consciously and deliberately circumventing a Security Council mandate, as called for in Art. 39, 42, 53 of the UN Charter—carried out military aggression against a sovereign state, which constitutes serious violation of prevailing International Law.

Neither can this aggression be justified through being—as the Federal Republic of Germany and other NATO member states allege—an act of emergency aid through a so-called humanitarian intervention. Aside from the fact that in prevailing International Law emergency aid to a state, which is a victim of aggression, exists only in the context of Article 51 of the UN Charter, which in the present case does not apply, this Tribunal has, after intensive examination of the evidence presented and the expert testimonies heard, arrived at the opinion, that even the concrete prerequisites for such a "humanitarian intervention" were non-existent.

The Tribunal reached the opinion, that there was no humanitarian catastrophe, as was particularly invoked by the German ministers [Joshka] Fischer and [Rudolph] Scharping. It is true that the civil war ignited between the KLA (Kosovo Liberation Army) separatist movement and the police and army of Yugoslavia had led to a large number of casualties on both sides, to the destruction of houses and villages, to the displacement of people—Albanians, as well as Serbs, Croats, and Romani—and to violations of human rights. As deplorable as these are, the plight of these victims does not justify the superlative characterization of being a "humanitarian catastrophe." NATO and its member governments stand exposed for their innumerable exaggerations, dramatizations and falsifications. But even if the Tribunal would assume—which it does not—that a "humanitarian catastrophe" had existed in the years 1998-1999, before the bombing, this would not have justified military intervention, as was carried out by NATO. In the customs of states, from which international common law has evolved, and in the vast majority of international legal opinion, humanitarian intervention is not recognized as an institution, legitimating an exemption from the absolute prohibition of the use of force.

The verdict handed down in 1986 by the World Court in the suit Nicaragua vs. the United States has lost nothing of its validity concerning "humanitarian interventions": "The use of force could not be the appropriate method to monitor or ensure respect for human rights. With regard to the steps actually taken, the protection of human rights, a strictly humanitarian objective, cannot be compatible with the mining of ports, the destruction of oil installations, (...). The Court concludes that the argument derived from the preservation of human rights in Nicaragua cannot afford a legal justification for the conduct of the United States."

In spite of what some would have us believe, this standpoint of International Law prevails. Even if "humanitarian intervention" could be admitted as a legitimate exemption from the absolute prohibition of the use of force,—which this Tribunal does not do—one cannot overlook the fact that NATO not only has failed to attain its proclaimed goal, the re-establishment of acceptable conditions for human rights, but has caused the already precarious situation to dramatically deteriorate. The number of fatalities, of wounded and of those robbed of all they possessed multiplied through the commencement of the bombing campaign. For this suffering of the Yugoslavian people, NATO, alone, stands to blame.

2) The bombing of Yugoslavia violated even the NATO Treaty itself. Art. 5 defines that the function of NATO is exclusively defensive, not military interventions in regions of civil war and domestic strife. Within the framework of the UN and OSCE, a multitude of non-violent, political and economical instruments are available for the prevention of or subsequent pacification of regions of crisis. These were deliberately circumvented.

The NATO Treaty does not mandate military intervention outside of the defense of the territorial boundaries of the alliance.

3) The Federal German Republic is guilty of violating the 1990 "4 + 2 Treaty," in which it committed itself to the principle that never again would war emanate from its territory and that it would engage itself militarily only in accordance with the norms established by the UN Charter. Through its substantial participation in the war against Yugoslavia, the FRG consciously violated its obligations.

4) The Tribunal is also of the opinion that the Federal German government violated German constitutional and penal law. This was substantiated by expert testimony. There are also good grounds for presuming violations of the laws of warfare by the German military. But in accordance with the limitations imposed by its Statutes, this Tribunal cannot pronounce a verdict concerning these violations. It would rather transfer these questions to subsequent investigations and Tribunals for the legal systems of all participating nations, and not just Germany, but also France, England, Italy, (...) and to appeal that this case not be considered closed but that the search for the truth about this war be continued.

5) This Tribunal would like to express its apprehension that the war against Yugoslavia has played a role in the elaboration of NATO's new strategic concept of April 1999, which has attained a geostrategic significance extending far beyond the Balkans and Eurasia as a model for a future military world order. To thwart the globalization of these military imperial instruments, it is absolutely necessary to further examine the prerequisites, objectives and consequences of the war against

Yugoslavia and simultaneously draw attention to the possible geostrategic perspectives.

6) After hearing extensive testimony of witnesses and experts, the Tribunal has arrived at the conviction that the methodology of warfare used by the accused constituted also serious and repeated violations of international humanitarian law, as spelled out in the Statutes of this Tribunal. The Tribunal intensively deliberated the question of whether responsibility for the violations of international law weighs as heavily on the parliamentarians of the German Federal Parliament, as they do on those members of the government administration, who had ordered the expansion of the bombing, going from targeting purely military to that of including civilian targets, as provided for in the so-called 3-phase plan. The members of the Tribunal could not ignore the fact, that even though the parliamentarians had not directly participated in deciding how the war would be waged, they themselves had also not taken any initiative to halt the gross violations of the law as the consequences of the bombing campaign became evident.

The Tribunal could not be convinced by arguments in NATO's and its member governments' defense, that the heavy damages of civilian objects were only unintentional, "collateral." All witnesses and experts confirm that the hospitals, villages or the RTS radio station were repeatedly attacked, which, due to the often reiterated praised precision of the bombs and guided missiles, excludes the element of accident. The prosecution sufficiently presented statements of high-ranking military and government representatives, to prove a strategic plan to destroy civil structures, in order to pressure the population into opposing, in one means or another, the Milosevic administration. Solely in the case of the bombing of the Dragisa Misovic Hospital Complex in Belgrade (point 3 in the indictment) could no evidence be presented substantiating repeated bombing attacks. On the other hand, the witness Sumkar brought forth evidence of multiple attacks carried out against his hospital in Belgrade.

The Tribunal has also arrived at the conclusion that none of the civilian targets listed in the indictment or mentioned by the experts and witnesses housed or were in the vicinity of military establishments. In only one case, was it reported that a police academy was at a distance of 6,000-8,000 meters, but the hospital in question was clearly discernible—also from the air—through the Red Cross sign.

These proceedings have led to the conclusion that the prosecution's selection of attacked civilian targets and persons simply exemplify a war strategy that in its third stage evidently sets out to systematically implicate the civilian population in order to reach its political goal—the overthrow of the administration of President Milosevic. This war strategy is in clear violation of the central norms of the 1949 Geneva Conventions and its Additional Protocol of 1977.

The use of depleted uranium and so-called cluster bombs constitutes a particularly serious violation. According to recent reports NATO is said to have disposed of approximately 10 tons of depleted uranium over the territory of Yugoslavia. Experiences with the use by the United States and Great Britain of this material in Iraq shows that this weapon constitutes a time bomb of incalculable health damages. Such weapons are inadmissible under terms of the avoidance of weapons inflicting superfluous injury and unnecessary and long-term suffering and the prohibition of weapons of indiscriminate destruction. The use of these weapons represents a grave violation of humanitarian international law as prescribed by the Additional Protocol to the Geneva Conventions. The same refers to the so-called cluster bombs, whose unexploded remnants left lying on the ground with the effect of landmines are also forbidden. Both of these weapons fall into the supplementary category of weapons prohibited because of being toxic and cruel.

The attack carried out against the radio/television station RTS represents not only a forbidden attack against a civilian installation, which, as confirmed by witness testimony, was never used for military communications, but also an infringement on the freedom of information. This was one of those targets which, as the bombing continued, was pushed ever higher on NATO's scale of priorities, not only in order to deprive the Yugoslav viewers and listeners, but also the viewers and listeners outside Yugoslavia of the information broadcast by the Yugoslav government. The question of the objectivity of this information is, in this respect, of no importance; in the final analysis the answer would hardly be different when raised concerning the information of NATO and the broadcasts of NATO states.

The Tribunal is well aware that the cases presented by the prosecution and those supplemented during the course of these proceedings represent only a segment of the war scenario that evolved during the seventy-eight days of bombardment—a scenario, which with the growing awareness of its failure, distanced itself ever further from the norms of humanitarian International Law, until finally placing might over right. That NATO propaganda was able to entice so many into passive—even active—support for this lawless war is a particularly sad aspect.

We cannot avoid mentioning that several of Yugoslavia's neighboring states, such as Macedonia, Bulgaria, Rumania, Albania, Bosnia-Herzegovina and others through according over-flight rights, through placing bases and other facilities at the disposal of the aggressors, have made themselves at least guilty of aiding and abetting these violations.

These Tribunal proceedings must not be allowed to constitute a finale in the efforts to learn the truth about the war against Yugoslavia. The problems that brought war to the entire region are far too serious and yet completely unresolved. It is imperative that not only the physical and material damage, but also the psychological wounds, the humiliation, be further investigated and unambiguously exposed to the public. This war must not be allowed to serve as a model for a new world order. We must make it finally clear to the politicians and the military that with war neither human rights nor civilization can be saved, that war can no longer be an instrument of politics.

Greeks Reject NATO

Massive, militant protests hit Clinton visit

BILL WAYLAND

Bill Clinton arrived in Greece November 19, 1999, like a thief in the night. His motorcade moved down darkened boulevards carefully cleared of people. Armies of police guarded him against any contact with ordinary Greeks. But the voice of the people could not be silenced.

While the U.S. president wined and dined with Greek Prime Minister Costas Simitis, police loosed barrages of tear gas against thousands of workers, students and retirees trying to march to the U.S. Embassy. Among those gassed were elderly veterans of the Greek anti-Nazi resistance in World War II.

Despite the gas and repeated police attacks, protesters regrouped again and again and marched through downtown Athens to the city's central Omonia Square. Over eighty people were arrested, many of them at pharmacies where they had gone for medical aid. As of this writing, they are still being held.

In the aftermath of the protest, the Greek government has mounted a violence-baiting campaign against the Greek Committee for Peace and the Communist Party of Greece (KKE), which was a major force in the demonstration. But it was the state and its heavily armed police that unleashed the violence that night.

CLINTON LEAVES TRAIL OF REPRESSION

The media have played up Clinton's carefully scripted comment about the "right to protest as long as it's peaceful." But at every stop on his Balkan tour, protests have been met with fascist-like violence.

While he was in Turkey, police beat and arrested hundreds of protesters in Ankara, the capital. They had not been released as of November 22.

In Sofia, Bulgaria, where Clinton went after leaving Athens, protests were also banned and over 100 people arrested. Blagoesta Doncheva, a former anti-communist "dissident" who has written eloquently about the Bulgarian people's suffering under the new capitalist regime, including a recent op-ed piece for the *New York Times*, was thrown into a mental ward.

Clinton will also visit the NATO-occupied Yugoslav province of Kosovo. There, Serbs, Roma people, Turks and other minorities are being systematically murdered and driven from their homes by NATO-sponsored gangs, even as the imperialist occupiers claim to be combating national oppression.

LONG HISTORY OF GREEK RESISTANCE

In Greece, too, the regime tried to stifle protest. In the week before Clinton's arrival, a masked gang attacked a Communist Party neighborhood office in Athens, beating three people. Another KKE office was firebombed. Officials and the media also created a climate of fear with constant warnings about violence. But their efforts at intimidation failed.

The Greek people hate NATO. Nearly 700,000 Greeks were murdered by Nazi occupiers during World War II. When the Communist-led Greek resistance, in alliance with Yugoslav and Albanian partisans, succeeded in driving Hitler's armies out of the Balkans, the imperialists feared a revolution and sent British troops to occupy the country.

Britain, a supposed ally, imposed on Greece a regime of Nazi collaborators headed by a hated royal family that had spent the war under British protection. In 1948 and 1949, tens of thousands of Greek anti-Nazi fighters were murdered, imprisoned or driven into exile by mercenary forces armed, trained and financed by the U.S. and British imperialist governments.

The Truman administration created NATO in conjunction with this war against Greece. The U.S. military's first use of napalm bombs was against Greek villages. U.S. planes also bombed Yugoslavia in this period. Over 100,000 anti-Nazi fighters were held in concentration camps for the next twenty years.

In 1967, when the Greek left had regained its strength, Greece's NATO military carried out a coup. Colonel George Papadopoulos, leader of the fascist junta that would rule the country for the next seven years, was on the direct payroll of the CIA. This was finally revealed by the *New York Times* in 1976.

Fascist /terror did not crush the people's resistance. On November 17, 1973, tens of thousands of university students defied tanks and guns to challenge the junta, which fell the following year.

That same spirit was very much alive in the streets of Athens and other Greek cities before and during Clinton's visit.

10,000 ACCUSE U.S./NATO OF WAR CRIMES

On November 8, some 10,000 people had stood in the rain in Athens's Constitution Square for a mass trial of the U.S. president and other NATO leaders. The judges were twenty justices of the Council of State—the Greek Supreme Court. Famous entertainers served as other officers of the court.

Clinton had ignored a subpoena delivered to the U.S. Embassy a week earlier by a march of several thousand people.

After hours of eyewitness testimony about the U.S. bombing of Yugoslavia, the presiding judge asked if Clinton were guilty of war crimes. The entire crowd responded "Guilty!"

On November 17, 1999, the anniversary of the 1973 student uprising, tens of thousands of marchers, mostly youth, filed past the U.S. Embassy. They loudly denounced Clinton as the butcher of the Balkans, called for an end to NATO and demanded that the U.S. military get its bases out of Greece and its troops out of Yugoslavia. The march was organized by the communists, but even youth from PASOK, the social-democratic governing party, felt compelled to join.

And then on November 19, the night of Clinton's arrival, tens of thousands of protesters, many waving red flags, gathered in three squares in downtown Athens in defiance of a police ban.

The main rally, in Constitution Square, was opened by Bill Doares of the International Action Center. Doares saluted the Greek people's history of resistance to fascism and war and their solidarity with the people of Yugoslavia.

"The profits of Wall Street depend on wars of destruction," he said, "and only mass action can stop the Pentagon's drive toward new and bigger wars. In this great task, the Greek people are leading the way." Doares also condemned Clinton's hypocrisy in preaching about "human rights" when the "U.S. has more people in prison than any other country—seventy percent are Black and Latin—and the biggest companies profit off their slave labor." He drew loud applause when he called for international action to stop the execution of U.S. political prisoner Mumia Abu-Jamal. Pictures of Mumia dotted the crowd.

The main speaker was Thanassis Pafilis, secretary of the Greek Committee for Peace and KKE central committee member. Pafilis condemned the "stability pact" signed at the conference of the Organization for Security and Cooperation in Europe in Istanbul. The pact asserts the "right" of the U.S. and NATO to intervene in any country where they deem there are "human rights violations."

Pafilis spoke of the long and bloody history of U.S. intervention in Greece and honored some of the country's anti-fascist martyrs, including Grigoris Lambrakis, a vice president of the Peace Committee, who was assassinated in 1963.

Pafilis asserted that the police had no right to stop the people of Greece from marching in protest down their own streets.

At 6:30 p.m., the moment Clinton's plane touched down, the minister of public order still refused to allow a march. The lead contingent of the demonstration, made up of construction workers and shipbuilders, then forced its way through police lines. The authorities responded with volleys of gas bombs.

Despite the police attack and arrests, the Greek people's opposition to NATO and the Pentagon's war plans was heard around the world. Clinton came to Greece from Turkey, where he had dominated the conference of the Organization for Security and Cooperation in Europe. Why the United States, which is not part of Europe, should have been there at all the president did not explain. But the reason is clearly that the continent is under U.S. military occupation. NATO is the justification for this relationship.

At a press conference, Clinton appealed to Greece's elite with visions of a partnership with U.S. corporations in robbing the rest of the Balkans. But for the Greek people, U.S. military and economic domination has meant high prices and a thirteen-percent unemployment rate.

It also means a $2-billion military budget, much of which is spent on U.S. arms. The November 21, 1999, *International Herald Tribune* admitted that military spending "exacts a heavy toll" on the Greek economy.

Clinton admitted that ninety-four percent of the Greek people opposed NATO and the war against Yugoslavia. He said that was "an example of democracy." He didn't explain why it was democratic for the U.S. to impose its war policies on Greece despite this overwhelming opposition.

Clinton also made the amazing statement that "southeast Europe is undivided and at peace for the first time in fifty years." Only a few months ago the U.S. launched the first war this region has seen since Washington's 1948 intervention in Greece.

Filip Karamalis, a young Communist worker who took part in the November 19 protests, told this writer, "U.S. imperialism will not pass. We shall stand fighting. All the Greek people are against NATO, against the European Union and U.S. policy. Clinton is trying to act like Hitler. But Hitler could not conquer the Balkans and neither will NATO."

(From Workers World, *December 2, 1999)*

Ukraine War Crimes tribunal

Washington, NATO, condemned

BILL WAYLAND

Kiev, Ukraine. President Bill Clinton and other NATO leaders were found guilty of crimes against peace by an International Peoples Tribunal on NATO War Crimes Against Yugoslavia that met January 23, 2000, in the parliament building of this beautiful ancient capital. The hearing was held in defiance of the U.S.-backed regime of President Leonid Kuchma, who wants to bring Ukraine into NATO.

Delegates from Ukraine, Belarus, Russia, Yugoslavia, the Czech Republic, Poland, Germany and the United States took part in the hearing. The United States was represented by Larissa Kritskaya and Bill Doares of the International Action Center.

Kritskaya and Doares were shown on the front page of the major daily newspaper *Kievsky Vedomosty* under the headline "Americans who dream of destroying NATO."

The Kiev tribunal was the second in a series of hearings organized by the International Peoples Tribunal (IPT), which was initiated in Russia by the All-Slavic Assembly. The first was held in the Russian city of Yaroslavl December 14, 1999. Others are planned for Belgrade, Warsaw and Minsk.

The Kiev tribunal focused on charges of crimes against peace and conspiracy to cause a war. IPT organizers plan to coordinate their efforts with the Commission of Inquiry on U.S./NATO War Crimes Against Yugoslavia, organized by the International Action Center and former U.S. Attorney General Ramsey Clark.

The Ukraine hearing, which was chaired by Professor Mikhail Kuznetsov of Moscow, got considerable support from the Socialist, Communist and other Ukrainian opposition parties. Socialist Party Deputy Vil Nikolayich Romashenko was vice president of the tribunal.

The judges and participants heard eyewitness testimony from Yugoslav delegates who told of the death and destruction inflicted by NATO bombs and missiles, which took 2,000 civilian lives. They also heard several parliamentarians who had visited Yugoslavia during the war.

Deputy Sergei Kaszian of the Belarus parliament told of his meetings with ethnic Albanian Kosovar leaders who condemned the NATO bombing and held the United States responsible for the destruction of their country. Kaszian said NATO forces had brutalized Kosovar refugees, separating children from mothers and sending them to different countries. He also testified to the large number of children killed or wounded by NATO bombs and missiles.

Ukrainian Communist Deputy Vladimir Moiseenko represents the Donbass coal-mining region and chairs the Ukraine Association to Restore the Soviet Union. He pointed out that NATO was from its inception an aggressive alliance aimed against East Europe and the Soviet Union. He compared the U.S.-NATO strategy to break up Yugoslavia with its current strategy toward Ukraine.

He quoted U.S. strategist Zbigniew Brzezinski's description of Ukraine as a "military platform" for NATO's expansion to the east. A NATO Ukraine would become a base to invade Belarus and later Russia, Moiseenko said.

He condemned Ukraine's U.S.-backed President Leonid Kuchma for facilitating NATO's expansion, but said, "The Ukrainian people are waking up to resist Ukraine's colonization."

NATO ALSO AGAINST ALBANIAN PEOPLE

Retired Soviet Adm. Anatoli Yurkovsky, now a member of Ukraine's parliament, testified that NATO was also aimed at the Albanian people. He told of the 1996 mass uprising in southern Albania against the U.S.-backed Berisha regime.

The insurgents "formed committees of national salvation that were like the workers' councils in Russia in 1917. But they were smothered by the massive intervention of NATO troops."

Larissa Kritskaya, a member of the International Action Center, said that "corporate America has dominated Ukraine long enough to deliver the country to the point of total destruction. But there is another U.S. inside the land of giant corporations. We are happy to be here today as your friends and supporters in your struggle against the coming colonization planned by U.S.-led NATO."

IAC spokesperson Bill Doares condemned the war against Yugoslavia as "a cynical maneuver carried out to enrich giant U.S. corporations that profit off death and destruction." He said: "Bombs and missiles are not the only agency of destruction. When the International Monetary Fund orders Ukraine to close down its coal mines and steel plants, reducing workers to starvation, is that not an act of war?"

He denounced NATO as "the strike force of the International Monetary Fund."

Yugoslav Ambassador to Ukraine Goiko Dapcevic said: "The fact that the war crimes tribunal took place here in Ukraine and the fact that many representatives of your country were willing to testify in the name of truth about the horrible crimes committed during this unlawful war speaks to our unity.

"Yet the war in Yugoslavia is still far from its end," he continued. "Though there are no missiles and bombs falling from the sky right now, there is also no peace for us. And the most difficult thing now is our incapacity to break the blockade on information.

"Therefore an event like the war crimes tribunal has special value in our struggle to tell the world the truth about this war and the present condition of my country."

From Workers World, *February 10, 2000*

German Government Sued

JOHN CATALINOTTO

Berlin anti-war lawyer Ulrich Dost has filed a civil lawsuit in German courts against his government, demanding damages for war crimes against individual Yugoslavs victimized by NATO bombing. He says Germany is responsible because its military actively participated in the U.S.-led NATO war and its government supported all NATO's actions.

U.S. imperialism and its NATO allies control the war-crimes court in The Hague. So no one has succeeded in charging NATO criminals in that court. Instead, Judge Carla del Ponte has blamed the victim by charging former Yugoslav President Slobodan Milosevic with war crimes. But Dost has experience trying war-crimes charges in "People's Tribunals" that the anti-war movement organized.

He was prosecutor for the European War Crimes Tribunal. In June 2000, that body found NATO leaders guilty of war crimes against Yugoslavia, including the crime of aggression for planning and starting the 1999 war. The European Tribunal worked cooperatively with those held by the U.S.-based International Action Center in 1999 and 2000 to expose NATO aggression.

Dost's office is now filing suit about a very specific crime. It involves the May 30, 1999, NATO bombing of a bridge in the town of Varvarin, about 125 miles south of Belgrade.

This bombing was only one of many atrocities the U.S./NATO bombers committed during the war of March 24-June 10, 1999. It is one, though, where there can be no doubt of criminal intent as well as action. And it is a violation of the Geneva Convention protecting civilians during hostilities.

Dost recently returned to Berlin from a two-week visit to Varvarin in April, 2001. There he interviewed and took depositions from victims to establish a legitimate suit for damages. On May 13, 2001, Dost told Workers World what he established from interviewing thirty-five witnesses and studying reports by local authorities.

VARVARIN: NO MILITARY TARGETS

Four thousand people live in Varvarin. There were no troops stationed nearby. There were no military facilities or factories. The bridge was not strong enough to support military traffic. A tank or armored car would have collapsed it. And there was no military movement in or near the town. "Thus the NATO claim that Varvarin was a 'military target' is a complete lie," said Dost.

Around 1:20 p.m. on May 30, 1999, three NATO fighters flew above Varvarin. One of them descended and launched a missile that hit the central part of the steel structure of the 620-foot-long bridge. The bridge collapsed. At the time there were three automobiles, some pedestrian traffic and bicyclists on the bridge. Dost says it was a "clear day, with sunshine and good visibility." The NATO fliers would have seen the civilians.

People at the town market ran to help the injured who were on the part of the bridge still above the water. A NATO plane attacked again, catching by surprise those who gave first aid. This added to the number of dead and wounded. A priest was decapitated by one of the missile blasts. In all, ten people were killed and sixteen severely wounded.

Some suffered severe burns or lost limbs. Many, said Dost, are unable to work or can only work under limited conditions. Many also have to care for their wounds every day.

Dost himself was shaken by what he described as "my first experience in seeing first-hand the horrors of war." He found it especially painful to experience the psychological difficulties and depression the victims were suffering from their trauma. "It is for them incomprehensible that they have been made victims by NATO for no good reason and they fear it could happen again."

He says the victims are aware that even if they are able to win the case, it may take years to go through the German courts. But they want to pursue it because it is painful for them that the NATO criminals go unpunished. And they hope to win a financial award to help them survive and take care of their medical needs.

Since the plaintiffs are unable to pay for the case, Dost and his supporters have had to raise money. They still need more to fund preparation of all the complaints. He hopes he'll be able to go through the medical reports of victims and all the other evidence in the next few months.

"If we are able to proceed smoothly, we'll be able to bring this before the courts in Germany some time in September this year," he concluded.

From Workers World, *May 24, 2001*

[There were some difficulties, but Dost was able to file charges in December 2001—Editor]

In the ʼ*White Book,*ʼ* facts accuse

MILOS PETROVIC

We now know that our country of South Slavs, Yugoslavia, was destroyed with two immediate aims: to divide and then conquer the Serbian nation and its territory.

Serbs make up the largest ethnic group of the former Yugoslavia, and one which always fought stubbornly for what history showed were just and universal causes— freedom, independence, national and cultural dignity, inter-ethnic coexistence and non-material values. Because of this, Serbs were to be neutralized as a military, economic and moral authority in the region.

The perpetrators of these aims, just as the aims themselves, were clear from the very beginning: an international oligarchy of certain countries, or more precisely, the elites of the United States and those countries of Europe that all together share a single economic, and thus political, aim—world domination. However, the new and experimental method they used to achieve these aims was not immediately clear.

We were learning, day after day, year after year, method after method. These include economic pressures, political exclusions, inter-ethnic provocations, mass media blockades and lies, covert actions and psychological operations, all part of one strategy and its aims. We now know that the point was to portray the victim as the aggressor, and the aggressor as the victim: Serbs became irredentists in their own homes, the Yugoslav Army became the force of occupation in its own country, Yugoslav laws and Constitution became lawless and unconstitutional.

On the other hand, the true intruders, the true forces of occupation, those truly lawless and unconstitutional put on the masks of their opposites in an attempt to deceive the people of Yugoslavia and world public opinion. It was a simple, but paradoxical, story of good and evil. Such a story was to provide these perpetrators, these true aggressors, with an alibi to divide, conquer and demonize, destroy in the name of uniting, liberating, and building a new and a very different social and economic order both for Serbs and other Yugoslav people, as well as for the rest of the world.

We now know what that new order that they impose on us consists of. Far from uniting, liberating, or building, it is selling of injustice for justice, totalitarianism for democracy, slavery for freedom, ugliness for beauty, despair for happiness. The aim is to eventually give nothing and take everything, to use us and reuse us, to mold us

---

* *NATO Crimes in Yugoslavia: Documentary Evidence* (the "*White Book*"), compiled by the Yugoslav Ministry of Foreign Affairs; this book catalogues with photographs, documents and testimonials the devastation NATO wreaked on Yugoslavia. Petrovic selected a portion of the evidence for reproduction here.

and remold us, to make us consume away our lives for their own benefit, and without resistance, which they hope to kill and crucify.

Yugoslavia and the Serbs, because of their size, multi-ethnic composition, their strategic geographic position, and their significant history, were the first to experience this new international regime. They became a convenient and symbolic laboratory for trying out those new economic, political, and cultural recipes.

Yet, we now know the weakness of that new order and its perpetrators: their method must rely on war, and war alone. It is the seed of their imminent defeat, and thus they are desperately, but unrealistically, trying to hide it behind euphemistic names and causes. They pretend not to see any wars, or that wars are not wars. They even have the arrogance to stage their own inquisition to indict and prosecute their own victims for their resistance. But such arrogance and disregard for law are only the signs of their pathological insecurity.

They are even afraid to mention the very word "war," their indictments are cleared of all war and bombs, of all inconveniences for their ruthless ideology. What remains on those indicting sheets of paper is their anger at their enemies, who they accuse of being their opponents and their victim, in wars that, according to them, never took place. They even try to mask war as its opposite, and thus accuse their opponents of obstructing peace.

But, we know that war is not peace. War is not humanitarian. We know that much. Behind every trick of theirs, behind their every mask, is their threat of power, a crime. The very need to resort to brute physical power shows the deviancy of their project and resistance to it. Look at Serbia: burnt down, lynched and disfigured, humiliated; lives taken away savagely, hospitals, homes, and school destroyed, roads and bridges erased to lead nowhere, churches desecrated, life depleted with uranium, people prosecuted for fighting back. And look at yourself: our lives, too, are under the immediate threat of being taken away savagely, destroyed, erased, desecrated, depleted, and we are all about to be prosecuted if we resist. This is no metaphor.

We now know and accuse, I accuse, the perpetrators of these crimes. We now know that they are guilty. War is not peace, that is all that we need to know in order to expose their responsibility and prove their guilt.

War is not peace. We have the evidence. The details are in the *White Book*, from which a selection follows on the next page.

NATO CRIMES IN THE TERRITORY OF THE FEDERAL REPUBLIC OF YUGOSLAVIA FROM 24 MARCH TO 10 JUNE 1999 (July 5, 1999)

Contents:

I. CIVILIAN CASUALTIES

Several thousand civilians were killed and more than 6,000 sustained serious injuries, while a large number of them will remain crippled for life. Children make up 30 percent of all casualties, as well as 40 percent of the total number of the injured, while 10 percent of all Yugoslav children (approximately 300,000) have suffered severe psychological traumas. For the most part, children have been victims of the sprinkle cluster bombs with delayed effect. What follows are the most tragic instances of civilian casualties and suffering as a result of the aggression of the NATO alliance on the FR of Yugoslavia:

Surdulica:
· in an attack on a peaceful provincial town 20 civilians were killed, including 12 children, and over 100 wounded of which 24 critically (27.4.1999);
· 20 civilians were killed and 88 injured in the attack on a Retirement Home and a Sanatorium (31.5.1999);
· in an attack on a refugee camp in which Serb refugees from the Republika Srpska Krajina (Croatia) were accommodated 10 refugees were killed (including 6 children) and 16 were wounded (21.4.1999);

Korisa:
· 87 civilians were killed and over 70 injured in NATO attack on a convoy of ethnic Albanian refugees returning to their homes (14.5.1999.);

Djakovica:
· Djakovica-Prizren road: in the attack on two ethnic Albanian refugee columns, with four cruise missiles, 75 civilians were killed (among them 19 children) and 100 wounded, of whom 26 critically (14.4.1999);

Grdelica gorge:
· in the attack on a international passenger train 55 passengers were killed, including one child, and 16 wounded (12.4.1999);

Village Luzani:
· 60 passengers were killed and 13 injured in an attack on a road bridge during which a passenger bus "Nis Expres" on the Pristina-Podujevo route was hit; at the same time a first aid doctor was injured during a consecutive attack on the bridge in which an ambulance, giving help to the injured, was destroyed (1.5.1999);

Istok:
· 100 inmates killed and 200 injured in several attacks, on consecutive days, on the Istok Penitentiary (19.-24.5.1999);

Varvarin:
· 24 civilians were killed and 74 wounded in the attack on a road on a busy market day (30.5.1999);

Belgrade:
· suburb of Batajnica: a three year old girl Milica Rakic was killed in the bathroom in her house, while five civilians were wounded (17.4.1999);
· in the attack on the Radio Television of Serbia office building, 16 employees were killed and 19 wounded (23.4.1999);
· in the attack on governmental buildings, commercial facilities and housing blocks in central Belgrade 3 civilians were killed and 38 wounded (30.04.1999.);
· 4 civilians (3 patients and a care-taker) have been killed and several injured in the attack on the hospital "Dr. Dragisa Misovic" (20.5.1999);

Nis:
· at least 16 civilians were killed and more than 80 injured in repeated attacks on housing flats, commercial premises and administrative buildings in central Nis (19.4.1999, 7.5.1999 and 12.5.1999) during which NATO planes dropped cluster bombs;

Savine Vode:
· 20 civilians were killed and 43 injured, out of which 24 sustained severe injuries, in an attack on a "Djakovica Prevoz" passenger bus on the Pec-Kula-Rozaje route (3-4.5.1999);

Aleksinac:
· 12 civilians were killed (among them two children) and more than 40 wounded in an attack on housing blocks, commercial premises and administrative buildings in downtown Aleksinac (5.4.1999);

Kursumlija:
· 13 dead (among them 9 children) and 25 wounded civilians in an attack on housing blocks, commercial premises and administrative buildings in central Kursumlija (27.4.1999);

Novi Pazar:
· 13 civilians were killed and 35 wounded in an attack on the residential area in the center of the town during which 25 buildings were completely destroyed (31.5.1999);

Village Nagavac:
· 11 civilians were killed and 5 wounded in an attack on the village (2.4.1999);

Pristina:
· 10 civilians were killed and 8 wounded in an attack on housing blocks, commercial premises and administrative buildings in downtown Pristina (7.4.1999);

Village Srbica:
· 10 civilians were killed, among whom 7 children, during an attack with cluster bombs upon this village;

Village Murino:
· 6 civilians, of whom two children, were killed and 8 injured in an attack on a road bridge in this village predominantly inhabited by ethnic Albanians (30.04.1999.);

Merdare:
· 5 civilians were killed, including an 11-month old baby, and several wounded when 8 containers, holding 1,920 cluster bombs, were dropped in an attack on the regional road Prokuplje-Pristina (10.4.1999);

Doganovici:
· 5 ethnic Albanian children were killed and two wounded when they stumbled upon an unexploded cluster bomb in an open field (27.4.1999);

Gnjilane:
· 4 civilians were killed and 19 wounded in an attack on the Agricultural Complex "Mladost" and transport company "Kosmet Prevoz" (19.5.1999);

Pancevo:
· 3 civilians were killed and 4 wounded in attacks on commercial/industrial facilities (4.4.1999);

Ralja:
· 3 civilians were killed (including 2 children) and 3 injured in the attack on the village of Ralja, near Sopot (25.5.1999);

Kragujevac:
· more than 160 workers, forming a live shield, were wounded in deliberate attack on the car factory "Crvena Zastava," while another 160,000 were left jobless in affiliated companies throughout Yugoslavia (9 & 12.4.1999);

Vranje:
· two civilians were killed and 23 wounded in an attack on downtown Vranje (22.4.1999);

Kraljevo:
· in attacks upon civilian targets in Vitanovac, Varca and Bogutovac, wider Kraljevo area, 14 civilians were wounded (30.4.1999);

Kraljevo-Godacica regional road:
in an attack on a passenger bus eight passengers were wounded, of whom four sustained heavy injuries (30.04.1999.);

Novi Sad:
· one civilian was killed and 45 injured in attacks on the Oil Refinery in Novi Sad during which residential suburbs Detelinara (6.5.1999) and Sangaj (7.06.1999) were hit;

Trstenik:
in the attack on a bridge one civilian was killed and 17 injured (30.04.1999.);

Vladicin Han:
· 2 civilians were killed and 5 wounded in an attack on a road bridge on the river Juzna Morava (11.5.1999);

Villag Radosta:
· 2 children were killed and one wounded in a NATO cluster bomb attack on this peaceful village near Orahovac (25.5.1999);

Cuprija:

· 1 civilian was killed and 14 injured in the attack on the central residential area of the town (over 800 housing units were demolished during attacks on 8.4. and 29.5.1999.);

Krk Bunar:
· one civilian was killed and 3 injured (French philosopher Daniel Schiffer, "Times" reporter Eve-Ann Prentis and "Corriera della Sera" Renzo Cianfanelli) in an attack on a foreign journalist convoy on the Prizren-Brezovica road (31.5.1999);

Mijatovac:
· 4 Romanian humanitarian workers were wounded in an attack on the bridge near Mijatovac (8.5.1999);

II. PUBLIC INSTITUTIONS

In NATO air strikes against public institutions and housing units in the Federal Republic of Yugoslavia, thousands of hospitals, health care centers, schools and housing units have been destroyed or damaged. For instance, in Leskovac, a town in the south of Serbia, more than 3,000 public buildings and housing units were either destroyed or damaged, while in the northern Serbian province of Vojvodina at least 3,650 public institutions and housing units met the same fate. Furthermore, residential areas on the outskirts of Belgrade (Rakovica, Batajnica, Kijevo-Knezevac, Borca), as well as in Pancevo, Novi Sad, Aleksinac, Kraljevo, Pristina, Kosovska Mitrovica, Prizren, Urosevac, Djakovica, etc. have been under perpetual attacks.

1) HOSPITALS AND HEALTH CARE INSTITUTIONS:

NATO strikes seriously damaged many clinical and hospital centers. NATO attacks did not cause only material damage to property (destruction of buildings and expensive medical equipment), but also provoked new health problems and intensified psychological traumas among the sick people, especially chronic patients and the terminally ill. The list of these institutions is very long and includes, among others, the following:

Belgrade:
· Neuropsychiatric Ward "Dr. Laza Lazarevic," Institute for urology and nephology and Central Pharmacy of the Clinical Center (3.4. & 8.5.1999);
· "Sveti Sava" hospital (7.4.1999);
· Army Medical Academy and Orthopaedic Clinic in Banjica, Belgrade (4.4. & 13.4.1999);
· Hospital "Dr. Dragisa Misovic," especially the Neuropsychiatric Ward which has been totally demolished (19.5.1999);
· Medical Center for Lung Diseases and Tuberculosis (28.4.1999);
· Gynaecological Hospital and Maternity Ward, Clinical Center (21.4.1999);
· City Hospital "Zvezdara" (5.4. & 30.4.1999);
· Health Care Center in the Belgrade suburb of Rakovica (15.4.1999);

Pancevo:
· City hospital including the Maternity Ward (30.4.1999.);

Novi Sad:
- City Hospital (1.4.1999);
- Medical station - Klisa (7.4.1999);

Vrsac:
- Neuropsychiatric Ward "Dr. Slavoljub Bakalovic" (30.4.1999.);

Kula:
- Medical station (25.3.1999);

Nis:
- Hospital and Poly-clinic (27.3.1999);
- Medical station of the Nis Machine Industry (24.4.1999);
- City hospital (7.5.1999);

Valjevo:
- City hospital (21.4.1999);
- Dispensary "Krusik" (14.4.-11.5.1999);
- Medical station, Druzetic, Koceljevo (23.4.1999);

Kraljevo:
- Medical Center;

Leskovac:
- Hospital and Medical Center in the Leskovac municipality (25.3.1999);
- Gerontological Center (25.3.1999);

Aleksinac:
- Medical Center and Ambulance Center (5.4.1999);

Kursumlija:
- Health Care Center;

Mt. Zlatibor
- Dispensary on Mount Zlatibor;
- Outpatient clinic and Medical station, Medjurecje - Ivanjica (12.4.1999);

Surdulica
- Sanatorium for treatment of lung diseases and Retirement Home (31.5.1999);

Vladicin Han:
- Medical Care Center (11.5.1999);

Novi Pazar:
- Hospital for treatment of dystrophia;

Kosovo and Metohija:
- Dentist station in Pristina (29.3.1999);
- Outpatient clinic in Prizren (19.4.1999);
- General Hospital in Djakovica;
- Outpatient clinic in Suva Reka (19.4.1999);

2) EDUCATIONAL INSTITUTIONS

The NATO aggression has abruptly put a stop to the education of close to one million pupils and students in the FR of Yugoslavia. More than 480 schools, faculties and facilities for students and children were badly damaged or destroyed (25 faculties, 15 colleges, 100 secondary, 320 elementary schools, 20 student dormitories), as well as more than 50 pre-school facilities. This list includes only those facilities that were destroyed:

Belgrade:
- Elementary schools "16. Oktobar" and "Vladimir Rolovic";
- Day-care center in the Belgrade suburb of Petlovo Brdo;
- Elementary school and Engineering secondary school center in the Belgrade suburb of Rakovica;
- Secondary music school "Stanislav Binicki" (7.5.1999);
- Building of the Faculty of Arts (7.5.1999);
- Elementary school "Marija Bursac" (31.5.1999);

Novi Sad:
- Elementary schools "Svetozar Markovic - Toza," "Djordje Natosevic,"

"Veljko Vlahovic," "Sangaj" and "Djuro Danicic" and a day-care center "Duga";
- Creches in Visarionova Street and in the Sangaj suburb in Novi Sad;
- Traffic School Center;- Faculty of Philosophy;

Sombor:
- Elementary schools "Ivo Lola Ribar," "A. Mrazovic," "N. Vukicevic" and "Nikola Tesla" in Kljajicevo;

Kula:
- School center;

Sabac:
- Elementary schools "Laza Lazarevic," "Kosta Abrasevic" (11. &18.5.1999.);

Valjevo:
- Agricultural school;

Nis:
- Two secondary schools;
- Faculty for construction and architecture;
- Faculty for machine-technical studies;
- Faculty for electro-technical studies;
- Faculty of Law and
- Faculty of Economics;
- Elementary school "Radoje Domanovic";

Kraljevo:
- Elementary schools in Kraljevo and the villages of Cvetka, Aketa and Ladjevci;

Leskovac:
- Four elementary schools and a Medical high school;

Vladicin Han:
- Elementary school "Branko Radicevic," high school "Jovan Skerlic" and two kindergartens (11.5.1999.);

Kosovo and Metohija:
- Elementary school in Lucani and great number of other educational institutions in Kosovo and Metohija;
- Elementary school in the village of Nabrdje, near Pec (11.5.1999);
- Elementary school in the township of Leposavic (11.5.1999);
- Elementary school "Miladin Popovic" in Pec (21.5.1999);

3) PUBLIC FACILITIES

The bombing of institutions and objects which symbolise the State and national identity was aimed at intimidating and insulting the dignity of the population. NATO aggressors had this in mind when making decisions to target the following facilities:

Belgrade:
· The residence of the President of the FR of Yugoslavia sustained heavy damages (22.4.1999);
· Building of the Federal Ministry of Foreign Affairs in center of the city (30.04. & 7.05.1999);
· Building of the Federal Ministry of Defence in central Belgrade (30.04. & 7.05.1999);
· Building of the Federal Ministry of the Interior in the center of the city (30.04. & 7.05.1999);
· Building of the Government of the Republic of Serbia in central Belgrade (30.04. & 7.05.1999);
· Building of the administrative and judicial authority of the Republic of Serbia in central Belgrade (7.4.1999);
· Building of the Ministry of the Interior of the Republic of Serbia in central Belgrade (30.4. & 7.5.1999);
· Damage to the building of the Institute for Security of the Ministry of the Interior (3.4.1999);
· Four libraries in the Belgrade suburb of Rakovica sustained heavy damage: "Radoje Dakic," "Isidora Sekulic," "Milos Crnjanski" and "Dusan Matic";
· Youth and children center in downtown Belgrade (23.4.1999);
· Youth theatre "Dusko Radovic" in central Belgrade (23.4.1999);

Novi Sad:
· Office building of the Provincial Executive Council of Vojvodina (18.04.1999.);
Sabac:
· Buildings of the Municipal and Republican authorities (22.5.1999);
Nis:
· Post Office (23.4.1999);
Uzice:
· Central Post Office (8.5.1999);
Kragujevac:
· Post Office (9.5.1999);
Kursumlija:
· Office building of the power distribution board "Elektrodistribucija" (20.4.1999);
Aleksinac:
· Heavily damaged administrative buildings of municipal and republican authorities (5.4.1999);
Paracin:
· Refugee camp "7 juli" has sustained heavy damages;

Varvarin:
· Building of the municipal authority (30.5.1999);
Vladicin Han:
· over 50 percent of housing facilities and state buildings have been destroyed or damaged (office buildings of the Republican and Municipal authorities, sport center, supermarkets, department stores, etc) /11.5.1999./;
Kosovo and Metohija:
Pristina: damaged or destroyed administrative buildings of municipal, provincial and republican authorities in downtown Pristina (29.3.1999);
· Destroyed Post Office in Pristina (7.4.1999);
· Destroyed Refugee center in Pristina (7.4.1999);
· Damaged refugee camp "Majino naselje" in Djakovica (21.4.1999);
· Seriously damaged post office in the township of Ponikve (14.5.1999);
· Sport hall in Pec was raised to the ground (2.6.1999);

Tourist facilities and mountain resorts:
· "Tornik" ski resort on Mount Zlatibor (8.4.1999);
· "Divcibare" mountain resort (11.4.1999);
· Hotel "Putnik" on Mount Kopaonik (12.4.1999);
· "Baciste" Hotel on Mount Kopaonik (12.4.1999);
· Hotel "Mineral" in Bogutovacka Banja sustained heavy damages (19.4.1999);
· Hotel "Jugoslavija" in Belgrade, has sustained heavy damages (7.5.1999);
· Hotel "Park" in Pec (19.5.1999):
· Hotel "Plaza" in the town of Varvarin (30.5.1999);

Meteorological stations:
· Heavy damage to Hydro-Meteorological Station Bukulja, near Arandjelovac;
· Meteorological Station on Mount Kopaonik sustained damages (13.4.1999);
· Meteorological station "Palic" near Subotica, was severely damaged (20-30.5.1999);

4) INFRASTRUCTURE:
Belgrade:
· Destruction of power supply transmitters in Belgrade suburbs of Resnik, Zemun Polje, Batajnica, Lestane (26.3.-2.6.1999);
· Damage to the water supply system in Zemun (5.4.1999);
· Damages to the power station 210-110 Beograd 3 and power station 110-35 Beograd 9 (23.4.1999);
· Damage to hydroelectric power station "Nikola Tesla" in the Belgrade suburb Obrenovac (3.- 22.5.1999);
· Damage to power stations Obrenovac, Beograd 8 and Beograd 3 (7.5.1999);
· Damage to the power plant in the Belgrade suburb Obrenovac (3.-23.5.1999);
· Damage to the long-distance power line /Boljevacka suma/ near Obrenovac (25.5.1999);
· Destruction of the power grid system in Lestane, suburb of Belgrade (23.5.-2.6.1999);
· Damage to the city power station (27.5.1999);

Novi Sad:
· Damage to the power plant Rimski Sancevi (23.5.1999);
Sombor:
· Severe damages to the water processing plant (30.05.1999);
Sremska Mitrovica:
· Damage to the water supply system and long-distance power line (24.5.1999);
Backi Petrovac:
· Destruction of the long-distance power line near Backi Petrovac (25.5.1999);
Smederevo:
· Destruction of the electical distribution station (15.5.1999);
Nis:
· Damage to the power grid system (23.5.1999);
Krusevac:
· Damage to the city power plant (12-13.4.1999);
Bogutovac:
· Damage to a power supply transmitter (10.4.1999);
· Telephone lines were cut off (10.4.1999);
Uzice:
· Damage to the postal transmitter station "Telecom" (27.5.1999);
Bajina Basta:
· Damage to the EPS facility (22.5.1999);
Bistrica:
· Damage to the Bistrica hydroelectric power station in Polinje (13.4.1999);
Bor:
· Destruction of the electrical distribution station (15.5.1999);
· Damage to the electrical distribution station within the mining complex Bor (22.5.1999);
Pristina:
· Damage to a electrical distribution station (12.4.1999);
Djakovica:
· Destruction of the long-distance power line near Djakovica (25.5.1999);
Facilities: "Drmno," "Kostolac A" and "Kolubara A"
· Damage to facilities "Drmno," power station Obrenovac, Bajina Basta, Nis and Novi Sad 3 (2.5.1999);
· Damage to distribution facilities "Drmno," power stations Beograd 8, Nis,
Bajina Basta
· distribution facilities and power plant "Kostolac A," as well as distribution facilities and power station of the thermal power plant "Kolubara A" (22.5.1999);
· Damage to distribution facilities "Drmno," power plants Nis 2 and Novi Sad 3 (23.5.1999);
· Damage to the thermo power plant "Kolubara" in the township of Veliki Crljeni (22.5.1999);

III. DESTRUCTION OF CULTURAL AND HISTORIC MONUMENTS AND RELIGIOUS SHRINES

The entire territory of the FR of Yugoslavia, and Kosovo and Metohija in particular, is a treasury of European culture and civilization since ancient times. By violating all international conventions on the protection of cultural and historical heritage and art, NATO destroyed or damaged during its two month long bombing, more than 365 monasteries, churches and other religious shrines, as well as other cultural and historic monuments of exceptional cultural and civilizational value, some under UNESCO protection. During frequent indiscriminate bombings not even cemeteries have been spared.

1) MEDIEVAL MONASTERIES AND RELIGIOUS SHRINES (59):

(a) Monasteries

1. Monastery Rakovica (16th century), Rakovica (24.3.1999);
2. Monastery Gracanica (14th century) under UNESCO protection, Pristina (30.3.-3.5.1999);
3. Patriarchate of Pec (13th century), Pec (31.3.-1.4.1999);
4. Monastery of St. Nicholas (12th century), Kursumlija (1/2.4.1999);
5. Monastery Vrdnik (16th century), Vrdnik (2/3.4.1999):
6. Vojlovica monastery (15th century) near Pancevo (3-12.4.1999);
7. Monastery Novo Hopovo (16th century), Fruska Gora (4/5.4.1999);
8. Monastery of Holy Mother (12th century) at the estuary of the Kosanica in the Toplica municipality of Kursumlija (4.4.1999);
9. Monastery Zociste (14th century), Orahovac (4.4.1999);
10. Monastery Nikolje (15th century), Ovcar (4/5.4.1999);
11. Monastery Zica (13th century) in Zica (7/8.4.1999);
12. Monastery Nova Pavlica (14th century) in Brvenik (7/8.4.1999);
13. Monastery Melentija (15th century), Kopaonik (13/14.4.1999);
14. Monastery Sisatovac (16th century), Fruska Gora (17.4.1999);
15. Monastery Staro Hopovo (16th century), Fruska Gora (17.4.1999);
16. Monastery Holly Trinity (16th century), Ovcar (22.4.1999);
17. Monastery Sretenje (16th century), Ovcar (22.4.1999);
18. Monastery Djurdjevi Stupovi (12th century), Novi Pazar (23.4.1999);
19. Monastery Kovilj (17th century), Kovilj (21.4.1999);
20. Monastery Sopocani (13th century), Novi Pazar (24.4.1999);
21. Monastery Ljubostinja (14th century), Trstenik (30.4.1999);
22. Monastery Draganac (19th century), Gnjilane (2.5.1999);
23. Monastery Decane (14th century), v. Istinic (2.5.1999);

(b) Churches

24. Roman Catholic Church St. Antonio in Djakovica (29.3.1999);
25. Monastery Church of St. Juraj (built in 1714) in Petrovaradin (1.4.1999);
26. Church of Virgin Mary (12th century), Kursumlija (1.4.1999);
27. Vavedenje Church (14th century), Lipljan (1.4.1999);
28. Church of Resurrection of Virgin Mary (15th century), Smederevo (3.4.1999);
29. St. Nicolas Church (16th century), Pec (3.4.1999);
30. Church of St. George (19th century), Smederevo (3/4.4.1999);
31. Church in Jelasnica near Surdulica (4.4.1999):
32. Chapel St. Archangel Gabriel (18th century), Zemun (5.4.1999);

33. Old Orthodox Church St. Stephen (17th century), Sremska Mitrovica (6/7.4.1999);

34. New Orthodox Church St. Stephen (18th century), Sremska Mitrovica (6/7.4.1999);

35. Roman Catholic Church (19th century), Sremska Mitrovica (6/7.4.1999);

36. Stara Pavlica Church (12th century), Brvenik (7.4.1999);

37. Old Church (19th century), Kragujevac (8.4.1999);

38. St. Petka Church (16th century), Klina (14.4.1999);

39. Monastery Church St. Archangel Michael in Rakovica (16.4.1999);

40. Church of St. Archangel Michailo (19th century), Ivanjica (19.4.1999);

41. Church of St. Peter (19th century), Belgrade (23.4.1999);

42. Orthodox Church St. Marco (20th century), Belgrade (23.4.1999);

43. Old Russian Orthodox Church Holly Trinity (20th century), Belgrade (23.4.1999);

44. Church of St. Peter (10th century), Novi Pazar (23.4.1999);

45. St. Nicholas Church (18th century), v. Krcmar, municipality Valjevo (29.4.1999);

46. Church of St. Archangel Mihajilo (19th century), Nis (5.5.1999);

47. St. Marco Church (19th century), Uzice (8.5.1999);

48. Church of St Mihajlo and Gavrilo (19th century), Zablace (10.5.1999);

49. Church of Virgin Mary (19th century), village Cvetke (10.5.1999);

50. St. Jovan Church (19th century), Nis (11.5.1999);

51. Church of St. Peter and Pavle (19th century), Mrcajevci (11.5.1999);

52. Church of St. Ilija (19th century), Pirot (12.5.1999);

53. Church of St. Dimitrije (16th century), Vranje (12.5.1999);

54. Church of St. Nicholas in Gornja Brnjica, near Pristina (25.5.1999);

55. Church of the Holy Mother in Varvarin (30.5.1999);

(c) Cemeteries

56. Orthodox cemetery in Gnjilane (30.3.1999);

57. Orthodox Christian cemetery in Pristina (7.4.· 31.5.1999);

58. Orthodox cemetery in Raska (11.5.1999);

59. Orthodox cemetery in Kosovska Vitina (29.5.1999);

2) CULTURAL-HISTORICAL MONUMENTS AND MUSEUMS (15):

1. Severe damage to the roof structure of the Fortress of Petrovaradin (1.4.1999);

2. Destroyed archives housed in one of the Government buildings in Belgrade (3.4.1999);

3. Heavy damage to "Tabacki bridge," four centuries old, in Djakovica (5.4.1999);

4. Substantial damage to the building in Stara Carsija (Old street) in Djakovica (5.4.1999);

5. Monuments destroyed in Bogutovac (8.4.1999);

6. "Kadinjaca" memorial complex (8.4.1999);

7. Memorial complex in Gucevo (Loznica);

8. Memorial complex "Sumarice" in Kragujevac;

9. Vojvodina Museum in Novi Sad;

10. Old Military Barracks in Kragujevac · under the protection of the State (16.4.1999);

11. Memorial complex Crveni Krst in Nis (21.4.1999);

12. Heavy damages to the "Stara Carsija" (Old street) in Pec (22.5.1999);

13. Memorial complex to the heroes of the battle of Kosovo, Gazimestan (24.5.1999);

14. Building of the Ethnographic museum in Belgrade (31.5.1999);

15. Medieval fortress "Markovo Kale" built in the 13th century, in Vranje (1.6.1999);

IV. MEDIA AND TELECOMMUNICATIONS

The destruction of more than ten private radio and television stations and over 50 TV transmitters and relay stations represents the most brutal aggression against freedom of speech and thought, and is a disgrace at the threshold of a third millennium. The production center of the Radio and Television of Serbia, in Belgrade, was bombed at the time of live broadcasting (23.4.1999) when 16 employees were brutally killed while 19 sustained severe injuries. The building of the RTV of Novi Sad which was bombed on several occasions was raised to the ground. Two times in six days the studios and transmitters located at the business center "Usce," which housed TV stations: BK TV, Pink, Kosava and SOS Channel, as well as several other radio stations, were bombed. The building was totally demolished. The aim of these crimes is more than obvious: suppression of the right to a different opinion and suppression of truth. Clearly, the intention of NATO aggressors was to prevent the world public from learning about the extent of their crimes and to impose their perception and interpretation of the aggression.

The list of destroyed facilities:

1) TELEVISION AND RADIO STATIONS

1. Business center "Usce" in Belgrade housing RTV Kosava, RTV Pink, SOS channel, TV BK and Radio S· Belgrade (21 & 27.4.1999);

2. Radio Television of Serbia building in Belgrade (23.4.1999);

3. Radio Television of Serbia building in Novi Sad (4-30.5.1999);

4. Facilities of the Radio Television Novi Sad in Sremska Kamenica (13.5.1999);

5. Severely damaged the TV RTS studio in Pristina;

2) TV TRANSMITTERS (44):

1. Jastrebac· Prokuplje (25.3.-26.5.1999;

2. Gucevo· Loznica (25-27.4.1999);

3. Cot· Fruska Gora (5-11.4.1999);

4. Grmija· Pristina (6.4.-10.5.1999);

5. Bogutovac· Pristina (29.4.1999);

6. TV transmitter on Mt Goles· Pristina (9.4.-13.5.1999);

7. Mokra Gora· Kosovska Mitrovica (17/18.4.1999);

8. Kutlovac· Stari Trg (4.4.-16.5.1999);

9. "Cigota"· Uzice (25.3.1999);

10. "Tornik"· Uzice (25.3.-15.4.1999);

11. Transmitter on Crni Vrh· Stara Planina (26.5.-3.6.1999);

12. Satellite station "Jugoslavija" · Prilike (13-30.4.1999);

13. TV masts and transmitters· Novi Sad (21.4.-11.5.1999);

14. TV transmitter on Mt Ovcar· Cacak (15.4.-11.5.1999);

15. TV transmitter in Kijevo· Belgrade (23-29.4.1999);

16. TV transmitter on Mt Cer (16.4.-8.5.1999);

17. Relay on Mt Jagodnja· Krupanj (15.4.1999);

18. TV transmitter "Iriski Venac"· Fruska Gora (21.4.-11.5.1999);

19. TV relay on Mt. Bukulja (25.3.1999);

20. Transmitter in Gazimestan· Pristina (13.4.1999);

21. RTV transmitter in Krnjaca· Belgrade (23-29.4.1999);

22. RTV transmitter on Mt. Gobelj on Mount Kopaonik (3.6.1999);

23. RTV transmitter on top of the business center "Usce" used by RTV Kosava, RTV Pink, SOS channel, TV BK and Radio S· Belgrade (21.& 27.4.1999);

24. RTV transmitter and scenic tower on Mount Avala (30.04.1999);

25. RTV transmitters (two) "Vrsacki breg"· Vrsac (30.04-11.5.1999);

26. RTV transmitter "Crveno selo"·· Subotica (10.5.1999);

27. RTV transmitter in Raska (19.5.1999);

28. RTV transmitter near Srbobran (20.5. & 3.6.1999);

29. Transmitter "Godominsko polje" of the Radio Smederevo (21.5.1999);

30. RTV transmitter "Prevovac" near Kursumlija (23.5.1999);

31. RTV transmitter and postal transmitter "Zabucje" · Bucje near Uzice (25.5.1999);

32. Transmission center of Radio Belgrade in the village of Zvecka, near Obrenovac (25-31.5.1999);

33. Radio transmitter of Radio Kragujevac· Kragujevac (29.5.1999);

34. RTV transmitter "Plackovica" near Vranje (29.5.1999);

35. RTV transmitter "Brdo Kozarica" near Dimitrovgrad (29.5.-3.6.1999);

36. RTV transmitter of Radio TV Serbia and RTV transmitter of Radio TV Priboj near the town of Priboj (29.5.1999);

37. RTV transmitters "Vucjamo" and "Brdo Jabuka" near the town of Leposavic (29.5.1999);

38. "Radio Yugoslavia" center in Stublina, near Obrenovac (30.5.1999);

39. RTV transmitter "Besna Kobila" near the town of Vranje (31.5.-3.6.1999);

40. RTV transmitter "Branko Brdo" near the town of Zubin Potok (31.5.1999);

41. RTV transmitter "Banjska" near the town of Zvecan (1.6.1999);

42. RTV transmitter "Nemic Brdo" near the town of Ljubovija (2.6.1999);

43. RTV transmitter "Kotelnik" near the town of Kraljevo (2.6.1999);

44. RTV transmitter "Rudnik" near the town of Gornji Milanovac (3.6.1999);

V. TRAFFIC AND COMMUNICATION LINKS

The road and railway network of the FR of Yugoslavia, especially road and rail bridges suffered extensive destruction and damage which will necessitate substantial investments for their reconstruction or repair. On the pretext of "neutralizing the military power of the Federal Republic of Yugoslavia," the NATO aggressor started systematic destruction of Yugoslav road and rail traffic routes: bridges, major and local roads, airports, railway tracks, railway and bus stations. Great number of civilians lost their lives in NATO attacks on passenger trains (e.g. 55 passengers in the Grdelicka gorge on 12 April) and buses (e.g. 65 passengers on a road bridge near Luzani on 1 May 1999). All demolished facilities were part of costly capital investments, into which the resources and the efforts of several generations of Yugoslav citizens were pooled. All the facilities are a strategic part of the European traffic infrastructure, and some of them are of historical and cultural importance (e.g. "The Wailing Bridge" in Novi Sad, on which the Fascists killed several thousand Jews in the Second World War). By the destruction of the bridges on the Danube river, including those at the strategic European E-75 corridor, the aggressors have blocked the entire river navigation at this traffic artery of the greatest importance for European economy and the shortest link between the Northern and Mediterranean sea (The Rhein-Mein-Danube route).

The targets of attacks were communication links such as:

1) BRIDGES (DESTROYED OR DAMAGED):
River Danube

1. The road bridge Varadin Bridge over the Danube, Novi Sad (1.4.1999);

2. The road bridge "Sloboda" (Freedom) over the Danube, Novi Sad (3.4.1999);

3. The road/railway bridge "Zezeljov" on the Danube, Novi Sad (5-26.4.1999);

4. The road bridge "Mladost" (Youth) over the Danube, connecting Backa Palanka with Ilok (3.4.1999);

5. The new railway/road bridge over the Danube connecting Bogojevo and Erdut (5.4.1999);

6. The road bridge on the Danube, between Smederevo and Kovin (16.4.1999);

7. The road bridge over the Danube along the Beograd-Novi Sad road, near Beska, Indjija municipality (21.4.1999);

Vrbas municipality

8. The old road bridge on the water channel in Vrbas, on the Vrbas-Srbobran and Vrbas-Feketic road (13.5.1999);

Vatin township

9. The railway bridge near the township of Vatin, on the railway line Belgrade-Timisoara (7.5.1999);

River Begej

10. The road bridge on the river Begej, near the township of Banatski Dvor· municipality Zitiste (20.5.1999);

Belgrade municipality

11. The railway bridge on the river Sava near Ostruznica (21, 23.4.1999);

River Nisava· Nis municipality

12. The bridge over the river Nisava, town of Nis (8.5.1999);

13. The road bridge on the highway Belgrade-Nis, near Mijatovac (8.-14.5.1999);

14. The road bridge on the Belgrade-Skopje highway, near the village Popovac, municipality Nis (13 & 29.5.1999);

15. The road bridge on the river Jasenica, on the Beograd· Nis highway near the township Orasja, municipality Velika Plana (21 25.5.1999);

16. The railway bridge on the railway line Nis-Sofia, near the town of Bela Palanka (29.5.1999);

17. The railway bridge on the river Nisava, on the railway line between Bela Palanka· Pirot (31.5.1999);

River Lugomir

18. The road bridge over the river Lugomir, on the Belgrade· Nis highway, near Jagodina (14.5.1999);

Kraljevo municipality

19. The railway bridge near the village of Rudnica in the vicinity of Raska, on the Kraljevo· Kosovo Polje railway line (4.4.1999);

20. The railway bridge on the Kraljevo · Raska railway line, near Kraljevo (23.4.1999);

21. The railway bridge on the river Lopatnica, v. Bogutovac, municipality Kraljevo (8.5.1999);

Usce municipality

22. The "Lozno" railway bridge near Usce (5.4.1999);

23. The road bridge on the road leading to Brvenik, near Usce (5.4.1999);

24. The road bridge over the river Brvenica, in Brvenik, on the regional road Kraljevo· Raska (17.5.1999);

Kursumlija municipality

25. The road bridge along the Nis-Pristina primary road, near Kursumlija (5.4.1999);

26. The road bridge over the Kosanica river near Kursumlija (13.4.1999);

27. The road bridge on the Prokuplje-Pristina road, village of Pepeljovac, municipality Kursumlija (14.4.1999);

Krusevac municipality

28. The old bridge on the river Rasina near the town of Krusevac (12-13.4.1999);

29. The new bridge on the river Rasina near the town of Krusevac (12-13.4.1999);

30. The road bridge on the regional road Krusevac-Razanj, near the village of Djunis (1.5.1999);

River Zapadna Morava

31. The Krusevac-Pojate road bridge on the river Zapadna Morava, near the village of Jasika (13.4.1999);

32. The road bridge on the river Zapadna Morava, in the town of Trstenik, regional road Trstenik· Velika Drenova (30.4.1999.);

River Juzna Morava

33. The Grdelicka gorge railway bridge, on the river Juzna Morava (12.4.1999);

34. "Sarajevo" Grdelica gorge road bridge, on the river Juzna Morava (12.4.-14.5.1999);

35. The road bridge near Vladicin Han, on the river Juzna Morava (11.5.1999);

River Velika Morava

36. The road bridge on the river Velika Morava, in the town of Varvarin (30.5.1999);

37. The road bridge on the river Toplica, on the Nis-Pristina road near the town of Kursumlija (14. and 19.4. & 11.5.1999);

38. The railway bridge over the river Toplica, railway line Nis-Prokuplje-Pristina, near the village of Podina, municipality of Zitoradja (1-14.4.1999);

39. The bridge on the Konjsko-Toplicane road over the Sitnica river, municipality Lipljan (14.5.1999);

River Kosanica

40. The railway bridge on the river Kosanica, village Rudari, municipality Kursumlija, railway line Prokuplje· Pristina (18.04. & 1.5.1999.);

41. The road bridge on the river Kosanica, at the village of Selo Visoko (18. & 30. 04.1999.);

Donja Bistrica

42. The railway bridge on the river Lim, between Priboj and Prijepolje, near the hydroelectric power station "Bistrica" (15.4.1999);

43. The bridge "Raskrsnica" near Donja Bistrica, on the route Priboj-Prijepolje-Nova Varos (20.4.1999);

Biljanovac municipality

44. The bridge over the railway track on the regional road Biljanovac · Mt. Kopaonik (29.4.1999);

45. The new road bridge in Biljanovac, village Zizovci (12.5.1999);

Nova Varos municipality

46. The road bridge "Uzicki" on the river Uvac, municipality Kokin Brod, primary road Uzice· Nova Varos (30.4.1999.)

47. The road bridge over the river Lim, at the village of Kucin, on the road Prijepolje-Nova Varos (1.5.1999);

48. The road bridge on the river Bistrica, regional road Nova Varos· Priboj, municipality Nova Varos (3.5.1999);

River Ibar

49. The road bridge "Lucice" over the Ibar river, Biljanovac municipality (4-13.4.1999);

50. The railway bridge on the river Ibar, v. Tuslici, municipality Rudnici (4.4.1999);

51. The road bridge on the river Ibar, at the village of Brvenik, linking Korlace and Raska (15.04.1999.);

52. The railway bridge on the river Ibar, in the village Bojiste (30.04.1999.)

Pristina municipality

53. The road bridge along the Magura· Belacevac road, 15 kilometres from Pristina (5.4.1999);

54. The road bridge on the river Lab, primary road Kosovska Mitrovica-Pristina, village Babin Most (27.4.1999.);

River Jablanica

55. The road bridge "Cekavacki" on the river Jablanica, near Lebane, on the regional road Leskovac· Pristina (27.5.1999);

Kosovska Mitrovica municipality

56. The road bridge over the Vrbicka river near Jezgrovici, on the road Ribarice-Kosovka Mitrovica (4.4.1999);

57. The road bridge near Zubin Potok, on the Kosovska Mitrovica – Ribarice road (5.4.1999);

58. The railway bridge near the village of Medari (1.5.1999);

59. The bridge over the river Vrapcevska Reka near the village of Ribarice, from the direction of Kosovska Mitrovica (12.5.1999);

River Istocka

60. The road bridge on the local Pec· Kosovska Mitrovica road over the Istocka river, near Djurakovac (17.5.1999);

Urosevac municipality

61. The bridge on the local road Gornje Nerodimlje-Jezerce, municipality Urosevac (12.5.1999);

2) RAILWAY TRACKS AND STATIONS:

(a) Railway tracks

Interstate routes:

1. The Belgrade· Thessaloniki rail, due to the destruction of the bridge over the river Zapadna Morava in the Grdelicka gorge (12.4.1999);

2. Railway track Belgrade· Bucharest, due to the destruction of the bridge near Vatin (7.05.1999);

3. Railway track Bogojevo· Vukovar, due to the destruction of the bridge on the river Danube (5.4.1999);

4. Railway track Nis· Sofia, due to the destruction of the railway bridge near the town of Bela Palanka (29.5.1999);

Primary routes:

5. The Belgrade· Bar rail, due to the destruction of the railway track near the village of Strbce and destruction of the bridge on the river Lim, between Priboj and Prijepolje (3.4.1999.);

6. The Nis· Pristina rail, due to the destruction of the bridge over the river Toplica at the village Podina, municipality of Zitoradja (1-14.4.1999);

7. The Kraljevo· Kosovo Polje rail, due to the destruction of the bridge near the village of Rudnica in the vicinity of Raska (4.4.1999);

8. The railway line and tunnel Prokuplje· Kosovo Polje, near Merdare, municipality Kursumlija (11.4.1999);

9. The railway line Prokuplje· Pristina, due to the destruction of the bridge on the river Kosanica at the village of Rudari, municipality Kursumlija (18.04. & 1.5.1999.);

Local routes:

10. Railway track and overpass (Josinacka Banja) near the town of Biljanovac (15.4.1999.);

11. Railway track on the Kosovska Mitrovica-Leposavic-Raska line, due to damages to the railway bridge at the village of Biljanovac (15.4.1999);

12. Railway track Uzice-Priboj, due to the destruction of the bridge over the river Lim (15.4.1999);

13. The Kursumlija· Prokuplje rail, damaged near the village of Pepeljevac;

14. The Kraljevo· Raska rail, due to the destruction of a bridge near Kraljevo (23.4.1999);

15. Railway track Kursumlija· Podujevo, due to damages on the railway bridge at Kursumlija;

16. Railway track Kraljevo· Kragujevac, due to damages to the section of the track near the village of Vitanovac;

17. Railway track Cacak· Kraljevo, damaged near Kraljevo (17.5.1999.);

18. Railway track Leskovac-Predejane;

19. "Sarpelj" tunnel, near Jerinje village, 15 km north of Leposavic towards Raska, was destroyed;

(b) Railway stations
1. Railway station in the township Lukicevo, near Zrenjanin (25.5.1999);
2. Railway station in Kraljevo· Bogutovac;
3. Railway station in Kosovo Polje;
4. Railway station in the town of Biljanovac;
5. The central railway station in Sabac (24.5.1999);

3) ROADS, BUS STATIONS AND TRANSPORT COMPANIES:
(a) Roads
Interstate routes:
1. The Belgrade-Novi Sad highway, section of the interstate route to Budapest (E-75), due to the destruction of the bridge "Mladost" (Youth) over the river Danube, connecting Backa Palanka with Ilok (3.4.1999);
2. The Bogojevo-Erdut road due to the destruction of the bridge on the river Danube (5.4.1999);
3. The primary road Zrenjanin-Srpska Crnja, section of the (M-7) interstate route to Romania, due to severe damages on the bridge over the river Stari Begej (20.5.1999);
4. Belgrade-Zagreb interstate highway (E-70), damaged near the town of Stari Banovci;
5. The Belgrade-Nis highway, section of the interstate route (E-75) to Macedonia and further to Greece, due to the destruction of the bridge over the river Jasenica near the town of Velika Plana (21-25.5.1999);
Primary roads:
6. The Kosovska Mitrovica-Ribarici section of the Adriatic highway, due to the destruction of the bridge over the Vrbicka river (4.4.1999.);
7. The primary road Prizren-Djakovica, damaged near the village Mala Krupa (14.4.1999.);
8. The road Smederevo-Kovin, due to the destruction of the bridge over the river Danube near Kovin 16.4.1999);
9. Kraljevo-Raska primary road damaged near the village Bogutovac, municipality Kraljevo (24.4.1999.);
10. Ibarska primary road, due to the destruction of four bridges near the towns of Biljanovac and Brvenik, as well as damages to entire sections on the Pozega-Cacak road and the Lipovica-Barajevo road (4.4.-28.5.1999);
11. The primary road Nis-Pristina due to severe damages on the bridge on the river Toplica, near the town of Kursumlija and destruction of an 8 kilometre long section of the road between Kursumlija and Rudare (14,19.4. & 11.5.1999);
Regional and local roads:
12. The road Ribarice-Kosovka Mitrovica, due to the destruction of the bridge over the Vrbicka river near Jezgrovic (4.4.1999);
13. The Leskovac-Vladicin Han road, due to the destruction of the bridge over the river Zapadna Morava at the entrance of the Grdelicka gorge (12.4.-14.5.1999);

14. The Krusevac-Pojate road (E-761), due to the destruction of the bridge on the river Rasina (12-13.4.1999.);

15. The Krusevac-Kragujevac road, due to the destruction of the bridge on the river Zapadna Morava, in the village of Jasika (13.4.1999.);

16. The Kursumlija-Podujevo road, due to the destruction of the bridge over the river Toplica (14,19.4. & 11.5.1999) and the bridge over the river Kosanica (18. & 30.04.1999.);

17. Regional road Priboj-Prijepolje-Nova Varos, due to damages on the bridge "Raskrsnica" near Donja Bistrica (20.4.1999);

18. The Srbobran-Sombor road, due to damages on the bridge near the town of Sombor;

19. The Pristina-Kosovska Mitrovica road, due to the destruction of the bridge over the river Lab near the village Babin Most (27.4.1999.);

20. The primary road Uzice-Nova Varos, due to the destruction of the bridge "Uzicki" on the river Uvac, municipality Kokin Brod (30.4.1999.);

21. The Krusevac-Razanj road, due to damages on the bridge near the village of Djunis (1.5.1999);

22. The Podujevo-Pristina road, due to damages on the bridge near Luzane (1.5.1999);

23. The regional road Murino-Cakor-Pec, due to the destruction of the bridge over the river Lim, near the township of Murino (1.5.1999);

24. The regional road Nova Varos-Priboj, due to the destruction of the bridge on the river Bistrica, municipality Nova Varos (3.5.1999);

25. The road Gornje Nerodimlje-Jezerce, due to the destruction of the bridge near Gornje Nerodimlje, municipality Urosevac (12.5.1999);

26. The Vrbas-Srbobran and Vrbas-Feketic road, due to the destruction of the old road bridge on the water channel in Vrbas (13.5.1999)

27. The Trupala-Popovac road, due to the destruction of the bridge on the river Nisava and the overpass near the town of Trupala (13.5.1999);

28. The Konjsko-Toplicane road, due to the destruction of the bridge over the Sitnica river, municipality Lipljan (14.5.1999);

29. The regional road Pristina-Pec, due to the destruction of the bridge over the river Beli Drim, near the township of Klina;

30. The local road Lapusnik-Kijevo, due to the destruction of a bridge near the village Djurdjica;

31. The Slatina-Zajecar-Negotin road, due to damages of the road surface near the town of Bor;

32. The local road Pec-Kosovska Mitrovica, due to the destruction of the bridge over the Istocka river, near Djurakovac (17.5.1999);

33. The regional road Leskovac-Lebane-Pristina, due to the destruction of the bridge on the river Jablanica, near the town of Cenovac (27.5.1999);

34. The Varvarin-Cicevac road, due to the destruction of the bridge over the river Velika Morava, near the town of Varvarin (30.5.1999);

(b) Bus stations and transport companies

1. "Jedinstvo" bus station in Vranje sustained extensive damage;
2. "Kosmet Prevoz" transporter in Gnjilane· hangar full of new buses has been destroyed (26.3.-19.5.1999);
3. Bus station in Pristina;
4. Road maintenance company "Magistrala" in Pristina;
5. The Nis Central Bus Station;
6. The Pristina Bus Station;
7. The "Jedinstvo" bus station in Vranje (18.5.1999);

4) AIRPORTS (14):

· Belgrade: "Batajnica" and "Surcin";
· Padinska Skela: "Lisicji Jarak" sports and agricultural airfield;
· Sombor: agricultural and sports airfield;
· Nis: city airport;
· Uzice: "Ponikve";
· Kraljevo: "Ladjevci" airport near Kraljevo;
· Leskovac: sports airfield in the v.Vinarce, municipality Leskovac;
· Novi Pazar: agricultural airfield in the village of Dubinje, municipality Novi Pazar;
· Pristina: "Slatina";
· Urosevac: agricultural airfield in village of Grlica, municipality Urosevac;
· Djakovica: agricultural airfield in the village of Jug Bunar, municipality Djakovica;
· Podgorica: "Golubovac";

VI. INDUSTRIAL, COMMERCIAL AND AGRICULTURAL FACILITIES

Great material damage was made in NATO air strikes against industrial, commercial and agricultural facilities throughout the territory of the Federal Republic of Yugoslavia. Great number of factories and entire industrial branches of vital importance for the population have been destroyed. A drastic example is the destruction of the Yugoslav petrochemical industry which has caused serious consequences on the environment. Industrial centers in Pristina, Novi Sad, Belgrade, Nis, Pancevo, Kragujevac, Krusevac, etc. have been systematically assaulted.

1) INDUSTRY:
Belgrade:

1 "Galenika" drug factory (12.4.1999.);
2. "Frikom" company (15.5.1999);
3. Industrial complex "Dvadeset Prvi Maj" in Rakovica (24.3.-3.5.1999);
4. Factory "Jugostroj" in Rakovica (24.4.-3.5.1999);
5. "Beogradska pekarska industrija" (bakery) corporation (24.3.-3.5.1999);
6. "Rekord" corporation (24.3.-3.5.1999);
7. "DMB" company (24.3.-3.5.1999);
8. "Minel" company (24.3.-3.5.1999);

9. Machine building plant "Industrija Motora Rakovica" in Rakovica (24.4.-3.5.1999);

10. Factory "Frigostroj" in Rakovica (24.4.-3.5.1999);

11. Construction company "Rakovica" (24.3.-3.5.1999);

12. "Udarnik promet" (24.3.-3.5.1999);

13. Holding company "Agropromet" · Krusevac, branch in Belgrade (27.4.1999);

14. Juice factory "Dunav grad" (29.4.1999);

15. "Jugoimport SDPR" (27.5.1999);

Pancevo:

16. "Lola Utva" agricultural aircraft factory (24-29.5.1999);

Smederevo:

17. Transport company Beograd, branch in Smederevo (29.4.1999)

18. "Sartid 1913" steel concern (15.5.1999);

19. Head office building "Zmaj" company (22.5.1999);

Novi Sad:

20. "Ciklonizacija" (28.3.1999);

21. "Tehnogas" (28.3.1999);

22. "Novograp" (28.3.1999);

23. "Gumins" (28.3.1999);

24. "Albus" (28.3.1999);

25. "Petar Drapsin" (28.3.1999);

26. Brewery Apatin, branch in Novi Sad (28.3.1999);

27. "Prevodnica" firm (28.3.1999);

28. "Niva" company (28.3.1999);

29. "Motins" (7.4.1999);

30. "Izolacija" (7.4.1999);

31. "Novokabel" (7.4.1999);

32. Trade company "Bazar" (7.4.1999);

33. "Zvezda" company (20-21.4.1999);

34. "Jugosped" company (20-21.4.1999);

35. "Stampa komerc" (20-21.4.1999);

Sremska Mitrovica:

36. "Dijana" shoe factory;

Kula:

37. "Istra" fittings factory (24.3.1999);

Bogojevo:

38. The port of Bogojevo;

Sabac:

39. Joint company "Mikromotor" (10.5.1999);

40. Storage house of "Agrocop" (22.5.1999);

Leskovac:

41. "Zdravlje" pharmaceutical plant (25.3.1999);

Aleksinac:

42. "Agrokolonijal" firm (5.4.1999);

43. "Empa" company (5.4.1999);

Cacak:

44. "Sloboda" home electrical appliances factory (26.3.-13.4.1999);
45. Thermo-technical appliances plant "Cer" (1-17.5.1999);
46. Technical and repair factory (1-15.5.1999);
47. "Hidrogradnja" company (1-10.5.1999);
48. Clothing factory "1. oktobar" (11.5.1999);

Nis:
49. "Din" tobacco factory (5.4.-12.5.1999);
50. "Elektronska industrija" factory;
51. "Jastrebac" machine industry;
52. "Masinska industrija" machine plant;
53. Facilities of the "Beograd" rail company;
54. Construction material depot "Ogrev Invest";
55. General merchandise depot "Kopaonik" (19.4.1999);
56. Production line of the tobacco factory "Nis" (5.4.-12.5.1999);
57. "Elektrotehna" warehouse;
58. Food storage facility "Fidelinka";
59. Facilities of the machine industry (24.4.1999);
60. Office building of the company "So Produkt" (24.4.1999);
61. "Proplanak" (24.4.1999);
62. "Elektro mang" company (24.4.1999);
63. "Elektro mehanika" company (24.4.1999);
64. "Frank komerc" firm (24.4.1999);
65. "Nis auto" (25.4.1999);
66. Holding company "Nana" (25.4.1999);
67. Holding company "Uzor" (25.4.1999);
68. "Birostroj" (25.4.1999);
69. "Agropromet" (25.4.1999);
70. Facilities of the pharmaceutical company "Velafarm";
71. "Feroks" company (12.5.1999);
72. "Nis elektro" (12.5.1999);

Kragujevac:
73. "Zastava" car factory, razed to the ground (9-12.4.1999);
Krusevac:
74. "14 Oktobar" machine factory (12 & 15.4.1999);
75. "Trayal" tire factory (14.5.1999);
Kursumlija:
76. Production line of the metal factory "Metalac" (20.4.1999);
Valjevo:
77. "Krusik" holding corporation (14.4.-11.5.1999);
Pozega:
78. "Prvi partizan· Lola Gama" factory (18.4.1999);
Jagodina:
79. "Juhor" meat processing plant (15.5.1999);
Vranje:
80. "Div" cigarette factory (2 & 5.4.1999);
81. "Nova Jugoslavija" printers (5.4.1999);
82. Furniture factory "Simpo";

83. Textile industry "Jumko";
Raska:
84. Wood-processing complex "27. November";
Novi Pazar:
85. "Polet" company (24.4.1999);
86. Holding company "Jugotrans" (24.4.1999);
87. Holding company "Vojin Pavlovic" (24.4.1999);
Kosijeric:
88. Public enterprise "Srbija Sume" (12.5.1999);
Lucani:
89. "Milan Blagojevic" chemical plant (5.4.-25.4.1999);
Klina:
90. "Volujak" mine (19.4.1999);
Pristina:
91. Plastics factory "Plastika" (25.3.-14.4.1999);
92. Cotton yarn factory;
93. Shock-absorber factory;
94. Surface coal mine "Belacevac" (11.4.-4.5.1999);
95. "Magistrala" company (12.4.1999);
96. Strip mine "Dobro Selo" in Obilic (4.5.1999);
Pec:
97. Facilities of the Pec Brewery (21.5.1999);
98. Facilities of the automobile spare parts plant "Zastava-Ramiz Sadiku" (21.5. & 2.6.1999);
99. Construction company "Ramiz Sadiku" (6.4.1999);
100. Facilities of the wood processing plant (21.5.1999);
101. Vehicle park of the transport company "Sloga prevoz" (21.5.1999);
Prizren:
102. Cement plant "Betonjerka" (6.4.1999);
103. Private firm "Limit-Duga" (8.4.1999);
104. "Star· proizvodi" company (2.5.1999);
105. "Kosovo vino" winery (6-12.5.1999);
106. "Famina· Trepca" State enterprise (13.5.1999);
107. "Printeks" company (13.5.1999);
Urosevac:
108. Tubes factory (28.3: 24.5.1999);
109. "Silkapora" factory (15.5.1999);
110. "Metohija vino" winery (19.5.1999);
Gnjilane:
111. "Binacka Morava" hydro construction company (10.4.-2.5.1999);
112. Cigarette factory (10.4.2.5.1999);
113. Battery factory (10.4.-2.5.1999);
Glogovac:
114. Plant Feronikl (29-30.04.1999);
Lipljan:
115. Plant Radioton (6.05.1999.);

Lebane:
116. "Jedinstvo company" (14.4.1999);
117. "Vocarstvo" unit (14.4.1999);
Djakovica:
118. Over 250 commercial and craft shops, predominately privately owned were destroyed (24.3.-3.6.1999);
Vucitrn:
119. Construction materials plant "Miloje Zakic" (28-29.5.1999);
Bujanovac:
120. "Integral" brick plant (13.5.1999);
Podujevo:
121. "Ciglana" brick plant (14.5.1999);

2) REFINERIES AND WAREHOUSES

The destruction of petrochemical installations and warehouses in Pancevo, Novi Sad, Sombor, Baric and elsewhere, has caused wide-spread contamination of soil and air, as well as significant adverse effects on the health of the population of the FR of Yugoslavia. Other countries of the region were also endangered for a longer or shorter period time and it was pure luck that an environmental catastrophe was not provoked, which could have had wide-spread effects on the entire European continent.

Belgrade:
1. Fuel storage in Lipovica, near Belgrade, which caused a great fire in the Lipovica forest (26.3.1999);
2. "Beopetrol" storage (4.4.1999);
3. Fuel storage of the boiler plant in Novi Beograd (4.4.1999);
4. Chemical plant "Prva Iskra" in Baric, near Belgrade· destruction of the production line (19.4 & 10.5.1999);
5. "Jugopetrol" pump station and storage facilities near Belgrade (16.5.1999);
6. "Jugopetrol" storage facilities in the Belgrade suburb Cukarica (18. & 20.5.1999.)
Pancevo:
7. Oil Refinery· totally demolished (4-7.6.1999);
8. Petrochemical industry "DP HIP PETROHEMIJA"· totally demolished (14-15.4.1999);
9. Fertilizer plant "DP HIP AZOTARA"· totally destroyed (14-15.4.1999);
Novi Sad:
10. Thermo electric power station/boiler plant (5.4.1999);
11. Oil Refinery (5.4.-07.6.1999);
Sombor:
12. Fuel storage "Naftagas promet" which is located 10 km from Sombor (5.4.· 20.5.1999);
13. "Naftagas" warehouse between Conoplje and Kljaicevo (6.4.-23.5.1999);
14. "Jugopetrol" storage (7.4.-24.5.1999);
Bogutovac:
15. "Beopetrol" storage (4.4.-25.5.1999);

Smederevo:
16. "Jugopetrol" installations (4.4.-31.5.1999);
17. "Jugopetrol" storage facilities in the township of Godominsko polje, municipality Smederevo (17.-22.5.1999);
Nis:
18. "Jugopetrol" storage facilities (11.5.1999);
Kragujevac:
19. Fuel depot in Gruza, near Kragujevac;
Bor:
20. "Jugopetrol" storage facilities (15.-27.5.1999);
Pristina:
21. "Beopetrol" fuel storage (7.4.1999);
22. Jugopetrol warehouse (12.4.1999);
23. Jugopetrol petrol station (13.4.1999);

3) AGRICULTURE:
Several thousand hectares of fertile land, many rivers, lakes and underground waters have been polluted due to the spillage of highly toxic petro-chemical substances which will, certainly, have long lasting effects on the health of the entire population of the FR of Yugoslavia.
Belgrade:
1. Agricultural complex "7. juli" (2.5.1999);
2. Agricultural complex PKB Corporation (15.5.1999);
Novi Sad:
3. Orchard institute (6.4.1999);
4. Agricultural complex "Petefi" (28.4.1999);
Indjija:
5. Agricultural complex "Agrounija" (1.5.1999);
Backi Petrovac:
6. Celarevo farm (21.4.1999);
7. "Podunavlje" agricultural and industrial complex (21.4.1999);
Subotica:
8. Agricultural complex (10.5.1999);
Nis:
9. Agricultural and industrial complex "Becej" (25.4.1999);
Kula:
10. Agricultural Complex "Djuro Strugar" (20.5.-3.6.1999);
Titel:
11. "Titel" agricultural complex (20.4.1999);
Sabac:
12. Warehouses of the agricultural complex "Agrocoop" (22.5.1999);
Kursumlija:
13. PIK " Despotovac:
14. Forestry Kopaonik";
Complex "Juzni Kucaj" (3.6.1999);
Boljevac:
15. Pig farm "Ekohrana" (8.6.1999);

Cuprija:
16. Agricultural farm "Dobricevo" (25.· 27.5.1999);
Dolac:
17. Agricultural Complex "Malizgan";
Ponosevac:
18. Pig breading farm (15.5.1999);
Sjenica:
19. Agricultural and food-processing plant and a cow-breeding farm with 220 milk cows "Pester" (6-8.4.1999);
Kosovo and Metohija:
20. Agricultural complex "Dubrava" in Pristina (30.5.1999);
21. Agricultural and industrial complex "Proges" in Prizren (8.4.1999);
22. Agricultural farm "Stocarstvo" in Prizren (2.6.1999);
23. Chicken farm "Juko" in Djakovica (12.4.1999);
24. Agricultural complex in Djakovica (4.5.1999);
25. PIK "Mladost" in Gnjilane (26.3. & 30.4.1999);
26. Chicken farm in Gnjilane (9.5.1999);
27. "Sumsko gazdinstvo" forest farm in Suva Reka (19.4.1999);
28. Agricultural Complex in the village of Svetlje housing refugees (11.5.1999);

VII. BOMBING OF DIPLOMATIC AND CONSULAR MISSIONS

The Embassy of the Peoples's Republic of China and the Chinese Ambassador's residence were bombed by NATO aircraft in the nights of 7-8 May. Three Chinese journalists died and eight other Embassy staff were seriously or lightly injured. The Embassy building and the Ambassador's residence, property of the PR of China, sustained heavy damages so that they cannot be used. During the bombing of central Belgrade in early May and in the period from 18 to 20 May 1999,
19 diplomatic missions, Embassies or residences suffered damages:
· Angolan Embassy;
· Royal Danish Embassy;
· Residence of the Egyptian Ambassador;
· Residence of the Indian Ambassador;
· Iraqi Embassy;
· Residence of the Iranian Ambassador;
· Residence of the Israeli Ambassador;
· Italian Embassy and the residence of the Italian Ambassador;
· Canadian Embassy;
· Residence of the Libyan Ambassador;
· Residence of the Hungarian Ambassador;
· Residence of the Norwegian Ambassador;
· Pakistan Embassy;
· Residence of the Polish Ambassador;
· Residence of the Syrian Ambassador;
· Residence of the Spanish Ambassador;
· Residence of the Swiss Ambassador;
· Residence of the Swedish Ambassador;
· Zimbabwean Embassy.

A

Abu-Jamal, Mumia, 82, 130-131
Adriatic Sea, 10, 47, 49, 257, 276, 309
Aegean Sea, 52, 222, 255, 257
aerosol particles, 231-232
Afghanistan, 35, 41, 66, 132, 165, 205
African Americans, 21, 78, 131
air campaign, 290, 293
Albania, 6, 9, 16-18, 37, 42, 51-52, 64-65,
     70, 95-103, 105, 107-110, 112, 118-
     123, 127, 155-156, 158-159, 164, 174,
     176-177, 183, 186, 253-258, 260-261,
     282, 299, 302-305, 308-311, 314-315
Albright, Madeleine, 4, 15, 34, 41, 73,
     105, 116, 121, 189-191, 193-194, 212,
     267-269, 273, 277
Aleksinac, 123, 186
Amnesty International, 26, 29, 131
Appendix B, 186, 192-194
anti-inflationary, 288
anti-personnel bombs, 125
Arabian Gulf, *see Persian/Arabian Gulf*
Asia Minor, 42, 256
austerity measures, 286
AWACS, 125
Azerbaijan, 47, 165-166, 168-170

B

Baker, James, 40, 185, 261
Baku, 166, 168-169, 257
Baku-Ceyhan Pipeline, 257
Balkan Task Force, 233-234
Balkans-Information, 90
Banja Luka, 269
Bar, Montenegro, 309
BBC, 110, 124, 172, 214, 255, 260, 277

Belgrade, 18-19, 28, 30, 40, 64, 71, 75, 95,
     103-104, 108, 113, 126, 151, 160-161,
     185-186, 189, 191, 212, 214-215, 219-
     222, 229-230, 233, 239, 242-244, 250,
     263-264, 266, 273-274, 276-279, 282,
     284, 289, 295-296, 302, 311
Berisha, Adan 302
Berisha, Hasim, 303
Berlin, *see Germany*
Bill 101-513, 47
bio-diversity, 218
black clouds, 218-219, 222
"Black Friday", 27
Black Sea, 222-223, 230, 257
Blair, Tony, 34
Bonn, *see Germany*
Bosnia, 5-6, 8-10, 15, 17-19, 31, 36, 42,
     47-54, 65-66, 73, 94, 103, 155, 157-
     158, 166, 169, 185, 189, 206, 234-235,
     248, 254-256, 258, 290, 295, 299
Bosporus, Straits of, 257
Britain, *see England*
Brooke, Sir James, 103, 291
Brussels, 126, 260, 283
Brzezinski, Zbigniew, 154, 258, 261
Budapest, *see Hungary*
Buendnis'90/Die Gruenen, 117
Bulgaria, 6, 28, 47, 85, 256-257, 260-261,
     265-266, 276, 287, 296, 314
Bundeswehr, 117
Burundi, 31
Bush, George (senior), 102, 132, 157-158,
     161, 173-174

C

Cacak, 273, 278
carcinogens, 220-221

International Action Center

The International Action Center was initiated in 1991 by former U.S. Attorney General Ramsey Clark and other anti-war activists who had rallied hundreds of thousands of people in the United States to oppose the U.S./UN war against Iraq, and then organized tribunal hearings in twenty countries and thirty U.S. cities against U.S. war crimes in Iraq. It incorporates opposition to U.S. militarism and domination around the world with the struggle to end poverty, racism, sexism, and oppression of lesbian, gay, bisexual and transgendered people in the United States.

Beginning 1993 the IAC anticipated the coming U.S./NATO assault on Yugoslavia, organizing discussions and writing a pamphlet exposing media lies demonizing Serbs and U.S. economic pressure on Belgrade, and demonstrating against U.S./NATO military intervention during the civil war in Bosnia. Early in 1998 the IAC published NATO in the Balkans, representing the work of the most astute activists and analysts. A month before the bombs started dropping in 1999, the IAC organized a national tour warning of the coming war.

When U.S.-NATO bombs and rockets hit Yugoslav cities, Ramsey Clark went with an IAC delegation to Belgrade to show solidarity with a people under attack. Inside the United States the IAC's weekly demonstrations of thousands and clear solidarity with the Yugoslav resistance, in alliance with the Yugoslav communities, distinguished its activities. It challenged the anti-Serb slanders spread by the U.S.-NATO propaganda machine and produced a video, NATO's Targets, to help mobilize the opposition.

Starting July 1999, the IAC organized hearings of an International Tribunal for U.S.-NATO War Crimes against Yugoslavia. Ramsey Clark drew up a list of nineteen charges against the political and military leaders of the major NATO countries and the officers who carried out these crimes. Similar tribunals in other NATO countries and in the former Warsaw Pact countries used these nineteen charges as a model as they exposed the criminal actions of the U.S. and NATO. The IAC joins with those who see the defense of Slobodan Milosevic against NATO's court in The Hague as a continuation of this struggle.

The IAC has fought the blockade against Cuba, led the movement to end the U.S./UN sanctions that caused the death of 1.5 million Iraqis, including a half million children, battled the use of radioactive "depleted-uranium" weapons that have endangered both the Middle East and the Balkans, fought "Plan Colombia" and other U.S. military intervention in Latin America. Since the 1999 Seattle anti-globalization protests the IAC has actively joined this growing and youthful movement in Washington and Quebec City.

SEPTEMBER 11, 2001

After the attacks on the Pentagon and World Trade Center on September 11, 2001, the IAC distinguished itself by immediately calling for protests against the coming U.S.-led war. It helped form the new coalition called A.N.S.W.E.R., or Act Now to Stop War and End Racism. This new group drew tens of thousands of youths to Washington and San Francisco on September 29, 2001, to say no to the war drive.

The IAC has played a leading role in the struggle to end the death penalty and especially the mobilizations to win freedom for Black liberation fighter and death-row political prisoner Mumia Abu-Jamal. IAC organizers coordinated a mass demonstration in Philadelphia in April 1999 and a rally in New York's Madison Square Garden in May 2000.

A major part of the IAC's work is to expose the intricate web of lies woven before, during and after each U.S. military intervention. It shows instead that U.S. intervention is dictated by the drive for profits and that as military funding expands, the money available for education, healthcare and needed social programs contracts. Much IAC material is published first on its increasingly popular web site, www.iacenter.org, which has made the "top one percent of web sites" list for the thousands of sites that link to it.

The IAC is a volunteer activist organization. In its campaigns opposing U.S. intervention, the center relies totally on the donations and assistance of supporters around the country. To be a part of a growing network, or to make a donation, request a speaker or volunteer your support, contact the IAC.

International Action Center
39 West 14th Street, Room 206, New York, N.Y. 10011 USA
Tel: 212-633-6646; fax 212-633-2889
Email: iacenter@iacenter.org
Web page: http://www.iacenter.org

Liar's Poker *The Great Powers, Yugoslavia and the Wars of the Future*

Combining sound research with inventive graphics, Michel Collon documents the plans of the NATO powers, especially Germany and the United States, to demonize the leadership and the entire population of Serbia and to destabilize and dismantle the Federal Republic of Yugoslavia. Collon's book closely exposes the media lies during the Bosnia conflict by contrasting what was printed and said to what was really taking place. Both scholars of that period and anti-war activists will find this book invaluable for understanding the background to NATO's first open aggression and the first war in Europe since 1945.

INTERNATIONAL ACTION CENTER, New 2002.212 oversize (8.5x11 inch) pages with extensive graphics indexed, softcover. $19.95

Hidden Agenda *U.S./NATO takeover of Yugoslavia*

The International Action Center's second full-length book on the Balkans conflict exposes the illegal roots and procedures of the International Criminal Tribunal for the Former Yugoslavia and its effort to stage a show trial of former Yugoslav President Slobodan Milosevic as an attempt to find the entire Serb and Yugoslav people guilty of resistance to NATO. Using evidence presented to dozens of popular international tribunal hearings in 1999 and 2000, it turns the tables on NATO by exposing and demonstrating the war crimes of Milosevic's accusers, including their decade-long conspiracy to wage war on Yugoslavia. With articles by Mumia Abu-Jamal, Former Yugoslav President Slobodon Milosevic, Former Attorney General Ramsey Clark, Michel Chossudovsky, Sara Flounders, Gloria La Riva, Michael Parenti, Michel Collon and other leading anti-war activists and analysts from many countries.

INTERNATIONAL ACTION CENTER, New 2002. 400 pages, pictures, indexed, cronology, maps, softcover. $19.95

NATO in the Balkans *Voices of Dissent*

Confused about the REAL reasons the United States bombed Yugoslavia? This book, released in 1998, will give you the secret background and hidden role of the U.S. and Germany in the dismemberment of Yugoslavia. *NATO in the Balkans* shows how sophisticated "Big Lie" war propaganda nearly silenced popular debate and opposition. Authors former U.S. Attorney General Ramsey Clark, Sean Gervasi, Sara Flounders, Thomas Deichmann, Gary Wilson, Richard Becker and Nadja Tesich will take you through the ins and the outs, the framework and media lies that led to the series of bloody conflicts that have characterized central Europe in the last years of this century.

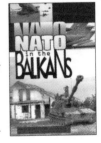

INTERNATIONAL ACTION CENTER, 1998. 230 pages, indexed, softcover. $15.95

NATO's Targets

Video

This video documents NATO's systematic destruction of civilian targets in Yugoslavia during the 1999 NATO bombing. Footage of bombed hospitals and schools and national resistance. Shot by award-winning videographer Gloria La Riva in the war zone while traveling with former U.S. Attorney General Ramsey Clark.

VHS, 1999, 29 min. $20 *individual* $50 *institutions*

The Fire This Time *U.S. War Crimes in the Gulf*

BY RAMSEY CLARK A book that tells the truth about the Gulf War tragedy–a sharp indictment of U.S. foreign policy that led to the Gulf War and its devastating human and environmental consequences. *The Fire This Time* stands out amid the deluge of self-congratulatory accounts which do injustice to history. *"A strong indictment of conduct of the war and especially of the needless deaths of civilians caused by bombing."* —New York Times *"Not academic…Clark risked his life by traveling through Iraqi cities at a time when the U.S. was staging 3,000 bombings a day".* —Los Angeles Times

INTERNATIONAL ACTION CENTER, 2002. 352 pages, indexed, pictures, softcover. $19.95

War, Lies & Videotape *How media monopoly stifles truth*

What passes as news today has been predigested by a handful of megamedia corporations. In this book, hard-hitting media critics, journalists, and activists examine:

- The ever-increasing media monopoly that stifles dissent and information
- Links between the government, the media and the military
- War propaganda & NATO's expanding role in Yugoslavia
- Role of Big Oil, the Pentagon & the media in the Gulf
- How new technologies can help break through the media monopoly

Edited by Lenora Foerstel. Chapters by: Jean-Bertrand Aristide, Scott Armstrong, Ben Bagdikian, Brian Becker, Ramsey Clark, Thomas Deichmann, Nawal El Saadawi, Sara Flounders, Diana Johnstone, Michael Parenti and others.

INTERNATIONAL ACTION CENTER, 2000. 288 pages, indexed, softcover. $15.95

Metal of Dishonor-Depleted Uranium
How the Pentagon Radiates Soldiers & Civilians with DU Weapons

A devastating exposé of the Pentagon's new weapons comprised of depleted uranium. This is the book you've heard about, but won't see in most bookstores. Now in its second printing. Gulf War veterans, leaders of environmental, anti-nuclear, anti-military and community movements discuss the connection of Depleted Uranium to Gulf War Syndrome and a new generation of radioactive conventional weapons. Understand how the bizarre Pentagon recycling plans of nuclear waste creates a new global threat. Authors include former U.S. Attorney General Ramsey Clark, Dr. Michio Kaku, Dr. Helen Caldicott, Dr. Rosalie Bertell, Dr. Jay M. Gould, Dan Fahey, Sara Flounders, Manuel Pino and many others.

INTERNATIONAL ACTION CENTER, 1997, 2nd edition 1999, 272 pages, indexed, photos, tables, softcover. $12.95

Metal of Dishonor

Interviews with noted scientists, doctors, and community activists explaining dangers of radioactive DU weapons. Explores consequences of DU from mining to production, testing, and combat use. Footage from Bikini and atomic war veterans.

PEOPLES VIDEO NETWORK, VHS, 1998, 50 min. $20   *PAL version for Europe $35*

Challenge To Genocide *Let Iraq Live*

Contains essays and detailed reports on the devastating effect of the economic sanctions on Iraq since the beginning of the Gulf War. It features "Fire and Ice," a chapter by former U.S. Attorney General Ramsey Clark. Also included are personal memoirs from many who defied the sanctions and U.S. law by taking medicines to Baghdad as part of the May 1998 Iraq Sanctions Challenge. Contributers include Ramsey Clark, Bishop Thomas Gumbleton, Rania Masri, Sara Flounders, Ahmed El-Sherif, Brian Becker, Barbara Nimri Aziz, Kathy Kelly, Monica Moorehead and Manzoor Ghori.

INTERNATIONAL ACTION CENTER, 1998. 264 pages, photos, indexed, resource lists, softcover. $12.95

Genocide By Sanctions

Video

Excellent for libraries, schools, and community groups and for cable-access television programs. This powerful video documents on a day-to-day, human level how sanctions kill. It contains important historical perspective that explains why the United States is so determined to maintain the sanctions. An important tool in the educational and humanitarian Medicine for Iraq campaign to collect medicine while educating people so U.S. policy will be changed. This excellent video by Gloria La Riva took second prize at the San Luis Obispo International Film Festival.

VHS, 1998, 28 min. $20 *individuals* $50 *institutions*

The Children Are Dying *The Impact of Sanctions on Iraq*

Report of the UN Food and Agriculture Organization, supporting documents, and articles by Ramsey Clark, Ahmed Ben Bella, Tony Benn, Margarita Papandreou, and other prominent international human rights figures. The human face of those targeted by the new weapon of sanctions. The UN FAO report showed with facts and statistics that over 500,000 Iraqi children under the age of five had died as a result of U.S./UN imposed sanctions. Photos and chapters define the social implications.

The impact of sanctions on Iraq

the children *are* dying

INTERNATIONAL ACTION CENTER, 1998. 170 pages, resource lists, photos, softcover. $10

Nowhere to Hide

Video

Traveling with Ramsey Clark in Iraq in 1991, award-winning video journalist Jon Alpert captured what it was like to be on the ground during the allied bombing. In dramatic, graphic scenes, *Nowhere to Hide* shows a different reality from what was on the nightly news. Tom Harpur wrote in the Toronto Star: "Only by knowing the true nature of Operation Desert Storm can similar wars be prevented...send for the video."

VHS, 28 min. $20 *individuals* $50 *institutions, plus $3 shipping*

Eyewitness Sudan

An expose of the 1998 U.S. bombing of the El Shifa, the small factory that produced more than half the medicine for Sudan. The smoking ruins are skillfully juxtaposed to footage of Clinton, Albright and Berger's charges. This documentary by Ellen Andors connects the years of sanctions to the cruise missiles sent against an African country.

PEOPLES VIDEO NETWORK VHS, 1998, 28 min.

The Prison Industrial Complex
An interview with Mumia Abu-Jamal on death row

Censored journalist, political activist and death-row inmate Mumia Abu-Jamal, framed for his ideas, speaks about the current political scene in the United States. In an excellent interview Mumia discusses racism, prison labor in the United States, youth, elections, economics and the state of the world. • See and hear "the Voice of the Voiceless" in this unique uncensored interview. • Interview by Monica Moorehead and Larry Holmes.

PEOPLES VIDEO NETWORK VHS, 1996, 28 min. $20

Mumia Speaks *An interview with Mumia Abu-Jamal*

BY MUMIA ABU-JAMAL with forwards by Monica Moorehead, Larry Holmes and Teresa Gutierrez.

Political prisoner and award-winning journalist Mumia Abu-Jamal speaks from his cell on Pennsylvania's Death Row. In this far ranging interview, Mumia talks about prisons, capitalism, politics, revolution and solidarity. The pamphlet also includes two articles—

"The oppressed nations, the poor and prisons," by Monica Moorehead. "The death penalty & the Texas killing machine," by Teresa Gutierrez.

WORLD VIEW FORUM, 2000, 33 pages, softcover. $3

ON A MOVE *The Story of Mumia Abu-Jamal*
BY TERRY BISSON

Covering Mumia Abu-Jamal's childhood in the North Philly projects, a turbulent youth in Oakland and New York, a promising career in radio journalism, and a fateful sidewalk altercation that changed everything, Bisson's colorful sketches tell the story of one of the stormiest periods in American history, and of a young rebel who came of age in its crucible. *"The next time you see Mumia demonized in the mainstream media, pick up this book. It chronicles the evolution of an eloquent advocate for the damned."* **— Martin Espada,** author, Zapata's Disciple

PLOUGH PUBLISHING, 2000, 240 pages, 36 photos, softcover. $12

TO ORDER: All mail orders must be pre-paid. Bulk orders of 20 or more items available at 40% off cover price. Include $4 U.S. shipping and handling for first item, $1 each additional item.

International shipping $10 for first item, $2 each additional item.

Send check or money order to:
INTERNATIONAL ACTION CENTER,
39 W. 14th St., Rm. 206, New York, NY 10011   (212) 633-6646
iacenter@iacenter.org.   www.iacenter.org

To place individual CREDIT CARD orders (VISA & MC only) order on-line at
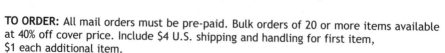
www.leftbooks.com or at www.booksuwant.com

For bookstore and university invoice orders and discounts, call the IAC in advance for specific information.